ID1006390

Business Research Solutions Series

NEW SERIES TITLES IN PREPARATION

INTRODUCTION TO ONLINE MARKET & INDUSTRY RESEARCH
Editor and Contributor Cynthia L. Shamel

INTRODUCTION TO ONLINE COMPANY RESEARCH
Editor and Contributor Chris Dobson

INTRODUCTION TO ONLINE INVESTMENT RESEARCH
Editor and Contributor Jan Davis

INTRODUCTION TO ONLINE LEGAL, REGULATORY & INTELLECTUAL PROPERTY RESEARCH
Editor and Contributor Genie Tyburski

INTRODUCTION TO ONLINE COMPETITIVE INTELLIGENCE RESEARCH
Editor and Contributor Conor Vibert

Produced by The Benjamin Group

THOMSON
™
TEXERE

EDITORIAL ADVISORY BOARD

The following group of national experts on business and financial information have formed an Editorial Advisory Board to work with editors and contributors to ensure content quality control and related professional research standards:

William A. Benjamin
The Benjamin Group

Jo Cooper
Goodwin Procter

Jan Davis
JT Research LLC

Christine B. Dobson
FI Services, Inc.

Lynn Ecklund
SEEK Information
Services, Inc.

Monica Ertel
Ertel Associates

Carol Galvin
Lotus Systems

Carol L. Ginsburg
CLG Consulting

Cynthia V. Hill
Sun Microsystems, Inc.

Mary Lee Kennedy
Microsoft Corporation

Susan M. Klopper
Goizueta Business Library

Sheri R. Lanza
Global Info Resources, Inc.

Anne P. Mintz
Forbes, Inc.

Barbara E. Quint
Searcher Magazine

Pam Rollo
LexisNexis

Jean Scanlan
PricewaterhouseCoopers

**Robert
Schwarzwalder, Jr.**
Ford Motor

Cynthia Shamel
Shamel Information
Services

Sandra Tung
Boeing Space &
Communications

Genie Tyburski
Web Manager, The
Virtual Chase

Masha Zipper
PricewaterhouseCoopers

DIRECTORY OF CONTRIBUTORS*

Melissa Barr
Cuyahoga County Public Library

Mary Ellen Bates
Bates Information Services, Inc.

Kathy Biehl
Independent Researcher

Polly D. Boruff-Jones
IUPUI University Library

Meryl Brodsky
Consultant

Helen P. Burwell
Burwell Enterprises

Cindy Carlson
Fried, Frank, Harris, Shriver & Jacobson

Margaret Metcalf Carr
Carr Research Group

Elena Carvajal
Ernst & Young

Donna Cavallini
Kilpatrick Stockton LLP

Dudee Chiang
Amgen, Inc.

Naomi Clifford
Consultant

Lynn Ecklund
SEEK Information Services, Inc.

Wes Edens
Thunderbird School of International Management

David Ernsthausen
Kenan-Flagler Business School

Michelle Fennimore
Competitive Insights

James Galbraith
Columbia University

James Harrington
Fujitsu Network Communications

Michelle Hartstrom
Columbia Financial Advisors, Inc.

Jean M. Heilig
Jones International University

Karl Kasca
Kasca & Associates

Wendy S. Katz
Factscope LLC

Hal P. Kirkwood, Jr.
Purdue University

Jan Knight
Bancroft Information Services

Margery A. Mackie
Mackie Research LLC

William S. Marriott
Marriott Research and Recruitment

Matthew J. McBride
Information Consultant

Karin Mohtadi
KZM LLC

Kathleen Morley
Independent Researcher

Rita W. Moss
University of North Carolina at Chapel Hill

Robin Neidorf
Electric Muse

Judith M. Nixon
Purdue University

Judith Parvez
Tax Analysts

Marcy M. Phelps
Phelps Research

Vicky Platt
Willamette Management Associates

Brenda Reeb
University of Rochester

Jan Rivers
Dorsey & Whitney LLP

Mary Rumsey
University of Minnesota Law School

Roger V. Skalbeck
George Mason University School of Law

Ann Spoth
A.T. Kearney

Kent A. Sutorius
Informed Solutions, Inc.

Jen Venable
Purdue University

Patricia A. Watkins
Thunderbird School of International Management

Susan F. Weiler
Weiler Information Services

Samuel Werberg
FIND/SVP, Inc.

Kim Whalen
Emory University

Morgan Wilson
Hamline University School of Law Library

* See Appendix D for more detailed biographies of most of the contributors.

Introduction to Online Accounting & Financial Research

SEARCH STRATEGIES, RESEARCH CASE STUDY, RESEARCH PROBLEMS, AND DATA SOURCE EVALUATIONS AND REVIEWS

Editor and Contributor Susan M. Klopper
Goizueta Business Library
Emory University

Produced by The Benjamin Group

THOMSON

™

TEXERE

Australia · Canada · Mexico · Singapore · Spain · United Kingdom · United States

HF5625.7
I58

THOMSON
TEXERE

Introduction to Online Accounting & Financial Research: Search Strategies, Research Case Study, Research Problems, and Data Source Evaluations and Reviews
Susan M. Klopper, Editor and Contributor

Vice President/ Editorial Director:
Jack Calhoun

Vice President/ Editor-in-Chief:
Dave Shaut

Acquisitions Editor:
Steve Momper

Channel Manager, Retail:
Chris McNamee

Channel Manager, Professional:
Mark Linton

Production Editor:
Todd McCoy

Production Manager:
Tricia Matthews Boies

Manufacturing Coordinator:
Charlene Taylor

Compositor:
GEX Publishing Services

Printer:
Phoenix Color Corp.
Hagerstown, MD

Design Project Manager:
Stacy Jenkins Shirley

Cover Designer:
Knapke Design
Mason, OH

Cover Photo:
Getty Images

COPYRIGHT © 2004 by South-Western, a division of Thomson Learning. Thomson Learning™ is a trademark used herein under license.

ISBN: 0-324-20314-4

Printed in the United States of America
1 2 3 4 5 07 06 05 04

ALL RIGHTS RESERVED.
No part of this work covered by the copyright hereon may be reproduced or used in any form or by any means—graphic, electronic, or mechanical, including photocopying, recording, taping, Web distribution or information storage and retrieval systems— without the written permission of the publisher.

For permission to use material from this text or product, contact us by
Tel (800) 730-2214
Fax (800) 730-2215
http://www.thomsonrights.com

For more information contact South-Western, 5191 Natorp Boulevard, Mason, Ohio 45040.
Or you can visit our Internet site at:
http://www.swlearning.com

Library of Congress Cataloging in Publication Data has been applied for.

PREFACE

The Business Research Solutions Series is intended to make online business and legal research easier to understand and practice. Taken together, all of the volumes serve both as a training tool and a reference resource for entry-level corporate personnel, undergraduate and graduate students of business and law, corporate and academic information professionals, and market researchers.

The Online Accounting and Financial Research volume specifically addresses information gathering related to the accounting and financial industries and the professional and regulatory marketplace within which they operate. This volume will provide valuable guidance for the corporate researcher seeking to understand the context in which accounting and related-financial information is needed, the best sources of information, and contextual strategies for accessing relevant content from those sources.

This volume is organized into five chapters to provide background and instruction as well as references to sample solutions and key sources. The researcher should consider reading Chapters One and Two in total. They lay the groundwork and provide context for understanding search strategies, particularly as they relate to accounting and financial research. Chapters Three and Four work well as reference sources for understanding the relevant types of research questions, and choosing appropriate sources. Here is a content summary:

1. RESEARCH DEFINITIONS, STRATEGIES, AND KEY SOURCE DESCRIPTIONS: This chapter introduces the reader to business research strategies and procedures. It also provides a plethora of practical advice and recommendations on better research techniques, dependable data sources, and industry best practices;

2. RESEARCH CASE STUDY: The second chapter takes an involved, multilevel research project and traces the solution from initial strategy to final data analysis and reporting. This provides real insight to the reader on professional research methodology and practices that are applicable to accounting and financial research;

3. **RESEARCH PROBLEMS AND SOLUTIONS:** The third chapter contains thirty-six "typical" research problems and their solutions. They apply specifically to accounting and financial research with practical advice on data source selection and content;

4. **RESEARCH DATA SOURCE EVALUATIONS AND REVIEWS:** In the final chapter, evaluations are presented for thirty-four information sources. The framework for the evaluations was developed in order to provide you with specific data about each product, such as cost and usability, as well as some general guidelines that you can apply when making product-purchasing decisions. While not every source identified in the prior three chapters is reviewed, those included represent the most important for consideration when conducting accounting and financial research.

5. **APPENDIX:** The four-part appendix contains valuable reference material that will be useful to any researcher. Included is a data source directory with contact names and the combined results of data source evaluations and ratings for the 102 business research sources that are (or will be) reviewed in this seven-volume series.

The topics, problems, solutions, and sources featured in this book were identified through the editor's experience, through the business literature, through the input and guidance of other series editors, and through the contributors who rely on their professional research skills and experiences every day to meet their customers' and clients' information needs.

Dozens of highly competent, motivated research professionals banded together to produce this volume. Their names appear either as members of the Editorial Advisory Board or as Contributors in the front matter. Detailed biographies of these experts appear in the Appendix of this volume. In particular, I wish to acknowledge and to thank both Jean Scanlan and Masha Zipper, respected colleagues and friends dating back to the golden era of corporate accounting firm libraries. I am most grateful for their advice and assistance, both of which were always delivered in kind spirit and with good humor. I would also like to thank the five contributors who crafted most of the problems and solutions and product data source evaluations for this volume: Naomi Clifford, Michelle Hartstrom, Brenda Reeb, Jan Rivers, and Kim Whalen. Your willingness to dedicate your free time to this project is greatly appreciated and the knowledge and different perspectives you brought to your work greatly enhanced the quality of this product. My personal thank-you as well to the editors of the other volumes in this series for their support and their willingness to share ideas and content, and to Helene Segal for her unwavering assistance, especially her attention to detail and patience.

When I was approached about working on this volume in July 2002, I had just walked out of the doors of the offices of the Atlanta office of Arthur Andersen for the last time. Not only was I leaving a job that satisfied my passion for my work many times over during the seventeen years I was there, but the worldwide community of Andersen practice who taught me everything I know about the accounting industry and the research process. I would like to dedicate this volume to that glorious firm. In particular, I wish to thank Susan Bell for the high value that she placed on my work during those years and for all of her time and help with the technical research content in this volume. My final thanks go to Steve Rubin, both for his pivotal article on the house of GAAP, which got me started on my love of accounting research, and for the friendship that he has extended to me these past few years.

A word is in order about the selection of online sources to be reviewed. Each editor provided a listing of key online data sources and the publishers were then contacted to ask for temporary passwords to assign to a specific reviewer and editor. While most of the publishers responded, we were surprised at the lack of interest on the part of several important business data sources, and hence there are some unavoidable omissions that the editors regret.

In the near future, the content for all of the books in the series will appear online as well as in print with the fervent hope that more and more useful material (as well as revisions) will be made available on a continual basis. There are also a number of additional volumes planned for inclusion in this Series so as to eventually address all special aspects (and vertical applications) of business research that cover international as well as domestic practices.

The Benjamin Group of Santa Barbara, California, developed the concept of this series with considerable help from the volume editors and the Advisory Board. We appreciate any and all suggestions for improvement in future editions and, of course, regret any shortcomings in the present content for which we are responsible.

Susan M. Klopper
Editor
July 19, 2003

The Editor

Susan M. Klopper is the manager of Research Services for Emory University's Goizueta Business School Library. Prior to joining Emory, she managed Arthur Andersen's Business Research Center for seventeen years. Susan is a frequent speaker on business research and management topics at international conferences for the information professional industry and regularly contributes articles to industry publications, such as *Online, Searcher,* and *Business Information Alert.* Susan is the recipient of several industry awards recognizing her knowledge and experience in the areas of business research and management.

TABLE OF CONTENTS

Chapter 4

Introduction to Accounting and Financial Research: Definitions, Research Strategies, and Key Source Descriptions

The corporate researcher is often asked to perform accounting and financial research. This may involve researching specific financial disclosures or identifying business ratios for a company and its peers. It may require one to find an SOP (Statements of Position), SFAS (Statement of Financial Accounting Standards), APB (Accounting Principles Board Opinions), or an EITF (Emerging Issues Task Force). The world of accounting and financial research is defined by acronyms, industry jargon, and a set of knowledge which has specific meaning and application for the accounting and financial professional. To successfully conduct accounting and financial research, you will need to put the request into context, understand the best choice of resources, and devise an effective search strategy.

This chapter describes the process by which technical accounting standards are created and examines the tools and techniques that support accounting and financial research. The chapter begins with an explanation of the purpose and applications for accounting standards: Where do you locate them and how are you assured that you have the most current versions? What are the connections between more broad-based financial and business information and these accounting standards?

We then turn to a discussion of the specific types of research questions that accountants and those requiring financial information typically ask: What client-specific accounting and financial-related issues do accountants normally address? What are the best research tools and strategies to use in order to address these information needs? And finally, what impact will the current focus on change within the accounting industry have on the standards-setting process, the roles and accountability of the CPA, and the information-gathering part of the equation?

Let's begin by defining who accountants are and what they do. Accountants record and report financial transactions. Businesses must keep track of all such transactions in order to demonstrate financial integrity and as a measurement of their success. This financial assessment is a critical basis on which concerned parties, such as investors, creditors, and the public at large, make important business decisions.

There are several main branches or divisions of accounting:

- *Financial Accounting.* Reports financial information to persons outside the business enterprise. The financial accounting methodology is determined by a set of rules, known as Generally Accepted Accounting Principles or GAAP, which consist of standards, interpretations of rules, and recommended practice set by authorized entities. GAAP will be discussed in greater detail.
- *Auditing.* Tests reliability of a company's financial information. An auditor examines a company's financial statements and reporting structure and attests to its accuracy, completeness of disclosure, appropriateness of methods, and general conformity to GAAP. A formal set of auditing standards, known as Generally Accepted Auditing Standards or GAAS, are promulgated by the American Institute of Certified Public Accountants (AICPA). GAAS will be discussed in greater detail.
- *Managerial Accounting,* Reports internal information to corporate managers. A management accountant maintains records, plans budgets, and advises top management. There are specializations within this field, such as cost accounting, which studies the costs and makes recommendations for cost-control measures. Managerial accounting will not be a focus of this volume.

- *Tax Accounting.* Focuses on developing business strategies based on tax consequences and compliance with the tax code and Internal Revenue Service (IRS) rules and regulations. Tax accounting and related research and resources will not be covered in this volume.[1]

Source: Laura M. Johnson, Suburban Library System. Reprinted with permission.

Now let's take a minute to introduce your clients, the individuals or departments for whom you might be asked to conduct accounting or related financial research within a corporate setting. In most cases, your clients will be accountants or financial advisors who need technical accounting or financial information for their own organization's internal accounting department, Comptroller, CFO, or CEO. If your organization is in the business of providing accounting or financial services to other companies, you will likely be responding to requests for information that the accountants working at the client site need in order to audit their clients' books, or to function in a financial advisory capacity to upper management, the Board of directors, or audit committee.

If your organization sells accounting and related services, you might receive requests for information from other internal departments, such as Marketing or Public Relations, which are focused on sustaining and growing the firm's competitive position in the marketplace. They might come to you seeking information about the market share of key competitors to target new client initiatives, or for background profiles on prospective clients used by partners in preparation for client presentations.

In the course of conducting research and gathering information for your clients, you will be called on to tap into both primary and secondary sources. Although the distinction may never formally be made by your client, it is implied and therefore important for you to understand. Primary information is the original source of that information without any additional interpretation or analysis. In the context of this volume, examples of primary sources would be Securities and Exchange Commission (SEC) filings, a company's annual report, technical accounting standards, or a company's press release. Secondary sources typically draw on primary information but present a layer of analysis, evaluation, or interpretation. Examples are articles that discuss the application of an accounting standard, aggregated financial data such as industry

---

1. Accounting, Part of Business Reference: A Cycle of Workshops, Suburban Library System, Burr Ridge, IL, *http://www.sls.lib.us/reference/workshop/business/account.html.*

ratios, and company and industry analysis such as investment analyst reports. Understanding the difference between primary and secondary sources will help you to provide your client with the appropriate balance of "raw" information and secondary discussions which help to place it in context.

You will learn more about your clients and why they request certain information in the sections that follow. Let's begin by introducing you to the world of technical accounting standards and related financial information.

UNDERSTANDING ACCOUNTING STANDARDS: THE BASICS

There exists a series of technical standards and a number of policy-setting bodies responsible for issuing these standards, responding to corporate financial reporting challenges, and in the case of the SEC, regulating and monitoring their applications in the business environment. You cannot effectively conduct accounting research without a good understanding of these basics. Let's take a look at this framework.

Accounting Standards: Why Have Them?

An established and accepted set of accounting standards exist in order to minimize bias, misinterpretation, inexactness, and ambiguity in financial statements, and to make financial reporting easily comparable between enterprises. Simply put, these standards govern the preparation of financial reports. The recognized need for such standards led to the creation of a common set of accounting practices that are "generally accepted" and universally used.

Generally Accepted Accounting Principles (GAAP) are binding rules, enforced by conformity to Rule 203 of the AICPA Code of Professional Ethics. Rule 203 requires that independent accountants determine whether a company's financial statements and disclosures are presented in accordance with promulgated GAAP before they can express an unqualified audit opinion on the financial statements. In other words, adherence to officially established accounting principles, to GAAP, results in financial statements that are not misleading.

These standards govern the preparation of financial reports and they define the financial accounting and reporting process that produces financial information critical to investment, credit, regulatory, and legislative decisions. Adherence to and belief in these standards are tied to business, consumer, and broader economic confidence and stability, as evidenced by the recent accounting scandals and resultant questions raised about accountant independence and corporate financial and managerial integrity.

Understanding Generally Accepted Accounting Principles: The House of GAAP

The role that accounting standards play in establishing the rules for disclosing both public and private financial reporting is defined by a hierarchy of authority that guides reliance on and weights the importance of the standards. Understanding this hierarchy is paramount to comprehending the meaning of GAAP. Understand it and the many mysteries of conducting accounting research become suddenly clear and logical.

One of the best explanations of the GAAP hierarchy appears in a 1984 article, "The House of GAAP."[2] In this article, Steven Rubin describes and defines the vast universe of accounting standards as a hierarchy structured along the lines of the floor plan of a house. In 1991 the AICPA's auditing standards board made significant revisions to this structure and remodeled the "house of GAAP" by changing some of the levels of authority of certain accounting pronouncements. Continuing on Rubin's theme, in 1991 Douglas Sauter published "Remodeling the House of GAAP" to update the hierarchy to reflect these revisions. Using Rubin's visual model of a house, following is a description of the floor plan adapted to the revised hierarchy:[3]

First Floor. Constitutes the highest level of GAAP authority; officially established, authoritative accounting principles; also referred to as authoritative literature or pronouncements, including:

- FASB Statements of Financial Accounting Standards (SFAS)
- FASB Interpretations (FIN) which modify, extend, clarify and elaborate on existing SFAS, AICPA Accounting Principles Board Opinions and Accounting Research Bulletins

---

2. Steven Rubin, "The House of GAAP," *Journal of Accountancy*, June 1984, ABI/Inform.

3. Douglas Sauter, "Remodeling the House of GAAP," *Journal of Accountancy*, July 1991, ABI/Inform. See also Adrian P. Fitzsimons and Marc H. Levine, "A Roadmap Through GAAP," *The Practical Accountant*, May 1993, pp. 47–52, ABI/Inform.

- AICPA Opinions and their Interpretations which have not been superseded
- AICPA Accounting Research Bulletins which have not been superseded
- Examples:
  - Statement of Financial Accounting Standards No. 131, Disclosures about Segments of an Enterprise and Related Information
  - APB Opinion No. 18, The Equity Method of Accounting for Investments in Common Stock

Second Floor. Pronouncements of organizations comprised of expert accountants who discuss and analyze accounting issues in public for the purpose of establishing accounting principles or describing existing accounting practices that are generally accepted and approved by FASB and GASB and have been exposed for public comment, including:

- FASB Technical Bulletins (TB)
- AICPA Industry Audit and Accounting Guides
- AICPA Statements of Position (SOP)
- Examples
  - SOP 97-2, Software Revenue Recognition
  - FASB Technical Bulletin No. 01-1, Effective Date for Certain Financial Institutions of Certain Provisions of Statement 140 Related to the Isolation of Transferred Financial Assets

Third Floor. Includes pronouncements of organizations comprised of expert accountants who discuss and debate accounting issues in public forums for the purpose of interpreting and establishing accounting principles or describing existing accounting practices that are generally accepted, including:

- FASB Emerging Issues Task Force (EITF) consensus position
- AICPA Practice Bulletins approved by the FASB
- Examples:
  - EITF Issue No. 98-10, Accounting for Contracts Involved in Energy Trading and Risk Management Activities
  - AICPA Practice Bulletin 14, Accounting and Reported by Limited Liability Companies and Limited Liability Partnerships

Fourth Floor. If an accounting treatment is not specified in a source from any of the first three floors, the accountant may consider other accounting literature. The appropriateness of the source depends on its relevance to particular circumstances, the specificity of the guidance, and the general recognition of the author as an authority, including:

- AICPA Accounting Interpretations
- FASB Implementation Guides in Q and A format
- Not yet cleared AICPA Statements of Position and Industry Audit and Accounting Guides
- Industry practices that are widely recognized and prevalent
- Examples
  - FASB Special Report, *A Guide to Implementation of Statement 125 on Accounting for Transfers and Servicing of Financial Assets and Extinguishments of Liabilities*
  - AICPA *Reporting the Results of Operations: Accounting Interpretations of APB Opinion No. 30*

Fifth Floor. When a generally accepted accounting pronouncement is not covered by floors 1 to 4, the independent auditor may use other sources of guidance as deemed relevant, including:

- FASB Financial Accounting Concepts (CON)
- AICPA Accounting Principles Board Statements
- AICPA Issues Papers
- Pronouncements of other professional associations or regulatory agencies
- AICPA Technical Practice Aids
- Accounting textbooks, handbooks, and articles
- Examples:
  - AICPA Issues Paper, *Identification and Discussion of Certain Financial Accounting and Reporting Issues Concerning LIFO Inventories*
  - FASB Concept No. 5, *Recognition and Measurement in Financial Statements of Business Enterprise*

Source: Copyright © 1991, 2002 from the Journal of Accountancy by the American Institute of Certified Public Accountants, Inc. Opinions of the authors are their own and do not necessarily reflect policies of the AICPA. Reprinted with permission.

Understanding the house of GAAP provides the researcher with a basic understanding of the accountant's context for practicing his or her profession and gives you a clear road map for understanding the documents and devising a research strategy.

THE STANDARDS-SETTING PROCESS

The Financial Accounting Standards Board (FASB), AICPA, SEC, and more recently, the International Accounting Standards Board (IASB) work together to create new and amend older standards in order to establish and maintain a common language for communicating financial information. They do so under the watchful eye of the larger business and economic community and related constituencies and stakeholders.

Who Sets the Standards?

Following is a brief introduction to the four important players in the accounting standards setting process:

AMERICAN INSTITUTE OF CERTIFIED PUBLIC ACCOUNTANTS. Originally, the AICPA, the membership association for Certified Public Accountants (CPA), was the body responsible for defining accounting standards. From 1939 to 1959 its Committee on Accounting Procedures issued Accounting Research Bulletins (ARBs); from 1959 to 1973 its Accounting Principles Board (APB) followed with a series of opinions. In 1973, facing concern that the AICPA was too member-focused and could not *objectively* represent a more broad-based business and consumer constituency, the APB was dissolved and the standards-setting responsibility was transferred to the FASB. At this time, the AICPA shifted its focus to supporting its membership and constituency and to bringing to the attention of the FASB and the SEC issues that it determined to be important to the accounting and auditing professional communities. While the AICPA has continued its role as the authoritative body for establishing auditing standards, this responsibility is now being assumed by the Public Company Accounting Oversight Board (PCAOB), a body created by the Sarbanes-Oxley Act of 2002. The oversight board's recent authorization to become directly involved with issuing auditing standards could have significant impact on the current standards-setting process. A discussion of the PCAOB and its potential impact on the industry follows in the sections below.

FINANCIAL ACCOUNTING STANDARDS BOARD. Since 1973 the FASB has been the organization designated to establish authoritative financial accounting and reporting standards for business and other private-sector entities. Its mission is to be responsive to the entire economic community, not just the public accounting profession, and to operate in full view of the community through a due-process system.

SECURITIES AND EXCHANGE COMMISSION. In addition to the AICPA and FASB, the SEC also plays a key role in the standards-setting process. Under the Securities Exchange Act of 1934, the SEC has statutory authority to establish financial accounting and reporting standards for publicly held companies. It supports as "de facto" the accounting standards established by the private sector, provides broad support to the FASB, and helps to identify emerging issues that it thinks FASB should address. Recent accounting-related scandals, such as the Enron collapse, have prompted the SEC, with the support of Congress, to become more directly involved in the oversight of the standards-setting process and the monitoring of corporate governance. In August 2002 as part of the Sarbanes-Oxley Act, the SEC's Public Company Accounting Oversight Board (PCAOB) was created by Congress to crack down on corporate accounting scandals. Authorized to conduct inspections and discipline accountants, the oversight board supplants the self-regulation of CPAs who audit public companies.

INTERNATIONAL ACCOUNTING STANDARDS BOARD. While international standards have traditionally taken a backseat to the national standards of the FASB, AICPA, and SEC, the increasing financial and economic demands and complexity of a global business environment are positioning them to play a more prominent role in the standards-setting process. Formed in January 2001, the ISAB replaced its predecessor, the International Accounting Standards Committee (IASC) as the international standards setter. Looking toward greater formalization of international accounting standards, IASB is structured similarly to the FASB. It is the intention of the IASB, in collaboration with the FASB and other accounting focused organizations, to "converge" standards and develop a single, universally accepted set of binding international accounting standards. The ISAC, and now ISAB, issue a series of standards known as International Financial Reporting Standards (IFRS), formerly called International Accounting Standards (IAS).

The Birth of a New FASB Accounting Standard

The final decision of the FASB to issue a new SFAS is the result of a deliberate and formal process. The FASB receives many requests for action on various financial accounting and reporting topics from all segments of its diverse constituency, including members of accounting firms, associations, lobbyists, the AICPA, and the SEC. Requests for action include both new issues and suggested review or reconsideration of existing pronouncements. The FASB remains alert to trends in financial reporting through observation of published reports, liaison with interested organizations, and discussions with the EITF.

In addition, FASB's staff receives technical inquires which may provide evidence that a particular topic or aspect of an existing pronouncement is in need of examination. The FASB is also alert to changes in the financial reporting environment that may be brought about by new legislation or regulatory decisions. FASB maintains an ongoing summary of current board projects on its Web site (*http://www.fasb.org/project/index.shtml*).[4]

Based on input from its constituency, the board works with its technical staff to establish an ongoing list of technical projects in preparation for the possible issuance of a new statement of financial accounting standards. The following five reports and publications document this process:

1. A *Discussion Memorandum* is prepared by the FASB staff, which defines the problem and scope of the project, identifies any related financial accounting and reporting issues, research findings and relevant literature, and proposes alternative solutions and implications. The Discussion Memorandum lays the foundation for a public hearing and analysis of oral and written comments on the issue.

2. The analysis and feedback are gathered into an *Exposure Draft* that explains the board's conclusions. At the end of a sixty-day comment period, the issue is further discussed and analyzed by the board and staff.

3. The completion of the process is signaled by the release of a new *Statement of Financial Accounting Standards*, technically known as an SFAS but commonly referred to as "a FASB." A sequential number is assigned to each newly released FASB, e.g., SFAS 133.

---

4. FASB Facts: How Topics Are Added to the FASB's Technical Agenda, *http://www.fasb.org/facts/tech_agenda.htm*.

4. An *Implementation* document may be issued to clarify, explain, or elaborate on the existing SFAS.

5. A *Technical Bulletin* may also be issued to address specific or technical issues not directly covered by the SFAS. *Technical Bulletins* are usually written in a Q&A format and offer practical clarification or guidance on a specific issue.

In 2002, as a direct result of a series of major corporate financial reporting scandals, the Sarbanes-Oxley Act was passed. This legislation directly impacts accountants and attorneys, officers and owners of publicly traded companies, as well as brokers, dealers, investment bankers, and financial analysts. The act, Public Law 107-204, established the PCAOB, responsible for registering, monitoring, investigating, and disciplining the activities of public accounting firms, including establishing the guidelines for the conduct of several key auditing procedures and delineating the types of services that CPAs are prohibited from providing to audit clients. The act additionally sets forth a number of requirements for corporations, their officers and board members by redefining working and reporting relationships with their internal audit committee and public accounting firms, creating changes in internal controls procedures, and enhancing financials disclosures. The passage of the Sarbanes-Oxley Act signals many significant forthcoming changes in GAAP and the current standards-setting process.[5]

Other Accounting Standards

Before concluding this discussion of accounting standards, it might be useful for the researcher to identify the other major accounting industry standards:

GENERALLY ACCEPTED AUDITING STANDARDS (GAAS). Established by the AICPA, these standards govern the conduct of exter-

---

5. For an excellent analysis of the Sarbanes-Oxley Act, the PCAOB, and their impact on corporate governance, reporting structures, and relationship with auditors, see the following articles:

- "Annual Update for Form 10-K and Proxy Statement Preparation, Part 1 of 2," James Carlson, Mondaq Business Briefing, February 28, 2003.
- "How the Sarbanes-Oxley Act of 2002 Impacts the Accounting Profession," AICPA, *http://www.aicpa.org/info/sarbanes-oxley2002.asp.*
- "Navigating the Sarbanes-Oxley Act of 2002: Overview and Observations," PricewaterhouseCoopers, March 2003, *http://www.pwcglobal.com.*
- "The Sarbanes-Oxley Act of 2002," NYSPA.org, *http://www.nysscpa.org/oxleyact2002.htm.*

nal audits by public accountants. The Statements of Auditing Standards (SASs) provide guidelines for the auditors' fieldwork and financial reporting. They frame the format and contents of the Auditor's Report or Opinion, which is the formal expression of their examination of a company's financial statements. In May 2003 the PCAOB was given the official go-ahead to assume responsibility for establishing GAAS. It remains to be seen exactly how the PCAOB's new role will play out, its impact on the AICPA's responsibilities, and the form in which the two entities will co-exist.

GOVERNMENTAL ACCOUNTING STANDARDS. While GAAP defines the accounting standards for public and private business entities, there also exist standards specific to government organizations. Organized in 1984 to establish standards of financial accounting and reporting for state and local governmental entities, the GASB's standards, known as governmental accounting standards (GAS), guide the preparation of external reports for these types of organizations. If your client is a governmental agency, you might need to reference one of the following special set of standards:

- *General Accounting Office (GAO)*. *Government Auditing Standards*, commonly referred to as the "Yellow Book," provides standards governing the audits of federal government and federal grants to local governments.
- *Office of Management & Budget (OMB)*. The OMB publishes several "circulars" which provide guidelines for federal audits of government entities.

INDUSTRY ACCOUNTING PRACTICES. Some industries have created their own accounting practices to fill in the gaps not covered by floors 1 to 4 of GAAP. These practices are often available in print publications issued by the overseeing industry association; on occasion they are also posted on the association's Web site. Examples of industries that have adopted their own practices are healthcare and insurance.

As this volume goes to press, the accounting industry is undergoing major changes that are having a significant impact on the accounting industry and the standards-setting process. Among the changes are:

- increased role of the SEC in legislating, monitoring, and sanctioning accounting standards and corporate governance matters;
- the PCAOB's assumption of responsibility for the auditing standards-setting process;
- increased financial accountability for public company corporate management, board of directors, and audit committees;
- an anticipated trickle down effect of the "spirit" of the Sarbanes-Oxley Act on privately held companies;
- FASB's creation of a User Advisory Council in 2003, made up of users rather than preparers of financial statements, to provide input for FASB's future standards-setting agenda;
- convergence of U.S. and international accounting standards to create global, universally accepted accounting standards along side the adoption by all European Union listed companies to follow a single set of international accounting standards (IAS) by 2005.

As these developments play out, it will be extremely important to monitor all of these changes in order to be responsive to your clients' information needs. Keeping abreast of these important industry events is paramount to ensuring that your research remains timely and accurate.

DEFINING THE ACCOUNTING RESEARCH PROBLEM: UNDERSTANDING WHAT ACCOUNTANTS ARE ASKING FOR AND WHY

Understanding the basics of the standards-setting process is a necessary starting point, but it is just one piece of the research puzzle. While it is not possible to document every variety of research requests your client might pose, there are predictable types which are common to virtually all accounting and financial research. In this section we will define and describe each of these, helping you to understand what the professional is asking for and why. Understanding the context behind the question is key to learning to speak your client's language and to delivering information that is responsive to real-world accounting and financial-related issues.

Before beginning this discussion, let's examine the questions you will need to ask the client to ensure that you understand exactly what is being asked of you and the purpose for the request. The research process really begins "offline" with a face-to-face reference interview with the client. Step one is taking the time to thoroughly discuss the topic with your client to make sure that you understand exactly what the client is asking for. In other words, what is the question at hand? Sometimes it is very straightforward. Your client wants to know who audits a particular public company or needs a print copy of a particular accounting standard. Unfortunately, most requests for information are not so easily answered and are rarely what they appear on the surface. Although unintentional, people rarely communicate exactly what they really need. That is where the power and the necessity of the reference interview come into play. As the researcher, it is your responsibility to initiate the essential two-way dialog that completely and accurately addresses the question or questions that you are being asked to answer.

When conducting any type of research, but especially technical research when you are not the content expert, begin by defining the scope of the project. Determine the information needed and the exact document types. For example, will you tap into primary sources such as SEC filings or secondary discussions such as journal articles? Determine key terminology and synonyms that will be essential for conducting effective searches. Don't hesitate to ask for any definitions or clarification of context that will help guide you through the process.

Once you thoroughly understand the project scope, discuss the context in which the information will be used. Is the client trying to support a particular recommendation, prepare for a marketing presentation, or provide guidance to less experienced staff on the engagement team? The answers to these questions will dictate how deep into the content you search, what format you deliver the results in, and even how much of your time should be invested in the process. For example, research that will be used for making important recommendations to a company's audit committee probably requires more time and specificity than a request for some background articles on a recent news event.

Be sure to address practical issues such as the amount budgeted, both for time (soft costs) and external expenses (hard costs), and a due date. Does your client simply want you to deliver the research results by a certain time or would it make sense to establish a series of "check points" for keeping in touch throughout the process. If you are conducting research on a topic for which you are not the expert or for which scope is especially complex, it might be appropriate to establish a schedule for providing regular updates on the project status. Some clients will prefer to have you push results out to them on agreed upon intervals. Make sure to verify your client's availability in case you need to ask questions or for points of clarification.

Always remember to play the skeptic. The more questions you ask—combined with some savvy fact checking on the side—the better prepared you will be to find the correct information efficiently. As you gain more experience conducting accounting and financial research, you will become familiar with the kinds of information your clients ask for and communication styles. However, no matter what your comfort level, it is a strongly recommended practice to review all the known facts or pieces of information before getting started. Become too comfortable and second-guess what your client needs and you are sure to make mistakes.

Now let's begin that discussion about the most common accounting and financial-related topics that you may be asked to research and some practical insights into the "why."

Requests for Accounting Standards

Accounting standards are the guidelines on which accountants rely for compliance with GAAP and you can expect many requests to focus on locating the full text and analysis of the following types of documents:

TECHNICAL PRONOUNCEMENTS. As described in the first section of this chapter, technical standards can derive from the FASB, AICPA, SEC, or ISAB, and in some circumstances, from industry practice. Often the request to you will be as basic as "can you locate an SFAS or SOP that discusses a particular topic." Before you start your search, you'll want to get some additional information: Does the requestor know the document's exact title or corresponding number? Is it in final form or still in the proposed stage? How did the requestor learn about this document? Asking upfront for the answers to these questions will help to direct your strategy for locating the documents. The accountant may not always know the answer, but it is still smart to ask. The more information you have, the less time you will waste.

By now, it is no secret that the accounting and financial industries have their own technical language. The more conversant you become with the many acronyms that will be tossed your way, the more efficiently you will be able to process your research requests and "talk the lingo" with your clients. You might want to consider purchasing a good handbook or dictionary to keep close at hand. Appendix 3: Reference Bookshelf identifies a few recommended publications, but there are many excellent choices on the market.

ARTICLES. In addition to relying on the relevant authoritative standards, accountants often turn to articles for thoughtful discussion on accounting pronouncements on a particular accounting-related topic. This approach can be helpful for a number of reasons. For instance, articles provide contextual analysis of a standard's application, including practical examples. They can demonstrate how a new or amended pronouncement changes the required disclosure, and highlight new and forthcoming standards and the anticipated impact on the accounting industry. When your clients asks you to locate articles, try and find out as much as possible about the topic and the type of information for which they are looking: How far back should you search? Should you target technical accounting journals, general business and finance publications, academic articles, industry white papers, Big Four accounting firm publications, or other types of sources?

Requests for Financial Disclosures

There are a great many circumstances under GAAP rules that require financial professionals to report additional information to accompany financial statements. Examples include disclosure of the principal accounting policies followed, such as the method of inventory valuation, type of depreciation calculation method applied, whether or not the lower of cost or market valuation approach is used for inventory costing purposes, or the disclosure of operating segments, including identification of the types of products that comprise each segment's revenue and the nature of any intercompany transactions between reporting segments.

When a company initiates a change in accounting, the accountant must also disclose the type of change, describe why it is being made, list the dollar impact caused by the change for the current and immediately preceding reporting period, as well as the amount of the change in earnings per share. In cases where the amount of information is either excessively detailed or only applies to a narrow range of possible situations, the applicable GAAP documents are clearly identified in the footnote.[6]

Source: *Accounting Reference Desktop*, Steven M. Bragg, John Wiley & Sons, Inc., 2002. This material is used by permission of John Wiley & Sons, Inc.

As support for financial disclosures they want to make, a public company's management often requires information about how other companies have disclosed similar transactions or events. It is common practice for individuals within the organization who have responsibility for financial reporting (such as director of financial reporting, CFO, comptroller) to ask the accountant to assist in drafting or reviewing financial statements and footnotes, and to recommend best practices in disclosure. While an official FASB pronouncement or other authoritative literature usually addresses general rules and principles of accounting or reporting, it does not necessarily address every specific situation. Therefore, when an accounting issue arises, management looks to the accountant to determine which authoritative guidelines best apply to the facts and circumstances.

In response to such requests, accountants may use a checklist of required disclosures that addresses currently existing GAAP and SEC reporting requirements; typically these are prepared by their accounting firm or by the AICPA. Such checklists generally indicate the "area" within the financial statement or the type of transaction, and reference the underlying authoritative literature that drives the disclosure requirements. This may be a specific financial line item, such as property and equipment or accounts receivable, or broader concerns, such as current, fixed, or intangible assets or accrued liabilities. These checklists generally reference financial statement issues both by category (for example, property and equipment) and by type of transaction (for example, acquisition of an asset). The auditors then help their clients determine the appropriate specific disclosures by providing them with the references to the technical standards and illustrations; in other words, to answer the question, "What is the required disclosure and why."

---

6. *Accounting Reference Desktop*, Steven M. Bragg, John Wiley & Sons, Inc., 2002, pp. 109–110, 119.

These recommendations are obtained using representative footnotes or examples of financial statements that cover similar issues and disclosures drawn from publicly filed 10-Ks. In these cases, you may be asked to locate examples of public companies that have disclosed a similar issue in the financial statements, footnotes, or the Management, Discussion & Analysis ("MD&A") sections of a 10-K. In some instances, based on knowledge of the client's specific circumstances or financial transactions, accountants may also suggest introducing original disclosure content.

Conducting accounting research requires a good working knowledge of SEC filings. You should understand the purpose of specific filings, what kinds of information they contain, where specific information is found, and what the SEC's required timetable is for making the filing. There are several excellent documents available in .pdf format for free on the Internet that explain the purpose of each SEC filings and their respective parts:

- Thomson Research (*http://www.primark.com*). Click on Guide to SEC Filings in the Content Support section
- SEC Web site (*http://www.sec.gov/info/edgar/forms.htm*). Click on Overview of the Most Common Corporate Filings
- LIVEDGAR (*http://www.gsionline.com*). Click on Free Resources

See Appendix 1: Guide to SEC Filings for detailed information about the more frequently referenced SEC filings and the particular sections which are heavily researched for accounting disclosures and financial information.

While accountants sometimes know the specific company whose SEC filing to target, more often they do not have a clue, leading them to ask you to perform keyword searches across the text of certain sections of company filings, such as the financial footnotes, auditor's opinion, or management discussion. To conduct these searches, you will require some very specific information: What type of SEC filing and what specific parts within that filing should you narrow your search to? You need to determine what combination of keywords to search for and their proximity to each other. Will any specific SFAS be mentioned, and if so, what is the number and title. Be sure to ask if the accountant really expects there to be any such disclosure? Discuss how exhaustive a search you are expected to conduct. In some cases there simply is no example of a disclosure that fits a particular issue. The possibility of this outcome should be incorporated into the reference interview. You do not want to expend unnecessary time and energy looking for an answer that cannot be found, but more importantly, you do not want to make any assumptions that may result in delivering to your client incomplete information.

Don't shy away from the fact that the accountant is the content expert; you need to tap fully into their knowledge of the language and context in order to conduct intelligent research. Ask the right questions and the answers will help direct you to the best sources, ensure that you maximize the power of the search interface, and make the best use of your time. Disclosure searches can be very difficult since the accountant is often unsure of the exact wording or even if the disclosure exists. Be patient, try out many different search strategies, and do not hesitate to contact your client throughout the process to discuss the results and explore other ways to approach the research problem.

Requests for Business Ratios

You might also be asked to locate business ratios. Analysis drawn from company financial statements (income statement, balance sheet, cash flow statement) is used to assess an organization's business condition and overall risk. Ratios provide useful aggregate comparative data on industry performance and are specifically used by accountants to benchmark the performance of their clients against their industry and peers. For example, analysis of a company's "day sales in receivables" is an important indicator of how quickly a company is collecting cash from its sales; those with quicker collections present less of a cash/liquidity risk than a peer which takes a longer than average amount of time to make sales collections. The benchmark data is now typically a part of the business performance review that accountants must complete as part of a financial statement audit.

To fully understand and properly apply the ratios, it is important to be aware of several internal and external factors: the company's business and its products, the company's performance within the context of the economic climate, any legal or regulatory issues that the company faces, its context within the competitive environment, and current and historic industry averages and ratio behavior.[7]

---

7. *The Essential of Finance and Accounting for Nonfinancial Managers*, Edward Fields, American Management Association, 2002, pp. 80–81.

When a company's ratios are compared with those of comparable industry peers, they provide an additional layer of insight about how a firm performs relative to its industry. Analysis of a company's ratios can help management monitor the company's performance and identify areas that are performing well and those that are in need of improvement.

Requests for Financial Market and Economic Data

Accountants regularly request foreign exchange rates, stock prices, treasury rates, bond values, selected interest rates (prime rate, London InterBank Offered Rate [LIBOR], federal funds, etc.), and economic indicators such as the Gross Domestic Product (GDP), Consumer Price Index (CPI), inflation, and the Producer Price Index (PPI). This type of information "independently" tests the reasonableness of client assertions about the value of assets and liabilities on their books as reported by the clients and that may be documented in bank and brokerage reports, loan documents, and other types of legal contracts.

If a company has a large number of investments, your client may use statistical sampling to select items to test in order to ensure that the value of the investments as reported by the client and supporting documentation are accurate. For example, the company's financial department provides the accountant with its monthly investment brokerage statements. These statements typically document the allocation of assets into cash, equity, and debt and detail each specific investment and their value as of a certain date. Based on this information, the accountant may select a sampling of stocks, bonds, and government treasuries and ask you to verify their value using an independent research tool.

Since a large part of the research that you may be called on to perform involves gathering financial market and economic data, let's flush out the "why" for using this type of information a bit more.

Financial market data may be requested by an accountant for a number of reasons, including:

- *Support for the historical cost or fair value recorded for an investment.* Investments in marketable securities, including government securities, are typically recorded as historical cost paid for the investment; they may subsequently be "marked to market" based on fair value. Pension fund investments are generally marked to market and must be based on fair values at the balance sheet dates; the auditor will seek independent data to verify the values assigned by the pension plan trustee or investment advisor.

- *Evidence that an investment has not declined in value below its original cost.* An investment whose value has declined below its original cost may need to be written down to its fair value.
- *Evidence of the value of a transaction.* For example, if a company's stock is issued to acquire an asset or a business, the fair value of the stock on the date issued may be the basis for the accounting of the transaction.

General economic data may be requested for some of the following reasons:

- *Foreign currency exchange translations.* If a U.S. company acquires an asset in a foreign currency, it generally must translate the value of the asset into U.S. dollars, as that is its "functional" currency.
- *Lease escalation provisions.* A company's lease may have a clause that states the rent expense escalates in correlation with a specified "standard" rate, such as the rate of inflation or tied to the CPI; the accountant may need to calculate the impact of that escalation on current year lease expense.
- *Calculation of interest expense.* A company's debt may bear interest at a rate based on the prime or LIBOR rate plus a certain percent; the auditor may want to independently test the company's calculation of those rates.

Before concluding this section, let's briefly discuss the time-frame in which this data is needed. The economic data requested may be historical (e.g., to test transactions recorded in the past), current (e.g., to test a value at a balance sheet date), or forecasted (e.g., to estimate the impact that a change in an interest rate or other factor may have on future expense for disclosure in a company's financial statements or press releases). Forecasted data may also be used to test a company's financial statement projections used for valuing a business or an asset, or for evaluating the company's ability to continue as a going concern. For example, if a company is in a precarious financial position, an auditor may want to test whether the "burn rate" of the company's cash might result in its running out of cash before a certain date. The company's burn rate will be derived from projected or forecasted financial statements that may include factors such as interest expense tied to an economic index (e.g., prime or LIBOR) or lease expense tied to the CPI.

Requests for Corporate Strategic and Operational Intelligence

In their capacity as accountants or financial advisors, your clients will need to review all matters and events that may impact the company's financial performance and health. These can include business segments, real estate holdings, and external factors such as the competitive marketplace, regulatory environment, the economy, internal and external risks, and future strategic directions. While identifying this level of company intelligence is common to many types of business research, it is highly relevant to the financial professional's financial reporting, analysis, and advisory capacity. Understanding the many nuances of gathering company and industry information will arm you with the questions that you will need to ask your clients so that you will provide them with just the right information. In this volume, we will focus on the sources that are most frequently referenced by the professional financial community. The *Introduction to Online Company Research* and *Introduction to Online Market & Industry Research* volumes in this series also discuss the many challenges and options for researching U.S. public and private companies in great detail.

Requests for Information about Corporate Governance

In the post-Enron era of accounting and corporate scandals, issues relating to corporate governance are in the forefront of the SEC, the accounting and financial industry, company management and boards, shareholders, and the public at large. The corporate researcher can expect to receive frequent requests for this type of information.

What is corporate governance? According to the Organization for Economic Cooperation and Development (OECD), corporate governance is the system that guides how companies are directed and controlled. Its structure specifies the framework for roles and responsibilities for the board, management, shareholders, and other stakeholders and spells out the rules and procedures for making decisions on corporate affairs. It also provides the structure through which company objectives are set and the means for attaining these objectives and monitoring performance.[8,9]

What does that mean within the context of this volume? Accountants regularly request information to identify and learn more about an organization's top management and members of its boards. This research supports financial professionals in their roles as accountants and financial advisors to company management, the board of directors, or the audit or compensation committees. Information about board members and executive management may also be requested by accounting professionals, internal marketing, and other support departments for the purpose of developing proposal initiatives for prospective clients or to target professional networking opportunities. Following are three examples of frequently requested corporate governance research applications:

1. *Corporate Management and Board Member Biographical Profiles.* Gathering biographical background information can include locating an individual's age, education, and employment history, activity on civic and business boards, and management style. Accountants and financial professionals use this information for professional networking and relationship building with current clients as well as for making sales presentations to prospective clients. Familiarity with an individual's background is useful for gaining a better understanding of that person's perspective as well as identifying possible

---

8. Economic Co-Operation and Development, *http://www.oecd.org.*
9. Following are some excellent discussions of what corporate governance is and the impact of the Sarbanes-Oxley Act on regulating corporate management:

- "Corporate Governance: The New Strategic Imperative," a white paper from the Economist Intelligence Unit, sponsored by KPMG International, *http://www.kpmg.com.*
- "Emerging Trends in Corporate Governance 2002," PricewaterhouseCoopers, *http://www.pwcglobal.com.*
- "Issues & Trends: Corporate Governance Reform: After the Fall," Dick Anderson and Anton van Wyk, *http://www.pwcglobal.com.*
- "Moving Forward—A Guide to Improving Corporate Governance Through Effective Internal Control: A Response to Sarbanes-Oxley," Deloitte & Touche, January 2003, *http://www.us.deloitte.com.*
- "Restrengthening Corporate Governance," Barry F. Kroeger, CrossCurrents, Winter 2002, *http://www.ey.com.*
- "Audit Committee Resource Guide," Deloitte & Touche, February 2003, *http://www.deloitte.com.*

connections with a mutual friend, colleague, or client. Tracing the path of "who knows who" and "who can influence whom" is extremely important to an organization's sustained and growing client base.

2. *Compensation and Benefits.* Compensation and benefits information requests may include an officer's salary, benefits, bonus and perks, such as stock options or other forms of equity compensation. This information is often used by accountants who specialize in compensation or financial planning advisory services that may apply this information to benchmarking executive compensation, designing equity compensation plans, or for demonstrating to a company the accounting and financial reporting implications of certain employee benefits. Perks, such as loans to executives (such loans may be for corporate relocations, to cover tax impacts of other compensation, or many other reasons), have come under particular scrutiny from a corporate governance perspective in the wake of recent accounting scandals.

3. *Audit Committees.* You might also be asked to identify the members of a company's audit committee. Accounting firm managers and partners meet with audit committees at least once a year to report on their findings and to present any recommendations. It is always smart business practice to "know your audience" by obtaining background information about the members of this or any committee before meeting with them.

Requests for Information about International Business

Reconciling accounting standards for companies headquartered or doing business in foreign countries is increasingly important in the global business economy. Accountants regularly need to identify existing accounting standards for specific countries and compare them with U.S. GAAP. Additionally, in their expanding roles as business advisors (for example, an accountant may advise clients on opening a new location or plant in a particular country), they need information on the accounting, tax, and corporate structures, local rules and regulations, and other risks related to conducting business abroad. There are two primary applications for using international information:

1. *International Accounting Standards.* You might be asked to identify standards or guidance comparing U.S. GAAP with another country's accounting standards. Companies that own foreign subsidiaries or are looking to acquire or merge with a foreign company will need to identify accounting and disclosure rules

for the target country in order to recognize potential accounting differences that might impact their financial results or to understand which disclosures are required in their annual reports. Financial reporting professionals have to reconcile a subsidiary's local country financial statements with the parent country's GAAP. In other cases, professionals involved with cross-border financial filings must reconcile the GAAP typically used by a company with the GAAP of the reporting country. This occurs, for example, when an international company lists its stock on a U.S. stock exchange and it becomes a "foreign registrant" for SEC reporting purposes.

2. *International Business Operations.* Accountants frequently function as business advisors for their clients and can be asked to locate information about "doing business" in an international context. For example, they might have a client who is considering acquiring a company based in another country or setting up a manufacturing or service plant on foreign territory. Their clients will be interested in obtaining key economic, financial, and regulatory data for that country, such as tax rates, rules for setting up a corporation, local labor laws, and more.

Requests for Competitive Intelligence

While accountants and other financial professionals seek out primary and secondary research to directly support their client's work, they also need information to maintain their own organization's competitive position in the marketplace. For example, your marketing department may want assistance developing target lists of prospective new clients. Depending on how your company focuses its practice, you may be asked to identify companies in a certain geographic area, grouped by a particular industry, or within a certain revenue size. In addition, you might be asked by managing partners to actively track local, regional, or national competitors so that they are better informed about the competitive business landscape.

While a certain amount of competitor information can be gleaned from company Web sites and electronic database searches, you will also need to tap into the soft kind of intelligence available only through personal contacts and professional networking through association, civic, or fraternal organizations. Unlike technical research for which there is clearly defined content and resources, competitive intelligence is as much about who you know as the sources you use. While competitive intelligence research is not the main focus of this volume, there are several types of competitive intelligence type requests that a client base of accountants and financial professionals might ask you to conduct. Following are a few examples:

- *Identifying Company Auditors.* For an organization that provides auditing and related services, knowing who your competition is and its share of a particular market is an essential step in formulating business plan and establishing targets and goals for sustained and future growth. For firms providing accounting services, this translates into defining the market or markets they want to compete in (generally determined by geographic and/or industry focus) and developing spreadsheets documenting the names of the firms that provide similar services to the companies making up that market. Marketing and communications departments regularly need this data to develop marketing pieces and to help management and sales teams with framing quarterly and annual goals.

- *Tracking Industry Trends and Competitors.* The current market for accounting and related financial services is extremely competitive and survival depends on sustaining a close watch over the many external factors that drive and impact the competitive marketplace. Internal departments such as marketing, public relations, and HR, plus upper management and those involved in developing sales plans, all need to be tracking significant events impacting the industry, including economic, regulatory, or political, as well as keeping an eye on the companies which are considered key competitors.

- *Audit Fees.* As a result of growing SEC concerns over risks to auditor independence, regulations were passed effective February 5, 2001, stating that all public companies were required to disclose in the company's annual proxy statement certain information relating to the fees paid by the company to its outside auditors. These rules were further impacted by the passage of the Sarbanes-Oxley Act of 2002 and resulting regulations have added further definition and limitations on the services that independent auditors are prohibited from providing to their audit clients. Audit fee disclosures must now be incorporated into the 10-K. These reported fees are broken out by: fees paid to the independent accountant for (1) audit services, (2) audit-related services, (3) tax services, and (4) other services.

  You might be asked to research audit fees for a number of reasons. Clients use this information as a leveraging tool when renegotiating contracts with their auditors and when considering outsourcing some of the nonaudit services their auditors are no longer allowed to provide. Accounting firms are aggressively using this information to ensure that their pricing remains competitive.

- *Accounting Salary Surveys.* Your accountant might be working with a client to help streamline its internal accounting department and will be asked to identity some salary benchmarks. To remain competitive with other local firms, your own organization's HR department may want to be kept informed about surveys that track salary ranges in the region for new and experienced accountants and financial managers.

Requests for Information about Accounting and Financial Software Packages: Annual Surveys and Product Reviews

Many accountants work with their clients to support financial-based technology needs, including recommending software for applications, such as accounts receivable, accounts payable, generating tax returns, or payroll, and provide technology-related training for the client's internal accounting department staff. As part of the limitations that the Sarbanes-Oxley Act of 2002 imposed on services that accountants can offer to publicly held companies, they can no longer provide financial information systems design and implementation services if they also serve as that company's auditor. It is allowable for accountants to provide these services if they are unrelated to the audit client's financial statements or accounting records if these services are preapproved by the audit committee. However, an accounting firm can still provide services to private companies and this remains a viable service that continues to be supplied.

Requests for Accounting Industry Certification

You might be called on to locate state requirements for licensing, certification, or continuing professional education requirements for accounting and financial management professionals. As accountants move beyond the standard CPA certification to remain competitive by offering more specialized services, there will be an increased need for information about certification requirements, course materials, and exam schedules.

RESOURCES AND RESEARCH STRATEGIES: DETERMINING THE BEST PATH FOR LOCATING INFORMATION

This discussion about sources for accounting and financial information focuses on both targeted subscription-based databases and free Web sites. However, it is important to note that several of the larger, broad-based database aggregators, such as LexisNexis and Factiva (see Chapter Four) also provide access to some of this information via their respective electronic interfaces. If you currently have contractual relationships with these vendors, you may already have access to the information or be able to add the content to your contracts for a reasonable cost. If your information requirements, however, are more targeted to accounting or financial information only and you cannot justify the cost of subscribing to any of these larger databases, you might want to explore purchasing a few of the products discussed in this section.

How much of the collective accounting standards can you locate on the free Web? Unfortunately, the majority of the AICPA, FASB, and IASB documents are only available electronically on a subscription or one-time purchase basis. (That said, the free Web never fails to surprise one, so it is always worth looking!) However, there is some good news. Much of the government-issued accounting and audit standards are accessible for free on their respective Web sites. The FASB and AICPA sites are effective avenues for free access to summaries and selective free text of recently issued or forthcoming accounting standards and their sites contain good links to timely industry news and related sites. There are a few print sources to recommend as well. If you need to reference accounting standards regularly, you might purchase a set of the core materials in hard copy (see Appendix 3: Reference Bookshelf, Primary Accounting and Audit Sources).

Sources for Accounting Standards

How do you locate the text of accounting standards or secondary analysis on their application? Fortunately, you have a variety of options, both print and electronic.

The technical documents outlined earlier in this chapter in the discussion about the house of GAAP can be divided into the following categories:

1. recently released and forthcoming documents,
2. core collections of documents,

3. articles and books,
4. University of Mississippi Accounting Collection (formerly AICPA library, and
5. accounting and related financial resource portals.

There are other sources that can help you find or learn about these standards. Some key print and electronic sources for locating and searching across these technical pronouncements are presented below. Although the focus of this volume is on corporate accounting and financial research, the most frequently requested government accounting standards are referenced in this section as well. Here is a detailed listing and description of these five categories.

RECENTLY RELEASED AND FORTHCOMING DOCUMENTS.

- *AICPA* (*http://www.aicpa.org*). Summaries and select full text of recently issued pronouncements are posted for free on the AICPA Web site; click on the links to Accounting Standards and Audit & Attest Standards. The Congressional & Financial Affairs section contains news and resources covering federal and state legislative and regulatory developments of interest to CPAs. Clicking on Online Newsletters provides quick access to recently issued documents and committee agendas for forthcoming accounting and audit standards. Although limited to AICPA releases, you could use this section for if you are not able to subscribe to the print *Journal of Accountancy* magazine (see discussion below).
- *FASB* (*http://www.fasb.org*). Click on the links to Project Activities and Exposure Drafts on the FASB Web site to display the summaries and text of the most recent documents, and agendas for forthcoming releases.
- *SEC* (*http://www.sec.gov*). Click on the link to Information for Accountants on the SEC home page to view all of the news and documents relating to accountants and auditors. The SEC Web site contains selective full text of SEC accounting statements, including Staff Accounting Bulletins, Accounting and Auditing Enforcement Releases, and Financial Reporting Releases.

CORE COLLECTIONS OF TECHNICAL DOCUMENTS.

- *AICPA reSOURCE* (*http://www.cpa2biz.com*). This subscription-based electronic database provides access to the full text of all AICPA's professional standards, technical practice aids, financial reporting trends, and standard-setting guidance. The authoritative accounting standards issued by the AICPA (ARBs and APBs) are not included in this database; they are available in a separate combination package that is available from either the AICPA or FASB. If you regularly need to locate the full text of a whole range of AICPA standards and your research requires that you conduct keyword searches across the text of these documents, you will want to subscribe to this product.

- *AICPA Print Publications.* If your requests are limited to accessing the text of specific documents by title or number, you can purchase the annual softbound editions of a particular series or subscribe to a loose-leaf service. A loose-leaf service is a subscription-based print service that delivers periodic updated content. Unlike the annual editions, which are only published once a year, loose-leaf services are filed in a ringed binder so that update pages can be interfiled throughout the subscription term. Since the print editions will lag behind, you will have to regularly check the AICPA Web site to keep up with new releases. The following print editions or loose-leaf subscriptions can be purchased from the AICPA:
  - Accounting and Audit Guides
  - Statements of Positions
  - Statements on Auditing Standards
  - Checklists and Illustrative Financial Statements
  - Statements on Standards for Accounting and Review Services
  - Statements on Standards for Attestation Engagements
  - Technical Practice Aids
  - Professional Standards
- *Financial Accounting Research System on CD ROM.* If your research requires keyword searches across the FASB materials, you will want to subscribe to FARS, a Folio-based CD ROM product containing the full text of the Original Pronouncements (OP), Current Text (CT), Emerging Issues Task Force Abstracts (EITF), and FASB Implementation Guides.

    OP is a chronological arrangement of the full text of the AICPA and FASB authoritative promulgations, including current and superseded sections. CT presents a topical arrangement of these standards organized into general standards, applicable across all enterprises, and industry standards, applicable to enterprises operating in specific industries. Both the OP and CT contain indexes pointing to relevant authoritative documents, EITF summaries and FASB Technical Bulletins. FARS is updated six times a year; you will need regularly to check the FASB Web site to keep up with the most recent releases.

- *FASB Print Publications.* If your requests only require that you locate the full text of the AICPA and FASB authoritative standards by title or number, you consider purchasing the annual softbound editions of the OP and CT or subscribing to a loose-leaf service. If you purchase annual editions, you will need to regularly check the FASB Web site to keep up with new releases.

- *Journal of Accountancy.* Published monthly by the AICPA, the *Journal of Accountancy* is the industry's premier magazine, containing articles on accounting standards, technology, marketing, and administration. In each issue the Exposure Drafts Outstanding and Official Releases section (located toward the back) charts all recently released and forthcoming documents by the AICPA, FASB, SEC, and IASB. This matrix offers the most comprehensive and efficient way to keep current with the status of all new, amended, and superseded accounting and auditing pronouncements.

  Beginning with 1996, the full text of most of the *Journal of Accountancy* articles is available for free on the AICPA Web site; click on the link Online Journal of Accountancy on the Home Page. Unfortunately, the Exposure Drafts Outstanding and Official Releases section is *not* accessible electronically; you will have to subscribe to the print magazine to view this useful matrix.

- *General Accounting Office Government Auditing Standards (http://www.gao.gov).* Known as "generally accepted government auditing standards" (GAGAS), this collection of standards is commonly referred to as the "Yellow Book." These standards apply to audits of government organizations, programs activities and functions, and government assistance received by contractors, nonprofit organizations, and other nongovernmental entities. They provide guidelines for the auditors' professional qualifications, quality of audit effort, and characteristics of professional and meaningful audit reports. The "Yellow Book" is periodically revised or supplemented, so be sure to check the GAO Web site for any updates. From the GAO home page, click on the link to Other Publications; Complete Listing. An alphabetical list of all GAO reports will display.

- *Office of Management Budget Audit Documents (http://www.whitehouse.gov/OMB/circulars).* OMB Circulars contain instructions or information issued by the OMB to federal agencies. These Circulars are frequently revised or supplemented so be sure regularly to check the OMB Web site for updates. Some of the most frequently requested audit-related circulars include:

- Circular A-21: Cost Principles for Education Opportunities
- Circular A-102: Grants and Cooperative Agreements with State and Local Government
- Circular A-110: Uniform Administration Requirements for Grants and Other Agreements with Institutions of Higher Education, Hospitals, and Other Non-Profit Organizations

ARTICLES AND BOOKS. Accounting and financial researchers often turn to journal articles and books for secondary discussion and analysis, and it is good to be familiar with some key resources. Many articles can be found online, either at the journal's Web site or through electronic online databases.

The coverage of full-text accounting and finance journals on electronic database services is excellent. Some of the key journals include:

- *Journal of Accountancy*
- *The CPA Journal*
- *Practical Accountant*
- *Corporate Accounting*
- *Financial Executive*
- *Journal of Accounting, Auditing & Finance*
- *Management Accounting*
- *Accounting Today*
- *CFO*

Electronic databases (see reviews in Chapter Four) like Lexis-Nexis and Factiva provide well-rounded representation of accounting industry-related publications through their electronic services. Both can be effectively used for "on-the-fly" searching as well as for creating saved searches that will push out timely, relevant articles to your e-mail. Factiva's News Pages feature has preformatted searches that automatically scan for current news on the accounting and financial industries and it displays the full text of the *Wall Street Journal* for easy scanning. Other excellent databases are ABI/Inform and Business Source Premier; these are sometimes available to community residents for free or a minimal cost through state and local public or academic libraries and community consortia.

ABI/Inform was one of the first electronic databases to provide access to abstracts and full text of the core accounting, tax, and financial magazines, and it remains to date the editor's favorite database for conducting secondary accounting research. While pieces of the database's content are available on LexisNexis and Factiva, the only way to gain full access to the current and back files (beginning with 1970) is by subscribing to ProQuest or Dialog. Unfortunately, access to both of these interfaces can be expensive. If you are being asked to consistently search across a particular body of accounting publications or to search for articles that predate the mid-1990s, you might want to consider evaluating this product. The other database that focuses primarily on the accounting industry is the Accounting & Tax Database, also only available in its complete version in ProQuest or Dialog. Consider evaluating this database for the same reasons outlined above for ABI/Inform.

A very popular series of annual GAAP reference books, the *Aspen-Miller GAAP Guides*, popularly referred to as the "Miller" guides, provide concise explanations of accounting and auditing standards. They can be purchased in print or CD-ROM directly from Aspen, but most of them are also now available on LexisNexis and CCH. At a cost of between $120 and $150 per volume, you might want to consider purchasing the print editions of the most relevant Miller titles for your collection. They are well organized and indexed, making them very efficient reference resources, and include the following titles:

- *GAAP Guide*
- *GAAS Guide*
- *Governmental GAAP Guide*
- *GAAP from the EITF*
- *Not-for-Profit Organization Audits*
- *European Accounting*

UNIVERSITY OF MISSISSIPPI ACCOUNTING COLLECTION.   In the late 1990s when the AICPA's library was downsized, the vast amount of its extensive collection of books, journals, treatises, special studies, and more was donated to the University of Mississippi Accounting School Library. In the early days of predominately print collections, the AICPA's library was considered the "Library of Congress" for accounting and tax research; its collection is rich and holds many unique resources. "Ole Miss" has a staff that is dedicated to supporting the usage of this collection and its services include loaning books and faxing articles. There are fees for these services, but they are quite reasonable. All the necessary information for tapping into this excellent collection is posted on its Web site, *http://www.olemiss.edu/depts/general_libary/aicpa/index. html.* Services are limited to AICPA membership, however. If you anticipate needing to contact the library to use its resources, obtain your client's AICPA membership number in advance. Additional contact information: Toll Free Number: 1-866-806-7477; Email: aicpalib@olemiss.edu; Fax Number: 622-915-7477.

ACCOUNTING AND RELATED FINANCIAL RESOURCE PORTALS. Web-based portals are collections of recommended links to sites and sources on similar topics or industries. There are many excellent accounting portals on the Internet. Associations and academic institutions do a particularly good job of developing collections of valuable links (see Appendix 2: Accounting and Related Industry Associations). Following is a short list of a few recommended portals:

- *AICPA* (*http://www.aicpa.org*). Clicking on CPA Links from the AICPA's home page yields a comprehensive series of links to broad groups of accounting related sites, including Accounting and Audit, Taxes, Government, and Securities Exchanges.
- *FASB* (*http://www.fasb.org*). Click on the link to Accounting Resources on the FASB site for its list of recommended links to accounting-related sites.
- KARL: The Official Kaplan's AuditNet Resource List (*http://www.auditnet.org/karl.htm*).
- Ohio State University, Fisher Department of Finance (*http://www.cob.ohio-state.edu/fin/journal/jogsites.htm*).
- *SmartPros* (*http://www.accountingnet.com*). Click on links to Resource Library, Professional Education, Accounting, A&A, Financial Planning, Technology, International, Tax, and more.
- *Electronic Accountant* (*http://www.electronicaccountant.com*). Click on link to Weblinks.

Sources for Financial Disclosures: Electronic Database Services

As discussed in the prior section, accountants are often asked by management to assist in drafting and reviewing financial footnotes and to recommend best practices in disclosure. For the researcher, requests to locate company financial footnote disclosures are among the most challenging and frustrating. Fortunately, there are several electronic research tools and print sources which are designed for the precision and flexibility necessary for conducting good disclosure research.

Key to conducting effective disclosure research is the ability to search for keywords within targeted sections of specific filings, for example the Financial Footnotes or MD&A sections of the 10-K. While virtually all of the free and subscription-based EDGAR databases allow you to conduct basic keyword searching across filings, and most even provide options for selecting the filing type (for example, 10-K, 10-Q, etc.), very few allow you to limit keywords to specific sections within the documents. Instead, most of the search engines will only look for all of your keywords to appear "somewhere" within the body of the text. Imagine searching for change in auditor and retrieving every 10-K in which the word "change" and the word "auditor" appeared anywhere throughout the text, including independently of each other.

The good news is that a few databases are exactly tailored to researching financial disclosures. And there are several others that, with some help from customer support, could be tweaked to yield reasonable results. In fact, with lots of patience and creative searching, you might even be able to yield promising results using some of the free EDGAR data. Remember to take advantage of the power of the Edit/Find option located at the top of your browser's menu bar. While usually limited to searching only one word, the Edit/Find option can be a very effective tool for quickly scanning a document or jumping to a particular section. It is a very handy tool when the Web site or database lacks its own targeted search options.

The most challenging aspect of conducting financial disclosure research remains developing the correct keyword search strategy. Work closely with your client to determine the best keywords and their proximity to each other within the relevant sections. Remember, in many instances, accountants request this type of search because they are treading on unfamiliar accounting territory; they may not know the exact search words. Talk through several different possible scenarios so that you have a back-up strategy if the first or second attempts are unsuccessful, and be prepared to conduct multiple searches.

You rarely find what you are looking for the first time around. Use the returned results from previous searches to help guide your strategy for refining the search. Remain in close contact with your client—and do not forget that in some instances, the answer is that there are *no* disclosure examples that fit the particular issue. The best solution for you will be determined largely by a combination of the cost of the risk of not conducting a thorough and comprehensive search weighed against the cost of subscribing to a particular product. For financial disclosure research, you do get what you pay for.

RESEARCH TIP

The section of the 10-K which contains the financial statements and footnotes can either be part of the "base" document or be included "by reference" as Exhibit 13. If you are asked to locate a company's financial statements and footnotes and you do not see these identified in the 10-K's table of contents, look at the detailed list of exhibits. If you do not see them in either place, you will have to locate the company's annual report. Since the annual report is not an official SEC filing, it will not be available on any of the free EDGAR sites. Check the company's Web site for a link to the annual report (usually in .pdf format).

So, with that caveat, let's take a look at some of these database choices, ranging from the most to least expensive. This is not meant to be a comprehensive list of all SEC filing databases, but rather a select look at a few of the best. If you already subscribe to a database not on this list that includes access to SEC filings, work with the vendor's customer service to determine if it meets your needs for financial disclosure research.

SUBSCRIPTION-BASED EDGAR DATABASES.

- *Thomson Research* (*http://research.thomson.com*). This database is the Cadillac of products for conducting financial disclosure research. Its interface contains all the necessary components to:
  - Target specific filings types by selecting one or multiple forms (e.g., 10-K, 8-K, etc.)
  - Select specific parts of the filings to search (e.g., Financial Footnotes, Financial Statements, MD&A, etc.)
  - Conduct complex keyword searching using Boolean connectors, proximity options, truncation, etc.
  - Specify range of filing dates (e.g., from 1/1/2001 to 12/31/2002)

- *LIVEDGAR* (*http://www.gsionline.com*). This product earns accolades for continually developing more versatile and creative options for searching across a large range of SEC filings. You have two main choices for searching disclosures: Using the Tax/Accounting Research Library section, you can select a preidentified filings section and run a sophisticated keyword search in that section combined with other limiters, such as date and industry. Examples of these sections include: 10-K, Item 9, Changes with Accountants; Adoption of Accounting Policies; FIFO Accounting Method Used; Purchase Method, etc.

  The other choice is a newly created "10-K Section Search" Text template. GSI has identified twenty-three sections (one for each Part of the 10-K and four for financial information). Sections you can designate to search include All Financials, Balance Sheet, Income Statement, Notes to Financial Statements, and Management's Discussion and Analysis. The search template displays each tagged section with a check box next to the description; you check the box of all relevant sections and enter keywords in the Free Text box at the top of the page. Additional boxes allow you to specify additional information, including SIC Code and Filing Date. Results are returned in a "keywords in context" view that allows for efficient scanning of the results.

- *LexisNexis* (*http://www.nexis.com*). To take advantage of targeting keywords within specific sections of SEC filings, you need to identify all of the segments that have been defined for each specific filing type. Unfortunately, obtaining this information is not always easy. The information guides (denoted by an "i" icon next to the file name) contain a list of the most frequently used segments, but they are not comprehensive and almost always exclude the sections required for disclosure research. There are two ways that you can identify all of the segments: contact Customer Service or look at the "Custom" view from the Power search template. Unfortunately, while many of the document sections are tagged for targeted searching, such as the MD&A, the financial footnotes section is not. The good news, however, is that LexisNexis does have one of the most powerful search engines in the business, combined with an outstanding Customer Service team. If you already subscribe to LexisNexis, work with your rep or Customer Service to learn the most effective strategies for conducting disclosure research. Taking advantage of LexisNexis' Focus and KWIC features will help you to minimize the time spent viewing the documents to determine relevant results.

Free **EDGAR** Databases.

- *EdgarScan* (*http://edgarscan.pwcglobal.com*). Created by Price WaterhouseCoopers' Technology Centre, this excellent SEC filing interface allows for multiple search access points. An advanced search template includes phrase and basic Boolean keyword searching, which you can combine with other limiters such as date and industry. Results from keywords searched are returned with a link to "Details"; clicking on this link displays the discreet sections of the filing containing your keywords. In addition, each filing is tagged with an excellent hyperlinked table of contents that is very useful for quickly jumping to the relevant sections of a filing. You can additionally isolate a particular document and conduct keyword searching just within it. Output options include .rtf and the financial sections are tagged for downloading into a spreadsheet. This database is constantly changing and improving so take the time to explore it and regularly check for new and improved features.
- *SEC Info* (*http://www.secinfo.com*). The first time you use SEC Info you will be required to register in order to create a personal id and password, but the site is free. Displayed on its home page are links to frequently searched sections of SEC filings, including Changes in Control, Changes in Accountants, Financial Statements. Click on one of the links and you can run a simple keyword search in that section across all relevant filing types. The results are returned with a portion of the relevant section containing your keywords highlighted; click on a link to that page and you can view the entire section. An especially nice feature is "Topics." Conduct a search for a specific company's filings and the results are returned with a link to "Topics" at the top of the page; clicking on this link displays a set of links to all the company filings organized alphabetically by section description. If you did not know which filings or sections within a filing contain specific information, this would be a quick way to find out. SEC Info allows output in .rtf and the financial sections are tagged for downloading into Excel. Each page is separately tagged so that you can view and output select pages if you do not need to print the entire document.

Databases for Researching SEC Regulation Fair Disclosure Material. Effective October 2000, the SEC's Regulation Fair Disclosure requires all public companies to release within 24 hours of its taking place the transcript of all quarterly earnings announcements and "morning conference call" discussions held with investment brokers, such as Merrill Lynch or Goldman Sachs.

The purpose of the rule is to ensure that there is complete and forthright disclosure of all significant company events and financial matters, and that brokers are not in a position to "sit on" or use inside knowledge to their advantage, the advantage of their clients, and to the potential detriment of shareholders and the public at large.

The text of the morning conference calls is filed as 8-Ks; the full text is also available on some for-pay electronic databases and loaded on company Web sites in the form of a Webcast. These calls are usually organized as a question-and-answer dialog between investment analysts and company management. They serve as forums for discussing company financial, operational, and strategic events and future directions, and are excellent sources of company accounting and financial intelligence.

For example, on February 6, 2003, analysts from Goldman Sachs held a "Discussion of Deferred Cost Accounting" conference call. Management representatives from American Greetings on the call included the CFO, corporate controller, and manager of investor relations. The call, as described in the Event Brief summary below, began with American Greetings' CFO introducing the primary topic of the discussion:[10]

OVERVIEW
Prepaid assets termed prepaid expenses represents deferred cost assets to be earned by the customer and amortized against gross sales over the next 12 months. Increases in this account result primarily from reclassification entries from other assets....
PRESENTATION SUMMARY
S1. OPENING COMMENTS (R.R.) 1. HIGHLIGHTS 1. The purpose of the call this morning is to bring clarity to unique operating characteristic of the co.'s business, the use of long-term contracts in the sales process. 2. The bulk of the discussions will involve a walk through of a hypothetical contract example.

American Greetings' management presentation is followed by the analyst question-and-answer sequence:

QUESTION AND ANSWER SUMMARY
Q1. One thing that you didn't discuss today is whether or not there are any reserves associated against the contracts for, like a retailer that may be in bankruptcy. Can you address that? (Jim Hoeg–Goldman Sachs)

---

10. "Event Brief of American Greetings Corp. Conference Call—Discussion of Deferred Cost Accounting—Final," FD (Fair Disclosure) Wire, February 6, 2003, Factiva.

A. (Robert Ryder) If you looked at our 10-K, we do disclose that every year. The answer is yes, we do have reserves against retailers and we do disclose that. I think it is Exhibit 2 in the 10-K. So you should be able to get that information. It actually shows the puts and takes during the year.

Q2. So you actually show, against the exact contracts, the level of reserve that you've taken? (Jim Hoeg–Goldman Sachs)

A. (Robert Ryder) No it's in aggregate. We wouldn't show reserves against specific contracts. I don't think anybody would do that. But you can see in aggregate reserves taken to contracts and reserves taken away in aggregate against customer contracts.

Q3. It looks like, if you follow the accounts that you made, at least it's implied a fairly large payment in 4Q02. I have to assume that this was for Albertson's. Is that correct? (Jim Hoeg–Goldman Sachs)

A. (Robert Ryder) It wouldn't be in our best interest to disclose any customer-specific information....

Reprinted with the permission of CCBN.

These conference calls are excellent sources for learning about company accounting, financial, operational, and strategic developments and directions. Some outlets for tapping into the transcripts of these conference calls include:

- *Factiva* (*http://global.factiva.com*). Use the following search strategy to locate Fair Disclosure documents: sn=fair disclosure and hd=company name. For example: sn=fair disclosure and hd= american greetings. SN searches for the source or publication name and hd looks for your keywords to appear in the headline or title.

- *Fair Disclosure Express* (*http://www.edgar-online.com/fdexpress*). Sponsored by EDGAR Online, this subscription-based EDGAR site contains free links to the text of the Fair Disclosure rule, definitions, and discussion about its future impact on shareholder, company, and analyst. It includes a free list of each day's 8-K and 425 filings, but you must be a subscriber to EDGAR Online to access the full text. Of course, unless you needed to access a large quantity, you could use this site to "view" the most recent filings and then turn to one of the free SEC filing sites, such as SEC Info or EdgarScan, and retrieve the filing for free.

- *SEC INFO* (*http://www.secinfo.com*). Click on the Fair Disclosure Per Regulation FD link on the home page to display a chronological list of all related filings. The list includes the filing company's name, date, and a number that ties to a legend located at the bottom of the page telling you the purpose of the filing. The number 9 represents Reg FD filings.

Sources for Financial Disclosures: Print Publications

Several print resources are staples for providing examples of financial disclosures. While not always substitutes for conducting a database search, they are heavily used by most practitioners and you might want to consider purchasing them for quick reference. In most cases, the print publications are updated annually and so they will not contain examples of disclosures for recently released accounting standards. Key print resources for financial disclosures include the following:

- *Accounting Trends and Techniques* (*http://www.cpa2biz.com*). This annual print publication is an industry standard. Each year the AICPA reviews approximately 600 public company annual reports and extracts sections of the financial statements and footnotes which illustrate both frequently used and unusual disclosures. It also identifies the best practices of established companies as well as newer firms. The content is organized into topics that are cross-referenced to an index located in the back of the volume; the index also includes references to all pronouncements discussed. *Accounting Trends and Techniques* is only available electronically as part of the AICPA's reSOURCE subscription database.
- *Aspen-Miller GAAP Financial Statement Disclosures Manual* (*http://www.aspenpublishers.com*). This annual publication contains more than 900 examples of realistic sample footnote disclosures used in the preparation of financial statements. The manual also includes a financial statement disclosure checklist that provides a centralized resource for the required and recommended GAAP disclosures currently in use. The book is accompanied by a CD-ROM; it is accessible on some electronic databases, including CCH's Tax Network's Accounting & Audit Library.

- *AICPA Checklists and Illustrative Financial Statement* (*http://www. cpa2biz.com*). Each year the AICPA updates a series of checklists that reflect AICPA, FASB, and GASB pronouncements and interpretations; SEC regulations are referenced where applicable. There are approximately 12 titles in the series, including: *Corporations, Banks and Savings Institutions, Defined Benefit Pension Plans, Employee Health and Welfare Benefit Plans, Life Insurance, and Not-for-Profit Organizations.* The checklists are only available in print.

Sources for Business Ratios

As discussed in the previous section, business ratios, also known as financial or operating ratios, are used to evaluate a company's financial position. The financial researcher can assess a company's performance by comparing its current ratios with ratios from previous years or with ratios for its industry as a whole.

AGGREGATE INDUSTRY RATIOS. Before beginning our discussion of sources for aggregate industry ratios, let's look at the two systems developed by the U.S. government to classify or group U.S. industry segments. You will need to be familiar with these systems in order to use sources of industry ratios. The two systems are the Standard Industrial Classification (SIC) and the North American Industry Classification (NAICS) systems.[11] Although the NAICS system, which was developed to more accurately represent specific business niches, "officially" superseded the older SIC system in 2001, it has been slow to catch on and most companies and business research tools continue to follow the older SIC code system.

How do these classification systems work? SIC codes use two-digit codes to describe a broad range of industries, three-digit codes to break these down to more narrow sectors, and finally four-digit codes for specific industry niches. For example, the SIC code for the broad industry group for Engineering & Management Services is 87; within that group, 871 is the code assigned to Engineering & Architectural Services, and 8713 is the SIC code for Surveying Services. NAICS uses a similar system, but goes further by expanding the industry to a five- and, if necessary, six-digit

---

11. *Standard Industrial Classification Manual, 1987,* Executive Office of the President, Office of Management and Budget; *North American Industry Classification System, United States, 2002,* Executive Office of the President, Office of Management and Budget.

number. For example, under the NAICS system Computer Systems
Design is classified under the two-digit code for Professional,
Scientific, and Technical Services, 541 is the code assigned
the same title, 5415 and 54151 represent Computer Systems
Design and Related Services, and the narrower niche of Custom
Computer Programming Services is assigned the 541511 code.

Since your requestor may not know the specific code for his or
her client's industry, be sure to ask for a good description of what
the company does. Virtually all business research tools using SIC or
NAICS codes contain cross-references between the code and the
description, enabling you to easily identify the specific code even if
you only know the organization's industry. However, be prepared
for the possibility that you may not be able to find an exact match
for the industry. Historically the SIC code system has erred in
the direction of being more broad than specific; for example,
there is no SIC code for a company engaged as an Internet Service
Provider; but NAICS accommodates this industry niche in its
classification system. Find the closest match possible, but be sure
to communicate the complete description of the code to your
clients so that they can gauge the need to account for any variations in the data.

If the industry is not a clean match with the client's business, it
is very important that they be made aware of that fact.

You may want to purchase print copies of both the *Standard
Industrial Classification Manual* and the *NAICS/SIC Code United
States Manual* because you are going to need to reference these
frequently, and constantly looking up the information on the
Internet will prove to be a poor use of your time. More importantly,
both print manuals contain additional levels of explanation of
each code, which is not always found online but is extremely
helpful for determining the best code to match a company's
business. However, if you prefer to look them up on the Web, both
the SIC codes (*http://www.osha.gov/oshstats/sicser.html*) and NAICS
codes (*http://www.census.gov/epcd/www/naics.html*) are posted for
free on the Internet, including tables which cross-reference one to
the other. Both sites provide access by keyword searching and
browsing.

Two standard sources for accessing aggregate industry ratios
are *RMA's Annual Statement Studies: Financial Ratio Benchmarks*
(*http://www.rmahq.com*) and *Dun & Bradstreet's Industry Norms &
Key Business Ratios* (*http://www.dnb.com*). Both sets of data are
available in print and electronically directly from the respective

publishers. They are the most reliable sources in terms of reputation, breadth of industry coverage, and range of data analysis and each one continues to be relied on heavily by accountants and financial advisors in the preparation of the required business performance review. Both are organized by SIC code, with RMA beginning its conversion to NAICS with its 2003/2004 edition. While there is some overlap in the industries covered, Dun's includes many additional industries since it draws the data from its company database of more than one million financial statements. RMA gathers its information from its membership. Each includes some different ratios and may present the data slightly differently.

Following are some examples of ratios you will find using these sources:

- *Liquidity Ratios.* Measure the quality and adequacy of current assets to meet current obligations as they come due. Types of liquidity ratios are Quick Ratio, Sales/Receivables, and Cost of Sales/Inventory.
- *Operating Ratios.* Assist in the evaluation of management performance. Types of operating ratios are Sales/Total Assets and % Profits Before Taxes/Tangible Net Worth.

You should consider purchasing both sets of data if you are regularly asked to locate this type of information. Should you purchase the print or electronic formats? The answer will depend on the size of your budget and the importance to your work to be able to download the data into a spreadsheet. Evaluate differences in cost of one format over the other. Are there any significant differences in the content? The print versions of both sources are well organized and data is very easy to locate. Consider if the electronic version is as efficient to use as the print. You may be surprised that the answer may be no.

Troy's Almanac of Business and Industrial Financial Ratios (*http://www.amazon.com*) is another frequently referenced source of financial ratios. The data is drawn from IRS tax return data for almost 5 million U.S. and international corporations; it is available in print and CD-ROM. The CD-ROM version presents the data in .pdf and is not formatted for downloading into spreadsheets. More importantly within the context of conducting accounting and financial research, although *Troy's Almanac* is published annually, the most recent data generally runs two years behind. Since it is appropriate for providing the timely financial analysis that accountants and financial advisors need for their clients, *Troy's Almanac* is not included in our list of recommended sources.

Integra's Industry Financial Analysis Reports (*http://www. integrainformation.com*) and BizMiner's Financial Analysis Profiles (*http://www.bizminer.com*) provide industry-specific analysis of financial statement and ratio trends and forecasts. Available only in electronic format, both have introduced several pricing models for their content, including one-off purchase of discreet reports directly from their Web sites. You can view samples of the reports for free. Some Integra data is also available to subscribers of the OneSource Business Browser suite of databases.

COMPANY-SPECIFIC RATIOS. A number of sources, both print and electronic, provide profitability ratios for specific companies. The range of ratios included will not be as extensive as found in the sources discussed above, but may still be valuable for your research:

- *Mergent Online* (*http://www.mergentonline.com*). A subscription-based database that includes company-specific key ratios drawn from U.S. and international public companies. In addition to viewing ratios for specific companies, you can also build custom reports that compare ratios for a selected list of company peers. The data can be downloaded into .pdf, Word, and Excel. You can select the number of periods or years for retrieving the data, ranging as far back as 15 years.
- *Standard & Poor's Industry Surveys* (*http://www.standardandpoors. com*). Available both in print and electronically, the "Comparative Company Analysis" section of each industry report contains approximately five years of ratios for a peer group of U.S. public companies. Many public and academic libraries have the print volumes in their collections.
- *Standard & Poor's Stock Reports* (*http://www.standardandpoors. com*). Available both in print and electronically, each company report includes some key ratios. Many public and academic libraries have the print volumes in their collections.
- *OneSource Business Browser* (*http://www.onesource.com*). A subscription-based company and industry database containing ratio comparisons for a company and its industry and S&P 500 group. The data is drawn from Integra's database of industry financial analysis.
- *Investment Analyst Reports* (*http://www.investext.com*). Both company and industry reports often contain comparative financial data and ratios for a peer group; look to longer reports (generally 10+ pages) for this type of information.

Sources for Financial Market Data

As discussed in the previous section, accountants regularly request financial market data to independently assess the reasonableness of client assertions about the value of their company's assets and liabilities.

Identification and descriptions of the many sources for accessing financial market equity, debt, and index pricing and ratings are covered in great depth in the *Investment Research* volume of this series. Refer to this source for a more in-depth discussion of resources and strategies for locating this type of information.

There are an abundance of free financial sites on the Web that "appear" to contain good information, and while some are excellent and worth using, many are not. Remember that appearances can be deceiving. Never forget that the information you are gathering will be used to validate and support important business decisions. Using information that is out of date, incorrect, or unsubstantiated can result in placing your firm and your firms' clients at risk. Chose carefully and do not yield to the lure of an attractive, information-packed Web site or the pressure of "getting it for free" on which to base your resource selections. Rather, carefully consider the cost of the risk of *not* using reputable, reliable sources as weighed against the cost of subscribing to a particular product.

The instructions that accountants will give you to locate financial market data will often come in the form of incomplete or "cryptic" information. You may be provided with a list of stocks and bonds that you need to look up in order to verify pricing values or ratings. Oftentimes, the key to locating these is to identify the unique number that has been assigned to that entity and which allows for its quick and precise retrieval. The requestor may not always know this number and so it will often be left up to your creative wiles to locate it. Following are a few resources that you will want to add to your bag of survival tricks:

- *CUSIP Number.* A CUSIP is a unique number assigned to common and preferred stocks, mutual funds, and corporate and municipal bonds for security identification on the exchanges and over-the-market markets. For example, Walt Disney's CUSIP number is 254687106 and Coca Cola's number is 10121600. Some CUSIPs, especially government issues, include letters combined with numbers. CUSIP numbers are often the easiest and most exact method for looking up equity and security values, and in some cases you simply will not be able to locate the exact entity without knowing it. Typically, accountants do not volunteer this information, so you might need to request that they look it up on their client's investment brokerage report or contact the broker directly. While company ticker symbols (see discussion below) are widely reproduced in most public company print and free Web-based information sources, CUSIP numbers remain elusive. One excellent source for looking up CUSIPs is the Form706.com Web site, *http://www.form706.com.* This site is free but you will have to register to use it. Its search engine allows for quick and easy lookup by company name or one or multiple ticker symbols. A "record" contains the entity name, ticker symbol, and CUSIP number.

- *Ticker Symbol.* Public companies are assigned a unique 2- to 4-letter acronym to facilitate trading on one of the exchanges. While each company has a ticker, it can be more problematic than CUSIP numbers for retrieving the exact match since one company can have multiple tickers, many of which look very similar. You can try to locate a ticker on the company Web site (look for the "Investor Relations" section) or by using the form706.com site described above. Company ticker symbols are widely reproduced in most public company print and free Web-based information sources.

- *Mutual Funds.* (*http://www.quicken.com/investments/quotes*). Mutual funds have their own brand of unique identifying symbols. Also referred to as ticker symbols, they usually consist of five letters; for example, FAIGX is the symbol for the Fidelity Advisor Balanced Fund group. A diverse Web site, Quicken can also be used to look up the ticker symbols for companies and equity indices, such as the Dow Jones Industrial Average.

Sources for Economic Data

Just as accountants are required to validate client assertions about stocks and bonds, so they also need to tap into economic and monetary data, such as foreign exchange rates, the prime and LIBOR rates, U.S. Treasury bills, the Consumer and Producer Price Indexes, and more. While the use of economic data is certainly not unique to accounting and financial professionals, its specific application has relevance to this community. In the following section, we will identify the types of economic data that accounting and financial professionals regularly tap into and the best sources for accessing them.

There are multiple sites on the free Web and many subscription-based databases which contain economic and monetary data. How do you know which is the best source to use? Some of them present the same data with different output options (for example, Adobe .pdf, or Excel). The data may be averaged on a monthly, quarterly, or annual basis. Some sources provide the most recent month or year's worth of data, while others display 10, 15, 20, or more year's run of the data. Which source you turn to will depend largely on your client's needs. The more knowledge you have of the choices of sources, the more likely you can deliver closely matched results.

It is more important that you use sources that provide reliable, authoritative data. A recommended research practice is to begin by turning to the original author or source of the information. For example, the Federal Reserve is the primary source for the prime rate and federal fund rate; The Bureau of Labor Statistics is the primary source for the Consumer and Producer Price Indexes. However, as we discussed above, you ideally want to match the data itself with other options, such as output or date range, which most closely approximates what your client needs. Matching up all of these criteria is one of the primary reasons why you need to leverage from awareness of multiple sources for "like" information.

HISTORICAL AND CURRENT DATA. Accountants use historical data to test their clients' financial transactions that are recorded in the past and current data to test a value as of the balance sheet date. Following are some recommended sources for tapping into this important information:

- *Federal Reserve Board* (*http://www.federalreserve.gov*). The FRB is the primary source of U.S. banking financial and economic data. It has a main home page, but each of its 12 Federal Reserve District Banks has their own sites as well. The regional sites are especially useful for looking up state and regional data. While we are going to focus on the main FRB Web site, you are strongly encouraged to check out the regional sites. They are all excellent and each one contains some unique information. Following is some of the most frequently requested economic data accessible on the Fed's Web site:
  - Prime Rate
  - Foreign Exchange Rates
  - Federal Funds Rate

- Commercial Paper
- Certificates of Deposit ("CDs")
- Treasury Bills
- Treasury Bonds

The data is published in the form of Daily, Weekly, Monthly, and Annual Releases; the monthly and annual releases are usually calculated as averages. To view the releases, from the Federal Reserve home page, click on links to Economic Research and Data, then Statistics: Releases and Historical Data. Some of the releases are available in .pdf format and most of the data is formatted for downloading into Excel.

Each release is assigned a combination letter and number. The FRB's releases are frequently referenced to and reproduced on the free Web. Familiarity with these assigned designations is very useful for verifying the validity of the data and for sourcing it back to the Federal Reserve. You can also use your knowledge of a release number to run a quick search on a Web-based search engine. For example, typing "federal reserve h.15" links you to the most recent release of selected interest rates. Following are the most frequently requested releases:

- *Daily and Weekly Releases*
  - H.10—Foreign Exchange Rates
  - H.15—Selected Interest Rates. Contain Prime Rate, Federal Funds Rate, Certificates of Deposit, Treasury Bills, Treasury Bonds, and Moody's Aaa and Baa Bonds
- *Monthly Releases*
  - G.5—Foreign Exchange Rates
  - G.15—Selected Interest Rates. *Note*: Release G.15 was discontinued in January 2002. All selected interest rate data is now incorporated into Release H.15.
- *Annual Releases*
  - G.5A—Foreign Exchange Rates

Let's spend some time discussing foreign exchange rates before looking at some other sources of economic and monetary data. The Federal Reserve's releases are the recommended first places to turn for locating exchange rates. The FRB publishes "noon buying rates," which is often specifically requested by accountants. As of January 3, 2002, the European Community's (EU) euro currency is reported in place of the individual euro-country currencies. These are: Austrian schilling, Belgian francs, Finnish markkas, French francs, German marks, Irish pounds, Italian lire, Luxembourg francs, Netherlands guilders, Portuguese escudos, and Spanish pesetas. Typically accountants will ask for the exchange rate in the specific country's currency rather than con-verted to the euro. You may then need to take the initiative to make the conversation from the euro rate, as reported on the release's main table, to the U.S. dollar.

While confusing at first sight, the process for performing this calculation is really very simple. Located at the bottom of each release is a table that contains the number of individual country currencies that equal 1 euro. For example, 1 euro = 1.95583 German marks. The same data is reported for each of the 11 countries. To calculate the conversion, you multiply the number of the country's individual currency that equals 1 euro by the number of euros for the desired date that equal 1 U.S. dollar. Following is an example of how you calculate the conversion:

What is the German mark's monthly average exchange rate in U.S. dollars in January 2003?

- 1 EURO = 1.95583 German marks
- 1 U.S. dollar = 1.0622 euros
- 1.95583 x 1.0622 = 2.07 German marks = 1 U.S. dollar

Now let's take a look at the primary sources of some of the most frequently requested economic and monetary data and recom-mended "other" sources for tapping into this data.

- *Additional sources of foreign exchange rates.*
  - *Statistical Abstract of the United States* (*http://www.census.gov/statab/www*). Annual average exchange rates are available in the "Comparative International Statistics" section in a table entitled "Foreign Exchange Rates." The most recent year's rates are published in each annual edition of the Statistical Abstract, with the full text available in .pdf from 1995 on the Web site.
  - *The Currency Site* (*http://www.oanda.com*). Click on the link to Historical Rates on the home page. Only daily rates are available but you can download them into Excel and use the spreadsheet's Function/Average option to calculate the desired data.
  - *Pacific Exchange Rate Service* (*http://pacific.commerce.ubc.ca/xr*). This site includes several options for accessing exchange rates, including Historical Annual Average Rates from 1948–present in .pdf. It also includes links to other exchange rate sources and a list of the currency name for each country.
  - *Bureau of Labor Statistics, Department of Commerce* (*http://stats.bls.gov*). The BLS is the primary source of key U.S. economic

indicators, such as the CPI,[12] inflation, PPI,[13] Employment Cost Index, Unemployment Rate, and more. Current and historical statistical data is aggregated nationally, regionally, and on a state level. You can retrieve particular data as published or run customized queries to retrieve specific data. From the BLS home page, click on the link to Get Detailed Statistics.

The BLS has worked hard to make this search process as user-friendly as possible, but it can be cumbersome and confusing the first time around. Try running a few test runs; the queries are free and run quickly. If you simply cannot make sense of it or need validation of the returned data, send an e-mail to the BLS Help Desk (labstat.helpdesk@bls.gov) or call your local or regional office (phone numbers will be posted on the BLS Web site).

- *Economic Indicators (http://www.access.gpo.gov/congress/cong002. html)*. A monthly government publication, Economic Indicators, is available in full text in .pdf on the Web. Individual issues dating back to 1998 and a searchable database dating back to 1995 are accessible on the site. The strength of this publication is that it pulls together in one place a great deal of the financial and economic data released by the Federal Reserve, the BLS, and other government and private-sector sources, such as Dow Jones, Standard & Poor's, and the major U.S. stock exchanges. Since it is only published monthly, the most recent data may be one to two months behind; you will still need to access the sites of the originating data sources for the most recent data releases.

- *Statistical Abstract of the United States (http://www.census. gov/prod/ww.statistical-abstract-01.html)*. Beginning with the 1995 edition, the content included in this annual publication is available for free on the Census Bureau's Web site. Drawing from most government and quasi-governmental agencies and some private-sector sources, it is a virtual cornucopia of local, state, national, and international government economic, financial, and statistical data. Since Statistical Abstracts is published annually, you will need to consult the originating data source to access the most recent releases.

---

12. The CPI is a measurement of consumer spending. The rate (percent) of change of the CPI is inflation. Often accountants will ask for the CPI when what they really want is the rate of inflation. Be sure to clarify exactly what information they are seeking.

13. PPI (*http://www.stats.bls.gov/ppi/home.htm*). Accountants frequently request the PPI index and percentage of change for a specific manufacturing sector. Fortunately, the PPI database, located at Get Detailed Statistics, allows you to search on specific criteria, such as the exact industry sector over a specified period of time. You can create customized output tables for one or multiple pieces of data.

- *Economic Report of the President* (*http://w3.access.gpo.gov/eop*). Considered a favorite source for referencing key economic and financial data, the *Economic Report of the President* is published annually in February or March. Each edition contains a section of tables that are lifted right out of Economic Indicators. The tables are accessible in Excel beginning with 1997. You might want to print out the frequently requested ones each year and keep them close by for quick reference. However, remember that the annual publication data will not contain the most recent year's data. The following tables will be the most relevant for your research:
  - Prices
  - Money Stock, Credit and Finance
  - Corporate Profits and Finance
  - International Statistics

FORECASTED DATA. A forecast is an educated perception of how a decision being contemplated will affect the future of the business. As discussed in the previous section, forecasted economic data may be used by the accountant to test a company's financial statement projects used for valuing a business or asset, or for evaluating the company's ability to demonstrate continued existence, referred to as "going concern." There are only a limited number of sources providing reliable forecasted economic data. Following are a few of the best:

- *The Budget and Economic Outlook, Congressional Budget Office* (*http://www.cbo.gov*). The CBO's Budget and Economic Outlook is published annually with a mid-year update. It is one of the best sources for forecasts of economic indicators, such CPI, PPI, GDP, and Treasury Rates. It also reports historical and current data. Links to the most Current Economic Projections and the Outlook are displayed on the CBO home page.
- *U.S. Outlook, Conference Board* (*http://www.conference-board.org*). The Conference Board posts the U.S. Outlook each quarter on its Web site. It contains quarterly data and forecasted data going back one year, with annual forecasted data going out two years. The data is reported as seasonally adjusted annual rates (%). Coverage includes: Real GDP, CPI/Inflation, 90-Day T-Bills, 10-Year Treasury Bonds, and more. To access U.S. Outlook, click on the Economic tab at the top of the home page; click on the link to U.S. Outlook.
- *BusinessWeek's Economic Forecast Survey* (*http://www.businessweek. com*). Published annually with a mid-year update, this forecast

covers the state of the economy and contains key current and forecasted data. It includes U.S. and global economic data and financial market indexes. You must be a subscriber to the print or electronic edition of BusinessWeek to access this data. To access the survey, type "Economic Forecast Survey" in the search box on the BusinessWeek home page.

- *Financial Forecast Center* (*http://www.forecasts.org*). Turn to this site for forecasts of stock indexes (Dow Jones Industrials, D&P 500, etc.), money rates, (Prime, Treasury Bills, etc.) exchange rates, and economic indicators (CPI, inflation, etc). The site also contains historical data.

INTERNATIONAL ECONOMIC DATA. The increased need for international economic data, of which the LIBOR rate is one of the most requested, is directly tied to the increased globalization of corporate business operations. Following are some reliable sources for tapping into international economic data.

- *London Interbank Offered Rate* (*http://www.bba.org.uk/media*). The LIBOR rate is a measurement of what major international banks charge each other for large-volume loans of Eurodollars or dollars on deposit outside the United States. It is a close equivalent to the U.S. prime rate. This site contains current and historical (dating back to 1987) LIBOR rates, reported as 1 month, 2 months, 3 months, 6 months, and 12 months. All the data is available in Excel.
- *World Economic Outlook Database* (*http://www.imf.org/external/pubs/ft/weo*). The WEO, published in May and October each year, aggregates annual country economic data. Each series contains annual data beginning with 1970 and projects out two to three years. All data is available in Excel. This site can be a bit trying to navigate but it is worth the effort. It contains an impressive amount of reputable data and most of it is available for free. The economic series included are:
  - Real Gross Domestic Product (annual percent change)
  - GDP (local currency and U.S. dollars)
  - Inflation (annual percent change)
- *Economist Intelligence Unit ViewsWire* (*http://www.eiu.com*). EIU is one of the most reputable names in the business for international economic data. Its subscription-based ViewsWire database includes a large range of data reported on a country-by-country and regional basis. The information includes economic structure, interest indicators, outlook, five-year forecasts, country risk ratings, and backgrounders.

- *Euromonitor's Global Market Information Database (http://www.euromonitor.com)*. Euromonitor specializes in collecting international economic, demographic, and consumer-focused data. The Country Data and Forecasts modules of this subscription-based database include consumer prices and costs, economic indicators, income and learning, labor, and external trade data reported on a country and regional basis. The strength of this interface is the ability to easily create customized data queries and reports and to download all the data to Excel.

Sources for Corporate Strategic and Operational Intelligence

In the capacity of accountant and financial advisor, your client might need to identify a number of internal and external business factors that impact an organization's financial performance. These can include a company's broad objectives and strategies, scope and description of lines of business, property and plants, and inherent and environmentally imposed external risks. Following are some of the most essential sources of that level of information:

ANNUAL REPORTS. Although not official SEC filings, annual reports are produced by virtually all U.S. public companies (and many private companies). These documents are usually available within three months after the fiscal year ends. For example, the majority of U.S. public companies have a December 31 year-end and March and April are when most public company annual reports are released.

The annual report contains some important financial information, including financial statements, financial footnotes, and the auditor's report. Its purpose is to tell its shareholders the story of the company's financial position, management and business successes and present challenges for the prior year, and strategies and opportunities for the future. Look here for information about a company's broad objectives and strategies, scope and description of lines of business, background on upper management, and merger and acquisition activity. In the President's Letter to the Shareholders, the CEO will recount the major events of the past year and set the tone for the year to come.

Annual reports are often used as marketing pieces and as such, are biased in favor of creating the most favorable picture for current and prospective shareholders. This natural bias does not detract from their value as long as you understand it and seek out additional sources to verify any information that your clients might rely on for important financial or business decisions.

How do you locate a company's annual report? Since they are not required SEC filings, they will not be available on free EDGAR sites. However, key sections, such as the financial statements, financial footnotes, MD&A, and Auditor's Opinion, are usually either introduced into the body of the 10-K or incorporated by reference into the 10-K's Exhibit 13. Many of the EDGAR sites call the 10-K the annual report, since technically the 10-K is the company's annual filing. Don't be mislead by this labeling; you are not accessing the entire annual report on these free sites.

Most public companies now post the past two to three years of their annual reports on their Web sites for free, usually in .pdf format. These are usually located in a section called "Investor Relations," "Financial Information," "About Us," or similar such descriptions. If you do not find a link to the report in .pdf, you are probably not viewing the entire document. If what you need is not located on the site and time is not of the essence, contact the company directly (ask for the Investor Relations Department) and they will send you a free copy. Report Gallery (*http://www. reportgallery.com*) is a free Web site that links to annual reports of many U.S. companies. Many public and academic libraries also have collections of historical SEC filings and annual reports on microform. If you are unable to locate the report for free, there are several subscription-based and for-pay electronic services that you can use to download annual reports, including LexisNexis, Thomson Research, and Mergent Online.

When deciding on the most appropriate outlet for accessing annual reports, consider if it is a high priority for you to view and output the documents in image format. If the answer is yes, then Thomson Research or Mergent Online are databases you should consider. Thomson Research contains the most comprehensive collection of annual report images on its Web site. As the original contractor with the SEC for its paper filings, a sister company, Disclosure, also has the largest and oldest repository of paper SEC filings and company annual reports. Accountants often need to access filings that are older than what is available in digital format (generally pre-early 1990s). If you regularly need older documents, you might want to set up an account with Disclosure; they can ship any documents to you. Mergent Online also provides access to annual report images through their subscription service.

There is, however, one important disadvantage to searching annual reports in .pdf format—they cannot be free-text searched. Instead, keywords are limited to basic search fields, such as company name and date. Most database vendors do not make this point clear. If you need to search across the full text of annual reports for your client research, LexisNexis and Dialog both provide text-only versions. However, keep in mind that while you benefit from the ability to conduct keyword searches across the complete document text, you also sacrifice the power of viewing and outputting the annual report in its original format with pictures, graphs, and colors.

COMPANY WEB SITES. Public company Web sites contain a wealth of information about an organization. Look for links to press releases, external articles, annual reports, management profiles, customer lists, product development, and other information that might provide you with critical insights into an organization's financial and strategic position and directions. Spend some time scouring the site; do not assume that what you are looking for will always be located in the obvious places.

Since private companies are not required to publicly disclose information, their Web sites often contain the most, and sometimes only, financial and strategic information that you will be able to locate. Sometimes the Web sites are duds! But do not neglect to check. The competitive marketplace is even driving private companies to reveal more about themselves.

INVESTMENT ANALYST REPORTS. Company and industry reports written by investment brokerage firms, such as Merrill Lynch, Goldman Sachs, or Deutsche Bank, are excellent sources of company strategic and operational intelligence. They often reflect a unique "inside" knowledge of the companies they track that you will not find in newspaper and magazine articles. These reports are rich sources of financial information, detailing a company's current, historical, and estimated projected financial health, comparative financial analysis with key industry competitors, analysis of the company's lines of business, risk analysis of continued performance, industry "hot" issues, and forecasts and strategies. Their focus on risk analysis is especially valuable to accountants and financial advisors.

Access to these reports is largely limited to fee-based electronic services, but most of these allow you to search for and view an individual report's table of contents (TOC) for free. You have the option of either purchasing an entire report or select pages. With a cost per page of $8.00 to $10.00 and a substantive report ranging from eight to several hundred pages, the purchase by discreet page is the best bang for your buck. You will need to ask your client upfront to define exactly what information is needed and the maximum amount of money available. Usually you will be able to determine the sections to purchase by scanning the TOC. If you are not sure, have your client select the relevant pages. You never want to make assumptions and risk making poor purchasing decisions. Your clients rely on your ability to manage their research budgets effectively.

Where do you locate analyst reports? While some current reports might be posted on a company or analyst's Web site (it is *always* worth a look), the majority must be purchased using an electronic database service. The best of these services include: Thomson's Research Bank on the Web (*http://www.investext.com*), Multex (*http://www.multex.com*), Factiva (*http://global.factiva.com*), LexisNexis (*http://www.lexisnexis.com*), and Dialog (*http://www.dialog.com*). These are the "best" because they contain the largest collections of U.S. and international brokerage firms and their analysts. Typically, financial professionals will seek reports written by recognized firms.

If purchasing analyst reports is not an option, an alternative is to look for articles in newspapers and trade magazines that contain data extracted or summarized from these reports. While not the same as accessing the full reports, journalists will often quote key financial, operational, and strategic passages and data from these reports. Factiva, LexisNexis, and Dialog are examples of electronic business databases that aggregate such articles from large collections of external business sources. Especially tailored for this type of research are two additional databases, Business & Industry and TableBase, both available on Dialog and other aggregators. The former specializes in company and market intelligence and the latter contains a collection of statistical and content-rich tables that are culled from articles, analyst reports, and other documents.

When searching Factiva, LexisNexis, and Dialog, consider incorporating keywords such as "annual report," "analyst," "trends," "outlook," "strategic," "strategy," or "future" into the article's headline and lead paragraph. If you know the particular analyst or brokerage house that tracks a company (this information is usually posted on the company's Web site), another useful strategy for locating insightful discussions is to introduce the analyst or brokerage house name into the search statement. Take advantage of Business & Industry and TableBase's excellent indexing to develop focused search strategies.

MANAGEMENT DISCUSSION & ANALYSIS. Recent accounting scandals have placed new emphasis on this section of the 10-K, found in Part II, Item 7 of the document body. Written by the CEO, the MD&A gives the investor an opportunity to examine the company's performance through the eyes of management by providing both a short- and long-term analysis of the business. It provides a narrative explanation of the financial statements in order to make the financial statements and accompanying footnotes understandable to a reader who is not a financial professional.

The MD&A usually begins with management's identification and evaluation of information, including the potential effects of known trends, commitments, events, and uncertainties—important issues for providing investors with an accurate understanding of the company's current and prospective financial position and operating results. Typically, it is included in both the company's 10-K and its annual report. Use any of the free EDGAR Web sites, such as SEC Info (*http://www.secinfo.com*) or EdgarScan (*http://edgarscan.pwcglobal.com/servlets/edgarscan*) to locate the 10-K. Click on links contained in the hyperlinked TOC to quickly locate the MD&A, either by the section name or the section part.

SEC FAIR DISCLOSURE. Discussed in the earlier section on financial disclosures, the transcripts of the analyst morning calls can also be extremely powerful for gleaning intelligence about a company's strategic and operational strengths, challenges, and future directions.

THE WALL STREET TRANSCRIPT (*HTTP://WWW.TWST.COM*). This subscription-based service provides several different vantage points for learning more about a company's management, strategies, and operations. Focused on seven industry sectors (technology, finance, health, consumer, industrial, natural, and investing), TWST contains analyst commentary on a company's performance, roundtable discussions of industry experts, and pithy CEO interviews offering a very personal and direct perspective on an organization's markets, competitors, management, and other important issues. You can subscribe to all seven sectors or individual ones. The *Wall Street Transcript* is accessible directly from its publisher or from several electronic database aggregators, including Research Bank on the Web and Factiva. This is an excellent service and so reasonably priced that it is worth subscribing to all of the available content directly from the publisher if you do not already have access via one of these databases.

Sources for Information about Corporate Governance

Corporate governance is certain to remain a pervasive issue for financial professionals, corporate management, outside advisors, shareholders, and employees. The close working relationship between accountants and a company's management, board, and committees, and the increased public and regulatory focus on accountability on both sides ensures that requests for corporate governance type information will remain a high priority. Some recommended Web sites for tracking corporate governance include: SEC (*http://www.sec.gov*), AICPA (*http://www.aicpa.org*), FASB (*http://www.fasb.org*), the Big Four Accounting Firms (Deloitte Touche, *http://www.deloitte.com*; PricewaterhouseCoopers, *http://www.pwcglobal.com*; KPMG, *http://www.kpmg.com*; and Ernst & Young, *http://www.ey.com*), the New York Stock Exchange (*http://www.nyse.com*), and the National Association of Securities Dealers (*http://www.nasd.com*). Financial newspapers, such as the *Wall Street Journal* and the *Financial Times*, and magazines, including the *Economist, Forbes, Fortune,* and *CFO Magazine*, will continue to heavily report on this important topic. Several research institutes are actively publishing white papers and sponsoring lecture series and conferences on corporate governance. These include

Harvard's Corporate Governance Initiative, *http://www.cglv. hbs.edu/index.html* and the International Institute for Corporate Governance, Yale School of Management, *http://iicg.som.yale. edu/index.shtml.*

CORPORATE MANAGEMENT AND BOARD MEMBER BIOGRAPHICAL PROFILES.

For U.S. public companies, both the 10-K and the annual proxy statement, officially known as SEC filing DEF 14A, are key sources of employment history and board activity for a company's upper management and members of the board of directors. The proxy statement is a written document that the SEC requires to be provided to shareholders before they vote by proxy on corporate matters. It typically contains proposed members of the board of directors, inside director's salaries, changes in company officers, and other management-related matters.

Top management are profiled in the 10-K (look for a section called Executive Officers) and the board of directors' biographies appear in the proxy statement when their elections are confirmed. Typically these profiles contain an individual's management-level positions, including title and years, and the current boards that he or she sit on. Most public companies now also post biographical information for upper management on their Web sites. Some private companies may also place biographical information on their sites; it is always worth a look.

Newspaper and magazine articles are also good sources for biographical profiles. Look for articles that profile a company or its CEO. When an executive is promoted or hired, an in-depth profile will often be published in the *Wall Street Journal* and in local or regional newspapers. Following are some recommended strategies for locating biographical profiles using electronic databases:

* Include the word "profile" or "interview" in the headline/title or lead paragraph. For example, if you want to locate a profile of Coca Cola's CEO, Douglas Daft, using Factiva, your search strategy would be: hlp=(doug* w/2 daft) and hlp=(profile or interview).
* Articles that profile a company will often contain background information on its top management within the body of the document text. Using the example from above, use the following search strategy to unearth these types of articles: hlp=(overview or outlook or profile or trend* or forecast or future) and doug* w/2 daft.

- If the individual has a middle name, you will need to develop a keyword search that allows for the possible occurrence of a middle name or initial. For example, searching for "james w/2 hamilton" will retrieve mention of james hamilton, james henry hamilton, or james h. hamilton. In most cases, options for conducting this level of complex searching is only available using one of the powerful subscription-based databases, such as LexisNexis or Factiva. Work with the database's customer service to understand its command language to determine the best strategy for allowing for a middle name or initial. When it comes to using one of the free EDGAR sites or Web search engines, your options for comprehensive name searches is greatly limited. In most cases, you can only search for the first and last name, and hope for the best. Unfortunately, you are virtually guaranteed of missing some potentially important information.

The company directories identified below include brief biographical sketches of company management and/or members of the board of directors. Available in print and electronically, most public and academic libraries should have the print versions in their reference collections.

- Standard & Poor's Register of Corporations, Directors and Executives Volume (*http://www.standardandpoors.com*)
- Dun & Bradstreet's Million Dollar Directory (*http://www.dnb.com*)

COMPENSATION AND BENEFITS. Salaries paid to corporate management, board, and committee members also fall under the umbrella of corporate governance. Financial advisors frequently work with both private and public companies to determine the best salary structure.

- *Public Companies.* Details about management's comprehensive compensation package, including salaries, perks, and other benefits for a public company's upper management, are spelled out in its annual proxy statement. The base salary is usually published in the 10-K, and can also be found in company directories and online databases, such as Standard & Poor's and Dun and Bradstreet.
- *Private Companies.* Since U.S. private companies are not required to disclose financial information, it is very difficult to find compensation data and to verify the accuracy of what you do find. If you are able to locate any data, it will be limited to straight salary. One possible source of information for private

companies is Dun & Bradstreet Business Information Reports (*http://www.dnb.com*). D&B's Information Reports, popularly referred to as "D&Bs," are available directly from D&B (*http://www.dnb.com*) on a subscription basis. They can also be accessed via some of the electronic business aggregators, such as Dialog and Factiva, or purchased as needed from many Web interfaces, including Hoovers (*http://www.hoovers.com*).

You can also try to locate salary data by identifying lists ranking the wealthiest executives or the top private companies. These lists can be found in local and regional newspapers, business chronicles, and business magazines, such as *Forbes* and *Fortune*. Gary Price's List of Lists (*http://www.specialissues.com*), a free Web-based directory, contains an excellent collection of links to many of these lists and rankings. Bizjournals (*http://www.bizjournals.com*) is the primary source for purchasing the business chronicle lists. They are also available in an annual publication called the Book of Lists and can be purchased in print or CD-ROM. Bizjournals has a search engine that does allow for simple keyword search in specific chronicles, but the search engine and full-text access is extremely limited.

Audit Committees. With the Sarbanes-Oxley Act now requiring that the auditor report solely to the audit committee, it is absolutely critical for accountants to perform good due diligence research on the individual committee members. The identification of the members is reported annually in the proxy statement, and the pressure of companies to demonstrate the independence of this committee to its management and the board will likely result in company press releases containing additional background information and any updated information. This information will likely be posted directly on the company's Web site. It can also be located by running a keyword search in electronic databases containing wire stores and press releases, such as Factiva and LexisNexis. For your search strategy, free text search the name of the company combined with the phrase "audit committee."

Sources for Information about International Business

As corporate boundaries continue to blur in our increasingly global economy, the research need is increasing for reconciling accounting standards for entities doing business in multiple countries, and for U.S.-based companies to attempt to reconcile international accounting standards with GAAP. Should the day come when there is true convergence of all accounting standards, the process will be greatly streamlined. In the meantime, the researcher trying to identify accounting standards for different countries is limited to a handful of print resources. While some of these documents are also available electronically, this remains largely a manual research task. If you are regularly required to locate international accounting standards, consider purchasing some of the print editions for your local library collections. See Appendix 3: Reference Bookshelf, for a recommended list of primary and secondary accounting and audit sources for international accounting standards.

One caveat: Accounting standards for some countries will not be accessible using any of these sources. In these cases, you will have to work through the accounting board for that country (relatively easy to identify using the free Web; for example: "argentina accounting board"), but be prepared for a possible language challenge as the Web site and the standards might only be available in the country's native language.

INTERNATIONAL BUSINESS OPERATIONS. As companies stretch to redefine themselves globally, they will continue to tap into accountants' financial insights and broad-based business knowledge to provide them with critical information about the international economic, financial, and regulatory data necessary to make international "doing business" types of decisions. There are two categories of sources to consider:

- *Books and Loose-leaf Services.* Several publishers are known for their "doing business" type publications: CCH (*http://www.cch.com*) and Matthew Bender (*http://www.matthewbender.com*) issue a series of loose-leaf services focused on accounting, legal, regulatory, and corporate matters; BNA's (*http://www.bna.com*), *Tax Management Portfolio* series includes a series of volumes on individual countries. Several of the Big Four accounting firms, most notably Ernst & Young (*http://www.ey.com*), publish an ongoing series of individual books on "doing business" in different countries.
- *Economist Intelligence Unit* (*http://www.eiu.com*). EIU is one of the most reputable publishers of "doing business" information. It publishes a numbers of newsletters and reports, all of which are available both in print and electronically. While EIU places

some current news stories and discreet economic data on its free site, most of the content is available on a subscription-basis only.

The EIU report that most closely addresses the accountant's research needs is *Country Commerce*, a guide to the business environment, regulatory framework, and trading risk for more than 60 countries. Each country report includes business and political climate, incentives, licensing requirements, corporate and personnel taxes, HR requirements, foreign trade regulations, e-commerce infrastructure, and more. Two other important EIU reports, *Country Risk Service* and *Risk Ratings Review*, focus on the business risks inherent in doing business in a particular country and geographic region.

Sources for Competitive Intelligence

The accounting and financial marketplace is becoming increasingly competitive and organizations engaged in providing these types of services are challenged to stay informed about and keep a step ahead of the competition. Following are some key areas in which you might be engaged by your firm's internal departments to activate regular environmental scans.

IDENTIFYING COMPANY AUDITORS. "Who audits who" is one of an accounting firm's primary sources of market share intelligence. In other words, what percentage of a particular market (typically defined geographically or by industry) do you and your competitors command? There are many reliable sources, both free and subscription-based, that you can turn to determine the most recent auditor of a U.S. public parent company. Here is a public company listing:

- *SEC Filings.* Look for the name of the company's auditor in several filings:
  - As the signature at the bottom of the auditor's report, located in the annual report, or incorporated as reference into the 10-K in Exhibit 13.
  - As an 8-K filing, Item 4, the required SEC disclosure about change in auditor; this 8-K must be filed within 10 days of the change taking place, and is often also publicly announced by the company as a press release.

- In the proxy statement is a statement affirming the continued services of the current accountant or a change of accountant.

Several of the EDGAR sites, including SEC Info (*http://www. secinfo.com*) and LIVEDGAR (*http://www.gsionline.com*), are now providing direct links to the change of auditor section of the SEC filing with an option to keyword search that section. If you conduct a keyword search across SEC filings, include all the following synonyms in the search statement: "auditor," "accounting firm," "accountant."

- *Public Company Directories and Databases.* The following print and electronic products cull financial data and text-based information from a public company's SEC filings. You can use any of them to identify a public company's auditor:
  - Mergent Online (*http://www.mergentonline.com*)
  - Standard & Poor's Register of Corporations, Executives and Directors (*http://www.standardandpoors.com*)
  - Dun's Million Dollar Directory (*http://www.dnb.com*)
  - Dun's Million Dollar Disc Plus (*http://www.dnb.com*)

When evaluating the use or purchase of any of the electronic databases, consider both the search strategy and required output. Let's say, for instance, that you have identified target companies for which you need to find out the name of the auditors. The targets may be specific companies or a group of companies that fit a desired profile, such as belonging to a particular geographic area or industry group. The database must allow you to specify the desired search criteria as well as to request a customized output that includes the company name and accounting firm.

In another search, however, you may want to identify all of the companies that use a particular auditor. In this scenario, the database must contain a field for accounting firm in which you can enter or select the firm name. You must also be able to request that the output contain this information.

Since U.S. private companies are not required to disclose their auditors, most do not. Private companies do not file with the SEC and so tapping into SEC filings is not an option. If you are trying to locate auditors of private companies, you are limited to a few sources, and what you will find is hit and miss at best. In most cases, the accounting firm information will not be included and when it is, it is often incorrect. It is important that you communicate these limitations to your requestor so that he or she is prepared for less than stellar results. Short of calling up the company and hoping that they will tell you who its auditor is, there is simply nothing else you can do to fill in the gaps except try the following directories:

- *Public Company Directories and Databases.* A very few vendors do attempt to identify private company auditors:
  - Standard & Poor's Register of Corporations, Executives and Directors (*http://www.standardandpoors.com*)
  - Dun's Million Dollar Directory (*http://www.dnb.com*)
  - Dun's Million Dollar Disc Plus (*http://www.dnb.com*)
- *Tracking Industry Trends and Competitors.* Remaining competitive requires careful scanning of the "business landscape;" in other words, knowing your industry's hot issues and key competitors. The following discussion highlights three of the best source categories and strategies for supporting your organization's efforts to sustain its own growth and guarantee success in the marketplace.
- *Newsletters and Newspapers.* There are a number of excellent newsletters and newspapers that specifically follow the events and key players in the accounting and related services industry. Typically, these contain profiles of specific companies, conduct annual rankings such as top firms, top people, and top regional firms, and track trends and hot issues. Each publication has a print edition and most are also available from the publisher as electronic subscriptions:
  - Public Accounting Report, Aspen Publishers (*http://www. aspenpublishers.com*)
  - Emerson's Professional Services Review, The Emerson Company
  - Accounting Today, Accountants Media Group, a Thomson Company (*http://www.electronicaccountant.com*)
  - International Accounting Bulletin, Lafferty (*http://www. lafferty.com*)

While some of these resources are available selectively on aggregators, such as Factiva and LexisNexis, the article coverage is very selective and usually does not include key competitor rankings and other tabular data. Exclusive reliance on these databases puts you at risk of missing important competitive intelligence. For comprehensive coverage, you will want to explore subscribing to electronic versions directly from the publishers.

All businesses, from the smaller boutique firms to the largest international organizations, are concerned about their local and regional market share. While the newsletters identified above typically focus on larger firms, the best sources for competitive information on smaller, private companies, are local newspapers and regional business chronicles. Both usually publish "top ranked lists" throughout the year, profile individual companies, and track corporate and management events and promotions within the business community.

Unfortunately, very little of this type of information, other than what can be found in more substantive, feature articles, is captured electronically. Solid competitive intelligence requires that these papers be visually scanned. Look for sections highlighting "People on the Move," or "Movers and Shakers." Often the coverage is just two or three sentences, but these can contain key competitive information that could make the difference in your organization's competitive positioning.

- *Company Web Sites.* Regularly scanning your competitors' Web sites can be an effective and free way to track competitor information. Keep in mind the source of the information—the company itself. While this means that the information is biased, that does not detract from its potential importance. As with all information, no matter what the source, you will want to weigh its value and always try to validate the facts using other sources. Companies sometimes reveal surprising pieces of information about themselves, often without meaning to. Scan a variety of areas on each Web site, especially those with these or similar headings:
  - About Us
  - Investor Relations
  - Financials
  - News
  - Products
  - Services
  - Customers/Clients
  - Awards/Recognition
  - Employment
- *Electronic Business Databases.* Running "on-the-fly" searches or setting up automatic alerts using aggregators, such as Lexis-Nexis or Factiva, can be very useful in tracking your competition. Keep in mind that depending on the level of competitive intelligence that you need to gather, searching across these large databases may be just one of several steps, including checking company Web sites, and scanning industry newsletters and local newspapers, as discussed above.

  These large business databases will not contain all of the sources you need to search and even the publications that are available in full text almost always only include selective articles. Step 1 is understanding the strengths and limitations of each of the of sources; step 2 is developing a search strategy which ensures that you retrieve all the relevant information. When developing your strategy, consider the following:

- *Name of target companies.* Verify the correct spelling, and never include in your search term endings such as co, corp, plc, llc, etc. Take into consideration mergers or other events which have resulted in name changes and, depending on the timeframe of your search, include all the possible name variations.

- *Specificity.* Be as specific as possible about what you are looking for without narrowing the query so much that you miss information. Easier said than done! Consider these techniques:

Work with the database customer service staff to ensure that you take full advantage of *all* the power search options that are available.

Inexact language is the bane of good searching. Use synonyms, Boolean logic, and nesting techniques to maximize your ability to "guess" the right keywords. If you are searching for specific company products or services or other events, study the company Web site and industry newsletters to make sure you are using the right terminology. For example, suppose you are interested in tracking your competitor's mergers and acquisitions advisory services. One company might label that service "corporate finance" while another calls it "financial services." Mergers and acquisitions are implied in the service description so those exact words may not be used by the company or anywhere in the article. Search too narrowly and you might miss key articles; search too broadly and you may find yourself scanning hundreds of irrelevant stories.

LOCATING AUDIT FEES. The good news is that beginning in 2001, public companies have been required to disclose the fees that are paid to their accounting firms for services provided. If you need that information prior to this period, or for any period for private companies, it is not available. When the SEC required that audit fees begin to be disclosed in 1991, they established the proxy statement as the official source for that information and defined how these fees were to be broken out. The Sarbanes-Oxley Act made some significant changes to this breakdown of fees and additionally required that beginning in December 2003, fee disclosures be included in both the proxy and 10-K filings.

How can you efficiently hone in on this information? If you need to identify fees paid by a specific company, your best approach is to locate the proxy statement for that company and use the hyperlinked table of contents to locate the relevant section of the filing. Unfortunately, the verbiage used to describe the fees is not always exactly the same, so limiting a keyword search to "audit fees" might not always yield good results. After December 2003, apply the same strategy described above to the 10-K. Since this is filed at least three to four months prior to the proxy, you will be able to locate the information more quickly.

If your research requires that you locate the information across multiple companies, your best bet is to hone in on the section of the filing in which audit fees are located, rather than on experimenting with multiple variations of keywords. Work with the vendor for the interface you are using to determine the most effective strategy. If keyword searching is the only option, try the following search statements: "audit* fee*", "accounting fee*, (fee* w/6 (accounting or audit* or accountant*)).

If your company needs to regularly scan for this data and to manipulate the data in spreadsheets, you might consider contacting The Emerson Company, the same company that publishes the *Professional Services Review* newsletter discussed above. Emerson maintains a complete database of all the data extracted from the filings and broken out per the SEC requirements. This resource is a subscription-based service.

SALARY AND ADMINISTRATIVE SURVEYS. Three good sources to consider are described below:

- *Institute of Management and Administration* (*http://www.ioma. com*). IOMA is a B2B publisher of management topics in Corporate Finance, Human Resources, Legal, Design & Construction, and CPA Firm Management. The following subscription newsletters contain select salary data in almost every issue:
  - "Accounting Office Management and Administration Report"
  - "Accounting Department Management and Administration Report"
  - "Partner's Report for CPA Firm Owners"
  - "Report on Salary Surveys"

- *Free e-Newsletter.* IOMA publishes several excellent monthly electronic newsletters containing good, quick management information and tips; you will be required to register on the site to subscribe. "Business Technology Update" will keep you informed on the latest CRM, ERP, or ASP product reviews and IT policies. Stay abreast of current business technology trends and learn about the latest Web-enabled accounting software or discover solutions for real-time accessibility for clients. Other e-Newsletters of interest include "Financial Management News" and "Consultant's Focus."
- *Robert Half Finance & Accounting and Accountemps Annual Salary Survey Guide* (*http://www.roberthalffinance.com*). This excellent free report includes national and regional salaries for professional and administrative personnel in the accounting and finance industries; available on the Web site in .pdf.

Sources for Information on Accounting and Financial Software Packages: Annual Surveys and Product Reviews

The following sources publish annual accounting and financial software reviews and rankings:

- *Accounting Technology* (*http://www.electronicaccountant.com*)
  - Subscription-based print and electronic editions.
  - Publishes a review of accounting software and technology in almost every monthly issue. If you need to subscribe to an accounting technology magazine, this is the one.
  - Reviews include: Professional Financial Planning; Payroll Software; Low-Cost Accounting Software; Time and Billing Software; Trial Balance Software; Fixed Assets Software; Tax Planning Software.
- *CFO.com* (*http://www.cfomagazine.com*)
  - CFO.com is the free, electronic version of the *CFO Magazine*. It is geared toward financial executives; its articles focus on new accounting standards, risk management, technology issues and solutions, and professional career development.
  - CFO publishes several important accounting software buyer's guides, including High-End Accounting Software Vendors, Midrange Accounting Software Vendors, and Value-Added Resellers (VARs).
  - Its Web site offers free topical e-mail alerts, notifying you when new articles are published on subjects you specify from a list, including accounting, auditing, cash management, disclosure, finance, software, tax, and risk management.

- *Accounting Today (http://www.electronicaccountant.com)*
  - Subscription-based print and electronic editions.
  - Addresses the integrating technology with accounting practice and technology products and services for client engagements.
  - Publishes annual list of "Top 100 Products," ranking the leading software solutions and Internet-based services marketed specifically to accounting professionals.
  - Reviews include: Tax Preparation Planning Software; Payroll Software; Low-Cost Accounting Software.
- *Institute of Management and Administration (http://www.ioma.com)*
  - Subscription-based print and electronic editions.
  - Publishes several accounting software buyer's guides throughout the year.

Sources for Information on Accounting Industry Certification

A wealth of information is available about certifications, licensing requirements, and examinations for an individual studying to become a CPA or looking to explore additional certifications in order to remain competitive in the marketplace. Examples of these certifications include:

- CPA—Certified Public Accountant
- CMA—Certified Management Accountant
- CFM—Certified in Financial Management
- CIA—Certified Internal Auditor
- EA—IRS Enrolled Agent

Some of the best Web sites to locate this important information include:

- CPA Exam (*http://www.aicpa.org*)
- CPA Links, located on the AICPA Web site (*http://www.aicpa.org*). Links include:
  - State Board of Accountancy. Contains links to all the State Boards of Accountancy
  - Associations—State CPA. Lists of links to each state's Society of CPAs
  - Accounting Associations. Extensive list of accounting and financial-related associations; useful for exploring associations supporting different career tracks; in many cases, specialized certifications are directly sponsored by associations

- Gleim Accounting Home Page (*http://www.gleim.com*). Gleim is the primary publisher for accounting certification review materials
- Pfeiffer Wiley (*http://www.pfeiffer.com*). Pfeiffer Wiley also publishes a heavily used series of CPA review materials, popularly referred to as "Delaney" after one of the authors
- CPAClass.com (*http://www.cpaclass.com*). A comprehensive source of information for students interested in becoming CPAs

CHAPTER SUMMARY

In this chapter we have provided you with the knowledge that you need to begin providing competent accounting and related financial research to your clients. We have done this by identifying and describing the key players, relevant terminology, and defined process by which technical accounting standards are created. As part of this discussion we have also provided some critical background information on recent significant changes in the accounting industry, and the impact that these will have on the regulation, monitoring, disclosure, and most importantly for you, researching of accounting issues.

Having provided you with the framework for understanding the very deliberate process by which accounting standards are created, we turned our focus to discussing the context in which this information is used by accountants and other financial professionals. We discuss why this information is needed, how is it being used, and what is your role in the dynamic of conducting research and providing information to your clients. As part of this section, we presented you with a series of suggestions and thought points for enabling you to engage your client in the level of dialog necessary to ensure that you fully understand what they are asking of you and simultaneously, to establish your credibility as a knowledgeable researcher.

In the final and most substantive section of the chapter, we identified and discussed the best print and electronic sources and strategies to use to address accounting and related financial research questions, drawing the application of each resource back to the context of the types of questions asked that were carefully detailed in the earlier section of the chapter. No single source is perfect and so we tried to provide a balanced perspective on both the strengths and limitations of each identified resource.

Ultimately, the decisions you make as to which source(s) to use will be drawn from the combination of all of the information shared in this chapter:

1. knowledge of the basics of the accounting standards setting process;
2. understanding who your requestor is and the context in which they are asking and will use the information;
3. a set of parameters for approaching the request which will be developed through dialog with your client; and finally
4. the selection of the sources you will use based on a complete understanding of the whole picture.

The process of learning how to conduct accounting and related financial research is multifaceted. This chapter describes what you need to know. The following chapter presents a real-life example and case study of an accounting research request and walks you through the entire process from the viewpoint of the auditor, her client, and you, the researcher. Pulling it all together in this format will help to highlight the challenges and complexity of conducting competent research, the critical role that communication plays for setting the stage and ensuring good results, and the roles that both technical and experienced-based search skill sets play in selecting the best sources, designing targeted strategies, and adjusting to the unexpected.

APPENDIX I: GUIDE TO SEC FILINGS

The following table (1) identifies the key filings you will access when conducting accounting and financial research; (2) describes each filing's functions; (3) indicates the SEC's timeline filing requirements; and (4) describes the most important sections within their respective filings.[14]

---

14. Appendix 1: Guide to SEC Filings, "Guide to SEC Filings," Disclosure, 1998; "An Overview of the SEC & Securities," LIVEDGAR, 1998.

FILING NAME	DESCRIPTION
10-K	
Annual report, which provides a comprehensive overview of the registrant's business. The report must be filed within 90 days after the end of the company's fiscal year.	
Part I, Item 1	Business. Identified principal products and services of the company, principal markets and methods of distribution and, if material, competitive importance of patents, licenses, and franchises, number of employees and effects of compliance with environmental laws
Part I, Item 2	Properties. Location and character of principal plants and other important properties
Part I, Item 3	Legal proceedings. Brief description of material legal proceedings pending
Part II, Item 6	Selected financial data. Five-year selected data including net sales and operating revenue, income or loss from continuing operations, total and per common share, total assets, long-term obligations. Also includes additional items that could enhance understanding of trends in financial condition and results of operations
Part II, Item 7	Management's discussion and analysis of financial conditions and results of operations
Part II, Item 8	Financial Statements and supplementary data. Two-year audited balance sheets and three-year audited statements of income and cash flow
Part II, Item 9	Changes in and disagreements with accountants on accounting and financial disclosure
Part III, Item 10	Directors and executive officers. Name, office, term, and specific background data
Part III, Item 11	Remuneration of directors and officers.
Part III, Item 12	Security ownership of certain beneficial owners and management. Identification of owners of 5% or more of registrant's stock
Part III, Item 13	Certain relationships and related transactions

FILING NAME	DESCRIPTION
Exhibit 13	Sometimes the financial statements and footnotes are incorporated into the 10-K by reference, originally published as part of the company's annual report. Be sure to always check the schedule of exhibits. If 13 is included, be sure to print it out, or you will essentially have downloaded a 10-K without any significant financial information.
10-Q *Quarterly financial report; although unaudited, it provides a continuing view of a company's financial position during the year. The 10-Q must be filed for each of the first three quarters and is due within 45 days of the close of the quarter.*	
Part I, Item 1	Quarterly financial statements
Part I, Item 2	Management discussion and analysis. Material changes in the amount of revenue and expense items in relation to previous quarters, including the effect of any changes in accounting principles.
8-K *A "current report" used to report the occurrence of any material events or corporate changes which are of importance to investors or security holders and previously have not been reported by the registrant. The report must be filed within 15 days of any event specified in the form.*	
Item 2	Acquisition or disposition of assets
Item 3	Bankruptcy or receivership
Item 4	Changes in registrant's certifying accountant
Item 7	Financial statements and/or exhibits
Item 8	Changes in fiscal year

Source: Thomson Financial. Global Securities Information, Inc.

APPENDIX 2: ACCOUNTING AND RELATED INDUSTRY ASSOCIATIONS

Associations are excellent sources of information across multiple industries and subjects. They are sources of timely and insightful information including trends and future outlooks, regulatory guidance, technical standards, statistical data, and more. Many publish key journals, informative studies, research reports, and host Web sites rich in content.

Always explore the association's site, but never hesitate to pick up the telephone to speak directly with someone on staff. Many associations are extremely knowledgeable about their industry; even if the association does not publish or track particular information, its staff can often direct you to the best sources for your information and most are very willing to share knowledge.

In addition, associations often post good data free on their sites and if you do have to purchase a report, they are generally relatively inexpensive. For example, an association's industry outlook might cost in the range of $25–$125 compared to the $800–$5,000 price tag to purchase a market research report.

Following are the associations that are either directly involved with accounting standards-setting or closely allied to the industry:

American Accounting Association (*http://accounting.rutgers. edu/raw/aaa*)
- Promotes excellence in accounting education, research, and practice. Publishes journals and research papers; strong academic bent

American Institute of Certified Public Accountants (*http:// www.aicpa.org*)
- A professional association supporting the interests of its membership, which is composed of CPAs. From 1939 to 1973, the AICPA was the organization designated to establish authoritative standards of financial accounting and reporting. The AICPA now functions as a lobbyists for issues of concern to its membership, including its code of ethics and continuing education guidelines

Association for Investment Managment and Research (*http://www.aimr.com*)
- Enables education opportunities, professional conduct and ethics, and standards of practice for portfolio managers, strategists, consultants, educators, and other investment specialists

Conference Board (*http://www.conference-board.org*)
- Creates and disseminates knowledge about management and global business practices; conducts research, convenes conferences, makes forecasts, assesses trends, and publish studies which discuss, analyze, and benchmark current management-driven practices of international organizations

Financial Accounting Standards Boards (*http://www.fasb.org*)
- Since 1973, FASB has been the organization designated to establish authoritative financial accounting and reporting standards for businesses and other private-sector organizations

Financial Executive Institute (*http://www.fei.org*)
- Membership-driven professional association for senior-level financial executives. Provides peer, networking opportunities, emerging issues alerts, professional development, and advocacy services; actively engages the FASB, IASB, SEC, and legislators in dialogs to represent viewpoints of its membership

Governmental Accounting Standards Board (*http://www.gasb.org*)
- Since 1984, GASB has been the organization designated to establish authoritative financial accounting and reporting standards for state and local government entities

The Institute of Internal Auditors (*http://www.theiia.org*)
- Serves as a watchdog and resource on significant issues concerning internal auditing, governance and internal control, IT audit, education, and security; promotes certification, education, research, and technological guidance

Institute of Management Accountants (*http://www.rutgers.edu/raw/ima*)
- Focuses on the practice of management accounting and financial management trends and new developments; publishes several key journals and research papers

International Accounting Standards Board (*http://www.iasc.org.uk*)
- Formed in January 2001, the IASB replaced its predecessor, the International Accounting Standards Committee (IASC) as the international standards setter. Looking toward greater

formalization of international standards, IASB is structured similarly to the FASB. It is the intention of the IASB, in collaboration with the FASB and other accounting focused organizations, to develop a single set of binding international accounting standards

National Association of State Auditors, Comptrollers, and Treasurers (*http://www.nasact.org*)
* A national advocate for financial industry excellence, NASACT addresses issues of education, training, technology, best practices and collaboration for state financial management and leadership

Securities and Exchange Commission (*http://www.sec.gov*)
* In addition to the AICPA and FASB, the SEC also plays a key role in the standards-setting process. Under the Securities Exchange Act of 1934, the SEC has statutory authority to establish financial accounting and reporting standards for publicly held companies. It supports as "de facto" the accounting standards established by the private sector, provides broad support to the FASB, and helps to identify emerging issues that it thinks FASB should address. However, with the recent number of accounting-related scandals (e.g. Enron), look for the SEC to get more directly involved in the oversight of the standards-setting process and the legislating and monitoring of corporate governance

Securities Industry Association (*http://www.sia.org*)
* Members include investment bankers, broker–dealers, and mutual fund managers; services include advocacy, education, codes of conduct and ethics, and discussion of current industry issues and challenges

APPENDIX 3: REFERENCE BOOKSHELF

Primary Accounting and Audit Sources

Following is a list of primary (e.g. authoritative and semi-authoritative) accounting and auditing resources. Complete purchasing information is available on the respective publishers' Web sites. Prices are not included as these are not static.

The AICPA and FASB now make virtually all of their content available in print and electronic formats. Most of the AICPA and FASB publications can be purchased as bundled subscription sets or as individual publications on a one-time purchase basis. CCH also provides subscription-based services containing some of this primary resource material, sometimes available both in print and on the Internet.

The following list of sources is grouped by the issuing organization, FASB, AICPA, IASB, and SEC, to reinforce the connection between the publication and its issuing body. A brief explanation of each of these titles is included in this chapter.

FINANCIAL ACCOUNTING STANDARDS BOARD

http://www.fasb.org; click on link to FASB Store
401 Merritt 7
P.O. Box 5116
Norwalk, CT 06856-5116
800/748-0659

Accounting Standards-Original Pronouncements
Contains all pronouncements, except those completely superseded, as they were originally issued, including:

- FASB Statements of Financial Standards
- Accounting Research Bulletins and related interpretations
- Accounting Principles Board Opinions and related interpretations
- FASB Statements of Financial Accounting Concepts
- FASB Interpretations (clarify, explain or elaborate on FASB Statements, Accounting Research Bulletins, or APB Opinions)
- FASB Technical Bulletins (staff documents that provide guidance on implementation and practice problems)
- Comprehensive cross-referenced topical index for this title and Current Text, EITF Abstracts, and FASB Technical Bulletins

Accounting Standards-Current Text
Codifies currently effective accounting and reporting standards into major subject categories.

Arranged by subject and fully indexed; divided into General Standards (generally applicable to all enterprises) and Industry Standards (applicable to enterprises operating in specific industries). Organized alphabetically by key topic, coverage includes comprehensive summaries of each subject plus applicable standards, illustration, and examples. Also includes a cross-referenced topical index to Original Pronouncements, EITF summaries, and FASB technical bulletins.

EITF Abstracts: A Summary of Proceedings of the FASB Emerging Issues Task Force

The abstracts comprise the task force's discussion and any consensus reached, as well as the issue's status and related subsequent developments.

Staff Implementation Guides

Question-and-answer formatted documents drawn from FASB Special Reports and other published implementation guidance.

Exposure Drafts

Proposed statements of financial accounting standards or proposed or interpretations issued for public comment prior to adoption.

Discussion Memorandums

Documents issues on major topics for public comment.

AMERICAN INSTITUTE OF CERTIFIED PUBLIC ACCOUNTANTS

http://www.cpa2biz.com; click on Store tab
Harborside Financial Center
201 Plaza Three, 3rd Floor
Jersey City, NJ 07311

Industry Audit and Accounting Guides

Includes descriptions of specialized accounting and reporting principles and practices for the particular industry they cover. Also contain recommendations on the application of the accounting principles and practices described, prepared by AICPA committees or task forces.

Audit Risk Alerts

Audit Alerts update CPAs on recent practice issues and professional standards that affect engagements. They are useful for planning and performing audits by identifying the significant business risks that may result in the material misstatement of financial statements.

Codification on Statement on Auditing Standards

The standards are indexed by subject, with amendments noted and superseded portions deleted.

Statements of Position

Issued to influence the development of financial accounting and reporting standards in directions that the AICPA believes are in the public interest. Some amend industry audit or accounting guides.

Technical Practice Aids

Question-and-answer formatted documents written to provide additional guidance and clarification on accounting issues.

Professional Standards

Contains all of the outstanding pronouncements on professional standards issued by the AICPA, the International Federation of Accountants, and the International Accounting Standards Board. These pronouncements are arranged by subject, with amendments noted and superseded portions deleted. Contents include:

- Statement on Auditing Standards and related interpretations
- Statements on Standards for Attestation Engagements and related interpretations
- Statements on Standards for Accounting and Reviews Services and related interpretations
- AICPA Code of Professional Conduct
- AICPA Bylaws
- International Accounting Standards and related interpretations
- International Standards on Auditing
- IFAC Code of Ethics
- Statement on Standards for Consulting Services
- Statements on Quality Control Standards
- Standards for Performing and Reporting on Peer Reviews and related interpretations
- Statements on Standards for Tax Services and related interpretations
- Statements on Responsibilities in Personal Financial Planning Practice
- Statement on Standards for Continuing Professional Education Programs and related policies and forms

INTERNATIONAL ACCOUNTING STANDARDS BOARD

http://www.iasb.org.uk; click on tab to Book Shop
30 Cannon Street
London EC4M 6XH
United Kingdom
International Accounting Standards

Includes all accounting standards, Implementation Questions and Answers, the IASC Framework, and Index.

SECURITIES AND EXCHANGE COMMISSION

CCH, Inc.
http://www.cch.com; click on link to Order Products
800/248-3248
Federal Securities Law Reporter

Covers laws administered by the SEC regulating the issuance of securities and the day-to-day handling of securities issues. Source materials include court decisions, the federal securities laws, and relevant takeover law, pleading decisions, and business judgment law decisions. Contains

- Accounting Series Releases
- Financial Reporting Releases
- Accounting and Auditing Enforcement Releases
- Staff Accounting Bulletins
- Regulation S-K
- Regulations S-X

Secondary Accounting and Audit Sources

Sources in this category provide contextual analysis and discussion of accounting pronouncements and issues. They are grouped by the type of information they contain, such as standards or dictionaries, in order for you to quickly identify the representative categories of secondary resources you should consider incorporating into your collections.

The primary publishers of accounting secondary sources include:

- CCH (*http://onlinestore.cch.com*)
- Aspen Publishers (*http://www. aspenpublishers.com*)
- Warren, Gorham & Lamont (*http://www.riatax.com*)
- John Wiley & Sons, Inc. (*http://www.wiley.com*)

U.S. ACCOUNTING AND AUDITING STANDARDS

Accounting Research Manager, Internet Version
Aspen Publishers
http://www.aspenpublishers.com
800/234-1660
Combines the text of authoritative and proposal-stage literature from the AICPA, FASB, SEC, EITF, and IASB, with interpretive
guidance and analysis; updated daily and includes a weekly summary of the latest developments.

Aspen-Miller Accounting Guides
Aspen Publishers
http://www.aspenpublishers.com
800/234-1660
Series includes: GAAP Guide, Not-for-Profit Guide, GAAS
Guide Single Audits, Audit Procedures, Restatement and Analysis
of Current FASB Standards.

Practitioner's Guide to GAAS (Dan M. Guy and D.R. Carmichael)
John Wiley & Sons, Inc.
http://www.wiley.com
800/225-5945
This annual publication is designed to help CPAs in the application of and compliance with authoritative standards. Reduces
the official language of Statement of Auditing Standards, Statements on Standards for Attestation Engagements, Statement on
Standards for Accounting and Review Services, and the interpretations of these standards to easy-to-read and understandable
advice.

FINANCIAL DISCLOSURES

Accounting Trends & Techniques
AICPA
http://www.cpa2biz.com; click on Store tab
Harborside Financial Center
201 Plaza Three, 3rd Floor
Jersey City, NJ 07311
This annual publication provides commentary, illustrations,
and examples of common and irregular financial disclosures
drawn from more than 600 company annual reports. An index
cross references all the pronouncements mentioned in the book.

Miller GAAP Financial Statement Disclosures Manual
Aspen Publishers
http://www.aspenpublishers.com

800/234-1660

Features hundreds of examples of real-world footnote disclosures. Includes executive summaries of GAAP, a detailed summary of disclosure requirements, and easy-to-follow examples.

Checklists and Illustrative Financial Statement Series
AICPA
http://www.cpa2biz.com; click on Store tab
Harborside Financial Center
201 Plaza Three, 3rd Floor
Jersey City, NJ 07311

Each checklist contains references to all applicable FASB, AICPA, and GASB pronouncements and interpretations, and where applicable, SEC regulations.

Series includes:

- Corporations
- Defined Contribution Pension Plans
- Employee Health and Welfare Benefit Plan
- Banks and Savings Institutions
- Investment Companies

Accounting and Auditing Disclosure Manual
Warren, Gorham & Lamont
http://www.riahome.com/financialreporting
800/950-1216

Requirements and examples needed to prepare financial statements and auditors' reports; compiles all relevant GAAP and GAAS requirements and integrated hundreds of illustrations and examples with specific disclosure requirements.

Designed as a reference source for all disclosures that GAAP requires; the manual incorporates currently effective pronouncements by major topics.

INTERNATIONAL STANDARDS

International Accounting Standards Explained
John Wiley & Sons, Inc.
http://www.wiley.com
800/225-5945

Presents an introduction to the IASB and to the requirements of the IAS. This publication outlines how the standards are used on a daily basis by companies in preparation of their financial statements. It examines the use of IAS from a practice orientation and looks at the main components of the financial statements, including questions of recognition and measurement of key financial statement items.

Applying International Accounting Standards (3rd ed.)
David H. Cairns
Tolley LexisNexis
http://www.iasb.org.uk; click on the link to Bookshop

All European Union listed companies will be required to issue financial statements using International Financial Reporting Standards beginning in 2005. This book is the authoritative guide. It presents practical coverage of how these companies will apply these standards and deal with recent developments.

IAS Illustrative Financial Statements and Disclosure Checklist
Ernst & Young/IASB
http://www.iasb.org.uk; click on the link to Bookshop

This new publication, compiled by the Financial Reporting Group of Ernst & Young, is a practical guide for preparers, students of accounting, and all those involved in the production of compliant financial statements. Professionals who require a detailed understanding of what IAS financial statements actually involve will also find this guide useful. Includes explanatory notes and commentary, setting out the authoritative IAS source for the required disclosure, cross-references to relevant IAS, interpretation, and guidance notes. Also includes a disclosure checklist, an essential tool for preparers to ensure that no required disclosures are missed.

IAS/US GAAP Comparison (2nd ed.)
Ernst & Young/IASB
http://www.iasb.org.uk; click on the link to Bookshop

Presents a comparison between IAS and U.S. accounting principles.

Aspen-Miller Accounting Guides
Aspen Publishers
http://www.aspenpublishers.com
800/234-1660
Series includes:

- European Accounting Guide
- International Accounting Standards Guide

SEC RULES AND REGULATIONS

SEC Guidelines: Rules and Regulations
Warren, Gorham & Lamont
http://www.riahome.com/financialreporting
800/950-1216
This annual publication contains regulations, forms, and official releases needed to prepare corporate financial statements and comply with SEC registration and reporting requirements, including:

- Regulations S-B, S-K, S-T, S-X
- Forms 8-K, 10-K,10-Q, 11-K Forms F-1, F-2, F-3, F-4, 20-F
- Regulation and Schedule 14A
- Forms SB-1, SB-2
- SEC Staff Accounting Bulletins
- Financial Reporting Releases

Sarbanes-Oxley Act of 2002: Law and Explanation
CCH, Inc.
http://www.cch.com; click on link to Order Products
800/248-3248
Law and explanation of this accounting reform legislation.
Accountants' SEC Practice Manual
CCH, Inc.
http://www.cch.com; click on link to Order Products
800/248-3248
Single source guidance for preparing and filing financial statements with the SEC.
SEC Accounting Rules
CCH, Inc.
http://www.cch.com; click on link to Order Products
800/248-3248

Covers accounting requirements imposed by the SEC.

SEC Handbook: Rules and Forms for Financial Statements and Related Disclosure
CCH, Inc.
http://www.cch.com; click on link to Order Products
800/248-3248

Reproduces current official materials that guide you through financial statement preparation requirements.

SEC Handbook II: Preparing Annual SEC Disclosure Documents
CCH, Inc.
http://www.cch.com; click on link to Order Products
800/248-3248

In-depth guide to the preparation of annual disclosure documents required by the Exchange Act and SEC regulation.

HANDBOOKS

U.S. Master Accounting Guide
CCH, Inc.
http://www.cch.com; click on link to Order Products
800/248-3248

This annual publication distills key accounting, business, legal, and financial information into a convenient reference book.

U.S. Master Auditing Guide
CCH, Inc.
http://www.cch.com; click on link to Order Products
800/248-3248

This annual publication explains complex auditing standards but also offers practical guidance on performing and managing both external and internal audits.

U.S. Master Tax Guide
CCH, Inc.
http://www.cch.com; click on link to Order Products
800/248-3248

This annual publication contains all the pertinent federal tax law changes that affect 2002 returns and provides fast and reliable answers to tax questions affecting individuals and business income tax.

Accounting Desk Book
Aspen Publishers
http://www.aspenpublishers.com
800/234-1660

This regularly updated publication is intended for the accounting and financial professional applying relevant accounting principles and standards as well as tax rules. It contains all the important pronouncements from FASB and the IASB, financial reporting presentation requirements, required and recommended disclosures, and specialized accounting topics.

TEXTBOOKS

Intermediate Accounting, Donald E. Kieso, Jerry J. Weygandt
John Wiley & Sons, Inc.
http://www.wiley.com
800/225-5945
Solid reference source for accounting rules and regulations; textbook used by many accounting majors.

Montgomery's Auditing, Vincent M. O'Reilly, Patrick J. McDonnell, et al.
John Wiley & Sons, Inc.
http://www.wiley.com
800/225-5945
Helps auditors develop more efficient audit plans, greater control over audit risk, effective audit tests, and sound audit reports. This book offers practice-tested guidance for every aspect of auditing, from standards and responsibilities, risk, and engagement strategy, through internal control, auditing specific cycles and accounts, and auditing reporting. In addition, detailed guidelines show the entire audit process and provide comprehensive auditing strategies and methods.

CPA EXAM

Wiley CPA Examination Review, Patrick R. Delaney
John Wiley & Sons, Inc.
http://www.wiley.com
800/225-5945
Popularly referred to as "Gleim," this book provides study outlines for the Uniform CPA Examination. Recent examination questions are organized by topic and there are explanations of AICPA unofficial answers.

BUSINESS RATIOS

Annual Statement Studies: Financial Ratio Benchmarks
RMA, Inc.
http://www.rmahq.com
800/677-7621
This annual publication contains financial ratio benchmarks derived directly from more than 150,000 statements of financial institution borrowers and prospects.
Industry Norms & Key Business Ratios Dun & Bradstreet
(*http://www.dnb.com*)
800/234-3867
Use this annual publication to research risk, understand industry trends, and measure how a company stacks up financially to its peers. Includes financial statement statistics measuring profitability, efficiency, liquidity, and solvency.

DICTIONARIES

Kohler's Dictionary for Accountants
Prentice-Hall, Inc. *http://www.amazon.com*
This remains the bible of accounting dictionaries. While it is now out-of-print, copies can still be purchased from amazon.com and other large book dealers. It is worth your while to try and locate a copy. If you have one in your collection, hold on to it.

There are many other accounting dictionaries available. Visit your local academic or public libraries to evaluate some of the publications. Following are a few examples:
International Dictionary of Accounting Acronyms

AMACOM

Dictionary of Accounting Terms (Barron's Business Dictionaries)
Joel G. Siegel, Jae K. Shim
http://www.amazon.com

2

Research Case Study on Accounting for the Impairment or Disposal of Long-Lived Assets in the Passenger Airlines Industry

According to Generally Accepted Accounting Principles (GAAP) set forth by the Financial Accounting Standards Board (FASB), company management is responsible for evaluating on an ongoing basis whether its long-lived assets are realizable. In other words, the company must determine if the value reflected on the balance sheet is correct. If the answer is no, then management may be required to calculate a financial write-down of the impaired assets. Such a write-down can occur both for assets that will continue to be used as well as for those that are being sold. In effect, a write-down results in a more truthful picture of an organization's assets as of the balance sheet date. The guidelines and criteria for making this assessment are spelled out in the FASB's Statement of Financial Accounting Standard (SFAS) No. 144, Accounting for the Impairment or Disposal of Long-Lived Assets.

The following case study presents a scenario in which an audit partner for a major passenger airline is working with the company's management to justify and account for the planned disposition of an impaired transport fleet in an effort to properly reflect the financial statements in accordance with GAAP.

BACKGROUND: STATE OF THE PASSENGER AIRLINES INDUSTRY

Beginning with the Gulf War in the early 1990s, the passenger airlines industry has been beset with a series of economic, political, and industry-specific challenges that have severely impacted its stability and financial performance. Just when the economy was showing signs of turning around, the events of September 11, 2001, reaffirmed the industry's precarious position. These days, it is not uncommon to pick up a major international newspaper and read a headline about a major airline declaring bankruptcy or struggling to emerge from it.

In the decades leading up to the 1990s, the major airlines took advantage of a booming economy by aggressively acquiring new and larger fleets of planes. An airline's fleet is one of its most important investments and in a healthy economic climate will result in a valuable asset that should reflect favorably on the company's balance sheet. Unfortunately, faced with a weak economy which adversely affected air travel, the rising cost of oil on the open market, and a mindset which equated flying with terrorism, these investments resulted in aging, fuel-inefficient, high maintenance, and obsolete inventories. To improve their bottom line, the major passenger airlines have been faced with the necessity of disposing of less productive and profitable assets in order to eliminate further financial drain. In other words, smart management and accounting practice dictate that they carefully scrutinize their fleets of aircraft to properly reflect their current fair values and, in some cases, to make the decision to sell some of them.

AUDITOR REFERENCE INTERVIEW: UNDERSTANDING WHAT THE CLIENT NEEDS

Emma Berke, a new partner in the accounting firm Vineberg, Hirschel, & Napoliello, LLC (VHN), has been tapped to lead the engagement of InterNational Air, a Chicago-based global passenger airline company. InterNational is a new client for the firm and the first major airline client of VHN's Chicago office. It selected VHN to be its new auditor after severing its 20-plus-year relationship with its former accounting firm. Based on a conversation with her firm's managing partner, Emma knows that InterNational was unhappy with its previous auditors due to significant turnover of personnel serving the account as well as some difficulty getting quick responses to certain questions related to its expanding global operations. InterNational specifically was looking for a firm with more global client-service experience.

Emma has just completed reviewing a stack of working papers and management correspondence as she prepares for her first meeting next week with InterNational's CEO, Marvin Heller, and CFO, Joshua Mitchell. She has created a spreadsheet for the engagement team identifying all the relevant accounting issues that need to be researched and the beginnings of a list of questions for which they will need to obtain answers from management. At a brief meeting with her team managers she reviews her findings and assigns the technical standards requiring research. After the meeting, Emma picks up the phone and calls the firm's Business Research Center (BRC) to schedule a time to discuss some additional information that she needs pertaining to the engagement.

At 3:00 PM, Susan Weiss, BRC's director, shows up at Emma's office. Emma explains that the firm has just taken on InterNational Air as a new client and that it represents not only a very large client for the firm but an opportunity to develop expertise and generate more clients in the airline industry. She asks Susan and her research team to provide her with several pieces of both technical and general business information that she needs in preparation for her meeting with the company's top management.

Emma explains to Susan that she has identified the company's aging and troubled C-223 aircraft fleet as a significant and long-time drain on the airline's profitability due to high labor and maintenance costs. Management has already indicated a strong desire to pursue selling the aircraft and Emma wants to be prepared with a thoroughly researched and appropriate set of recommendations for them. SFAS 144 is the technical accounting standard that provides the guidelines for assessing impairment of long-lived assets. Emma explains that SFAS 144 sets forth criteria that assist management in determining the accounting implications of potentially disposing of less productive and profitable assets that are negatively impacting the company's financial results.

Specifically, SFAS 144 describes a number of "trigger" events or environmental conditions that must exist in order for an asset to be considered impaired, qualifying for a write-down:

- Significant decrease in the market price of a long-lived asset
- Significant adverse change in the extent of manner in which a long-lived asset is being used or in its physical condition

- Significant adverse change in legal factors or in the business climate that could affect the value of a long-lived asset, including an adverse action or assessment by a regulator
- Accumulation of costs in excess of the amount originally expected for the acquisitions or construction of a long-lived asset
- Current period operation or cash flow combined with a history of operating or cash flow losses, or a projection or forecast that demonstrates continuing losses associated with the use of a long-lived asset
- Current expectation that, more likely than not, a long-lived asset will be sold or otherwise disposed of significantly before the end of its previously estimated useful life[1]

Source: FASB Statement No. 144, Accounting for the Impairment or Disposal of Long-Lived Assets, is copyrighted by the Financial Accounting Standards Board, 401 Merritt 7, P.O. Box 5116, Norwalk, Connecticut 06856-5116, U.S.A. Portions are reprinted with permission. Complete copies of this document are available from the FASB.

To put this into a context which will help Susan to better understand the accounting issues at hand, Emma explains that InterNational introduced the C-223 aircraft, popularly called Millennium in 1979, touting it in the press as "the world's fastest, most high-class airplane which would revolutionize cross-continental travel for the traveling elite." Unfortunately, save for the first few years when the novelty of flying the plane motivated a large number of bookings, it has failed to live up to management's expectations. Passenger tickets ran approximately $10,000 for a round-trip from New York to Hong Kong, a price tag that proved hard to swallow by even the more wealthy business and pleasure travelers, and over time the plane became a money-loser for the company.

The fleet's viability was further impacted by an increasingly unstable economy that severely hampered air travel, high fuel and maintenance costs, and other environmental factors, such as war and increased threats of terrorist activities. The Millennium experienced its first—and only—accident two years ago, which resulted in the death of all 89 aboard. Although InterNational was able to locate the mechanical cause of the accident, the age of the plane

---

1. Statement of Financial Accounting Standards No. 144, Accounting for the Impairment or Disposal of Long-Lived Assets, Paragraph 8, FASB.

and expense of fixing the problem for the entire fleet was determined an unwise business investment. InterNational's CEO and board of directors are anxious to put the C-223 fleet behind them and move on.

Emma explained to Susan that she would like the BRC to provide her with the following two sets of data in preparation for her meeting next week with the CEO and InterNational's management team:

1. *Technical Accounting Standards and Related Information*
   a. Articles published in accounting journals in the past two years that provide substantive discussion, analysis, and examples for applications of SFAS 144
   b. Examples of airline industry footnote disclosures related to SFAS 144 policies and write-downs, and management's comments on it in the Management Discussion & Analysis (MD&A) section of the 10-K
   c. Any information on fair market values for comparable aging airline fleets
2. *Market Trigger Conditions*
   a. Articles published in newspapers and news wire stories dating back two years about InterNational Air and any problems with its Millennium aircraft
   b. Articles from airline industry trade journals, major newspapers, and airline company press releases dating back approximately two years that describe the state of the industry and key factors that have impacted the industry's performance (trigger events)
   c. Articles from airlines industry trade journals, major newspapers, and airline company press releases discussing obsolescence of airline fleets in general, and this aircraft type in particular

RESEARCH STRATEGY AND RESULTS

Reviewing Emma's list of topics to research, Susan decides to begin with the first market trigger, background on InterNational Air and the Millennium. She wants to understand more about the company and the challenges it has faced with this fleet before jumping into researching the technical accounting issue. She divides the research into six steps:

1. background on InterNational Air and the Millennium aircraft,
2. technical accounting articles on SFAS No. 144,

3. financial footnote disclosures,
4. determination of aging airline fleet fair market value,
5. state of the industry, and
6. airplane fleet obsolescence.

Step 1: Background on InterNational Air and the Millennium Aircraft

To locate articles on the Millennium's struggles to sustain a profit for InterNational Air, Susan turned to Factiva, a fee-based electronic database. Factiva contains full-text articles from a deep repository of national and international wires, press releases, newspapers, and industry magazines. Factiva is an excellent search interface for the level of content retrieval that the audit partner requires for this project. It combines an impressive collection of reputable source documents and a powerful search engine with the ability to browse results using a keyword in context (KWIC) format, which "pushes out" the sections of the articles containing the search terms.

After logging onto the database, Susan enters the following search statement:

- **hlp=(international air and millennium).** In the **Select Date** drop-down box, she chooses **"in the last 2 years"**

Limiting the keywords to the headline (h), which is another name for the title, and the first few paragraphs (lp) of the article is a good strategy for retrieving articles that focus on a particular topic. While Susan is also tempted to include keywords that will look for discussions about problems or challenges with the aircraft, she decides to begin the search with a broad approach. Rather than risk missing relevant articles due to using incorrect or limiting keywords, she opts to start broad and look for "clues" such as frequently used keywords to direct modifications in the search strategy.

The initial search results in 1,586 returned articles, clearly more than a reasonable number to read. Using the View As "Keyword in Context" format, Susan scans the first 150 hits, gathering a short list of recurring keywords that capture the concepts for which she is looking. Returning to Factiva's search box, she revises the search strategy to incorporate the keywords as follows:

- hlp=(international air and millennium) **and (downturn or econom* or problem or challeng* or fuel or price or cost or trigger* or demise or decreas* or business travel* or crash* or loss* or struggl*)**

Unfortunately, this tactic only brings the article count down to 1,318. After scanning the first few pages of returned article citations, Susan makes two observations. First, many of the articles are very short. Factiva reports the word count (for example, 346 words) for each article, a very effective piece of intelligence when strategizing ways to narrow down search results to the most substantive discussions on a topic. Second, the shorter articles appear to be wire stories that only regurgitate news covered in greater detail in newspapers and company press releases.

Based on what she has learned from the second search results, Susan modifies the search a third time, limiting the articles to those with a count of more than 600 words. While there is no "magic" number, articles greater than 600 words tend to be meatier rather then merely rehash the facts. With the new addition of the word count limitation, the third modified search strategy is:

- hlp=(international air and millennium) and (downturn or econom* or problem* or challenge* or fuel or price or cost or trigger* or demise or decreas* or business travel* or crash* or loss* or struggl*) and **wc > 600**.

This time the search engine responds with 184 articles. Selecting the Sort by "Relevance" option pushes the most relevant articles to the head of the list (the default display is "Publication date, most recent first"). While Susan will scan all 184 articles to ensure that she does not miss any information that Emma might need to see, viewing them in order of relevance should capture the "best" articles first, allowing her the flexibility of "quicker scanning" as she works her way down the list of articles.

Following are some of the articles Susan found on Inter-National Air and Millennium:

- "Is the Age of Supersonic Passenger Travel Well and Truly Over?" *The Guardian*, April 17, 2003. This article discusses the fact that Millennium's problems were triggered by the two problems of not enough passengers buying seats and spiraling maintenance costs."[2]
- "Concorde Operations to End in the Fall," *Aviation Daily*, April 11, 2003. The article notes that Millennium's fleet was grounded following the crash of one of the planes in which more than 100 people were killed. But commercially the plane did not recover from the crash. Demand has diminished due to the worsening economic situation, the fleet is aging, and maintenance costs have increased, thus making further investment hard to justify. Operating the Millennium has "become a severely and structurally loss-making operation," according to InterNational Air's CEO.[3]
- "Concorde Is Not a Viable Proposition," Bary Noakes, *Travel Trade Gazette UK*, April 14, 2003. The article states that, "Millennium's declining fortunes are due to the fall in business travel following September 11, safety fears after the New York crash and rising maintenance costs. InterNational Air's year-on-year premium traffic fell nearly 69% last year. It had been due to be phased out in 2012 but talks with its supplier confirming the need for a $80 million maintenance program has caused the company to seriously consider escalating that the timeframe."[4]

Source: Travel Trade Gazette UK. Reprinted with permission.

Step 2: Technical Accounting Articles on SFAS No. 144

Now that Susan understands more about the factors contributing to InterNational Air's decision to consider selling its Millennium fleet, she is ready to conduct the technical accounting research that Emma requested. Susan will complete researching the market trigger conditions when she completes this phase of the project.

---

2. "Is the Age of Supersonic Passenger Travel Well and Truly Over?" *The Guardian*, April 17, 2003, Factiva (*http://global.factiva.com*).

3. "Concorde Operations to End in the Fall," *Aviation Daily*, April 11, 2003, Factiva (*http://global.factiva.com*).

4. "Concorde Is Not a Viable Proposition," Bary Noakes, *Travel Trade Gazette UK*, April 14, 2003, Factiva (*http://global.factiva.com*).

Emma had requested some articles discussing the application of SFAS 144. The source for that level of analysis is technical accounting journals and ABI/Inform is, without question, the best repository of full-text articles from accounting publications, such as the *Journal of Accountancy, Practical Accountant,* and the *CPA Journal.* ABI was one of the first generation of full-text electronic databases; it was also one of the earliest databases to provide article access in .pdf format. Many accounting articles include detailed examples of financial computations and footnotes and a great deal of this level of detail is lost to the reader when the article text is viewed in ASCII format. Retrieving the articles in ABI will ensure that that Emma will benefit from the full value of the technical discussions.

After logging on to ABI/Inform, Susan begins by highlighting the Search Methods button at the top of the page and clicking on the link to Guided search. In addition to its excellent accounting and related financial content, ABI also provides the searcher with several options for keyword searching, including simple, natural language, advanced, and guided search. The Guided selection allows the searcher to combine using Boolean logic with the application of keywords to specific sections of the article, such as Article Title, Abstract, Publication Name, and Author. This puts a tremendous amount of control into the hands of the searcher by providing options for "feeling out" where the best occurrences of the keywords appear within the body of the article. For example, similar to employing the "hlp" technique discussed above in the Factiva search on InterNational Air and the Millennium planes, targeting the Article Title and Abstract sections in ABI/Inform can aid the searcher in retrieving more focused discussions on a topic.

Susan begins her search using the following strategy:

- **(financial accounting or sfas) and (144 or long lived assets)** appearing in *either* the **Article Title** or **Abstract sections.**

Why introduce this combination of keywords? Based on experience researching accounting standards' articles, Susan has learned the following lessons:

1. The Statement of Financial Accounting Standards can be expressed as its formal name or the acronym, SFAS. The safest search strategy is to allow for either form of expression. Since "financial accounting" is part of the formal name, searching on that portion alone combined with other relevant keywords should be sufficient. In addition, limiting the keywords to these two adjacent words allows the searcher to avoid the nasty

problem of introducing adjacency logic into the search (for example, statement w/1 financial accounting standards, where w/1 replaces "of," a noise word which most search engines will not search). If possible, it is always preferable to create a strategy that works around combining adjacency logic with Boolean connectors.

2. If possible, create a search statement which uses the Boolean connector "and" rather than an adjacency connector to tie the SFAS number to the statement. For example, typing "SFAS 144" will eliminate some results since the formal designation is "SFAS No. 144." Will "No." be expressed as No. or Number? And consider what happens if you type "SFAS No. 144," you run into systems interpretation challenges. Will the search engine treat the period following No. as a space or ignore it? If you use an adjacency connector, "SFAS w/1 144" to get around this problem, you run into the same issues described above.

3. Although the actual SFAS number is likely included some-where in the body of the article, you cannot assume it will appear in the title. The best approach is to require that either the SFAS number or keywords from the SFAS title appear, hence including both "144 or long lived asset" in the strategy.

The bottom line is that keyword searching is wrought with perils. Your best offense is to develop a search statement that is as uncomplicated as possible without being so simple or broad as to negate retrieving the desired results. How do you accomplish this feat? The answer lies in maintaining a balance between carefully reading search engine help documentation to understand allow-able search options, including any tips on how the system inter-prets commands, sustaining a healthy skepticism about any search engine's ability to accurately interpret your search commands, and building on lessons learned based on personal experience.

Emma instructed Susan to limit the search to the past two years since the SFAS was not issued until August 2001. Since ABI will default to displaying the returned articles in order of most recent date first, Susan decides not to build in a date limitation as part of her strategy. Experience has taught her that keyword searching almost always yields unexpected surprises and limiting by date is one of the main culprits contributing to missing relevant content. Better to leave the date open for now and see what the returned results tell her about the need for any modifications in the strategy.

Returning to the search template, Susan clicks on the search button and the result is more than 100 articles! Quickly scanning the list of citations, Susan gleans some important intelligence.

Apparently SFAS 144 superseded an earlier standard, SFAS 121, "Accounting for the Impairment of Long-Lived Assets and for Long-Lived Assets to be Disposed Of." According to the AICPA's "Official Releases" column appearing in the March 2002 *Journal of Accountancy*, "Because Statement 121 did not address the accounting for a segment of a business accounted for as a discontinued operation under Opinion 30, two accounting models existed for long-lived assets to be disposed of. The FASB decided to establish a single accounting model, based on the framework established in Statement 121 for long-lived assets to be disposed of by sale. The board also decided to resolve significant implementation issues related to Statement 121."[5]

Source: FASB Statement No. 144, Accounting for the Impairment or Disposal of Long-Lived Assets, is copyrighted by the Financial Accounting Standards Board, 401 Merritt 7, P.O. Box 5116, Norwalk, Connecticut 06856-5116, U.S.A. Portions are reprinted with permission. Complete copies of this document are available from the FASB.

Susan did not recall Emma mentioning SFAS 121 during their reference interview and wonders if the audit partner also needs her to research this statement. Not willing to risk missing any important information but also sensitive to her billable time, Susan makes a note of the ABI search strategy, logs off, and calls Emma to discuss the results and get further direction. Emma happens to be at her desk and picks up the phone. She explains that she had experience implementing SFAS 121 for several of her telecommunications clients prior to the release of SFAS 144 and so was comfortable with her knowledge of the standard. However, giving the question a second thought, she asks Susan to include a list of all the returned article citations for both SFAS 144 and 121 and tells her to go ahead and retrieve the full text of the most substantive discussions of SFAS 121, along with those she was pulling for SFAS 144. Background on SFAS 121 would probably be useful for some of the junior managers on the engagement who had no prior practical experience on the technical issues relating to impairment of long-lived assets.

Returning to her research, Susan logs back onto ABI/Inform and recreates her search strategy. Scanning the returned articles, she selects nine articles to download in full text, including two on

---

5. "Official Releases, FASB No. 144," *Journal of Accountancy*, March 2002, ABI/Inform.

SFAS 121. All of the articles on SFAS 144 include references and comparison to 121 as well. Although most of the articles are too technical for Susan to understand, scanning them does help to provide her with some additional "comfort level" on the general topic. She identifies several passages that provide more context supporting InterNational Air accounting issues. The following executive summary appears in the March 2002 *Journal of Accountancy* article, "New Accounting Guidance for Long-Lived Assets: Asset Impairment and Disposal," David T. Meeting and Randall W. Luecke:

> Businesses recognize impairment when the financial statement carrying amount of a long-lived asset or asset group exceeds its fair value and is not recoverable. A carrying amount is not recoverable if it is greater than the sum of the undiscounted cash flows expected from the asset's use and eventual disposal. FASB defines impairment loss as the amount by which the carrying value exceeds an asset's fair value.
>
> Impairment exists when the carrying amount of a long-lived asset or asset group exceeds its fair value and is nonrecoverable. CPAs should test for impairment when certain changes occur, including a significant decrease in the market price of a long-lived asset, a change in how the company uses an asset or changes in the business climate that could affect the asset's value.
>
> Fair value is the amount an asset could be bought or sold for in a current transaction between willing parties. Quoted prices in active markets are the best evidence of fair values. Because market prices are not always available, CPAs should base fair-value estimates on the best information available or use valuation techniques such as the expected present-value method or the traditional-present-value method.

Since Emma also asked Susan to locate examples of companies that have disclosed SFAS 144 in their financial footnotes, she was especially glad to find the following paragraphs in the same article. Searching footnotes is always tricky and it provided her with some useful guidance in preparation for researching footnotes:

> When a company recognizes an impairment loss for an asset group, it must allocate the loss to the assets in the group on a pro rata basis. It must also disclose in the notes to the financial statements a description of the impairment asset and the facts and circumstances leading to the impairment . . . the manner and timing and the gain or loss on sale. . . . If not separately presented on the face of the statement, the

amount of the impairment loss and the caption in the income statement or the statement of activities that includes the loss. The method or methods used to determine fair value.[6]

Source: Copyright © 1991, 2002 from the Journal of Accountancy by the American Institute of Certified Public Accountants, Inc. Opinions of the authors are their own and do not necessarily reflect policies of the AICPA. Reprinted with permission.

Following are some additional articles from ABI/Inform. All of them include technical analysis and implementation examples for SFAS 144 or 121:

"SFAS 144 Revises Asset Writedowns: Why Good Assets Go Bad," *The CPA Journal*, December 2002, Jalal Soroosh and Jack T. Cieskielski.

"SFAS No. 121 Illustrated," *NPA*, February 1996, Quinton Booker.

"How Can Auditors Make Sure the Requirements Are Applied Correctly: Auditing Considerations of FASB 121," *Journal of Accountancy*, July 1996, Hugo Nurnberg and Nelson W. Dittmar, Jr.

"The Practitioner's Role in Accounting for Asset Impairment," *NPA*, July 1997, Gale Newell and Jerry Kreuze.

Step 3: Financial Footnote Disclosures

With a bit more understanding of SFAS 144, Susan turns her attention to locating examples of disclosures in airlines companies' annual financial footnotes and MD&A. Since SFAS 144's effective date was for financial statements issued for fiscal years beginning after December 15, 2001, the first annual filings would not be available until the end of the first quarter of 2003. The majority of the larger passenger airlines has a fiscal year end of December 31 and therefore would not be required to file their annual 10-K until March 31. Emma had requested that the BRC try to locate at least six examples of disclosures, although given that it was not yet the end of the first quarter, she understood this might be difficult.

Researching financial footnote disclosures is always an adventure, requiring knowledge about the appropriate document type, relevant sections within the filings to search, and the correct combination of keywords. Fortunately, while creating the perfect search strategy often takes time, there is no guesswork involved

---

6. "New Accounting Guidance for Long-Lived Assets: Asset Impairment and Disposal," David T. Meeting and Randall W. Luecke, *Journal of Accountancy*, March 2002, ABI/Inform.

when selecting the best database. Thomson Research, formerly known as Global Access, allows for targeted keyword searching in each of the key sections of the major Securities and Exchange Commission (SEC) filings; there is currently no other electronic database on the market which allows for the level of focused searching necessary for conducting financial accounting research.

Logging on to Thomson Research, Susan clicks on the Documents tab at the top of the page and then selects EDGAR Free Text. The Thomson Research platform contains a wealth of financial information on public U.S. and international companies. The site can be a bit confusing to navigate, but Susan knows by heart where to click to locate the template for searching across SEC filings.

During the reference interview, Susan sought guidance from Emma on developing the best strategy for the search. Which sections of the 10-K should be searched, what combination of keywords should be used, and what SIC codes should be included? Although Susan is very experienced using Thomson Research's electronic database and conducting disclosure searches, a successful query is dependent on using the correct technical accounting terminology and targeting the appropriate filing sections. This know-how requires the technical knowledge of an accountant. Susan would never conduct this type of research without carefully reviewing the search strategy with the financial professional. Unlike searching for articles in a general business database, such as Factiva where more "common" language is used and a certain amount of experimenting with keywords and context is allowable and often preferable, footnote disclosure requires precision of both language and context.

Based on the feedback from Emma, Susan developed an initial search strategy. After four slight modifications, she finally arrived at the optimum strategy. Following is the search statement and a brief explanation of the process:

- **Filing Type**: 10-K
- **SIC Codes**: 4500 or 4510 or 4512 or 4513 or 4520 or 4522 or 4580 or 4581
- **Receipt Date From**: 01/01/1994
- **Receipt Date To**: 3/25/2003
- **Filing Sections**: Financial Footnotes or Management Discussion
- **Keywords**: ("long lived assets" or "long-lived assets") and (fleet or airplane or plane or aircraft)

The SIC codes for the passenger airlines are 4510 and 4512, "Air Transportation Scheduled." Initially Susan selected just these two codes but with dismal results. This should not have come as a complete surprise since the assignment of SIC codes to companies is far from a science; in fact, it is virtually impossible to gather together a complete and accurate list of companies in the same industry based purely on their assigned SIC code. To ensure that no possible companies were missed, Susan decided to include all of the SIC codes for the broad group of 4500, "Transportation by Air."

The choice of keywords to use was a practical compromise based on a combination of Emma's recommendations for accounting language and Susan's knowledge of limitations in the Thomson Research SEC filings search template. While Thomson's search documentation explains that it allows for advanced features, such as Boolean and adjacency connectors, doing so does not always result in smooth sailing for the searcher. Using too many connectors or combining Boolean and adjacency connectors in the same statement typically results in either a timed-out message or an error message. For example, it could not process a search such as (sfas or financial accounting) w/5 144). The system simply cannot process complex search statements. The only solution is to develop a search string that is as streamlined as possible and which does not incorporate more than a few connectors. In addition, while it would have been desirable to include reference to the statement number, 144, without the ability to connect it directly to SFAS, consider how many "false drops" would have resulted from all the occurrences of 144 showing up in the income statement or balance sheet!

According to Emma, "long-lived assets" is a key accounting concept. The best solution to targeting mention of SFAS disclosures, given the challenges discussed above, was to combine these keywords with the description of the particular asset (for example, fleet or airplane or plane or aircraft). The first search included the expression "long-lived assets" with the first two words hyphenated. Concerned about so few a number of returned results, Susan reran the search but entered "long lived" as two words without the hyphen. The results were better but she noticed that one of the companies retrieved from the initial search was now missing from the list. Modifying the statement a third time, she entered both expressions, with and without the hyphen, yielding the best results.

Some electronic databases, such as LexisNexis, essentially ignore hyphens and treat them as a space, so that searching for either of these expressions in that database would yield the same and correct number of results. Based on her experience with Thomson, Susan realized that its search engine treated the two expressions as distinct from each other, and that since she could not control their being spelled differently (for example, with and without the hyphen) in the SEC filings, she would need to use her knowledge of the search system to make sure her search yielded the maximum results.

In addition to searching the financial footnotes section of the 10-K, Emma instructed Susan to search the MD&A section as well. She was looking to management's discussion of the impairment of its fleet's long-lived assets to provide her with some of the contextual background that would explain more about the environmental factors leading up to the write-down, as well as its impact on the company's future financial performance. Based on the earlier conversation concerning SFAS 122, Emma also decided to have Susan expand the search back to 1994 to identify which companies disclosed SFAS 121. For now, however, Emma asked Susan to supply her with the list of returned companies predating 2002 filing dates; she only wants Susan to capture the text of the relevant footnotes for those disclosing SFAS 144.

Thomson's search results page includes the following information for each company: name, filing type, description, number of pages, receipt date, filing date, links to view the documents in several formats, including Word and Excel, and a column titled "View Keywords" with a check box next to each company name. Checking this box allows you to view search results in a KWIC format. We discussed the power of this option in the Factiva search conducted above; it is equally effective for scanning SEC filings, especially considering the large size of these documents.

Eighteen companies with a 2002 or 2003 filing were listed, including JetBlue Air Corp., Southwest Airlines, Northwest Airlines, and Alaska Airlines. Using the "View Keywords" option, Susan scanned the sections of the relevant financial footnotes and MD&A sections for reach of the 18 companies. As it turns out, the majority of the companies simply reported the following statement: "The company adopted SFAS No. 144 on January 1, 2000. Adoption of this statement did not have a significant effect on the company's financial position or results of operations." Only three companies, Northwest Airlines Corp., Continental Airlines, and

Airbourne Inc., recorded impairment loses on long-lived assets in accordance with SFAS 144. Within the footnotes, the disclosures were incorporated in a note titled "Impairment of Long-Lived Assets." The MD&A section also provided, as Emma suspected, a tremendous amount of substantiating background information.

Following is Northwest Airline's footnote:

Impairment of Long-Lived Assets: The Company evaluates long-lived assets for potential impairment in compliance with SFAS No.144, *Accounting for the Impairment or Disposal of Long-Lived Assets.* The Company records, in depreciation expense, impairment losses on long-lived assets used in operations when events and circumstances indicate the assets might be impaired and the undiscounted cash flows estimated to be generated by those assets are less than their carrying amounts. The current fair market value of the assets is determined by recent transactions involving sales of similar aircraft, outside appraisals, asset utilization, expected remaining useful lives, future market trends and projected salvage values to determine the fair market value of these assets. Impairment losses are measured by comparing the fair value of the asset to its carrying amount.

In December 2002, the Company revised its fleet plan, accelerating the retirement of nine Boeing 747-200 and 13 DC10-30 aircraft. The Company recorded non-cash impairment charges of $352 million to reflect reductions in the estimated market values of certain aircraft, engines and related inventory in the fourth quarter of 2002. These charges consisted of $294 million related to the aircraft, $23 million write-down of spare engines, and $35 million of related inventory.[7]

Source: Thomson Financial.

Continental Airline's Management Discussion includes an excellent summary of the trigger events negatively impacting the airlines industry.

Among the many factors that threaten us and the airline industry generally are the following:

- A weak global and domestic economy has significantly decreased our revenue. Business traffic, our most profitable source of revenue, and yields are down significantly, as well as leisure traffic and yields. Some of our competitors are significantly changing all or a portion of their pricing structures in a manner that is revenue dilative to us.

---

7. Northwest Airlines Corp., 10-K, 12/31/2002, Thomson Research (*http://www.thomsonlib.com*).

Although we have been successful in decreasing our unit cost as our unit revenue has declined, we expect our operating margin to be negative for at least the first quarter of 2003 and to incur significant losses in that quarter and for the full year 2003.

- We believe that reduced demand persists not only because of the weak economy, but also because of some customers' concerns about further terrorist attacks and reprisals. The continued specter of a war with Iraq and unrest in the Middle East may decrease demand for air travel just as the Persian Gulf War did in 1990 and 1991. We believe that demand is further weakened by customer dissatisfaction with the hassles and delays of heightened airport security and screening procedures.

- Fuel costs rose significantly at the end of 2002 and are, and could remain, at historically high levels. Even though we have hedged approximately 95% of our fuel requirements for the first quarter of 2003, a war with Iraq, other conflicts in the Middle East, political events in Venezuela, or significant events in other oil-producing nations could cause fuel prices to increase further (or be sustained at current high levels) and may impact the availability of fuel. Based on gallons consumed in 2002, for every one dollar increase in the price of crude oil, our annual fuel expense would be approximately $40 million higher.

- The terrorist attacks of 2001 have caused security costs to increase significantly, many of which have been passed on to airlines. Security costs are likely to continue rising for the foreseeable future. In the current environment of lower consumer demand and discounted pricing, these costs cannot effectively be passed on to customers. Insurance costs have also risen sharply, in part due to greater perceived risks and in part due to the reduced availability of insurance coverage. We must absorb these additional expenses in the current pricing environment.

- The nature of the airline industry is changing dramatically as business travelers change their spending patterns and low-cost carriers continue to gain market share. We have announced and are implementing plans to modify our product for the large segment of our customers who are not willing to pay for a premium product, to reduce costs and to generate additional revenue. Other carriers have announced similar plans to create lower-cost products, or to offer separate low cost products (such as a low-cost *"airline within an airline"*). In addition, carriers emerging from bankruptcy will have significantly reduced cost structures and operational flexibility that will allow them to compete more effectively.

- Current conditions may cause consolidation of the airline industry, domestically and globally. The extremity of current conditions could result in a reduction of some of the regulatory hurdles that historically have limited consolidation. Depending on the nature of the consolidation, we could benefit from it or be harmed by it. We continue to monitor developments throughout the industry and recently entered into a marketing alliance (implementation of which is subject to certain conditions) with Northwest and Delta to permit us to compete more effectively with other carriers and alliance groups, although the DOT has announced that it intends to bring an enforcement proceeding against us with respect to the alliance.
- We are engaged in labor negotiations with the union representing our pilots. We cannot predict the outcome of these negotiations or the financial impact on us of any new labor contract with our pilots. Recent significant concession agreements with labor groups at USAir and United Air Lines have had the effect of lowering industry standard wages and benefits, and our negotiations may be influenced by these and other labor cost developments.[8]

Source: Thomson Financial.

As Emma suspected, searching for these annual filings before the filing date had resulted in only a few examples, but Susan had an idea on how to possibly identify a few more. In the current accounting climate of corporate governance and forthcoming disclosure, she wondered if some additional companies might have announced in press releases that they were intending to make changes to their assets of aircraft fleet. Logging on to Factiva, Susan typed the following search strategy:

- **((sfas or financial accounting) w/5 144) and (fleet or airplane or plane or aircraft) and (long lived asset or write-down or impairment).**
- **Source Browser** option, limited the sources searched to **Press Release Wires**
- **Enter Date Range: From: 01/01/2002 To: 3/09/2003**

---

8. Continental Airlines Inc., 10-K, 12/31/2002, Thomson Research (*http://www.thomsonlib.com*).

Success! Four additional airlines companies issued press releases in the third quarter of 2002 to announce their intentions to conduct asset write-downs of their airplane fleet, including a very lengthy discussion by Delta Air Lines in an article entitled, "Delta Air Lines Reports Third Quarter Results," found in *PR Newswire*, October 15, 2002.

Step 4: Determination of Aging Airline Fleet Fair Market Value

SFAS 144 defines fair value as follows:

> The fair value of an asset is the amount at which that asset could be bought or sold in a current transaction between willing parties, that is, other than in a forced or liquidation sale. Quotes market prices in active markets are the best evidence of fair value and shall be used as the basis for the measurement, if available. However, in many instances, quotes market prices in active markets will not be available for the long-lived assets covered by this Statement. In those instances, the estimate of fair value shall be based on the best information available, including prices for similar assets and the results of using other valuation techniques.

Source: FASB Statement No. 144, Accounting for the Impairment or Disposal of Long-Lived Assets, is copyrighted by the Financial Accounting Standards Board, 401 Merritt 7, P.O. Box 5116, Norwalk, Connecticut 06856-5116, U.S.A. Portions are reprinted with permission. Complete copies of this document are available from the FASB.

During the reference interview, Emma said she suspected that industry standards already existed for valuing airplane fleets, as they do for most other industries in which a substantial amount of their liabilities is tied up in tangible assets. She asked if Susan could identify the source or sources of these standards. She was not sure how much of them would be available "for free" but she was not concerned about that. She knew that she would be able to tap into these sources at InterNational Air, but she did not want to enter into her meeting with its CEO without specific knowledge of these standards.

Susan's gut reaction told her that this was a perfect application for a free Web-based search engine such as Google (*http://www.google.com*). Without any specific clues as the names of sources of fleet valuation, she hoped that running a simple search in Google would push out some good leads. She typed the following search statement in Google's basic search box:

- **airplane fleet valuation**

Scanning the first few pages of returned results, Susan immediately identified some potential sources:

1. *Desktop Valuation Report* (*http://www.aviationspecialistsgroup. com/sample%20pages.pdf*). This report is a summary of a more in-depth report containing base value, current market value (fair market value), and future base values for commercial aircraft. While the summary itself was brief and of limited value, it provided Susan with an important lead. Taking her first clue from the main domain name in the summary URL, she types *http://www.aviationspecialistsgroup.com* and displays the home page for Aviation Specialists Group (ASG). Navigating the Web site, she learns that ASG is an airlines industry consulting group specializing in "high quality, cost effective aircraft appraisals, market analysis, and aviation industry insight. ASG has valued billions of dollars worth of jetliners, . . . engines, simulators and spare parts and has extensive practical industry experience in such areas as finance, operating leasing, asset management, airframe and engine maintenance and market analysis."

   ASG publishes a semiannual report, *The Guide*, which covers more than five dozen jetliners manufactured by the industry's main aircraft manufacturers, including Airbus, the manufacturer of the Millennium fleet. *The Guide* contains current market and base values, future values (with and without inflation), manufacturer's list price for current production models, operating lease rental costs, payload and weight data, and more.

2. *Primedia Price Digests* (*http://www.pricedigests.com*). Primedia publishes the *Aircraft Bluebook*, which provides retail and wholesale aircraft prices. The companion volume, *Aircraft Historical Reference Valuation Bluebook*, contains 20 years of historical aircraft data. Both publications are issued quarterly.

3. *Federal Aviation Administration (FAA)*, Economic Values for Evaluation of Federal Aviation Administration Investment and Regulatory Decisions (*http://www.api.faa.gov*). This report presents economic values, often referred to as "critical values," for use in the conduct of benefit-cost and other evaluations of investments. It includes aircraft-related values such as aircraft capacity and utilization factors, aircraft operating and ownership costs, and aircraft replacement and restoration costs. For

aircraft-related values, detail for most measures is available by specific aircraft, generic aircraft classification, and use profiles, such as scheduled commercial service. Scanning the lengthy report which contained more than 100 detailed aircraft valuation data tables, Susan noted that most of the data is based on ASG's *The Guide* and Price Digests' *Aircraft Bluebook.*

Based on verification that the FAA was citing the *Bluebook* and ASG as its primary sources of data, Susan concluded that she had successfully identified the sources of industry standards for valuing airplane fleets. She also noted one additional source, *The Aircraft Cost Evaluator* by Conklin and deDecker Associates, that was additionally cited throughout the FAA report.

Having completed her research of the three technical accounting standards issues that Emma requested, Susan turns her attention to locating the market trigger events impacting the airlines industry.

Step 5: State of the Industry

Susan had initially planned to use Factiva to locate articles, but reconsidered her strategy. The Google search on airplane fleet valuation had retrieved some links relating to the general state of the industry that looked very promising. Returning to the Google Web site, Susan typed the following search statement with excellent results:

- **airlines industry state of**
- *Boeing Commercial Airplanes' Current Market Outlook 2000: World Demand for Commercial Airplanes* (http://www.boeing.com/ commercial/cmo). "Every year Boeing publishes its latest assessment of the demand for world air travel. This assessment estimates the jet airplane capacity to meet the projected growth in travel demand, plus the replacement market for older in-service airplanes." This in-depth, 47-page report contains the following sections: State of the Industry (Airline Profitability, Decline in Traffic, Capacity Reduction, Cycle and Forecast), Demand for Air Travel (Economics and Traffic, Impact of Base Year on the Forecast, Traffic Growth by Region), Demand for Commercial Airplanes (Traffic and Fleet, Network Development Strategies, Fleet Growth, Airplane Replacement, Noise Standards, Deliveries, Demand for Freighter Airplanes, Regional Deliveries), Regional Overviews, and Appendices.
- *FAA Aerospace Forecast Fiscal Years 2003-2014* (http://apo. faa.gov/foreca02/content_5.htm). The Executive Summary looks

at the United States and world economic activity, commercial aviation, world and U.S. travel demand, U.S. air carrier financial results, and more. According to the section on U.S. commercial air carrier fleets, "in the immediate aftermath of the terrorist attacks, many larger airlines grounded large numbers of older less efficient aircraft and deferred scheduled delivery of new aircraft after the next several years. Many of the larger carriers continued to ground aircraft throughout the year as they restructured to cut costs. At the end of CY 2002, . . . The large carrier passenger jet fleet has fallen by 292 aircraft since 2000—down 137 craft in 2001 and 155 aircraft in 2002. . . . Orders for commercial jet aircraft worldwide totaled only 407 during the first 3 quarters of 2002, a 51.4 percent decline from the same period in 2001. . . . Manufacturers delivered 719 commercial jet aircraft worldwide during the first 3 quarters of 2002, a 17.3 percent decline over the same period in 2001."[9] A detailed table of contents contains a series of links to Excel data spreadsheets. The report also cited two additional sources of major airline passenger statistical data that might be useful: Year-End Review and Forecast—An Analysis, Aerospace Industries Association of America (*http://www.aia-aerospace. org/stats/stats.cfm*) and Bureau of Transportation Statistics (*http://www.bts.gov/oai*).

Source: Reprinted courtesy of the Federal Aviation Administration.

- *State of the Airline Industry One Year After 9/11,* Air Transportation Association (http://*www.delta.com/pdfs/senateLFM_1002.pdf*). This series of slides summarizes operations and other performance-related measures of the major U.S. passenger airlines.
- *Iraq War Could Cost Airlines $10 Billion,* Karen Padley, Reuters, March 22, 2003 (*http://biz.yahoo.com/rb/030322/airlines_ iata_losses_4.html*). The article discusses the impact of the war with Iraq on an already devastated airlines industry. The International Air Transport Association states that the "war in Iraq could easily add $10 billion to world airlines losses and deepen what is already the worst crisis in the history of commercial aviation. . . . In the gloomiest forecast yet of the impact of the war on the industry, the association said it expects international passenger travel to drop 15 to 20 percent during the war. . . . Airlines have already reported accumulated losses of $30 billion since the Sept. 11, 2001 attacks in the United States reduced air travel. . . . Three major airlines, United Airlines, US

---

9. FAA Aerospace Forecast Fiscal Years 2003–2014, Chapter I, Executive Summary, "U.S. Commercial Air Carrier Fleets," p. I-9–I-10. *http://apo.faa.gov/foreca02/content_5.htm*

Airways and Hawaiian Airlines are already in bankruptcy protection and the world's largest airline, AMR's American is on the brink."[10]

Source: © Reuters. Reprinted with permission.

Step 6: Airplane Fleet Obsolescence

The final market trigger condition that Emma requested information about is focused on the major passenger airlines replacing aging or obsolete airplane fleet. She wanted articles that demonstrated clear patterns of this occurrence over the past two years and consistency in the rationale.

Returning to Factiva, Susan typed the following search statement:

- **hlp=(airplane or aircraft or fleet) and hlp=(aging or obsole* or replac*) and airlines**
  The search resulted in 202 articles over the most recent two years. Resorting them in relevance order, Susan began the process of scanning the text. The patterns that Emma described in the reference interview quickly emerged. Virtually all of the major airlines are selling one or more of their older fleets and the key reasons all point to overcoming the economic downturn: anticipated reductions in fuel, maintenance and repair costs, and crew training time due to the need to learn to operate few types of planes.
  Following are highlights from some of the articles:

Major U.S. airlines have been retiring older, less fuel efficient airplanes in large numbers since Sept. 11 attacks led to sharp capacity cuts across the industry. They have also sought to cut back the number of different models they fly in order to reduce the cost of maintenance and crew training.[11]

Source: © Reuters. Reprinted with permission.

AirTran Airways is in the process of replacing its aging DC-9-30 fleet with Boeing 717s, a later generation of the DC-9 family. The change should increase the airline's standing because B-717s are a more fuel-efficient aircraft than their predecessors introduced in the mid-1960s. . . . Despite the capital outlay to replace its fleet, the change will improve the

---

10. "Iraq War Could Cost Airlines $10 Billion," Karen Padley, Reuters, March 22, 2003, Yahoo! Finance, *http://biz.yahoo.com/rb/030322/airlines_iata_losses_4.html.*
11. "Delta Retires Last of Aging Boeing 727s," Reuters News, April 8, 2003, Factiva (*http://global.factiva.com*).

company's overall costs. . . . The Sept. 11 terrorist attacks spurred to speed up its replacement schedule.[12]

Source: Reprinted with the permission of Commonwealth Business Media, Inc.

DELIVERING THE RESEARCH RESULTS

Per Emma's request, Susan printed out the relevant documents as she worked through all the research issues. She divided the content into the broad areas of technical accounting standards and market trigger conditions and then created individual packets for each of the corresponding research topics. She attached a cover page to each individual packet, outlining the resources used, search strategy employed, and identification of any additional sources that Emma might want to know about but for which the text was not included in the packets. Susan scheduled a meeting with Emma the afternoon the research was due to review the results and to make sure that Emma was satisfied with her approach and the outcome.

FOLLOW UP: THE AUDITOR'S RECOMMENDATIONS TO THE CLIENT

Based on the research that the BRC provided Emma, she was able to summarize the SFAS 144 issues that InterNational's management should consider in order to make a final determination on selling the Millennium fleet. Her discussion agenda for the client meeting included:

1. Applicable triggering events under SFAS 144.
2. Specific SFAS 144 technical criteria to be applied in assessing realizability and possibly recording a write-down.
3. Reference for determining fair market value if the company's SFAS 144 technical assessment requires a write-down.
4. Examples of financial statement footnote disclosures that InterNational may use as a model.

Subsequent to the client meeting, Emma dropped by the BRC to let Susan know that the preparation and knowledge that Emma and her team displayed in the initial meeting with the client demonstrated to the CEO and CFO that they had, indeed, selected the right accounting firm.

---

12. "Easier Said Than Done," Angela Greiling Keane, *Traffic World*, March 24, 2003, Factiva (*http://global.factiva.com*).

APPENDIX I: AIRLINE COMPANIES' IMPAIRMENT DISCLOSURES

Northwest Airlines Corp., 10-K, 12/31/2002, Thomson Research[13]

Aircraft Valuation and Impairments. The Company has evaluated its long-lived assets for possible impairments in compliance with SFAS No. 144, *Accounting for the Impairment or Disposal of Long-Lived Assets.* The Company records impairment losses on long-lived assets used in operations when events and circumstances indicate the assets might be impaired and the undiscounted cash flows estimated to be generated by those assets are less than their carrying amounts. Impairment losses are measured by comparing the fair value of the assets to their carrying amounts. In determining the need to record impairment charges, the Company is required to make certain estimates regarding such things as the current fair market value of the asset and future net cash flows to be generated by the asset. The current fair market value of the asset is determined by independent appraisal, and the future net cash flows are based on assumptions such as asset utilization, expected remaining useful lives, future market trends and projected salvage values. Impairment charges are recorded in depreciation and amortization expense on the Company's Consolidated Statements of Operations. If there are subsequent changes in these estimates, or if actual results differ from these estimates, such changes could impact the Consolidated Financial Statements.

In December 2002, the Company revised its fleet plan, accelerating the retirement of 13 DC10-30 and nine Boeing 747-200 aircraft by an average of five and six years respectively. The Company recorded impairment charges of $352 million associated with these aircraft, engines and related inventory as a result of the retirement acceleration. See Note 1 to the Consolidated Financial Statements for additional discussion of impairment of long-lived assets.

The Company's 2003 operating results will also be impacted by an estimated $20 million of additional depreciation expense, reflecting the combined result of the reduced average lives, a decrease in net book values and lower salvage values. If the current fair market values and salvage values of the impaired aircraft were decreased by 10%, the aircraft impairment charge would have increased by $17 million and the 2003 depreciation expense would decrease by $7 million.

13. Northwest Airlines Corp., 10-K, 12/31/2002, Thomson Research (*http://www.thomsonlib.com*).

Impairment of Long-Lived Assets: The Company evaluates long-lived assets for potential impairment in compliance with SFAS No. 144, *Accounting for the Impairment or Disposal of Long-Lived Assets.* The Company records, in depreciation expense, impairment losses on long-lived assets used in operations when events and circumstances indicate the assets might be impaired and the undiscounted cash flows estimated to be generated by those assets are less than their carrying amounts. The current fair market value of the assets is determined by recent transactions involving sales of similar aircraft, outside appraisals, asset utilization, expected remaining useful lives, future market trends and projected salvage values to determine the fair market value of these assets. Impairment losses are measured by comparing the fair value of the asset to its carrying amount.

In December 2002, the Company revised its fleet plan, accelerating the retirement of nine Boeing 747-200 and 13 DC10-30 aircraft. The Company recorded non-cash impairment charges of $352 million to reflect reductions in the estimated market values of certain aircraft, engines, and related inventory in the fourth quarter of 2002. These charges consisted of $294 million related to the aircraft, $23 million write-down of spare engines, and $35 million of related inventory.

In the third and fourth quarters of 2001, the Company recorded non-cash impairment charges of $161 million to reflect reductions in the estimated market values of certain aircraft and related inventory due to reduced demand resulting from the events of September 11, 2001. The impairment charges consisted of a $96 million write-down to the estimated market value of 25 Boeing 727 aircraft and five Boeing 747 freighter aircraft. The remaining $65 million of impairment charges related to seven non-operating aircraft that had been stored for future sale, two DC9 aircraft and three Boeing 727 aircraft retired during 2001, and four Boeing 747-200 aircraft retired or scheduled to be retired by 2004. These impairment charges included $9 million to write-down related spare parts to their estimated fair market value.

In December 2000, the Company accelerated the retirement of 21 DC10-40 and six DC10-30 aircraft in anticipation of the replacement of these aircraft with Airbus A330 and Boeing 757-300 aircraft. As a result, the Company recorded a non-cash fleet disposition charge of $125 million in depreciation and amortization. The fleet disposition charge included a $29 million write-down of related spare parts to their estimated fair market value.

Item 7. MANAGEMENT'S DISCUSSION AND ANALYSIS OF FINANCIAL CONDITION AND RESULTS OF OPERATIONS
Overview

Northwest Airlines Corporation (*"NWA Corp."*) is a holding company whose principal indirect operating subsidiary is Northwest Airlines, Inc. (*"Northwest"*). The Consolidated Financial Statements include the accounts of NWA Corp. and all consolidated subsidiaries (collectively, the *"Company"*). The Company reported a net loss of $798 million for the year ended December 31, 2002, compared with a net loss of $423 million in 2001. Loss per common share was $9.32 in 2002 compared with loss per common share of $5.03 in 2001. Operating loss was $846 million in 2002 compared with operating loss of $868 million in 2001. Operating revenues for the year ended December 31, 2002 decreased by $416 million compared to 2001 primarily due to a decline in business travel caused by an economic slowdown in the United States, weakness in the Asian economies and reduced demand for travel resulting from the September 11, 2001 terrorist attacks.

Full year 2002 results included $464 million in unusual pre-tax charges, principally comprised of $352 million attributable to the accelerated retirement of certain Boeing 747-200 and DC10-30 aircraft, $53 million of costs associated with the closure of several facilities, $32 million related to benefit costs and other asset write-downs, and a $27 million partial write-down of the Company's receivable from the U.S. Government related to the grant under the Air Transportation Safety and System Stabilization Act (*"Airline Stabilization Act"*). In addition, the effective tax rate reflected a provision of $15 million for tax credits the Company expects to expire unused.

Full year 2001 results included $300 million in unusual pre-tax charges related to $161 million of reductions in the estimated market values of aircraft, $89 million retroactive wages and benefits as a result of labor contract settlements, $27 million of employee severance costs following the events of September 11, 2001 and $23 million in other non-operating charges. These charges were offset by $461 million of grant income from the U.S. government under the Airline Stabilization Act and a $27 million gain from the sale of the Company's investment in Continental Airlines, Inc.

Substantially all of the Company's results of operations are attributable to its principal indirect operating subsidiary, Northwest, which accounted for approximately 95% of the Company's

2002 consolidated operating revenues and expenses. The Company's results of operations also include other subsidiaries, of which MLT Inc. (*"MLT"*) and Pinnacle Airlines, Inc. (*"Pinnacle Airlines"*) are the most significant. The following discussion pertains primarily to Northwest and, where indicated, MLT and Pinnacle Airlines.

Northwest and Airline Industry Current Status

The current U.S. airline industry environment is the worst in history. Since early 2001, the U.S. airline industry has suffered a significant decline in revenues versus what would have been expected based on historical growth trends. This shortfall has been caused by a number of factors.

The rapid growth of low cost airlines has had a profound impact on industry revenues. Using the advantage of low unit costs, these carriers offer lower fares, particularly those targeted at business passengers, in order to shift demand from larger, more-established airlines. As a result of growth, these low cost carriers now transport nearly 25% of all domestic U.S. passengers compared to less than 10% a decade ago. They now compete for, and thus influence industry pricing on, approximately 75% of all domestic U.S. passenger ticket sales compared to less than 20% a decade ago. As a result of their better financial performance, low cost carriers are expected to continue to grow their market share.

While the advent of Internet travel Web sites has driven significant distribution cost savings for airlines, it has had a large negative impact on airline revenues. Having access to *"perfect pricing information"*, air travel consumers have become more efficient at finding lower fare alternatives than in the past. The increased price consciousness of travelers, as well as the proliferation of distribution channels, has further motivated airlines to price more aggressively to gain fare advantages through certain channels.

The U.S. airline industry is one of the most heavily taxed of all industries. Taxes and fees now represent approximately 25% of what a passenger pays for an average domestic airline ticket, a percentage even greater than that for alcohol and tobacco products. These taxes and fees have grown significantly in the past decade, most recently with the introduction of a $2.50 security fee imposed on each passenger flight segment, subject to a $10 per roundtrip cap. The company believes that every dollar of tax or fee increase imposed on airline passengers roughly translates into a dollar of reduced airline revenue, particularly over the long run.

The attacks of September 11, 2001 materially impacted and continue to impact air travel. Concerns about further terrorist attacks, which are unlikely to abate any time soon, have had a negative impact on air travel demand. Furthermore, security procedures introduced at airports since the attacks have increased, both in reality and in perception, the inconvenience of flying and thus further reduced demand.

While the factors noted are believed to be lasting, if not permanent, and could in fact worsen over time, some of the current airline industry revenue shortfall is believed to be cyclical in nature. U.S. airline revenues have historically been and continue to be influenced by the strength of the U.S. economy. Furthermore, airline business revenues are greatly influenced by the growth in corporate profitability. The current sluggishness of both the economy and corporate profitability is adversely affecting airline revenues.

The airline industry revenue decline has been further exacerbated in early 2003. In January, United Airlines introduced a new pricing structure, reducing its highest business fares by 40-50%. This action and the resulting match by other airlines has reduced average fares without a corresponding increase in demand. The threat of a war with Iraq has also materially affected future airline bookings, particularly for international travel.

In addition to the impact on industry revenue, the September 11, 2001 events caused a significant rise in certain operating costs, particularly for aviation and property insurance. Total aviation and property insurance expense nearly tripled in 2002, to $121 million. These costs could rise further should coverage presently provided by the government under the Homeland Security Act, which has been extended until August 31, 2003, no longer be available.

During the past year, two major U.S. airlines, US Air, Inc. and United Air Lines, Inc., have filed for Chapter 11 bankruptcy protection. Current trends make it likely that the airline industry will continue to post significant losses, at least through 2003.

In response to the industry environment, the Company has taken several steps to mitigate the impact on its results of operations and financial condition. These steps included a significant reduction in scheduled capacity on an available seat mile basis, a reduction in work force of 12,000 employees, deferral of certain aircraft orders previously scheduled for delivery in 2003 through 2005 for an average of two years, closure of maintenance facilities, flight crew bases, reservations and sales facilities, and deferrals and cancellations of discretionary and other non-operationally critical spending. For the year ended December 31, 2002, capacity was 9.6% below 2000 levels.

While the Company has already taken these significant cost reduction steps, it believes additional measures will be necessary in this new and permanently changed revenue environment. Wages, salaries and benefits made up 41% of the Company 's 2002 operating revenues and will need to be a major component of future cost reduction initiatives. The Company has begun discussions with its labor unions in an effort to align wages, benefits and work rules with the new revenue environment and to remain competitive with those airlines achieving permanent cost reductions through bankruptcy proceedings.

Source: Thomson Financial.

Continental Airlines Inc., 10-K, 12/31/2002, Thomson Research[14]

ITEM 7. MANAGEMENT'S DISCUSSION AND ANALYSIS OF FINANCIAL CONDITION AND RESULTS OF OPERATIONS.

The following discussion contains forward-looking statements that are not limited to historical facts, but reflect our current beliefs, expectations or intentions regarding future events. All forward-looking statements involve risks and uncertainties that could cause actual results to differ materially from those in the forward-looking statements. For examples of such risks and uncertainties, please see the cautionary statements contained in Item 1. *"Business - Risk Factors - Terrorist Attacks and International Hostilities"*, *"Business - Risk Factors Relating to the Company"* and *"Business - Risk Factors Relating to the Airline Industry"*. We undertake no obligation to publicly update or revise any forward-looking statements to reflect events or circumstances that may arise after the date of this report. Hereinafter, the terms *"Continental"*, *"we"*, *"us"*, *"our"* and similar terms refer to Continental Airlines, Inc. and its subsidiaries, unless the context indicates otherwise.

---

14.   Continental Airlines Inc., 10-K, 12/31/2002, Thomson Research (*http://www. thomsonlib.com*).

Overview

We incurred a consolidated net loss of $451 million for the year ended December 31, 2002 as compared to a consolidated net loss of $95 million for the year ended December 31, 2001. Results for 2002 include a $242 million charge for the impairment of owned aircraft and the accrual of future obligations for leased aircraft permanently grounded. Results for 2001 included a $146 million charge for the impairment of owned aircraft and the accrual of future obligations for leased aircraft permanently grounded, costs associated with furloughs and company-offered leaves, and other charges related to special items. In addition, 2001 results included a $417 million grant under the Air Transportation Safety and System Stabilization Act (the *"Stabilization Act"*).

The current U.S. domestic airline environment is the worst in our history. Prior to September 2001, we were profitable, although many U.S. air carriers were losing money and our profitability was declining. The terrorist attacks of September 11, 2001 dramatically worsened the difficult financial environment and presented new and greater challenges for the airline industry. Since the terrorist attacks, several airlines, including United Air Lines and US Air, have filed for bankruptcy. Although we have been able to raise capital, downsize our operations and reduce our expenses significantly, we have reported significant losses since the terrorist attacks, and current trends in the airline industry make it likely that we will continue to post significant losses for the foreseeable future. The revenue environment continues to be weak in light of changing pricing models, excess capacity in the market, reduced corporate travel spending and other issues. In addition, fuel prices have significantly escalated due to the threat of imminent military action against Iraq and continued political tension in Venezuela.

Absent adverse factors outside our control such as those described herein, we believe that our liquidity and access to cash will be sufficient to fund our current operations through 2003 (and beyond if we are successful in implementing our previously announced revenue generation and cost cutting measures, as well as additional measures currently being developed). However, we believe that the economic environment must improve for us to continue to operate at our current size and expense level beyond that time. We may find it necessary to further downsize our operations, ground additional aircraft and further reduce our expenses. We anticipate that our previously announced capacity and cost reductions, together with the capacity reductions announced by other carriers and capacity reductions that could come from restructurings within the industry, should result in a better financial environment by the end of 2003, absent adverse factors outside our control such as a further economic recession, additional terrorist attacks, a war affecting the United States, decreased consumer demand or sustained high fuel prices. However, we expect to incur a significant loss in 2003, regardless of such adverse factors.

Due in part to the lack of predictability of future traffic, business mix and yields, we are currently unable to estimate the long-term effect on us of the events of September 11, 2001, or the impact of any further terrorist attacks or a war involving United States forces against Iraq. However, given the magnitude of the unprecedented events of September 11, 2001 and their continuing aftermath, the adverse impact to our financial condition, results of operations, liquidity and prospects may continue to be material, and our financial resources might not be sufficient to absorb it or that of any further terrorist attacks or a war involving United States forces if the war were prolonged.

Among the many factors that threaten us and the airline industry generally are the following:

- A weak global and domestic economy has significantly decreased our revenue. Business traffic, our most profitable source of revenue, and yields are down significantly, as well as leisure traffic and yields. Some of our competitors are significantly changing all or a portion of their pricing structures in a manner that is revenue dilutive to us. Although we have been successful in decreasing our unit cost as our unit revenue has declined, we expect our operating margin to be negative for at least the first quarter of 2003 and to incur significant losses in that quarter and for the full year 2003.
- We believe that reduced demand persists not only because of the weak economy, but also because of some customers' concerns about further terrorist attacks and reprisals. The continued specter of a war with Iraq and unrest in the Middle East may decrease demand for air travel just as the Persian Gulf War did in 1990 and 1991. We believe that demand is further weakened by customer dissatisfaction with the hassles and delays of heightened airport security and screening procedures.
- Fuel costs rose significantly at the end of 2002 and are, and could remain, at historically high levels. Even though we have hedged approximately 95% of our fuel requirements for the first quarter of 2003, a war with Iraq, other conflicts in the

Middle East, political events in Venezuela, or significant events in other oil-producing nations could cause fuel prices to increase further (or be sustained at current high levels) and may impact the availability of fuel. Based on gallons consumed in 2002, for every one dollar increase in the price of crude oil, our annual fuel expense would be approximately $40 million higher.

- The terrorist attacks of 2001 have caused security costs to increase significantly, many of which have been passed on to airlines. Security costs are likely to continue rising for the foreseeable future. In the current environment of lower consumer demand and discounted pricing, these costs cannot effectively be passed on to customers. Insurance costs have also risen sharply, in part due to greater perceived risks and in part due to the reduced availability of insurance coverage. We must absorb these additional expenses in the current pricing environment.

- Although we reduced some of our costs during the last year and continue to implement cost-cutting measures, our costs cannot be decreased as quickly as our revenue has declined. In addition, as is the case with many of our competitors, we are highly leveraged, and have few assets that remain unpledged to support any new debt. Combined with reduced access to the capital markets, themselves already weakened by the state of the economy, there is the potential for insufficient liquidity if current conditions continue unabated for a sufficiently long period of time. We had approximately $1.3 billion of cash, cash equivalents and short-term investments at December 31, 2002. During the first quarter of 2003, we anticipate our cash balance will decline by approximately $1.5 million per day taking into account all expected sources and uses of cash, including required debt payments and capital expenditures. We continue to hold 53.1% of the outstanding stock of ExpressJet Holdings, Inc. ("Holdings"), the publicly traded parent of our regional jet subsidiary, which stock is not pledged to creditors. We intend to sell or otherwise dispose of some or all of our interest in Holdings, subject to market conditions.

- The nature of the airline industry is changing dramatically as business travelers change their spending patterns and low-cost carriers continue to gain market share. We have announced and are implementing plans to modify our product for the large segment of our customers who are not willing to pay for a premium product, to reduce costs and to generate additional revenue. Other carriers have announced similar plans to create lower-cost products, or to offer separate low cost products (such as a low-cost *"airline within an airline"*). In addition, carriers emerging from bankruptcy will have significantly reduced cost structures and operational flexibility that will allow them to compete more effectively.

- Current conditions may cause consolidation of the airline industry, domestically and globally. The extremity of current conditions could result in a reduction of some of the regulatory hurdles that historically have limited consolidation. Depending on the nature of the consolidation, we could benefit from it or be harmed by it. We continue to monitor developments throughout the industry and recently entered into a marketing alliance (implementation of which is subject to certain conditions) with Northwest and Delta to permit us to compete more effectively with other carriers and alliance groups, although the DOT has announced that it intends to bring an enforcement proceeding against us with respect to the alliance.

- We are engaged in labor negotiations with the union representing our pilots. We cannot predict the outcome of these negotiations or the financial impact on us of any new labor contract with our pilots. Recent significant concession agreements with labor groups at US Air and United Air Lines have had the effect of lowering industry standard wages and benefits, and our negotiations may be influenced by these and other labor cost developments.

- As a result of continuing declines in interest rates and the market value of our defined benefit pension plans' assets, we were required to increase the minimum pension liability and reduce stockholders' equity at December 31, 2002 by $250 million. This adjustment did not impact current earnings, the actual funding requirements of the plans, or our compliance with debt covenants. However, because of the decline in interest rates and the market value of the plans' assets, we anticipate that pension expense and required pension contributions will increase in 2003. Pension expense for the year 2002 was approximately $185 million. Pension expense for 2003 is expected to be approximately $326 million. We contributed $150 million of cash to our pension plans in 2002 and expect our cash contribution to our pension plans to be $141 million in 2003.

• Under our two principal bank loans, we are required to maintain a minimum unrestricted cash balance of $500 million and, beginning in June 2003, we will also be required to maintain a 1:1 ratio of EBITDAR (earnings before interest, income taxes, depreciation, amortization, and aircraft rentals) to fixed charges, which consist of interest expense, aircraft rental expense, cash income taxes and cash dividends, for the previous four quarters. These bank loans had an outstanding balance of $250 million at December 31, 2002. We anticipate that the outstanding balance will be approximately $158 million at the time the EBITDAR to fixed charges ratio covenant becomes effective and $74 million at December 31, 2003. If we are unable to meet the required ratio and are unsuccessful in renegotiating the terms of these bank loans, we will have the option of repaying the debt at that time.

Results of Operations

The following discussion provides an analysis of our results of operations and reasons for material changes therein for the three years ended December 31, 2002.

Comparison of 2002 to 2001. Passenger revenue decreased 7.0%, $595 million, during 2002 as compared to 2001, which was principally due to a decrease in both traffic and yields subsequent to the September 11, 2001 attacks, as well as the continuing weak economy. Yield was 6.4% lower in 2002 compared to 2001.

Comparisons of passenger revenue, revenue per available seat mile (RASM) and available seat miles (ASMs) by geographic region for our mainline jet and regional jet and turboprop (which were removed entirely from our fleet in 2002) operations are shown below:

Increase (Decrease) for Year Ended December 31, 2002 vs. December 31, 2001

	PASSENGER REVENUE	RASM	ASMS
Domestic	(12.3)%	(5.8)%	(6.8)%
Latin America	(5.4)%	(4.4)%	(1.1)%
Trans-Atlantic	2.6 %	4.5 %	(1.9)%
Pacific	(8.6)%	(3.6)%	(5.2)%
Total Mainline Jet Operations	(9.1)%	(4.1)%	(5.2)%
Regional Jet and Turboprop	10.9 %	(3.0)%	14.4 %

Cargo, mail and other revenue increased 5.5%, $28 million, in 2002 compared to 2001, primarily due to increased charter revenue and passenger related fees, offset by new security restrictions that reduced mail volumes.

Wages, salaries and related costs decreased 2.1%, $62 million, during 2002 as compared to 2001, primarily due to a reduction in the average number of employees and lower employee incentives, partially offset by higher wage rates.

Aircraft fuel expense decreased 16.8%, $206 million, in 2002 as compared to 2001. The average price per gallon decreased 10.6% from 78.24 cents in 2001 to 69.97 cents in 2002. Jet fuel consumption decreased 9.1% principally reflecting decreased flight operations due to the current industry environment and the fuel efficiency of our younger fleet.

Aircraft rentals decreased 0.1%, $1 million, in 2002 compared to 2001, due to aircraft rent on grounded aircraft no longer requiring accrual since such amounts have been recognized as part of the fleet impairment charge, offset by increased rental expense related to the delivery of new aircraft.

Landing fees and other rentals increased 9.0%, $52 million, in 2002 as compared to 2001 primarily due to higher landing fees resulting from rate increases and higher facilities rent, partially attributable to the completion of substantial portions of the Global Gateway project at Newark Liberty International Airport.

Maintenance, materials and repairs expense decreased 16.2%, $92 million, during 2002 as compared to 2001 primarily due to the replacement of older aircraft with new aircraft that generally require less maintenance.

Depreciation and amortization expense decreased 4.9%, $23 million, in 2002 compared to 2001, primarily due to lower depreciation expense on grounded aircraft which have been written down to fair market value and $22 million related to the discontinuation of amortization of routes following the adoption of SFAS 142, partially offset by the addition of new owned aircraft and related spare parts.

Reservations and sales expense decreased 14.6%, $65 million, in 2002 as compared to 2001 principally due to lower credit card fees as a result of lower revenue.

Commissions expense decreased 41.8%, $152 million, in 2002 compared to 2001 due to elimination of domestic base commissions and lower revenue.

Passenger services expense decreased 14.7%, $51 million, in 2002 as compared to 2001 primarily due to improved baggage performance and a decrease in food costs caused by a decrease in passengers.

Fleet impairment, severance and other special charges in 2002 consisted of a $242 million charge primarily related to the impairment (owned aircraft) and accrual of lease exit costs (leased aircraft) of our DC-10-30, MD-80 and turboprop fleets. Fleet impairment, severance and other special charges in 2001 totaling $124 million include costs associated with impairment of various owned aircraft and spare engines, furloughs and company-offered leaves, a charge for environmental remediation and costs associated with the closure and under-utilization of certain facilities and for certain uncollectible receivables.

Financial Footnotes

a. Measurement of Impairment of Long-Lived Assets

Effective January 1, 2002, we adopted SFAS 144, *"Accounting for the Impairment or Disposal of Long-Lived Assets"*. SFAS 144 superceded SFAS 121, *"Accounting for the Impairment of Long-Lived Assets and for Long-Lived Assets to be Disposed Of"*. The adoption of SFAS 144 had no effect on our results of operations. We record impairment losses on long-lived assets used in operations, consisting principally of property and equipment and airport operating rights, when events and circumstances indicate that the assets might be impaired and the undiscounted cash flows estimated to be generated by those assets are less than the carrying amount of those assets. The net carrying value of assets not recoverable is reduced to fair value if lower than carrying value. In determining the fair market value of the assets, we consider market trends and recent transactions involving sales of similar assets.

Source: Thomson Financial.

Airbourne Inc.., 10-K, 12/31/2002, Thomson Research[15]
Property and Equipment

Property and equipment is stated at cost. The cost and accumulated depreciation of property and equipment disposed of are removed from the accounts with any related gain or loss reflected in earnings from operations.

For financial reporting purposes, depreciation of property and equipment is provided on a straight-line basis over the lesser of the asset's useful life or lease term. The Company periodically evaluates the estimated service lives and residual values used to depreciate its property and equipment. This evaluation may result in changes in estimated loss and residual values. Depreciable lives are as follows:

Flight equipment	5 to 18 years
Buildings, runways, and leasehold improvements	5 to 40 years
Package handling and ground support equipment	3 to 10 years
Vehicles and other equipment	3 to 8 years

---

15. Airbourne Inc., 10-K, 12/31/2002, Thomson Research (*http://www.thomsonlib.com*).

DC-9 aircraft generally carry residual values of 15% of asset cost. All other property and equipment have no assigned residual values.

When an aircraft is removed from service and considered impaired, as was the case with a DC-8 aircraft removed from domestic operations in 2002, the assets residual value is adjusted to its fair value, which is the equivalent of an estimated parts value in accordance with the provisions of Statement of Financial Accounting Standards ("SFAS") No. 144, "Accounting for the Impairment or Disposal of Long-Lived Assets". A fair value adjustment charge of $3,068,000 was included in depreciation and amortization expense in 2002.

Major engine overhauls as well as ordinary engine maintenance and repairs for DC-8 and 767 aircraft are performed by third-party service providers under long-term contracts. In July 2001, a third party service provider began performing major engine overhauls on the Company's DC-9 aircraft. Service costs under the contracts are based upon hourly rates for engine usage and are charged to expense in the period utilization occurs.

The Company adopted SFAS No. 144 on January 1, 2002. Adoption of this statement did not have a significant effect on the Company's financial position or results of operations.

Source: Thomson Financial.

3

Accounting and Financial Research Problems and Solutions

Chapter One laid the foundation for understanding the basics of accounting and related financial research, while focusing on the types of questions posed, and the context in which they are asked. Based on this information, Chapter Two's case study presented a complex research project. The case study offered an opportunity to delve into the solution to an accounting research issue, thus providing the researcher with clear directions on the time, resources, and budget necessary to develop a complete and thorough answer/response.

In the real world, however, researchers are usually required to respond to a client's request for information with less than optimal conditions: time, resources, and budgets are all open for negotiation, with the researcher often expected to demonstrate that he or she can produce the desired results with minimum expenditure of all three. This means the researcher must be: (1) knowledgeable about a broad range of resources and keenly aware of his or her strengths and limitations, (2) equally adept in appropriately selecting and using both free and for-pay sources, (3) able to approach problem solving with flexibility and creativity, and (4) comfortably adjusting to the unexpected. Hence the problems and solutions reviewed in this chapter present a number of differing strategies for approaching and answering a series of real-life accounting and related financial research queries.

The five individuals contributing to these pieces come from different backgrounds: four are information professionals, two from corporate environments (Susan Klopper and Jan Rivers) and two from academic (Brenda Reeb and Kim Whalen); the fifth is a financial analyst (Michelle Hartstrom). Considering their differing backgrounds, it is not surprising that each takes a slightly different approach to their problems, and yet each arrives at a successful solution which matches the specific information needed within the client-defined perimeters for time and budget. Each adeptly combines the four important research qualities defined in the previous paragraph.

The problems and solutions are organized to parallel the structure of the discussion about accounting and related financial resources and research strategies in Chapter One and are summarized below.

ACCOUNTING STANDARDS. Problems 1 and 2 illustrate typical requests to locate the text of technical accounting standards, a Financial Accounting Standards Board (FASB) Technical Bulletin (FTB) and FASB Exposure Draft. In both cases, the client identifies the documents by their subject but it is up to the researcher to determine the specific numbers or titles, and to locate the documents in a format that meets the specified delivery and turnaround times. For Problems 3 and 4 the client is looking for secondary analysis that discusses and presents examples of applying two specific FASB financial accounting standards. Problem 5, the final activity in this set, requires the researcher to locate current news and discussion on the trend toward the converging of all accounting standards. While articles are expected to address the accounting boards' technical agendas for tackling this complex process, they will likely also discuss broader trends and implications for this movement.

FINANCIAL DISCLOSURES. Problems 6, 7, and 8 illustrate classic examples of financial disclosure research. Each problem requires knowledge of the technical language combined with familiarity with the parts of Security and Exchange Commission (SEC) filings and the electronic databases that allow for this level of precise, targeted research. Problems 9 and 10 test the researcher's comfort with the types of information contained with the 8-K SEC filings as well as the strengths and limitations of using free vs. fee-based electronic databases for this type of research.

BUSINESS RATIOS. Problems 11 and 12 illustrate the importance of using SIC (Standard Industrial Classification) codes for locating comparable industry ratios and the need to include your client in the process to minimize the risk of identifying an incorrect code. Problem 11 highlights the importance of knowing when it is more efficient to use a print resource while Problem 12 allows the researcher to benefit from the power of an electronic database.

FINANCIAL MARKET DATA. All three problems in this set illustrate the power of the free Web. While the researcher used a subscription-based service to solve Problem 13, per the request of her client, she was also able to provide directions for using a free site to locate the same data. Problems 14 and 15 illustrate the value that the free Web can play in locating information. It also demonstrates that your knowledge of reputable sources helps to recognize and distinguish between good and bad information. When basing important business decisions on the use of the free Web, this lesson can mean the difference between research success and disaster.

ECONOMIC DATA. The solutions to all seven problems in this set were arrived at through intelligent and creative use of the free Web. Intelligent because either the researchers already knew the authoritative source for the data and were using the Web as an instrument for identifying the URL, or they used the Web to lead them to some possible choices, tapping into their knowledge of how to separate quality information from bad data to determine which sources were reliable. Problems 20 and 21 additionally draw on international data while Problem 22 targets forecasted data. This set also illustrates the different research strategies used by information and financial professionals, each of whom brings to the table slightly different experiences, skills, and mindsets for approaching the research process.

CORPORATE STRATEGIC AND OPERATIONAL INTELLIGENCE. Problems 23 and 24 illustrate the wealth of rich public company information that is available for free via the Internet. In Problem 23, the researcher tapped into her knowledge about SEC filing disclosure and the content of the company's annual report to target management's discussion about its organization's outlook. A scan of the company's Web site Investor Relations section revealed some additional important intelligence. A well-rounded answer to Problem 24 required the persistent scan of the BEA's Web site combined with fee-based investment banking analysis. Problems 25 and 26 specifically required use of investment banking company reports, rich sources of corporate strategic and operational analysis, but hardly free.

CORPORATE GOVERNANCE. Problems 27, 28, and 29 illustrate the power of corporate disclosure, tapping into the wealth of management-focused information disclosed in 10-K SEC filings and the proxy statement. These are all available using free EDGAR sites and enable the level of due diligence research that is now necessary in the post-Enron world. Problem 30 illustrates the value of a resourceful electronic business aggregator, such as Factiva, for efficiently employing credible corporate intelligence. The necessity for accurate due diligence overshadows the lure of relying purely on the free Web for reliable information. Providing a comprehensive answer to Problem 31 highlights the need to balance access to primary information with secondary analysis.

INTERNATIONAL BUSINESS. The answer to Problem 32 required tapping into a standard source of international accounting standards, combined with using the free Web, to identify a relevant international accounting standards board and benefiting from the wealth of analysis available on its Web site. Familiarity with core secondary accounting research publications, and a general understanding of the parallels between international and U.S. standards-setting processes, was invaluable for the researcher.

COMPETITIVE INTELLIGENCE. Problem 33 illustrates the value of subscribing to targeted business research tools; this problem could simply never have been solved without investing in the necessary fee-based resources. Problem 34, which asks for information about a public company's auditor and its fees, appears an easy find. But as is often the case when conducting research, there is a catch. Not to be deterred, the researcher used creativity and intelligent sleuthing to resolve the problem to the client's satisfaction. Problem 35 illustrates yet another example of creative use of the free Web.

ACCOUNTING INDUSTRY CERTIFICATION. By being familiar with the different areas of accounting specialization, the researcher easily solved Problem 36 by identifying the appropriate association and tapping into the wealth of information on its Web site.

PROBLEM NUMBER 1: LOCATE A FASB TECHNICAL BULLETIN THAT DEALS WITH EMPLOYEE STOCK PURCHASE PLANS

RESEARCH BACKGROUND: You receive a frantic call from an audit partner who needs to meet with a client this afternoon concerning an issue with employee stock purchase plans, and specifically a "look-back option." The client is interested in offering his employees several different plan options and wants the auditor to present him with a relatively easy-to-understand explanation of the differences so that he can finalize his decision and present something to his firm's employees. The auditor has looked over the FASB but is concerned that it is too technical for the client and is hoping that FASB has issued a FTB on this issue that is more simplified. You are authorized to spend up to $200 to locate the information.

RESEARCH STRATEGY EMPLOYED: While on the phone with the auditor, you asked specifically which FASB this related to. He was not positive of the number but knew that it had to do with accounting for stock based compensation. You know that the text of the Financial Accounting Statements and Technical Bulletins are included in the *Original Pronouncements* (OP), and that the OP contains excellent cross-references to all related documents. You opt instead to use CCH Tax Research Network (*http://www.taxgroup.com*) as you already subscribe to the full text of the OP in its Accounting and Auditing Library.

Logging onto CCH, you click on the tab to Accounting/Audit and display the page listing all the sources you subscribe to within that library. You click on the box to the left of OP and decide also to select the *Aspen-Miller GAAP Guides*. "Miller's" guide contains good discussion and examples and so perhaps it will provide a level of explanation that will be helpful to the client.

CCH's interface is very accommodating, allowing you to select the specific resources you want to search and conduct a keyword search across those sources. You enter the keywords "look back option" in the search box, hoping that it is specific enough to retrieve relevant documents. The search returns eight documents, of which the first three are to a Miller commentary, SFAS 123, Accounting for Stock Based Compensation, and FASB FTB

97-1, Accounting under Statement 123 for Certain Employee Stock Purchase Plans with a Look-Back Option.

You spend a few minutes scanning the Miller commentary and the FTB, and although you do not fully understand the technical discussion, it is apparent that they provide further explanation and guidance as to how to implement and calculate these plans for employees.

RESEARCH RESULTS: Both Miller's Commentary and the FTB appear to contain the type of discussion that the partner was looking for so you download both documents. You also save the CCH results list in case he is interested in any of the additional documents that were returned; several of them also contain Miller Commentary. Attaching the documents to an e-mail, you include a note explaining your search strategy and leave the door open for possibly trying to locate some journal articles in case the attached documents are not all that the partner needs.

SUMMARY OF RESULTS: The technical scope of this issue was a bit out of your area of expertise so you began the research process by spending a few minutes talking with the partner to better understand the issue and learn more about the relevant SFAS. The ability to search for the information using CCH's electronic database made it much quicker to locate the information and to be able to deliver it in the format requested. Had you not had access to CCH Tax Research Network, however, the exact same research could just as easily have been conducted using print editions of the OP and the *Aspen-Miller GAAP Guide*. Both include excellent indexes at the back which contain cross-references to other relevant documents.

CONTRIBUTOR NAME: Susan M. Klopper

AFFILIATION: Goizueta Business Library

PROBLEM NUMBER 2: LOCATE A RECENTLY RELEASED FASB EXPOSURE DRAFT ON ACCOUNTING FOR STOCK-BASED COMPENSATION

RESEARCH BACKGROUND: An audit partner has heard that an Exposure Draft relating to disclosure and accounting for stock-based compensation was recently released by the FASB. He is going to be meeting with a client in the afternoon about this topic and wants to read the draft beforehand. He needs a full-text version of the Exposure Draft within an hour, since he will not have any other time to review it before the meeting. There is no budget for this request since it is for the partner's review and educational purposes.

RESEARCH STRATEGY EMPLOYED: The quickest way to locate the Exposure Draft is via the FASB Web site (*http://www.fasb.org*). The site contains a link to recently released drafts; they are downloadable for free in full-text .pdf format. From the FASB Web site, perform the following steps:

- Locate the Exposure Draft link on the left side of the FASB home page and click on it to access the Exposure Draft page.
- The Exposure Draft home page lists current Exposure Drafts by title in chronological order according to their release dates, with the most recently released drafts appearing first. The release date appears directly below the draft's title.
- Scan down the list of Exposure Draft titles to locate the one the partner is requesting. It was released on October 4, 2002, and is entitled, "Accounting for Stock-Based Compensation—Transition and Disclosure—an amendment of FASB Statement No. 123."
- Under the date of release is a download link. Click on it to access the full-text, .pdf version of the document. The document will appear via Adobe Acrobat Reader.

SUMMARY OF SOLUTION: A tax partner wanted a copy of a FASB Exposure Draft about disclosure and accounting for stock-based compensation so that he could read it before a client meeting that afternoon. Due to the partner's schedule, he needed it within the hour. Also, there was no budget for the request. FASB posts the full texts of its Exposure Drafts on its Web site in .pdf format and for free. They are easily accessible via the Exposure Drafts link on the FASB home page.

This presented an excellent opportunity to tap into the wealth of full-text authoritative pronouncements accessible via the FASB's Web site; Exposure Drafts are posted on the site dating back to 1999. Earlier drafts, dating back to 1978, can be ordered by clicking on the FASB Store link at the top of the home page. To locate the draft you need, you have the options of either conducting a keyword search or clicking on the Publications link on the left menu and browsing a list of publications. The list is sorted by "publication type"; scroll down the list and click on Exposure Drafts. This will result in a list of drafts in descending order by issue date. If an item is available for free download, it will contain a link for that purpose.

What if the requestor did not know the correct title of the Exposure Draft but only the subject matter? Simple. Use the search box that appears on each page in the site. Conducting a simple search yields a results list that pushes out your keywords "in context," highlighting portions of the document text in which they appear. The results list also contains a hyperlinked title and the document's publication or release date. Search results can be sorted by keyword relevancy or time, in other words, the document's release or publication date. A series of stars denoting degree of relevancy appear next to each returned document on the list; the more stars, the more relevant the document.

The FASB Web site is an excellent resource for keeping current on the organization's activities, including new developments and current and forthcoming publication release. The home page features announcements of new releases and publications, as well as board-related meeting notices and other information. The link to Action Alerts takes you to FASB's weekly news alert, which contains more comprehensive coverage of board activities, both current and upcoming. Emerging Issues Task Force (EITF) proposals are also directly accessible from the FASB home page.

CONTRIBUTOR NAME: Jan Rivers
AFFILIATION: Dorsey & Whitney LLP

USEFUL TIPS

- Click on the News Center link at the top of the FASB home page to access press releases announcing newly released FASB statements. Exposure Drafts become FASB Statements upon final board approval, so tracking newly announcement Exposure Drafts is an excellent way to learn about forthcoming FASB Statements of Financial Standards.
- Keep current on FASB developments by registering for free, weekly Action Alert e-mail newsletters. Click on the Action Alert link on the FASB home page and follow the directions to sign up.
- Exposure Drafts are available in full text on the FASB site, dating back to 1999 in .pdf format. They may be printed by clicking on the printer icon in Adobe Acrobat or saved. To save the Exposure Draft in .pdf format, click on the Save icon in Adobe Acrobat.

PROBLEM NUMBER 3: LOCATE ARTICLES FROM KEY ACCOUNTING JOURNALS THAT DISCUSS STATEMENT OF ACCOUNTING STANDARDS 86, "ACCOUNTING FOR COSTS OF COMPUTER SOFTWARE TO BE SOLD, LEASED, OR OTHERWISE MARKETED"

RESEARCH BACKGROUND: John, an audit manager, needs to bone up on the disclosure of costs for computer software. His client is selling and leasing software and needs some guidance on how to account for this on his books. John leaves you a brief voice-mail asking if you would locate some substantive articles appearing in accounting industry magazines that will provide him with some explanation of the SFAS and examples of how to apply it. He is on the road and does not have his copy of OP with him, but knows that Computer Software is in the title and that it was released sometime in the 1980s. Please e-mail him the copies of four to six substantive articles and the copy of the actual SFAS as well. It is Tuesday morning and he would like to review your research when he returns to the office on Thursday afternoon.

RESEARCH BUDGET: John gives you the go-ahead to spend up to $100 for the research. If you need to incur more expenses, send him a voice-mail with the estimated additional costs before spending the money.

RESEARCH STRATEGY EMPLOYED: ABI/Inform is one of the best electronic databases for conducting accounting article searches. An early generation of databases to provide full-text articles, it is especially strong in its collection of accounting, finance, and business magazines and it contains articles dating back to the 1970s. Your firm subscribes to ProQuest Direct, the "official" database name, so you know that you are in good standing to locate the type of articles John requires.

Before jumping online, you grab your shelf copy of the OP and look up the SFAS. True to John's word, it is entitled "Accounting for the Costs of Computer Software to Be Sold, Leased, or Otherwise Marketed" and was released in August 1985. The first page of each SFAS in the OP also includes any updated information that might indicate if the SFAS has since been amended or superseded, or if there are any relevant EITF issues or supplementary FASB publications that relate to the SFAS. According to the OP, the SFAS is still current and has not been altered; there are five EITF issues and a FASB highlight (from February 1986) that might be useful. You make a note of the citations for possible use when conducting your research.

Now that you have the exact SFAS number, title, and release date, you log onto ABI/Inform and begin your search. Based on experience conducting accounting article searches, you know that usually the most substantive discussions of a new FASB are written within a few years after it is has been released. Of course, if the SFAS is later changed, newer articles would likely be written to reflect the changes. Since this was not the case with SFAS 86, you focus your search on the dates surrounding its issue.

You basically need to sit back and make a list of any and all sources of articles from accounting magazines and journals to which you have, evaluate the sources for coverage of accounting practices, and keyword search in the best ones. You do not need to be 100 percent exhaustive (you don't have time) but you do need to present all of the interpretations or implications of SFAS 86. Interestingly, in this problem you need to capture comments made before, during, and several years after SFAS 86 went into effect in 1986. Not everything from the mid-1980s is online.

Logging onto ABI/Inform, you select the option to conduct a "Guided" search since this allows you to limit keywords to specific parts of the article, such as subject, title, or publication name. You repeat the search string to appear in either the Basic Search Fields, which will include the title or subjects, or the article abstract. Since you are looking for substantive discussions on the topic, limiting the keywords to any of these fields will eliminate the possibility of getting lots of articles that may mention the topic but only as a more casual reference. Your search strategy is: "(fasb or accounting or sfas) and 86 and computer* and software." Typically, a particular FASB statement can be referenced in a number of ways, identifying the source (fasb), the technical abbreviation (sfas) or spelling the abbreviation out (standards of financial accounting standard). Generally requiring that either "fasb or accounting or sfas" appear, along with the number, picks up on any of the several ways it might be expressed. It is a tried-and-true strategy when conducting searches for discussions about particular SFASs. Last, you limit the search to the range from 1984–1987 since there is often preliminary discussion about the statement before it is actually released.

Clicking the Search button yields 16 citations. Since John is looking for more lengthy discussions, you scan the titles and, combined with the inclusion of the total number of pages in the citation, select several articles that appear to be right on point. Unfortunately, only one of the articles is available in full text online; given the age of the articles, this is not entirely surprising.

Checking the catalog of a local university library located nearby, you determine that it has the print editions of the magazines, and you contact a local "jobber" to go to the library and make copies of the articles. Based on the jobber's pricing structure, you can get all the articles for $60, which is below the approved budgeted amount. You place the order and ask to have the articles delivered to you by the end of the next day.

Since you only have one article available electronically, and John was not going to read them until he physically returned to the office, you go ahead and print out that article, make a hard copy of SFAS 86 from the OP and deliver the full packet of articles to his desk by Thursday morning. You also include a list of all the returned article citations in case he decides to look at other articles. Just to cover all of your bases, you also run the search again, but this time for the period from 1988–present; there were a few additional articles although none of them seemed very substantive or to offer anything new. This does not come as a surprise since there has been no change to the SFAS, but it is worth looking. You also provide John with the returned cite list of the updated search.

RESEARCH RESULTS: You located the following articles for John:

- "Software Struggle: Statement 86 Has Helped Software Designers but Confused Corporate Comptrollers," *Financial Executive,* March 1987.
- "Some Implications as to Capitalization and Amortization of Intangibles," *The CPA Journal,* November 1986.
- "Accounting for Software Costs: A Guide to FASB Statement No. 86," *Journal of Accountancy,* June 1986.
- "New Rules of the Game for Computer Software Companies," *Corporate Accounting,* Spring 1986.
- "Statement 86 May Affect Many Firms' Software Costs," *FE,* January 1986.
- "Accounting for the Costs of Certain Computer Software," *The CPA Journal,* January 1986.
- "Statement of Financial Accounting Standards No 86— Accounting for the Costs of Computer Software to be Sold, Leased, or Otherwise Marketed," *Journal of Accountancy,* November 1985.

SUMMARY OF SOLUTION: ABI/Inform is an especially powerful database for accounting article research. If you did not have access to it, LexisNexis or Factiva could also be used although they might not have as much coverage dating back to the timeframe of this particular SFAS.

If accessing articles on electronic databases is not an option, consider using the accounting collection at the University of Mississippi AICPA Library Services *http://www.olemiss.edu/depts/ general_library/aicpa*. Available to CPAs for a very reasonable fee, this library, now holding the collection of the American Institute of Certified Public Accountants (AICPA) library, makes research and article delivery services available to CPAs. Be sure to have the CPA's AICPA membership number with you when calling to request information.

CONTRIBUTOR NAME: Brenda Reeb

AFFILIATION: University of Rochester

USEFUL TIPS

- Use public or nearby college or university libraries to photocopy articles published prior to full-text coverage on the Web.

PROBLEM NUMBER 4: LOCATE ARTICLES THAT EXPLAIN AND ANALYZE APPLICATIONS FOR SFAS 133

RESEARCH BACKGROUND: You receive a call from Jeff, an auditor who needs some background information about financial hedging for one of his client engagements. The effective date for application of SFAS 133, "Accounting for Derivative Instruments and Hedging Activities," is in a few months and Jeff wants to make sure that he is fully aware of the disclosure requirements and the implications for his client's financial statements. He would like you to locate some articles that will provide him with guidance. He already has a copy of the SFAS; all he needs from you are a handful of timely and relevant articles.

RESEARCH BUDGET: The engagement is budgeted for research but Jeff asks if you could try and keep expenses under $200 and not to spend more than two hours of your time. He would like the research by the end of the week; if possible, just e-mail him the full text of the articles.

RESEARCH STRATEGY EMPLOYED: Jeff has given you both the number and the name of the SFAS, but even though he has a good track record for getting his facts right, you grab a shelf copy of FASB's OP to make sure his information is correct. You also take a quick look at the summary of the SFAS that appears at the very beginning of the statement. Although you are not an accountant and your technical understanding is very limited, you want to try to understand the context of the SFAS a bit more. You also want to develop a good search strategy and recognize articles that will help Jeff who asked that you send him a small number of "on point" articles.

You know that the AICPA's monthly magazine, *Journal of Accountancy*, contains regular topical articles, as well as a special section which focuses on discussing and analyzing new accounting standards so you decide to start there. Beginning with 1996, the full text of this magazine is available for free on the AICPA's Web site. Going to *http://www.aicpa.org*, you follow these steps from the home page: Click on the link to Online Journal of Accountancy; click on the Search Site button at the top of the next page; and click on the Search All of AICPA Online link. The AICPA's search engine is basic, so you type the following search expression in the search box: FASB and "derivative instruments."

Your search yields 94 matches, each displayed with the title and summary. The first article is "Practical Issues in Implementing FASB 133." Scanning the article it appears to be exactly what you are looking for, providing background to its creation, risk management issues, the implementation process, and a real-life example for corporate application. You also select several other articles, including one that discusses the AICPA's release of a new Statement of Auditing Standards on auditing derivative instruments and hedging activities.

Now that you have a few solid articles from the AICPA, you turn your attention to ProQuest Direct's ABI/Inform database. ABI has the best collection of full-text accounting and finance journals, combing both academic and business-focused publications. Using the Guided search option, you begin with a broad search that will look for your keywords in "all basic search fields." These fields would include the title, subtitle, subject terms, and abstract, but would exclude the full text. ABI is known for its excellent indexing and abstracting and this strategy would enable you to tap into articles that focused on your topic. Oftentimes searching across the full text of articles can retrieve a high volume of less critical discussions. Following is your keyword expression:

- (fasb or sfas or accounting standards or accounting statement) and (133 and derivative instrument)

You used this strategy because you know from experience that FASB statements are not universally referred to the same way. By requiring that either "fasb or sfas or accounting standards or accounting statement," be present, you were more assured of locating relevant articles. The FASB number, however, is almost always mentioned, and to ensure that the context of the number was this particular FASB, you added "derivative instrument" since this is part of the FASB title.

Only one article was returned. Surprised, you looked at the subject keywords that ABI applied to the article and saw that the term derivative was used, but not instrument. Using this "inside" knowledge, you revised the search to include derivative (without instrument) and the results were much more promising—more than 50 articles. Scanning the results list, you identified several additional articles that you downloaded in full text and e-mailed to Jeff. The articles found discussed alternative approaches to testing hedging effectiveness, the impact of FASB 138 on amending FASB 133, and several discussions of practical applications in the corporate setting. The sources of the articles selected were primarily accounting industry journals, but several of the real-life discussions came from business and finance sources.

SUMMARY OF SOLUTION: In preparation to researching substantive articles on FASB 133, you first scanned the summary of the financial statement in an effort to gain a little more insight into the accounting issues and to makes notes about any terminology or jargon you might need to build into the search strategy. You then turned to the AICPA's *Journal of Accountancy*, a mainstream practical accounting magazine, and searched the site for articles that might provide some analysis of implementing the standard and managing client risk. You ended the search by using ABI/Inform, the best source for locating key accounting and finance articles. The entire search took about two hours, including the time needed to scan articles for relevancy and e-mail them to Jeff. The AICPA search was free and since you have a flat-rate subscription to ABI/Inform, you did not incur any additional costs. However, if you had needed to "purchase" the articles selected for Jeff, the total cost would have been approximately $25 dollars ($3/article for 7 articles).

Jeff had also asked you to send him some pointers for locating these articles on his own. You explained to him how to use the AICPA Web site and also recommended that he use Factiva for locating additional articles. Since Jeff has desktop access to Factiva, access would be easy. You included the following suggestions for refining his Factiva search:

- Refine the source list: From the Factiva Search template, click on the Source Browser link. Displaying the Publications tab, click on the link to Industry and select "Accounting & Consulting." Saving this set of articles will limit his search to related magazines, newspapers, and newsletters. If he clicks on the + sign to the left of "Accounting & Consulting," a list of the individual titles are displayed and he can chose specific publications. He might want to consider this approach for some searches, such as the one he requested on FASB 133. For example, by selecting specific accounting and finance titles (such as *The CPA Journal* and *Financial Executive*), you narrowed the results to the most appropriate sources and greatly limited the number of extraneous, returned matches.

CONTRIBUTOR NAME: Susan M. Klopper
AFFILIATION: Goizueta Business Library

USEFUL TIPS

- Do a little fact checking on your own before jumping into a search. Even if the requestor has provided you with good information, familiarizing yourself a little more with the topic, verifying spelling, and so on will save you time, ensure better results, and impress the requestor.
- If you conduct a lot of serious accounting-related article research, consider subscribing to ABI/Inform. If you cannot justify the expense, check with local public and academic libraries to explore availability.
- Familiarize yourself with the "key" accounting industry journals. This knowledge will be useful for performing targeted research. If you are not sure what the sources are, try running a few searches in a database and make note of the publications which regularly appear.

PROBLEM NUMBER 5: LOCATE SOME ARTICLES THAT DISCUSS CURRENT TRENDS ABOUT "CONVERGENCE" IN THE ACCOUNTING INDUSTRY

RESEARCH BACKGROUND: One of the partners in your accounting firm has asked you to locate articles on this topic because several of her clients are expanding their operations to Europe, and one is contemplating a merger with a French company. The partner needs to learn more about how convergence will impact the reporting process, and she needs to learn fast! She has worked as an accountant for about five years and has a good understanding of accounting language and how the industry currently works.

RESEARCH BUDGET: This is a basic "find out about xyz topic" request. It is expected that reputable sources will be consulted. A vast, exhaustive treatment of the topic is not necessary, so that will keep the price down—under $100 should do. The partner would like a citation list and selected full-text articles by the end of the day.

RESEARCH STRATEGY EMPLOYED: You were a little familiar with the topic, but started out by asking the partner to discuss any sites that she recommended. Basically, after years of discussion between the accounting bodies about creating a system of GAAP that truly was universal across countries, the creation of the European Union (EU) was forcing the issue beyond discussion into reality. By 2005, all the countries in the EU will be required to adopt the same, "universal" accounting standards. As part of this movement, the International Accounting Standards Board (IASB) had been elevated in stature in the United States and was finally getting buy-in from the FASB, AICPA, and SEC to work toward expanding the concept of "universal" standards to include the U.S. GAAP.

Based on her very useful explanation, you determined that there were some core questions you needed to try and answer for her: Why was convergence important to the accounting industry? What stage was it at now, and what were the anticipated challenges and hot buttons in the next few years, especially as related to the United States jumping on the bandwagon? Who were the different stakeholders and what did each one need to get out of adoption of convergence? Who was more likely to influence the outcome?

With those questions in mind, you decided to start on the Web sites of the IASB, FASB, AICPA, and SEC to see what they had to say about it since clearly they were stakeholders in this huge undertaking. Hopefully not only would their respective sites contain good information but they might also lead to additional sources. From these sites you planned to search at least two electronic databases:

ABI/Inform, since it contains the best collection of full-text articles from the accounting and finance journals, and Factiva, for its well-rounded representation of business and economic news from major international newspapers.

Sure enough, both the FASB and IASB Web sites contained some excellent information. For example, directly on the FASB home page was a prominent link to an October 22, 2002, press release that contained a link to the "memorandum of understanding" signed jointly by FASB and IASB.

When you were ready to turn your attention to the electronic databases, you decided to begin with a simple search statement: convergence and accounting. Because of the currency of the issue and the unique context within the accounting industry, it proved to be a very effective search strategy. ABI/Inform contained several excellent articles from sources such as *Accountancy, Investor Relations Business,* and *Financial Executive.* These sources provided a very interesting discussion on the problems and challenges ahead for the regulating bodies, and for companies struggling to accommodate all of the potential changes in reporting structures.

Factiva was useful in presenting more of the global perspective. You started out by running a broad search dating back one year, looking for the words convergence and accounting in the headline and lead paragraph (in Factiva terms: hlp=convergence and accounting). The results were overwhelming and so you regrouped and opted to restrict the search to some key publications, namely the *Wall Street Journal* and *Financial Times* (sn=wall street journal and financial times). That was much better, and in fact by conducting a narrower search and taking advantage of Factiva's "more like this" link to jump to similar articles, you not only found some excellent articles but also were able to expand the search to other sources. Had using the "More like this" option not worked out, you were prepared to click on the link to Source Browser located in the Search template, and expand the category for Region to identify some newspapers from EU countries.

RESEARCH RESULTS: Convergence seems to be a topic whose time has come to the U.S. accounting industry. The term "convergence" refers to converging, or making more similar, the accounting standards of various nations. In the wake of several accounting scandals in past few years, the U.S. accounting industry has renewed interest in harmonizing U.S. accounting standards with European standards. In the past, the United States did not want to converge because it felt its standards were superior to those of

IASB. However, in the wake of recent scandals that position is no longer popular. The United States renewed interest began in the second half of 2002. Joint meetings of FASB and IASB were held in late 2002. Differences in the two systems of accounting will be identified in 2003 with those differences resolved by 2005.

SUMMARY OF SOLUTION: Since the partner requesting this information was so knowledgeable, you started out by getting some background information directly from her. This enabled you to immediately hone in on the key points and to determine specifically what she wanted. Had you not had this conversation with her, you might have gathered more general information then she really wanted. Starting with the sites of the accounting organizations most involved in convergence led me to many "official" documents that contained excellent discussion and references. Targeted keyword searching using ABI/Inform and Factiva provided insightful secondary and "real-world" analysis from the business community that would be most impacted by the changes in the accounting structure. As part of the process of scanning the articles, you also learned of a Web site you had not visited before: International Forum on Accountancy Development at *http://www.ifad.net.*

CONTRIBUTOR NAME: Brenda Reeb
AFFILIATION: University of Rochester

USEFUL TIPS

- Whenever possible, tap into the knowledge and expertise of your requestor. And don't hesitate to ask them the objective of the research. Often that provides you with critical clues that help direct your strategy.
- When exploring a hot topic, identify who the stakeholders are and what they want.
- When searching electronic databases, look for a feature like "More like this" to help you to navigate from one article that is right on point to additional, related discussions.

PROBLEM NUMBER 6: LOCATE EXAMPLES OF FINANCIAL FOOTNOTE DISCLOSURES ON ACCOUNTING FOR EXPLOITATION COSTS

RESEARCH BACKGROUND: A partner has asked you to locate examples of footnotes relating to exploitation costs. He has recently acquired a new audit client in the film production industry and needs to find some examples of how to disclose this accounting issue. Hopefully by focusing your search on other film and video production corporations, you can find some good examples. He goes on to explain that exploitation costs include advertising and marketing costs. A Statement of Position was released by the AICPA addressing these costs and the partner would like to find recent examples of how other companies have disclosed the treatment of these costs as well as make sure that he addresses his client's disclosure in a manner that will be acceptable to the SEC.

RESEARCH BUDGET: You are authorized to spend up to $200 on this request and the client would like to see some examples by the end of the day.

RESEARCH STRATEGY EMPLOYED: Footnotes are found after the financial statements in a 10-K and are formally called Notes to Consolidated Financial Statements. The notes are sequentially numbered, and Note 2, which covers "Accounting Policies and Procedures" is where the disclosure of exploitation costs is found. Typically, you will find verbiage about how the company accounts for and discloses its exploitation costs and it should also contain a reference to Statement of Position 00-2 (SOP 00-2) "Accounting by Producers or Distributors of Films."

Financial footnotes are usually published as part of the Annual Report and while most companies do reproduce them in the 10-K, in some instances, they will just be "referenced" in the 10-K body but included as Exhibit 13. If you do not find the financial statements and footnotes incorporated into the main 10-K document, be sure to review the Exhibit 13 section that always includes financial information.

The most efficient way to conduct financial disclosure research is to use a subscription-based SEC filings database such Thomson Research (*http://research.thomsonlib.com*). Thomson Research contains a powerful search engine that allows you to conduct complex keyword searches within specific portions of filing documents. It would be extremely time-consuming and, in some cases, impossible to conduct these searches using a free EDGAR Web site.

Log into Thomson Research and click on the Documents tab appearing at the top of the screen and then select the EDGAR Free Text link that appears beneath this tab to search across SEC filings using keywords. In the Full-Text Query box, select the "Fin. Footnotes" option from the drop-down menu next to the first text box and enter **exploitation w/2 costs** into the text box. Enter the SIC code 7812 into the SIC field box; this is the industry code for the

Motion Picture and Video Production industry, allowing you to narrow your search to just the filings of companies in the same industry as the client. Since the partner wants recent examples of filings, select the "last year" option for Receipt Date. Finally, select 10-K Annual Financials for the Filing Type, elect to sort your search results in descending order by receipt date, and click the search button.

The power of this interface is how easily it accommodates the many layers of search criteria needed to find the applicable results: search only specific sections of the filing, develop complex but flexible keyword strategies, specify one or more filing types, narrow your search to a specific time frame, and request results to be displayed in a desired order. The ability to use proximity operators, such as w/2 (which means within two words of) as part of your search strategy is also extremely important for financial disclosure research. While the presence of certain words might be known in advance, the order in which the words appear is usually not so clear. Flexibility in requesting how the words are laid out within the text is critical to maximizing the best results.

Your search yielded six documents. To see your search terms in context within each filing, check the View Keywords box next to each filing, and then click on the View Keywords button. You can then browse your keywords in context within the filings. The partner only wanted to see the relevant footnote so, rather then downloading the entire 10-K, you use Thomson Research's "custom" option. This allows you to customize the output. Select the option "Using Word Processor (RTF format)" and check the box next to Financial Footnotes, then click on the View button at the bottom of the page. This retrieves just the Financial Footnotes, a cover sheet and table of contents.

RESEARCH RESULTS: Your search resulted in six examples (Walt Disney Co., Fortune Diversified Industries, Family Run Entertainment, Lion's Gate Entertainment, and the two latest 10-Ks for MGM). You print the Financial Footnote sections for each one using Thomson Research's Custom Filing format and deliver them to the partner.

CONTRIBUTOR NAME: Jan Rivers

AFFILIATION: Dorsey & Whitney LLP

USEFUL TIPS

- Examples of footnotes can also be found in the print publication *Accounting Trends and Techniques.*
- The Full-Text Query search can be temperamental whenever more than two keywords are combined with a proximity operator within one text search box. You may need to spread out your search statement between the two text search boxes in the Full-Text Query search template for your search to run.
- It is not clear how to download formatted (RTF) filings. The Save As feature in the browser does not allow for saving as RTF, only HTML. The View using Word Processor option does not bring up a Save icon along with the formatted document, and the mouse right-click/save as option does not work.
- If you do not know the SIC code for a specific industry, the Full-Text Query template contains a look-up feature if you click on the field label SIC.

PROBLEM NUMBER 7: SEARCH THE MANAGEMENT DISCUSSION AND ANALYSIS SECTION OF THE 10-K FOR IMPAIRMENT CHARGES RELATING TO THE AMORTIZATION OF GOODWILL

RESEARCH BACKGROUND: An audit manager is requesting a search of the Management Discussion and Analysis (MD&A) section of company 10-K filings to find examples of how farm machinery and equipment manufacturing companies are reporting impairment charges relating to the amortization of goodwill. The manager is working with a client who manufactures large outdoor farming tractors and would like to see how other companies are reporting these issues (he would like you to locate about six examples within the next few days). You can spend up to $200 on this request.

RESEARCH STRATEGY EMPLOYED: The MD&A section of the 10-K contains key information as to the company's current viability and business operations and practices, including comments on its financial condition and outlook, discussion of its business segment performance, product lines, legal proceedings, merger and acquisition activity, changes in accounting practices or disputes with its outside accounting firm. It also includes other information relating to the financial and business events the company experienced in the course of the year, and always appears as Item 7 in Part II of the main body of the 10-K filing.

Because this search requires that you target a specific section of the 10-K and will require some fancy keyword searching, you decide to use a database called Thomson Research (formerly known as Global Access). This database is one of the best suited for the type of text-specific searches that accountants regularly require. It is also ideal for searching financial footnote disclosures, auditor's reports, and other key SEC filing sections. After logging on, you click on the Documents tab appearing at the top of the screen, and then click on the link to EDGAR Free Text to display the customizable SEC filings search template. In the first Full-Text Query box, select the "Mgt. Discussion" option from the drop-down menu and type (**impairment w/2 charge) and (amortiz* w/2 goodwill**) in the text box.

Another benefit of using Thomson Research is the ability to take advantage of powerful search tools such as Boolean and proximity connectors and word truncation. Good disclosure searches require a combination of knowing the right words to search on combined with a search statement that is flexible enough to capture variations in word endings and the variations in the placement of one word in relationship with another. If you develop a search statement that is too specific and inflexible, you are very likely to get bad results.

If the Thomson search engine has difficulty processing a long search statement, take advantage of two drop-down Full-Text Query boxes and break up the search. In this example, Select "Mgt. Discussion" and enter **impairment w/2 charge** in the first text box; keep the "and" option, select "Mgt. Discussion" in the second Full-text Query box and type **amortize* w/2 goodwill** in the second text box. The results should be the same but it might take the system less time to process.

Now that you have defined the search statement, you also need to narrow the universe of companies you search against those in the same industry as the client. This is simply done by entering the SIC code 3523 in the SIC code box. Since the manager wanted recent examples of filings, you select the "last year" option for Receipt Date. Last, you choose "10-K Annual Financials" for the Filing Type, elect to sort your search results in descending order by receipt date, and click the search button.

The search only yields two company filings so you modify the search by expanding the date range to cover receipt dates from January 1, 2001, to the present. You decide to take a quick look to see if these match what the auditor is looking for. Another excellent Thomson Research search feature is the option to view the results in "keyword in context;" selecting this viewing option enables you to view just the sections of the MD&A that contained your search terms. This is an extremely efficient way to quickly glean the relevance of the search results. A quick look tells you that these results are on point.

Still concerned that you only have located two examples, you check back with the audit manager and explain your search strategy and the returned results. Given the relevance of the two examples, he is satisfied with what you find and sees no reason to conduct more searches. Since the manager only needed the MD&A section, you return to your results list and click on the C icon next to the first company name. This allows you to create a "custom" filing where you select only those parts of the filing you need. Select the option Using Word Processor (RTF format), check the box next to Management Discussion, and then click on the View button at the bottom of the page. This retrieves just the Management Discussion section and includes a cover sheet and table of contents, which you print and deliver to the manager.

RESEARCH RESULTS: Despite expanding the query to include two years more than the requested one, the search results in only two companies from the same industry as the client whose MD&A sections discuss impairment charges relating to the amortization of goodwill: Agco Corp and CTB International Corp. After conferring with the manager to discuss further modifying the search strategy, he reviews the two results and determines that he has exactly the information that he needs to complete his client work.

SUMMARY OF SOLUTION: While there are several excellent electronic databases that allow for complex keyword searching within SEC filings, such as LexisNexis and LIVEDGAR, Thomson Research is one of the very few that allows you to limit searches to specific sections of the filings. This is extremely valuable for conducting disclosure research and other, accounting-related SEC filing searches. Although these types of searches can be conducted using other databases, it would take much more time to target and output just the relevant sections.

CONTRIBUTOR NAME: Jan Rivers
AFFILIATION: Dorsey & Whitney LLP

USEFUL TIPS

- If you don't know the SIC code for a specific industry, the Full-Text Query template contains a look-up feature if you click on the field label SIC.

PROBLEM NUMBER 8: LOCATE AN EXAMPLE OF AN AUDITOR'S QUALIFIED OPINION

RESEARCH BACKGROUND: A company wants to hire your firm as its external auditor since its previous auditor has resigned. The financial condition of the potential client appears precarious and the risk management partner at your firm has asked you to check to see if the company was issued a qualified opinion by its previous auditors in the past three years. You can spend up to $100 on this request; the information is needed within two days.

RESEARCH STRATEGY EMPLOYED: All 10-K filings contain the independent auditor's report and consent. The auditor's report is usually included in the 10-K "by reference" from the annual report. In the future, due to stricter SEC filing requirements, virtually all 10-K filings will include this report; however, older reports may not include it in which case you will need to locate the company's annual report.

The report and consent attests to the auditor's examination of the company's financials and accounting practices, as well as discloses any concerns the auditor may have about the company's financial condition, accounting practices, or business practices. If the auditor has any reservations about the company's ability to remain in business, a standard phrase is introduced into the report, stating that the auditor has "substantial doubt" as to the company's ability to remain a "going concern" due to large financial losses or other factors. This is a qualified opinion.

To search for the qualified opinion, you use LIVEDGAR (*http://www.gsionline.com*) since your company has a subscription to this well-designed product. You select the full-text search option because the auditor's report generally appears within the 10-K's section containing the financial statements and footnotes. The auditor's consent is usually contained in Exhibit 23 or Exhibit 24. To capture both the report and concern sections, you decide that conducting a well-crafted keyword search will be the most efficient way to access both sections simultaneously.

Limiting the search to 10-K filings, you enter the following search in the free-text search box: **substantial w/2 doubt w/10 going w/2 concern**, combined with the company name in the appropriate box. A qualified opinion will use boilerplate phrasing stating the auditors have substantial doubt as to the company's ability to remain a going concern. Why? When a company changes auditors (Item 8 in the 10-K, "Change in Accountant"), that section generally contains a statement indicating that the auditor did not issue any "qualified opinion" about the company prior to the change. Conducting a keyword search on "qualified opinion," therefore, would yield a great many "false hits;" "going concern" is a common accounting phrase and searching on this phrase alone would also have yielded many incorrect results.

The returned results contained hyperlinks to portions of the 10-K that contained the keywords specified. You quickly scan the sections to verify that they were what the accountant was looking for. You print the relevant sections and e-mail them to the accountant, including information about the search strategy and the database used. In addition, you also download the full 10-K filings for all three years and send those as well. You believe likely that the accountant would want to take a closer look at the filings as part of her analysis of whether she would want to take the company on as a client.

RESEARCH RESULTS: The previous auditor had issued a qualified opinion on the company the previous year. If no qualified opinion had been issued, you would have gone ahead and sent the accountant the most recent year's 10-K filing for her analysis of the company's financial and business position.

SUMMARY OF SOLUTION: A partner with a potential client wants to know if the company's previous auditors had ever issued a qualified opinion on that company. You accessed LIVEDGAR and conducted a free-text search of that company's filings using the search: **substantial w/2 doubt w/10 going w2/ concern**. The returned results indicated that the auditor did have some concerns about the company.

LIVEDGAR has created a set of preformatted search queries that capture some frequently requested, popular search topics. This "Topical Research Library" is accessible once you have logged on to the product. In the Library's "Tax/Accounting" category, there is a search for "Accountant Opinion." These preformatted searches can be very helpful, but in this case, using this "Accountant Opinion" search would not have resulted in the desired information because the search retrieves ALL auditor consents, not just the qualified opinions. This type of search could also have been successfully done using some other SEC filing search products, including LexisNexis. Due to the need to search for a combination of words within close proximity to each other, this particular search is not easily accomplished using many of the free EDGAR Web sites. It might require scanning many individual documents and relying on a rudimentary search engine and/or the Edit/Find search option.

CONTRIBUTOR NAME: Jan Rivers

AFFILIATION: Dorsey & Whitney LLP

USEFUL TIPS

- Knowledge of accurate verbiage and phrasing can be extremely important when conducting searches within SEC filings. Be sure to review terminology and information context within the documents with the requestor before beginning your search.

PROBLEM NUMBER 9: SEARCH XEROX CORPORATION'S RECENT 8-K FOR DISCUSSION ABOUT A FORTHCOMING RESTATEMENT OF EARNINGS

RESEARCH BACKGROUND: A partner read recently that Xerox Corporation announced it will be restating its earnings. He would like a copy of the 8-K filing containing this announcement so that he can read the way the restatement was announced to the SEC. He has just taken over a client from another firm that is going to need a restatement of earnings done for the past three years and the partner thinks it would be very useful to how it was formatted.

RESEARCH STRATEGY EMPLOYED: You can access company 8-K information for free via the SEC's Web site (*http://www.sec.gov*). From the SEC home page, click on the Search for Company Filings link under Filings & Forms (EDGAR). This will take you to the SEC's EDGAR database of company filings (EDGAR is an acronym for Electronic Data Gathering and Retrieval, which represented digitized version of U.S. public company SEC filings). Once you are on the EDGAR Database home page, click on the Search Companies and Filings to display the search page. Enter the company's name or ticker symbol to obtain a list of its filings in reverse chronological order.

Scroll down the list to locate recent 8-K filings. Click on the link for HTML next to the 8-K filing entry to obtain an information page about that filing. 8-Ks are filed with the SEC for a variety of purposes, such as announcing a change in auditor or newly released financial statements or a change in leadership. Usually, this type of information is identified in this filing information page under Item Information. A company announcement or press release-related 8-K filing will have "Other Events" listed for the Item Information identifier.

For those recent 8-Ks with "Other Events" as the Item Information identifier, click on the document link that appears on the filing information page. Filings with attached press releases will also have a link to an Exhibit 99, which contains the body of the press release. You can print a copy of the filing from the Web site itself, or you can copy and paste it into a Word document.

Since the 8-K was not accompanied by a press release, you decide to take a quick look on the company's Web site to see if there is any additional information that might be useful to the partner. Under Xerox's Investor Relations section of its Web site, you did locate a press release that the company issued explaining the reasons for the restatement and its impact on the company. Hoping to identify a more "objective" perspective on the matter, you also conduct a quick query in Factiva, using the keywords of "Xerox and restated," limiting the timeframe to 90 days around the filing of the 8-K, and specifying the *Wall Street Journal* and *New York Times* as the sources. You locate four excellent articles. These articles not only discuss the facts leading up to Xerox's 8-K filing, but also identify a few other companies that were restating their financial for similar reasons. You save these articles and e-mail them, along with the 8-K and the Xerox's press release, to the partner. Since your firm has a flat-rate contract with Factiva, you did not incur any additional costs to access these articles.

RESEARCH RESULTS: The 8-K announcing the forthcoming restatement of earnings was filed on December 20, 2002. The section denoted as Item 5: Other Events contains the announcement about the planned restatement in its body that the partner requested. This particular 8-K filing does not contain a press release attachment, nor is the Item 5 information in the form of a press release.

There are many viable options on the market for locating SEC filings. If your primary objective is to retrieve a filing when you already know the company name and approximate timeframe, you always get good and quick results using one of the many free EDGAR Web sites. Examples of others are SEC Info (*http:// www.secinfo.com*) and EdgarScan (*http://edgarscan.pwcglobal.com*). You can, of course, also retrieve filings using subscription-based electronic databases such as Dialog, LexisNexis, and LIVEDGAR, although you really leverage the power and value of these databases when you need to conduct complex keyword searching across multiple company filings.

CONTRIBUTOR NAME: Jan Rivers
AFFILIATION: Dorsey & Whitney LLP

USEFUL TIPS

* 8-Ks frequently contain copies of press releases as attached exhibit 99s.
* 8-K/A filings are amended versions of previously released 8-K filings. You may want to check any 8-K/A filings that appear closely after the date of the 8-K in which you are interested to see if any amendments have occurred.
* The SEC Web site has no keyword searching capability. It is most useful for retrieving specific filings from particular companies, such as Microsoft's most recent 10-K filing or 3M's latest proxy statement.
* For the best formatted filings via the SEC Web site, always use the HTML links instead of the Text links.

PROBLEM NUMBER 10: IDENTIFY THREE COMPANIES THAT CHANGED AUDITORS LAST YEAR

RESEARCH BACKGROUND: A partner wants a rough statistic for a meeting he is having with his staff next week. He was wondering approximately how many companies changed auditors in the past year due to the auditor resigning from the client engagement. You can spend up to $100 on this request.

RESEARCH STRATEGY EMPLOYED: U.S. public parent companies are required to file an 8-K with the SEC whenever they change their auditor. This information is always disclosed as Item 4 in the body of the 8-K. While the decision to change auditors is usually based on mutual agreement between the auditor and its client, there can be many reasons why it occurs. An auditor may resign due to a lack of faith in the client's ability to remain a going concern or there may have been a falling out with the client over accounting practices and financial disclosure. But whatever the reason, since it is considered a significant event and would be important for the investor to know about, it must be publicly disclosed in an SEC filing.

The only efficient way to conduct this search is by using a fine-tuned subscription-based electronic SEC filing database, such as LIVEDGAR, LexisNexis, or Thomson Research. Each of these products contains a powerful search engine that allows you to conduct complex keyword searches within specific portions of filing documents. It would be extremely time-consuming, and, in some cases, impossible to conduct these searches using a free EDGAR Web site.

Since your firm has a flat-rate contract with Thomson, you select this interface. Log into Thomson Research, click on the Documents tab appearing at the top of the screen, and then select the EDGAR free text link that appears beneath this tab to search across SEC filings using keywords.

In the Full-Text Query box, select the "Full Filing" option from the drop-down menu next to the first text box and enter **auditor w/5 resign*** in the text box. Since the partner is looking for a rough number estimate across all industries, do not enter anything in the SIC box. Select the "last year" option for Receipt Date and 8-K for the Filing Type, and last, elect to sort your search results in descending order by receipt date and click the search button.

The ability to use proximity operations, such as w/5 (which means within five words of) and truncation (adding * to the end of the root word will search for resignation, resigned, resigning) as part of your search strategy is extremely important for conducting keyword searching across any large bodies of text. The more you can control the relationship of the words to each other, the more likely that the documents returned will be relevant.

A list of 253 documents is returned. To quickly scan your search terms in context with each filing, check the View Keywords box next to each filing, and then click on the View Keywords button. Since your partner does not need to see the filings, but rather just wants the total number returned from the search, you print off the search results page so that he can review which companies changed auditors and highlight the total number that appears at the top.

RESEARCH RESULTS: Your search resulted in a list of 253 companies that filed an 8-K last year to disclose the resignation of the auditor, including U.S. Energy Corp, Maxxis Group, and Appiant Technologies.

CONTRIBUTOR NAME: Jan Rivers
AFFILIATION: Dorsey & Whitney LLP

USEFUL TIPS

- 8-Ks announcing auditor changes are frequently, but not always, accompanied by letters to the SEC from the former auditor. These letters are Exhibit 99.

PROBLEM NUMBER 11: LOCATE THE MOST RECENT BUSINESS NORMS FOR THE TEXTILE INDUSTRY

RESEARCH BACKGROUND: A team of auditors is analyzing a client in the textile industry and Megan, the team leader, has requested the most recent business norms for the industry. She is completing her client's business audit review and must meet the requirement of benchmarking the client against its industry peers. Megan asks that you find information by the end of the day. Though you have a client number to charge, you are expected to obtain the best information as economically as possible; Megan puts a limit of $100 on the research and your time.

RESEARCH STRATEGY EMPLOYED: Since gathering this data is required for the business audit review, you are well acquainted with the two standard sources used for industry business norms: Dun & Bradstreet's *Industry Norms & Key Business Ratios* and RMA's *Annual Statement Studies*. Each source provides some different ratios and has gathered the data against different peer group types. RMA bases its data on its private company membership, and D&B's on its huge repository of more than one million company financial statements. In addition, while they overlap in some SIC coverage, D&B's includes some industry ranges that are not found in RMA. For both of these reasons, it is recommended practice to provide the auditor with data from both sources.

From experience you know that industry ratios are collected and organized by SIC and/or NAICS (North American Industry Classification System) codes. Since the whole point of this research is to gather comparable norms for your client's industry, it is very important that you identify the correct industry code. If the audit team is unsure of the correct code, do not try and guess. Rather, refer to the *Standard Industrial Classification Manual* and/or *NAICS/SIC Code United States Manual* and provide the auditor with the written descriptions contained in these manuals so that they can approve the appropriate code. In discussing this issue with Megan, she was able to confirm that their client's industry was Fabric Mills, Cotton, SIC 2211.

With that important information in hand, you turn to both books and look up the industry code 2211; the data is available in both publications. D&B's *Industry Norms* is organized chronologically by the SIC code number; the code is clearly noted at the top of each page. RMA is not organized by code, and so you must use the SIC Numbers Appearing in the Statement Studies Code reference table located toward the beginning of the book to identify the correct pages. If you base availability of a particular code in RMA on finding it by scanning the contents chronologically, you will likely miss important information.

RESEARCH RESULTS: D&B's *Industry Norms & Key Business Ratios* provides an easy-to-read column of the ratios most commonly used by financial analysts:

- Each column of ratios begins with the SIC code, the name of the industry, the year of the data and the number of companies included in the industry sample. The data that follows the description is organized in two separate sections—the industry norm format and the key business ratios. The industry norm format includes a balance sheet and income statement described by D&B as a "Common-Size Financial Statement." Each statement item has an industry average in dollars ($) and percentage (%). For example, the industry norm for SIC 2211's Accounts Receivable is $345,103 or 26.3 percent.
- The 14 key business ratios have median figures, an upper quartile and a lower quartile. The ratios are divided into three subsections: Solvency, Efficiency, and Profitability. Solvency ratios include Quick Ratio, Current Ratio, Current Liabilities to Net Worth, Current Liabilities to Inventory, Total Liabilities to Net Worth, and Fixed Assets to Net Worth. Efficiency ratios include Collection Period, Sales to Inventory, Asset to Sales, Sales to Net Working Capital, and Accounts Payable to Sales. Profitability Ratios include Return on Sales (Profit Margin), Return on Assets, and Return on Net Worth (Return on Equity).

Annual Statement Studies by RMA provide the following data:

- Each SIC code is covered in two pages beginning with the name of the industry, SIC code, corresponding NAICS codes, dates of the data, and the number of company statements by size included in the industry sample.

- The industry norm data is divided into three main sections and organized by the headings, Current Data Sorted by Assets, Comparative Historical Data, and Current Data Sorted by Sales. Each statement item in RMA's "Common Size Balance Sheet and Income Statement" is defined only as a percentage (%). For example, the industry norm for SIC 2211's Trade Receivables is 19.3 percent for a $2 to 10 million company, 16.6 percent for a $10 to 50 million company, and 17.3 percent for a $50 to 100 million company. This norm information differs from the D&B norm because the data is further broken down by the size of company in the industry sample.

- The 16 key business ratios have median figures, an upper quartile and a lower quartile. Liquidity ratios include the Current Ratio, Quick Ratio, Sales/Receivables, Cost of Sales/Inventory, Cost of Sales/Payables, and Sales/Working Capital. Coverage ratios include Earnings Before Interest and Taxes (EBIT)/Interest and Net Profit plus Depreciation, Depletion, Amortization/Current Maturities Long-Term Debt. Leverage ratios include Fixed/Worth and Debt/Worth. Operating ratios include % Profits Before Taxes/Tangible Net Worth, % Profit Before Taxes/Total Assets Sales/Net Fixed Assets, and Sales/Total Assets. Expense to sales ratios include % Depreciation, Depletion, Amortization/Sales, and % Officers,' Directors,' Owners' Compensation/Sales.

SUMMARY OF SOLUTION: RMA's *Annual Statement Studies* and D&B's *Industry Norms & Key Business Ratios* are industry standards. Both considered reliable and consistent data sources by accounting professionals. The print sources are very easy to use and provide quick access to this information; they are also both reasonably priced.

Both publishers now also provide most of their data electronically, with RMA's accessible via CD-ROM and D&B's ratio data available as a Web-based product. Differences in content coverage, format, and pricing may or may not present the electronic versions of these publications as viable options. While there is certainly a push to obtain as much information as possible electronically, in the editor's opinion, these remain two resources that are equally effective in their traditional print editions.

In addition to D&B and RMA, another frequently referenced source of industry norms and ratios is Troy's *Almanac of Business and Industrial Financial Ratios.* Troy's contains 50 data points of data derived from IRS tax returns for more than 192 industries. The reliance on IRS data generally results in print editions that contain information approximately three to four years old. For example, the figures for the 2002 edition were taken from tax returns filed between July 1998 through June 1999. For this reason, it would be problematic for an auditor to rely on this data for the business audit review.

CONTRIBUTOR NAME: Kim Whalen

AFFILIATION: Emory University

USEFUL TIPS

- It is very useful to have a print copy of both the SIC code and NAICS manual close at hand. Both SIC and NAICS codes are also available online although the descriptions are not always as complete as found in the print versions. For a complete list, visit *http://www.census.gov* and click on the link to NAICS.
- At the time of the request, clarify with the audit team the exact SIC code to use when looking up the data. If they are unsure, provide them with descriptive information from SIC and NAICS code manuals and work with them to select the closest match to the client's industry.
- Both D&B and RMA print resources have very useful introductions. Each explains the industries covered, calculations of the ratios, and how and why the ratios are used in financial evaluations. Written in an easy-to-understand style, they can be quite helpful to your research. It is often very useful to supply copies of this information to the auditor to include in the client's working papers for clarification of calculation of the data.

PROBLEM NUMBER 12: CONDUCT A FINANCIAL COMPARATIVE PEER ANALYSIS FOR COOPER COMPANIES AND ITS TOP THREE COMPETITORS

RESEARCH BACKGROUND: As part of his client's business audit review, Michael, a manager, needs to conduct a comparison of the client's financial statements and ratios to its top competitors. He is under a time crunch and needs you to deliver the information to him by the end of the day. Michael authorizes you to spend up to $100 and one hour of your time. You have gathered this type of information for him before and so he is confident that this is a reasonable budget and time allotment.

RESEARCH STRATEGY EMPLOYED: While you have Michael on the phone, you go ahead and ask him what Cooper's primary line of business is and the names of any of its competitors. You know from past experience that the auditors already have a good idea about their clients' business landscape. Asking Michael directly and tapping into his knowledge base not only saves you valuable time, but also provides you with useful clues about how to proceed. Many public companies have multiple lines of business and a few cues from Michael will ensure that you follow the right path.

Based on your conversation with Michael, you know that you are to focus on the contact lens aspect of Cooper's business. He mentioned Bausch & Lomb as one of the competitors. Cooper is a public parent company and it is a given that you will need to limit its competitors to public companies if you are to locate the level of financial data that Michael has requested.

Your organization recently picked up a subscription to Mergent Online, the "old" Moody's database of public company financial and descriptive data. It tags the financial statements and ratios for all of its companies and since all financial data can be downloaded into Excel, you decide to use this product. However, you also know from experience that you will have to use its Advanced Search option to come up with a list of competitors. While good to use if you have no other options, there are several alternative sources that you decide to tap into for your list of three of Cooper's main competitors. Once you have gathered these names, you will return to Mergent Online to generate the comparative financial data.

The sources you can turn to for a quick list of competitors are Hoover's, Factiva's Quick Company Profiles (actually pulls the information from Hoover's), and Standard & Poor's Industry Surveys. Navigating to Hoover's Web site (*http://www.hoovers.com*), you access Cooper Companies free company capsule and quickly locate a list of top competitors: Bausch & Lomb, Essilor International, Hologic, Novartis, Ocular Sciences, and Vistakon. Unfamiliar with all of these except for Bausch & Lomb, you still need to learn more about what these companies do to come up with your top three competitors list. Logging into Mergent Online, you click on the Advanced Search tab and conduct a keyword search for "contact lens" in the Business description; you also limit your search to U.S. companies. A quick glance at some of the returned companies tells you that several are on the retail side of the contact lens industry. Since you need to limit your search to those companies that manufacture lenses, you try a different tact. You pull up the Mergent record for Cooper Companies and note that 3851 is the SIC code for manufacturing ophthalmic goods. Returning to the Advanced Search template, you delete your earlier search and now select Primary SIC Code and enter 3851; the returned list looks much better.

You click on the link at the top of the page to move all the companies to Mergent's Company Analysis List, select Create Comparison Report, pick Total Revenue from the Financial Summary, and click on the Create Report button. This displays a table of the seven companies ranked in descending order by Total Revenues. You make note of the top three companies (Bausch & Lomb, Oakley Inc., and Ocular Sciences) but also go ahead and download the list just in case the manager is interested in knowing which other competitors are on the list.

Turning your attention to the real objective of this research, you return to the Company Analysis List, check the four companies you now want to compare, and click Create Multiple Company Report. A new template appears and you select four output options: Income Statement, Balance Sheet, Cash Flow, and Profitability Ratios, and request three years of annual data. Selecting Excel as your software of choice, you click on the button to Create Multiple Company Report and, within two minutes, you have the full financials and ratios for the four companies downloaded into Excel. Saving the results, you forward this and the short list of seven companies to Michael with a brief explanation of the sources used and your strategy for conducting the research.

SUMMARY OF SOLUTION: There are many sources that you can look to for deriving a list of company peers. For example, Hoover's and Factiva display a quick list as part of their company profile. While these lists are very helpful for getting you grounded and giving you some company names to begin searching, you must be careful not to assume that the companies are all comparable matches. Without knowing what criterion was used to gather the list, you cannot be positive that they match your criteria. Hoover's list contained several companies that did not appear as a result of the Mergent list. Why? Some possibilities are: (1) the lists included all companies that shared at least one of Cooper's lines of business and (2) the companies are not limited to public parent companies.

In the case of this request, locating the financial data was the easy part. If you do not subscribe to Mergent Online or one of its competitors, such as Thomson Research, you could also have used one of the free SEC filing sites, such as SEC Info or EdgarScan, both of which have tagged the financial data for downloading into Excel. The tricky part is defining the peer list. It is an imprecise process because the ways we define industry are so precarious. SIC and NAICS codes do not always exactly describe what the company does, and in many cases, are improperly applied. The written description of the business is even more susceptible to inconsistencies and error. The bottom line is that when conducting research that requires you to define a list of "comparable companies," and line of business is one of the criteria, be sure to use several reliable sources to generate your list and verify your findings.

CONTRIBUTOR NAME: Brenda Reeb
AFFILIATION: University of Rochester

USEFUL TIPS

- Solid spreadsheet skills are important for conducting accounting, financial, and really any type of business research. At a minimum, you need to understand how to download data into a spreadsheet, how to format the data once it is in Excel, and how to make minor adjustments in cell and row alignment. If possible, consider taking a class in Excel.

PROBLEM NUMBER 13: LOCATE PAST QUARTERLY AVERAGES FOR COMPANY STOCK PRICES

RESEARCH BACKGROUND: The auditor is trying to finish up some independent sampling of some of his client's equity investments and explains that he is missing some stock values for December 31, 2001, that he needs to complete his analysis. He asks you to look it up for him and send him the information. He also would like you to tell him how he could look it up himself for the next time he needs such data. You have been allotted $200 to purchase the information needed.

RESEARCH STRATEGY EMPLOYED: There are many sources, fee-based and free, that you can turn to for this information. Any source that provides daily or month-end closing prices will give you the answer to the stock price on December 31, 2001, for example. Most free and even most subscription sources do not calculate the averages, but no problem. As long as the data is downloadable into Excel, or can be copied and pasted into Excel, you can easily find the daily pricing for each quarter and use the Function/Average feature on the spreadsheet to calculate the averages.

One important question comes up: Does the auditor want the information already "adjusted" for stock splits and dividends? Most stock price interfaces assume adjusted pricing. Since the auditor already knew that there were no stock splits or dividend payments in 2001, he replied that unadjusted value would be fine.

You usually use Factiva to access this information, as the query is clean and easy on this service. Selecting the Quotes tab at the top of the Factiva Search page, you specify the date range, data type (stocks), and format (comma delimited). You do not know the ticker symbols off hand, but that is not a problem since Factiva gives the choice of typing in the ticker symbol or conducting a company name lookup. The comma-delimited output automatically displays the results in Excel. You look up each company and run the requested data; you can only generate a spreadsheet for one company at a time. You note the December 31, 2001, closing price and use the Average function to determine the fourth quarter averages. You also save each spreadsheet to send to the auditor for his working papers and in case he needs some additional information from this data. The entire request takes you approximately 20 minutes from beginning until you hit the send button and e-mail the results.

RESEARCH RESULTS: The e-mail you send the requestor includes the pricing spreadsheets you generated for each company along with your summary of the results. You also include the name of the database you used in case you are asked to check or rerun any of the numbers and so that next year the same source can be used for consistency sake.

COMPANY	12/31/2001	2001 QUARTERLY AVERAGES
Apple Computer	21.80	Q1 19.62; Q2 22.60; Q3 19.12; Q4 19.44
Sun Microsystems	12.30	Q1 24.51; Q2 17.23; Q3 13.63; Q4 11.62 (These are unadjusted, from Yahoo!)
Georgia Pacific	26.74	Q1 28.65; Q2 31.50; Q3 33.06; Q4 28.19
IBM	119.84	Q1 101.65; Q2 110.30; Q3 101.87; Q4 110.85
SunTrust Bank	61.04	Q1 61.45; Q2 60.52; Q3 65.14; Q4 60.75

SUMMARY OF SOLUTION: Locating current and historical company stock prices is an easy exercise. Many subscription-based databases and free Internet sites contain the daily, weekly, and monthly pricing. As long as you have the daily pricing and the ability to download or copy and paste the information into a spreadsheet, you can quickly calculate the data you need. Be sure to clarify whether the data is needed as adjusted or unadjusted. Having the ticker symbols at hand will make the look-up process a bit quicker, but it is not required since most interfaces also have a company name look up feature.

Since the auditor also requested that you tell him how to look up the information on his own, you also send him the instructions on using Yahoo! Finance (*http://finance.yahoo.com*), one of the free and most easy sites to use for stock price information. Daily historical prices go back to 1970 and all the data is automatically downloaded into Excel. Just enter the company ticker symbol (or conduct a company lookup) at the top of the page. A page with the most current quote will be returned. Click on the link to Historical Quotes directly below this to view the Historical Quotes page. From this page you can select a date range, data that is reported daily, weekly, monthly, or dividends, and you can enter ticker symbols in a box on this page to look up different company pricing. A link to Download Spreadsheet Format at the bottom of the page opens the data into Excel.

CONTRIBUTOR NAME: Brenda Reeb
AFFILIATION: University of Rochester

USEFUL TIPS

- If ######### appears in the Excel spreadsheet, it simply means that the data is too large for the cell. Use your cursor to widen the Excel column and the ###### will be replaced with the data.
- Practice the export method in Excel with one company before attempting to save multiple companies at the same time.
- Obtaining the ticker symbol up front will move the search along more quickly, but fall back on the company name look-up feature available on most interfaces if you do not know it.

PROBLEM NUMBER 14: WHAT WAS THE AVERAGE AAA CORPORATE BOND YIELD FOR THE THIRD QUARTER 2001 AND FOR THE ENTIRE YEAR 2001?

RESEARCH BACKGROUND: As part of the normal workflow, auditors are regularly expected to locate investment data. While there is a budget for external data the client expects the auditor to tap into these sources selectively; the more the auditor can get "for free," the better. Since auditors bill for their time, they also need to take into consideration the most efficient path to the information.

RESEARCH STRATEGY EMPLOYED: More and more economic and financial-type data seems to be available on the free Web, so you decide to start with a quick search. Using the Google search engine (*http://www.google.com*), you type "aaa corporate bond" in the search box. The first returned link is to the Financial Forecast Center Web site (*http://www.forecasts.org/interest-rate/ moodys-corporate-bond-yield.htm*). The returned page contains a link to Moody's Aaa Corporate Bond Yields Historical Data. Clicking on this link yields Moody's monthly Aaa corporate bond rates from 1919 to the present. The data credits Moody's Investor Services as the source of the data so you are comfortable that this is reputable data and not just some numbers posted on the free Web. From beginning to end, you spent approximately 15 minutes on this request and incurred no external data costs for these results:

- The Aaa corporate bond yield for the third quarter of 2001 is 7.17 percent.
- The average Aaa corporate bond yield for 2001 is 7.1 percent.
  - To simplify calculating the annual rate, you copied the range of data from January 2001 through December 2001, pasted it into Excel, and applied the function for "Average."

SUMMARY OF RESULTS: In this instance, your approach of using a search engine to locate the information on the free Web worked in your favor. There are some alternatives to consider. For example running a simple search in Google will provide quick access to a reliable source. To access the Aaa Corporate Bond Yields directly from the Financial Forecasts Center home page, click on the links to Money Rates>Aaa Corporate Bond Yields. Because the data was tied back to Moody's, an authoritative resource for this type of information, you felt comfortable relying on it for client work.

Google's returned search results list some other sources for the Aaa corporate bond yields:

- *The Bond Market Association (http://www.bondmarkets.com/research).* Contains Moody's Aaa, Aa, A, Baa, and Average Corporate Bond Yield Averages from 1980–2002. From the home page, click on the link to Moody's Corporate Bond Yield Averages. The data is sourced back to Moody's Investors Service. This site contains a wide range of bond market statistical data: Cross Market, Asset-Backed Securities, Corporate, European Securitization, Federal Agency Debt, Funding, Money Market Instruments, Mortgage-Backed Securities, Municipal Securities, and U.S. Treasury Securities.
- *Federal Reserve Bank of St. Louis, Economic Research (http://www.stlouisfed.org/fred).* Contains the same data as was posted in the Financial Forecasts Center, with the added value of already being formatted to download into Excel. From the home page, click on the link to Economic Data – FRED II>Interest Rates. The Federal Reserve Bank sites contain a wealth of economic, financial, and banking information. They usually contain value-added applications that are responsive to the need to work efficiently with statistical data. Categories of data included on the St. Louis site include: Business/Fiscal, Commercial Banking, Consumer Price Indexes, Employment and Population, Exchange Rate and Trade Data, Gross Domestic Product, Interest Rates, Producer Price Indexes, Regional (including Employment and Banking Data), and U.S. Financial Data.

CONTRIBUTOR NAME: Susan M. Klopper
AFFILIATION: Goizueta Business Library

USEFUL TIPS

- For quick searches, use your browser's address bar. Remember to enclose phrases in quotes ("").
- When using the free Web for any time of research, check to make sure the original provider of the data is sourced and that you recognize the source as authoritative and reliable.
- When using a search engine to locate information, take the time to explore several of the returned sites. Several sites may contain the same information but offer different options for using it, such as downloading features. Depending on what you need, having several sites to select from can make the research process run more smoothly and your time to be utilized more efficiently.

PROBLEM NUMBER 15: WHAT WAS THE YIELD ON THE ONE-, FIVE-, AND TWENTY-YEAR TREASURY BOND RATES ON DECEMBER 31, 2001?

RESEARCH BACKGROUND: An auditor calls you from the client site to verify the value of some client investments as reported on the client's brokerage report.

RESEARCH STRATEGY EMPLOYED: The logical choice is the Federal Reserve Bank (*http://www.federalreserve.gov*). It is the originating, authoritative source of this data. The content is easily accessible on the FRB Web site; it is free, easy to navigate, current, and reliable—everything the researcher could hope for. From the FRB home page, the following steps were followed:

- Click on the link to Economic Research and Data.
- Next, click on the link to Statistics: Releases, and Historical Data. This section contains all the Fed's daily, weekly, monthly, quarterly, and annual economic and banking data, including the prime rate, federal fund rate, foreign exchange rates, and Treasury bill, and bond rates.
- Scroll down to the "Weekly Releases" section; click on the link to Releases for document "H.15, Selected Interest Rates." Document H.15 contains links, in reverse chronological order, to each week's release. Clicking on the link to December 31, 2001 will display data for the week ending on the last business day of 2001. Scroll down the document and beneath the heading "U.S. Government Securities" are Treasury bond rates (called "Treasury Constant Maturities") and yields for a range of years, including one, five, and twenty years.

The displayed page is in HTML formatting; when you print it, some of the data is likely to run off the page. To ensure that you print the complete page, look to the top of the page, and click on the link to PDF. Clicking on this link will open the page in Adobe, for ease of printing as well as attaching the document to an e-mail if your client has specified that you send it electronically.

SUMMARY OF SOLUTION: An audit senior needed you to help her locate some Treasury bond rates so that she could independently test the accuracy of the client's financial position as reported on its books. Since December 31 is often *not* the actual last day of the year, you should verify exactly what the last date is (for example, 12/28/2001) so that the auditor will report it correctly in their client documentation. Treasury bond rates (yields) are published by the Federal Reserve, making the FRB's Web site the logical first place to access. It is extremely easy and quick to navigate and the document you needed could be saved in a format that enabled clean printing and easy electronic delivery.

CONTRIBUTOR NAME: Susan M. Klopper
AFFILIATION: Goizueta Business Library

USEFUL TIPS

- The FRB (*http://www.federalreserve.gov*) Web site should be one of your bookmarks if you do a lot of accounting and financial research.
- Take advantage of the ability to output the release pages in Adobe .pdf format.
- Check out the 12 Federal Reserve District Web sites. They contain excellent information not found on the FRB home site, including regional data, and more. To locate links to these other sites, click on the link to Federal Reserve Districts and Banks located on the FRB home page.

PROBLEM NUMBER 16: ON WHAT DATES IN 2001 DID THE PRIME RATE CHANGE AND WHAT WERE THE RATE CHANGES?

RESEARCH BACKGROUND: An audit senior is conducting a sampling to validate the client's assertions about expenses related to a loan; the terms of the loan are tied to the daily prime rate. To verify what is recorded on the client's books, the auditor needs to know each date that the prime rate changed and what the rate change was.

RESEARCH STRATEGY EMPLOYED: You know that the FRB determines the prime rate so you decided to look there first, although you do not recall ever seeing a list of the prime rates for every day of the year. Your library subscribed to a weekly publication called *Selected Interest Rates*, which you used in the past, but you are pretty sure that it only listed the daily rate for a week at a time. The prospect of looking up 52 weeks of this release is rather unappealing, but it is worth a quick look at this site:

- You "guess" that the URL is *http://www.federalreservebank.gov*, but unfortunately you guess wrong. Instead, you type "federal reserve bank" in Explorer's address bar with success. The correct URL is *http://www.federalreserve.gov*.
- Once at the FRB home page, click on the following links: Economic Research and Data>Statistics: Releases and Historical Data. Under the section for Daily Releases, click on Daily Update next to H.15. You are pretty sure that H.15 is that weekly release the library used to keep and you are right!
- At the top of the page is a link for Historical Data; clicking on this yields a table of updates to all the FRB's data. Scrolling down you see Bank Prime Loan and a link for Daily. Clicking on this displays a table of the daily prime rate from 1955 to the present.

RESEARCH RESULTS: It is easy to scan the table and find the information you need. Since the data comes directly from the Federal Reserve, an authoritative source, you feel confident using this for client engagement work. Just to make sure you have not transcribed any of the numbers, you also copy and paste all the daily rates for 2001 into Excel and place a copy of this in the working papers as follows:

- Dates and rate changes in 2001: 1/4=9.00%; 2/1=8.50%; 3/21=8.00%; 4/19=7.50%; 5/16=7.00%; 6/28=6.75%; 8/22=6.5%; 9/18=6.00%; 10/3=5.50%; 11/7=5.00%; 12/12=4.75%

SUMMARY OF SOLUTION: Fortunately, the researcher knew that the FRB published the prime rate, so she had some clue as to where to start looking. In the course of locating the prime on the site, she also discovered that historical tables of the prime's average on a monthly and annual basis are also available. If the researcher had not known that the FRB was the source to turn to for changes in the prime's rate, how might her strategy have changed? Typing "daily prime rate" in the browser address bar or search engine of choice displays an excellent list of possible leads. Exploring them unearthed the following great sites to know about and save as Favorites:

- *New York Federal Reserve Bank Prime Rate As It Changed, 1929–Present* (*http://ftp.ny.frb.org/prime/prime.txt*). Maintains a running table of only the dates that the prime changed and the new rate, beginning with 1929. From the home page, click on the link to Prime Rate in the "Historical" section. Since this data is coming directly from the prime, some researchers consider this the "optimal" source to use when needing this information.

- *HSH Associates Web Site* (*http://www.hsh.com/indices/prime.html*). Maintains a running table of only the dates that the prime changed and the new rate, beginning with 1975; a separate table just for the 21st century is located at (*http://www. hsh.com/indices/prime00s.html*). HSH cites the *Wall Street Journal* as its source and even includes some brief information explaining what the prime is and why rate changes occur. HSH Associates is an unknown name and looking on the Web site for additional information about them did not provide enough evidence of credibility. Running a sampling of this data against the Federal Reserve daily prime confirms that it is accurate, and therefore this site can be used for client work.

- *Economagic.com Economic Time Series* (*http://www. economagic. com/em-cgi/data/exe/fedbog/day-prime*). This daily list of the prime rate from 1955 to the present is taken directly from the Federal Reserve site, with the added value of providing a link to download it directly into Excel.

- *Dallas Federal Reserve Bank Prime Interest Rate* (*http://www. dallasfed.org/htm/data/data/rmbkprim.tab.htm*). The average monthly and annual, with year-over-year percent change, prime rate is pulled together in one table. Not applicable to the daily rate change need but eliminates the need to look at two different tables to glean these averages.

CONTRIBUTOR NAME: Susan M. Klopper
AFFILIATION: Goizueta Business Library

USEFUL TIPS

- The FRB (*http://www.federalreserve.gov*) Web site should be one of your bookmarks if you do a lot of accounting and financial research.
- Check out the 12 Federal Reserve District Web sites; they contain excellent information not found on the FRB home site, including regional data, and more. To locate links to these other sites, click on the link to Federal Reserve Districts and Banks located on the FRB home page.
- Even when you know the source to turn to, it is worth exploring alternative options on the free Web. Using your browser's address bar or a favorite search engine to display a list of possible sites and then taking a little time to explore three to five of the top sites is an effective strategy to identify new sites and to hone in on unique applications.

PROBLEM NUMBER 17: WHAT WAS THE QUARTERLY AND ANNUAL AVERAGE FOR THE PRIME RATE IN 1999?

RESEARCH BACKGROUND: You are engaged by a client to provide historical financial analysis for their fiscal 1999 results. The client has debt rates tied to the prime rate and your supervisor has requested data for the prime rate in 1999.

RESEARCH STRATEGY EMPLOYED: You decide to cast a broad net by going to Google (*http://www.google.com*) and typing in "prime rate historical data." You could have conducted a slightly more narrow search such as "Federal Reserve prime rate," but you decide to search more broadly to find all options.

The first entry from the search results turns out to be the Federal Reserve. Clicking on the link to FRB: Federal Reserve Statistical Release H.15: Historical Data (*http://www. federalreserve.gov/releases/h15/data.htm*) leads to a series of links to all of the Fed's economic data. The section for the prime tells you that the data is available on a Daily, Business, Weekly (Wednesday), Monthly, and Annual basis. For this request you need the prime rate calculated on a quarterly and annual basis. You can estimate the quarterly data by averaging the monthly rates; the annual data is already calculated.

RESEARCH RESULTS: The following rates were in effect at month-end for January through March of 1999: 7.75 percent, 7.75 percent, and 7.75 percent (average of 7.75 percent). The following rates were in effect in April through June of 1999: 7.75 percent, 7.75 percent, and 7.75 percent (average of 7.75 percent). The following rates were in effect in July through September of 1999: 8.00 percent, 8.06 percent, and 8.25 percent (average of 8.10 percent). The following rates were in effect in October through December of 1999: 8.25 percent, 8.37 percent, and 8.50 percent (average of 8.37 percent). The average of all 12 monthly figures is 7.99 percent.

SUMMARY OF SOLUTION: You were not sure of the exact Web address but knowing that the Federal Reserve was the primary source, you used Google to run a broad search. The first link brought you directly to the Federal Reserve Statistical Release, which contains the information. Because quarterly data is not already calculated, you drew your results by averaging the monthly data. If you had needed to conduct the calculations for several years, it would have been easy to copy/paste the data into Excel and use the Function/Average feature to conduct the calculations. The Fed already provides the annual data.

Familiarity with the primary source of the data was a big help, but conducting a good search strategy using Google would have pointed you to the right source also. The same information was found on the Financial Forecast Center Web site (*http://www. financialforecastcenter.com*), but it is important to note that it refers back to the originating source, the Fed.

CONTRIBUTOR NAME: Michelle Hartstrom
AFFILIATION: Columbia Financial Advisors, Inc.

USEFUL TIPS

- Economic data is often available on many Web sites; before relying on it, make sure that it sources the data back to the originating source. If you are looking for very current data, you are best looking on the site of the primary source of the data.
- Take advantage of application software, such as Excel, to help with calculations if the raw data is not available in the form that you need.

PROBLEM NUMBER 18: WHAT WAS THE INFLATION RATE EACH MONTH IN 2000 AND WHAT WAS THE ANNUAL RATE IN 2001?

RESEARCH BACKGROUND: Your company is signing a network support contract with an outside vendor and the annual service fee will fluctuate based on the inflation rate. You want to know how much fluctuation you can expect, based on previous inflation rate movement.

RESEARCH STRATEGY: The U.S. government determines the inflation rate and as a service to taxpayers the data is freely available on government Web sites. Inflation is the *percentage of change* in the Consumer Price Index (CPI). The CPI measures the prices that working people pay for basic goods and services and it is measured by the Bureau of Labor Statistics (BLS), a bureau of the U.S. Department of Labor. A visit to the BLS home page (*http://www.bls.gov*) shows a prominent link to the CPI home page (*http://www.bls.gov/cpi*). The CPI home page provides the data for the index and its database allows you to query calculations on its change from month to month or year to year. The site also contains some very useful and well-written explanations about the data.

There is a difference between the CPI "Index" and the percentage of its change over time (for example, rate of inflation). It is important to understand the basic difference between the two and to make sure that you and your requestor are in agreement about exactly which type of information is being sought. It is very common for people to ask for the CPI when what they really mean is the percentage of its change. Be sure to ask up front.

Without prior familiarity of inflation and the CPI, you would not necessarily know to go to the BLS government Web site. Using your ISP address bar or a free search engine, such as Google (*http://www.google.com*), is a quick way to get to the source. Running two different searches through Google: "inflation rate" and "rate of inflation," both yielded a number of sites. Interestingly, in neither case did the BLS site come up within the first eight sites displayed. What did appear were some sites that might provide explanations of what it was and others that seemed to contain the information. If you carefully read the summaries, CPI and BLS are finally mentioned in the seventh document. This is perfect evidence of how important it is to be patient, and not just jump to the first site you find. Presumably the sites that appeared to contain CPI data would reference or link you to the government site, but maybe not. When conducting business research, you *always* want to try and access the data from the originating source; if this is not an option, than use reputable sources that will report the data accurately.

The interesting part really begins once you load the BLS home page: it contains a mind-boggling array of CPI data choices. To determine which version of the data is best for your needs, click on the link CPI-U for the U.S. City Average for All Items, Not Seasonally Adjusted. The network services company wants to use the inflation rate to escalate the monthly or annual service contract paid by your company. The BLS Web site recommends using this data set for escalator clauses in contracts because it represents the broadest, most comprehensive CPI.

To locate a link to the CPI-U, U.S. City Average for All Items, Not Seasonally Adjusted series, go to the box of quick links on the right side of the CPI home page. Below the heading CPI-U, All Cities, All Items, select the link to historical data for this series by clicking the dinosaur icon for the first link, Not Seasonally Adjusted, monthly change data. A page is returned with monthly and annual data from 1992–current that reflects the percent change in CPI from month to month. Using drop boxes at the top of the page, modify the date range to calculate its inflation for the period of 2000–2001.

RESEARCH RESULTS: In 2000 the CPI fluctuated between 2.7 and 3.8. In 2001 the annual percent change was 2.8. This is not unreasonable, so your company decides to sign the contract with that clause. Moreover, the wide application of CPI in contracts is apparent after studying material on the CPI Web site and this awareness gives the contract signers confidence that they can agree to a reasonable clause in the contract.

	2000	2001
Jan	2.7	3.7
Feb	3.2	3.5
Mar	3.8	2.9
Apr	3.1	3.3
May	3.2	3.6
Jun	3.7	3.2
Jul	3.7	2.7
Aug	3.4	2.7

	2000	2001
Sep	3.5	2.6
Oct	3.4	2.1
Nov	3.4	1.9
Dec	3.4	1.6
Annual	3.4	2.8
Half1	3.3	3.4
Half2	3.5	2.2

SUMMARY OF SOLUTION: With prior knowledge of CPI data, this process would take less than 10 minutes to complete. Without prior knowledge of CPI data, it could take up to an hour exploring the CPI home page to determine which data series is appropriate for escalator contracts. A crash course in CPI data can be self-taught if you read the FAQ or other support material on the CPI site. If you are unfamiliar with where to go for this information, use your browser address bar or your favorite free search engine to run a simple search. Carefully read through the returned results to determine the best (that is, more reliable) source of data. The monthly and annual rate of inflation is also reported in several other sources, all of which glean the data from the CPI. Depending on what you need, these can be more user-friendly than running the calculations using the BLS CPI database query system:

- *Economic Indicators* (*http://www.access.gpo.gov/congress/cong002.html*). This is a monthly report compiled by the Council of Economic Advisors for the Joint Economic Committee to provide information on wages, prices, production, business activity, credit, money, purchasing power, and Federal finance.
- *Economic Report of the President* (*http://w3.access.gpo.gov/cop*). This is an annual publication so you can not rely on it for recently released data.

CONTRIBUTOR NAME: Brenda Reeb
AFFILIATION: University of Rochester

USEFUL TIPS

- When using Web sites to learn about important topics, verify the credentials of the site authors and note the currency of information. Perhaps visit a few "expert" sites to compare the data. You know you have explored the topic completely when the information begins to repeat itself.

- The CPI Index and rate of inflation is announced by the BLS each month. The BLS offers an e-mail service of the press release. A few other shortcuts for frequent users of CPI data include the "Create Customized Tables" on the CPI home page or the "series report shortcut." Each series has a unique code number; if you enter the code you can go straight to that table.

PROBLEM NUMBER 19: WHAT WAS THE PRODUCER PRICE INDEX FOR NATURAL GAS EACH MONTH AND ANNUALLY IN 2001?

RESEARCH BACKGROUND: A staff auditor working on an engagement has requested the Producer Price Index (PPI) for natural gas for each month in 2001, as well as the annual 2001 PPI figure. She needs to compare this data with information received from the client and would like it in Excel format, if possible.

RESEARCH STRATEGY EMPLOYED: PPI information is available for free via the U.S. Department of Labor's BLS PPI Web site (*http://www.bls.gov/ppi/home.htm*). Click on the Get Detailed Statistics link in the body of the PPI home page, and then click on the Commodity Data link appearing under the heading "Most Requested Series." This is the quickest way to access frequently requested PPI data. Do not click on the Get Detailed Statistics link in the banner of the PPI home page. This link is for all BLS data; the link in the body of the PPI home page is targeted to just PPI information.

Scroll down the Producer Price Index–Commodities list and click in the box next to Natural Gas–WPU0531. Then click on the Retrieve Data button. You will receive a table of PPI information by month for natural gas covering 1992–2002. You can limit this data to only 2001 by changing the output options appearing above the table. Since the staff auditor requested the data be in an Excel spreadsheet, do not change the output options on this screen, but instead, click on the More Formatting Options link.

Here you can format the PPI data so that you can put it into Excel format. The formatting options page automatically defaults to have Original Data Value checked and Table Format highlighted for view type. Specify the year range for only 2001. For output type, select HTML Table. Click on the Retrieve Data button. Copy and paste the resulting table into Excel.

RESEARCH RESULTS: You obtained a table containing the monthly and annual PPI data for natural gas and put it into an Excel spreadsheet. You saved the spreadsheet and e-mailed it to the client with these results:

- Series Id: WPU0531, Not Seasonally Adjusted, Group: Fuels and related products and power, Item: Natural Gas, Base Date: 8200
- 2001   Jan(393.8)   Feb(262.3)   Mar(215.8)   Apr(220.6)   May(203.6)   Jun(153.4)   Jul(121.1)   Aug(120.9)   Sept (93.0)   Oct(72.9)   Nov(114.0)   Dec(90.5)   Annual(171.8)

CONTRIBUTOR NAME: Jan Rivers

AFFILIATION: Dorsey & Whitney LLP

USEFUL TIPS

- All PPI items have a series number. For example, natural gas is WPU0531. You can use this number to locate PPI information as well. From the PPI home page, click on Series Report to obtain information by series number.
- You can view your results in column or table format.
- Optional graphs are available with your search results.
- If you have a print subscription to PPI releases, you can locate information by commodity name in them as well.

PROBLEM NUMBER 20: WHAT WERE THE ANNUAL FOREIGN EXCHANGE RATES FOR FRANCE, ENGLAND, NETHERLANDS, JAPAN, AND CANADA IN 2001?

RESEARCH BACKGROUND: Janice, an audit senior, needs to verify independently the value of some investments her client has made in foreign stocks. The client has provided her team with the value converted to U.S. dollars, but she needs to validate the conversion rate using another source.

RESEARCH STRATEGY EMPLOYED: The FRB is one of the primary sources of foreign exchange data and all of its data is available for free on its Web site, *http://www.federalreserve.gov*. If you did not know exactly where the exchange rates were located on the site, the home page provides several useful search aids. Clicking on the link to Search and typing: **foreign exchange rates Netherlands** in the search box will take you directly to the official releases. Another approach is clicking on the Subject Index link and scrolling down to the topic "Foreign Exchange." If you were familiar with the FRB site and how its content is located, you would follow the path Economic Research and Data>Statistics: Releases and Historical Data, or jump directly to the page, *http://www.federalreserve.gov/releases.*

The Statistics: Releases and Historical Data page contains links to several categories of data identified by a "Release" number and available for daily, weekly, monthly, and annual frequency. Scrolling down to the section labeled "Annual Releases," you click on the link to document G.5A, "Foreign Exchange Rates." You click on the link to the most recent date and discover that it contains the most recent four years of annual average exchange rates for a number of key countries. You can print the page or save it as a text document.

The top of the releases contains the following explanation:

THE TABLE BELOW SHOWS THE AVERAGE RATES OF EXCHANGE IN 2002 TOGETHER WITH COMPARABLE FIGURES FOR OTHER YEARS. AVERAGES ARE BASED ON DAILY NOON BUYING RATES FOR CABLE TRANSFERS IN NEW YORK CITY CERTIFIED FOR CUSTOMS PURPOSES BY THE FEDERAL RESERVE BANK OF NEW YORK.

Often, accountants will specifically ask for the "noon" exchange rates; this is unique to the Federal Reserve and verifies that this release is the appropriate source to use. At the bottom of the page is some information that, while confusing at first glance, is extremely important for anyone needing foreign exchange rates to understand:

- As of the January 3, 2000 release, the euro is reported in place of the individual euro-area currencies. These currency rates can be derived from the euro rate by using the fixed conversion rates (in currencies per euro) given below:
- EUR = 13.7603 AUSTRIAN SCHILLINGS
  - = 40.3399 BELGIAN FRANCS
  - = 5.94573 FINNISH MARKKAS
  - = 6.55957 FRENCH FRANCS
  - = 1.95583 GERMAN MARKS
  - = .787564 IRISH POUNDS
  - = 1936.27 ITALIAN LIRE
  - = 40.3399 LUXEMBOURG FRANCS
  - = 2.20371 NETHERLANDS GUILDERS
  - = 200.482 PORTUGUESE ESCUDOS
  - = 166.386 SPANISH PESETAS

Reprinted courtesy of U.S. Board of Governors, Federal Reserve System.

Glancing at the table of countries, you see that neither France nor the Netherlands are broken out as individual countries, an important signal that they are part of the European Community and their "official" currency is the euro. The above list provides the information that you need to "reconvert" the French franc from the euro to the U.S. dollar. Here is what you need to know to calculate this conversion:

- You need to determine the rate between the euro and the French franc and Netherlands guilder. According to the table: 6.55957 francs = 1 euro. The main listing of the individual currencies indicates that $1 U.S. dollar = .8952 euros. To calculate how many francs equal $1 U.S. dollar, you multiply 6.55957 (number of francs = 1 euro) by .8952 (number of euro = $1 U.S. dollar). The answer is 5.87212. This is the exchange rate that you will forward to Janice.
- Working through the same process to determine the exchange rate of the Netherlands guilder: 2.20371 guilders = 1 euro and $1 U.S. dollar = .8952 euros. Multiply 2.20371 by .8952 to arrive at 1.97272. Again, it is the latter number that you will provide to the auditor.

RESEARCH RESULTS:

COUNTRY	ANNUAL EXCHANGE RATE WITH U.S. $1; 2001
Canada	1.5487 dollar
England (called U.K. in the Fed chart)	1.4396 pound
France	5.87212 franc, translated from the euro
Japan	121.57 yen
Netherlands	1.97276 guilder, translated from the euro

SUMMARY OF SOLUTION: The FRB's Statistical Releases is the primary source of locating many country exchange rates. One "slight" complication is the need to convert a country's euro rate to the U.S. dollar. Once you understand the necessary calculations, however, it is an easy conversion process to work through. If your country is not included in the FRB's release, you can turn to several other sources, including:

- *International Monetary Fund (IMF)* (*http://www.imf.org/external/fin.htm*). The IMF tracks a larger range of countries than the Federal Reserve, approximately 100 countries compared to about 25 covered by the Federal Reserve.

- *United States Statistical Abstract.* This source, free on the Web at *http://www.census.gov/statab/www*, uses IMF data. Exchange rates are contained in the "Comparative International Statistics" section in a table titled "Foreign Exchange Rates." The most recent year's average annual rates are published in each edition of the *Statistical Abstract* and publication is available on the Web site beginning with 1995.

- *The Currency Site* (*http://www.oanda.com*). Click on the link to Historical Rates on the home page. Only daily rates are available, but you can save them in Excel and use the Function option to calculate the average.

- *Pacific Exchange Rate Service* (*http://pacific.commerce.ubc.ca/xr*). This site contains several options for accessing exchange rates, including Historical Annual Average Rates from 1948–present in .pdf. It also includes links to other exchange rate sources and a list of currency for each country.

Whichever site you use, be sure to document its name and URL and the source that it identifies as the primary source of the data. If at all possible, try to obtain all or as much of the data from one source. Begin with the Federal Reserve releases and then turn to the IMF as a second source.

CONTRIBUTOR NAME: Brenda Reeb

AFFILIATION: University of Rochester

USEFUL TIPS

- Many sites on the free Web offer foreign exchange rates; be careful about using "just any source." Remember, the information you provide is being relied on to make business decisions. Always try to use a reliable source and document all the sources you do for the audit working papers. When the auditor returns next year for similar information, it is always preferable to use the same sources.

PROBLEM NUMBER 21: WHAT WAS THE THREE-MONTH LIBOR RATE ON DECEMBER 31, 2001?

RESEARCH BACKGROUND: You are working for a client to perform a review of financial statements for the company's fiscal year ending December 31, 2001. The company has bank debt with a rate tied to LIBOR, the London Interbank Offered Rate. You need to research the rate as of year-end for the preparation of footnotes to the client's financial statements.

RESEARCH STRATEGY EMPLOYED: Since this the first time you have been requested to locate LIBOR rates, you do not already have a site in mind to use. One strategy is to go to Google (*http://www.google.com*), and type the following keywords in the search box: libor historical data. The search returned many possible Web sites from which to choose. It is very important that you obtain the information from a reliable source. You also hope to access it for free, although you are willing to pay a reasonable amount to ensure that it is accurate.

Based on the keyword search performed, you checked several sources based on promising Web site descriptions provided by Google. The following two sites were found to be very thorough and reliable:

1. *Financial Forecast Center* (*http://www.financialforecastcenter.com*). Clicking on the Google link took you directly to the current forecast for the three-month LIBOR rate and some current interest rates. By scrolling down to the bottom of the current page, you saw a link to Historical Data. Clicking on this link displayed a page linking to a large range of historical economic and banking data. From the list on the left column, you select Interest Rates. Again you look to the left column and select 3 Month LIBOR which displays the month-end LIBOR rate on a historical basis from the last day of each month beginning with September 1989.

2. *Investopedia* (*http://www.investopedia.com*). Investopedia provided the following information on LIBOR: "This is the rate of interest at which banks borrow funds from other banks, in marketable size, in the London interbank market. In other words, LIBOR is the international rate that banks borrow from other banks at. This is the most widely used benchmark or reference rate for short term interest rates."

http://www.investopedia.com. Reprinted with the permission of Equade Internet.

In addition to this definition, which was very helpful since you were new to researching the LIBOR, the site also pointed to Economagic.com (*http://www.economagic.com*). This site posted the LIBOR in several different currencies. You click on the link to U.S. dollars. The next option allowed for selecting the LIBOR increments from one week to 12 months and clicking on three months displays the desired information. This site is very impressive. The LIBOR is available on a daily basis beginning with January 2, 1987, and it is available for downloading in several formats, including Excel. The LIBOR rate on December 31, 2001, was 1.88125 percent.

SUMMARY OF SOLUTION: Not sure where to look for the LIBOR, you ran an effective search using Google. The results pointed to many different sites. You took the time to look at several of them before you determined the two that appeared to offer the most complete information. By comparing the results from each site, you were also able to validate the information.

Another excellent source for LIBOR is the British Bankers Association (*http://www.bba.org.uk/media*). This site contains current and historical rates, dating back to 1987. The LIBOR is reported as one month, two months, three months, six months, and twelve months, and is available for downloading into Excel.

CONTRIBUTOR NAME: Michelle Hartstrom
AFFILIATION: Columbia Financial Advisors, Inc.

USEFUL TIPS

- Another site to try for interest rate information on a current, one-month, two-month, three-month, six-month, and one-year basis is *http://www.Bloomberg.com* under "Key Rates."
- *http://www.Bankrate.com* also provides interest rate information in the same time frames as Bloomberg under "Rates & News."

PROBLEM NUMBER 22: LOCATE 2005 FORECASTS FOR INFLATION AND GDP

RESEARCH BACKGROUND: You are working on a financial forecast for a client. You are asked to perform a discounted future returns analysis and you need to estimate the long-term growth of the company. You need to find the long-term estimates for inflation and GDP as of the valuation date.

RESEARCH BUDGET: You have a client charge number for any costs, but are expected to obtain the best information as economically as possible.

RESEARCH STRATEGY EMPLOYED: Before you can move forward with this research, you need to understand exactly what discounted future analysis means and what it is used for. Speaking with one of your colleagues, you learn that discounted future (sometimes referred to as discounted cash flow analysis) is an income approach to performing a company valuation. The long-term growth estimate is used in the terminal year of the cash flow analysis and is the estimated growth for the company into perpetuity. Often, estimates of long-term real GDP and inflation are used in arriving at the long-term growth rate for a company. Understanding that, you now have to determine what source of information to use for this research. You know of several historical sources for this type of macroeconomic information but forecast data is unfamiliar to you. You ask some colleagues and they suggest you may find it through some branch of the FRB but they do not know exactly the source. You decide to perform a search using your best "guess" as to the correct search terms.

You search Google (*http://www.google.com*) using the terms "federal reserve bank and inflation forecast." You review the listings and decide to try *http://www.valuationresources.com/EconomicData* since its summary refers to FRB data and inflation information. The site proves to be a very useful source of economic data. It refers searchers to the FRB of St. Louis for historical and current bond yields and interest rate data (*http//research.stlouisfed.org/fred*). The site also points to the FRB of Philadelphia and the publication *Livingston Survey* (*http://www.phil.frb.org/econ/respubs*). According to the description from the Web site, the *Livingston Survey* was started in 1946 by columnist Joseph Livingston and is the oldest continuous survey of economists' expectations. It summarizes the forecasts of economists from industry, government, banking, and academia.

Clicking on the link to the *Livingston Survey*, you learn that it is published twice annually. Since you are performing a current analysis, you select the most recent publication (December 2002). The *Livingston Survey* data presents half-year inflation data through 2003 and annual average CPI inflation data through 2004. The survey also provides an estimate of long-term inflation and real GDP based on what forecasters think will happen over the next 10 years. This 10-year estimate is a good long-term estimate for inflation and real growth.

RESEARCH RESULTS: Based on the December 2002 issue of the *Livingston Survey* from the FRB of Philadelphia, forecasters think that inflation will average 2.5 percent over the next 10 years. The survey estimates annual growth of real GDP will be 3.2 percent annually over the next 10 years. These two estimates are appropriate estimates for the years 2005 and beyond for the client project. The publication is presented in PDF format. Print the December 2002 issue and save it in your file for future reference.

In the course of working on this project, you also identified some additional, excellent sources for economic forecasts, all of which are accessible on the free Web:

* The Budget and Economic Outlook, Congressional Budget Office (*http://www.sbo.gov*)
* Conference Board U.S. Outlook (*http://www.conference-board.org*)
* Financial Forecast Center (*http://www.forecasts.org*)

CONTRIBUTOR NAME: Michelle Hartstrom

AFFILIATION: Columbia Financial Advisors, Inc.

USEFUL TIPS

* Bookmark the following Web sites: *http://www.phil.frb.org/econ/respubs, http://research.stlouis.org/fred, http://www.valuationresouces.com.*
* You may want to print back issues of the *Livingston Survey* and keep your file updated with future issues. People in professions like business valuation use this type of information on a regular basis and may need the forecast data on a historical basis.

PROBLEM NUMBER 23: CORPORATE REPORTING TO SHAREHOLDERS ABOUT THE CHALLENGES OF THE CURRENT YEAR AND ITS FUTURE OUTLOOK

RESEARCH BACKGROUND: Your client wants to diversify her stock investments and is interested in investing in American Greetings. You already have a good handle on the company's financial performance and have read a few investment banking reports. Now you want to know what American Greetings' leadership is saying about its current and future financial health and strategic direction. Since American Greetings is a public company, most of this information will be available for free.

RESEARCH STRATEGY EMPLOYED: To learn what the leaders of American Greetings tell shareholders about its future, go straight to the horse's mouth and visit the company's Web site. The Management Discussion and Analysis (MD&A) section of the 10-K, usually Item 7, is an excellent source of this information. This is where a company's management is expected to reflect on the past year's activities and events, and discuss its direction for the next year. As the SEC has been placing greater accountability on management to monitor and disclose critical information about its organization, the MD&A section has become more substantive, informative, and revealing. Another source of future direction is the President's Letter to the Shareholder, traditionally a part of the company's annual report. While there is an increasingly large degree of duplication between the 10-K and the annual report, each contains unique information and so both should be consulted. Since virtually all public companies now post their SEC filings and annual reports on their Web sites, accessing this information has become very convenient.

A second source to plumb for the company's view of its future and accomplishments are its press releases. Again, these are almost always posted right on the Web site, generally in the same section, Investor Relations, as contains the SEC filings. While in some instances an organization's own press releases might be considered "biased," in this instance, it is this internal bias that is exactly what you want to tap.

Press releases, as a type of information source, are readily accessible on multiple electronic databases, including Factiva, LexisNexis, and OneSource. Oftentimes, however, these databases combine internal press releases and externally written wire stories, resulting in a lot of hits and the challenge of separating the two perspectives. *Business Wire* is a source which focuses on publishing company released press releases. Since it can be more efficient to access and download a number of stories using electronic databases versus viewing and outputting them one-by-one from a company Web site, try limiting your publication source to *Business Wire* to eliminate all the external wire stores. For example, in Factiva, you could try the following strategy: sn=businesswire and hl=American greetings.

RESEARCH RESULTS: In his Letter to the Shareholders, American Greetings' CEO communicates that in the past year the company reached its earnings projections and successfully restructured the organization. The restructuring accomplished three main goals: reducing the product line by one third, streamlining work processes to more nimbly bring new product lines to the retail outlet within weeks of the initial idea instead of months, and restructuring pricing to offer more inexpensive cards. On the finance side, the company completed debt refinancing and acquired BlueMountain.com, which bolstered its already existing Internet storefront at AmericanGreetings.com.

The MD&A echoed the comments from the President's Letter but in much greater detail, dedicating 15 pages to a more in-depth explanation of the restructuring initiative, segment profits, accounting changes, and other financial events. The last section contains some observations about the prospects for the year ahead. The outlook is conservative, calling for a year of stabilization coming off the restructuring. It reported that while sales could fall off on the retail end due to the soft economy, American Greetings has favorable contracts and other long-term agreements with big retailers that should serve to cushion the impact on the company if people do not buy as many cards as usual.

A very interesting press release, titled "American Greetings Announces Leadership Transition and Implementation of New Strategic Initiatives," discusses a significant organizational change on top of the restructuring of 2002. Halfway through the release, four key strategic initiatives are outlined: cut supply chain costs by $50–$75 million, continue to improve speed to market with new ideas, commit to growing the core social expression business, and adopt a performance-based evaluation program for employees.

SUMMARY OF SOLUTION: This is an unusual research problem in that researchers are usually cautioned against the positive bias that companies spin on themselves in their annual reports or other communication with shareholders. In this instance, however, that bias is exactly what you want to balance the external analysis of the company. Company Web sites can be designed to serve multiple purposes and oftentimes you have to persevere to locate the information about the organization's financial performance and strategic direction. Since American Greeting's Web site is focused primarily on promoting its online greeting card business line, it is not very apparent where to look for information about the parent company. If you scroll down to the very bottom of the home page, there is a very small link to the parent Web site. Clicking on this eventually leads you to the Investor Relations section, which is the source of the parent company information. It is very easy to get distracted by what a company is trying to sell or promote on its Web site; however, if it is a public parent company, be assured that complete financial information is there, somewhere!

Several additional sources that you can turn to glean insight from a company's management about the organization's outlook include:

- *Fair Disclosure.* These are transcripts of the "morning calls" between investment banking analysts and a company's top management. Typically the analyst will ask the officers a series of questions that are intended to draw out management's opinions about the company's financial, competitive, and strategic outlook. These transcripts typically run 10 to 15 pages and are excellent for gleaning insight into an organization. You can access these from Factiva by including the statement: sn=fair disclosure in your search statement.
- *The Wall Street Transcript.* This subscription-based service includes investment banking analyst interviews with the CEOs of public companies.

CONTRIBUTOR NAME: Brenda Reeb
AFFILIATION: University of Rochester

USEFUL TIPS

- Be sure to balance any research you do, considering information that is filtered through a number of channels, including the original source itself. With increasing pressure by the SEC for public companies to full disclosure, and in understandable language, any significant events impacting their organizations, a company's Web site, SEC filings, press releases, and annual reports have taken on a great importance and should not be taken casually.

PROBLEM NUMBER 24: RESEARCHING CUSTOMERS OF BEA SYSTEMS, A LARGE ENTERPRISE SOFTWARE COMPANY

RESEARCH BACKGROUND: Your client, a company similar to BEA, wants to increase its customer base and market share. As the senior partner on the audit engagement, you and several members of your firm's M&A practice have been asked to help the client develop a marketing strategy. As a first step, you have been asked to supply a customer list of BEA. Since this project is still in the preliminary stages, the partner does not want to invest too much in research and asked you to try and limit costs to $200.

RESEARCH STRATEGY EMPLOYED: Companies vary in the amount of customer intelligence they will make public. Some flaunt it; others hold it close to the vest. The quickest way to gauge BEA's philosophy about sharing this information is to start with its Web site. Hoping you can guess the URL, you type *http://www.beasystems.com* in the browser. You guessed wrong, with the address taking you to a Japanese company. Instead, you type "bea systems" in the browser address bar and are pointed to *http://www.bea.com.*

A quick scan of the site tells you that it is publicly traded; you make a mental note to check the annual report for a customer list. The site is very busy and at a quick glance, it is not too obvious where customer information might be located, so you decide to use the site's search engine and type "customers" in the box. The results are great, leading you directly to a very full page that focuses on the company's key customers. According to the introduction, BEA's customer count is more than 13,000 companies. The site provides options for browsing customers by industry, product, and Global Fortune 500 Number. Exploring a bit further, you click on the link to the Global Fortune 500 list and learn that it is organized using an A–Z format.

While the Global Fortune list represents a subset of the company's entire customer database, the other two lists are more complete and organize BEA customers into a series of industry and product subcategories. For example, the industry section is broken down into 14 categories with 10–60 companies in each category. Turning to the View by Product section, it is clear that the categories are designed to correspond with BEA products, allowing you to learn which companies use which products. The number of customers and categorization of them is far more extensive then you had anticipated. Usually you are lucky to find a short list you can simply print off. Not sure exactly which information would be useful for the partner, but guessing that it might be worth some staff time to read this section of the BEA site carefully, you decide to just print the Customer home page which describes the options for viewing customer lists and review it with the partner. In addition to the customer lists, there are also some glowing customer reviews included on the site. You print off a few examples of these as well to show to the partner.

Before leaving the site you turn to the Investor Relations section, hoping to locate BEA's annual report. You are surprised that it is not there since this has become a standard feature of so many public company Web sites. However, since your firm subscribes to Thomson Research, you quickly locate and download the .pdf version. Running a quick search in the Adobe search box brings up several sections dedicated to BEA's customers and, perhaps more important, some information about BEA's strategies for distinguishing itself from its competition. This should be very useful information for the client.

Both the company Web site and the annual report have produced excellent information about BEA's customers, in fact, much better than you could have even expected. But there remains one more step, and that is to locate some newspaper and trade journal articles. You are hoping to locate some additional intelligence about BEA's customers: Who are its largest customers; whom have they recently acquired; what do customers say about it (ideally, you would like to find some negative as well as positive comments); and does BEA have any corporate sponsors? Since you subscribe to Factiva, you construct a search using that interface, however LexisNexis or Dialog would have also been good choices to use.

Running a quick free-text search using keywords "BEA Systems" and "customer" in articles dating back two years yields way too many results. Since you already have so much good information, you decide to use a more focused approach. You limit all the keywords to the headline and lead paragraph (title and first two paragraphs), hoping that this approach will limit the results to articles in which these are the primary topics of discussion. Clicking the search button displays 250 articles and a quick scan of the first 15 tells you that the strategy worked.

For example, one article highlights a conference sponsored by BEA that showcases a dozen customers and the success they enjoyed thanks to BEA's software. Taking advantage of Factiva's ability to allow you to view and print articles using a "keyword in context" format, you decide on two output options. First, you print out the standard Factiva citation, which includes the title, date, source, and first sentence from the lead paragraph. This will ensure that the partner will see all of the returned articles. Second, you can view all 250 articles and select around 50 that you thought were especially useful, and you print those out using the "keyword in context" option.

SUMMARY OF SOLUTION: Identifying a company's customers can be very challenging because companies vary in the amount of customer information they reveal. In BEA's case, however, quite a bit of information was readily accessible directly on its Web site. Combing this information with a targeted database of business and news sources provided a substantive amount of competitive information about BEA's customers. Ideally, once the partner has completed reading the articles and identifying any customers with whom his firm has a relationship, he will have learned about BEA's strategies for customer relationship management and product support that he can share with the client to help develop a successful marketing campaign.

CONTRIBUTOR NAME: Brenda Reeb

AFFILIATION: University of Rochester

USEFUL TIPS

- When you come across information that you did not expect, take a break from the research and check back with the requestor to clarify what is needed. You cannot always anticipate everything when you initially discuss the project and so the "door" should always be left open for returning with additional questions or points of clarification. Better to ask before investing significant time and money.

PROBLEM NUMBER 25: LOCATE ESTIMATED FINANCIAL PROJECTIONS FOR BP PLC

RESEARCH BACKGROUND: A senior accountant called you because he needs to present a comparison between his client's estimated financials and his major competitor. You explained to the senior that analyst reports cost approximately $10 per page, but that you can generally use a detailed Table of Contents to identify and pay for just the pages that are needed. He agrees with that strategy and allows you a budget of up to $200. He gives his approval to download the requested financial data as well as any analyst commentary that might explain the estimated projections. You also ask him if there are any particular analysts that he wants you to target, but he says no.

RESEARCH STRATEGY EMPLOYED: Investment banking analyst reports are available on many electronic databases, including Thomson Research (formerly known as Investext), OneSource, Dialog, and LexisNexis. Your firm has a contract with Thomson that allows you to search and scan a report's Table of Contents for free. The cost per page to view, print, or download a report is approximately $8–$10 per page, depending on the currency of the report. You have the option to select the entire report or any discreet pages.

Thomson's interface will allow you to conduct a search by company name and quickly display a list of all analyst reports for BP, sorted in reverse chronological order so that you can see the most recent reports first. Although Thomson's interface has a fairly powerful search engine, trying to locate this type of information by searching for keywords such as "estimated" or "projections" might actually return fewer results since the data is generally contained within tables that are not usually searchable. Rather, by taking advantage of Thomson's company name search option, you are sure to locate all the possible reports. Once the results list is displayed, you simply hone in on the substantive reports (generally more than pages) because these are the ones more likely to have estimated projections for the financial statements. After you have identified the report you want, it only takes a few minutes to select the desired pages and download them in .pdf.

Using this approach, you identify three reports that look favorable. Morgan Stanley's report on BP from February 12, 2003, contains estimated projections for the full financials, all captured on one page. Downloading the entire report would cost $150, but you only have to purchase two pages, the page with the projections plus the following page that contains the continuation of the analyst's commentary. From the same date, you found a report by Dresdner Kleinwort Wasserstein, a London-based investment banking firm. Page 18 contains its estimated projections, although they are reported in pounds. Since BP is a UK company, however, you decide this report might be useful and so you print two pages (tables plus analysis) and look up the exchange rate for the year-end date of the most recent financials so that the partner can calculate the necessary conversion.

One last report from A.G. Edwards, dated February 14, 2003, also looked promising. Its Table of Contents indicates that page 15 contains earnings, fundamentals, and operating budget data from 2002–2004. Unfortunately, the data is exactly as reported and not as detailed as you needed. However, purchasing the one page only cost you $10 so it was not a great loss and a useful lesson about "reading" the tables. In the future, you will try to only purchase reports or pages whose descriptions fit exactly what you need.

SUMMARY OF SOLUTION: Investment banking company research reports are extremely valuable and used by accountants on a regular basis for tracking commentary and forecasted projections on their client, their clients' peers, and overall performance within an industry. While they are not generally free, they are available through multiple electronic interfaces, some subscription-based and some pay-as-you go. To get the most bang for your buck, consider these strategies:

- Before committing to use an interface, make sure that each report contains a detailed Table of Contents which reports section headings and specific details about any graphs, tables, or charts, including number of years covered and the focus of the data (for example, "Estimated Projections, Income Statement and Balance Sheet, 2002–2007"). Also verify everything for which you will be charged. Ideally, the search and the browsing of the Table of Contents should be free; with you incurring a charge only to read, print, or output a page.
- Verify that all the reports are available in .pdf format.
- Find out exactly what type of information the requestors are interested in purchasing before you begin. The more you understand about what they *really* want to see (and remember, what they say they need is not always want they want), the smarter purchasing decision you can make. Also be sure to communicate the pricing structure with them. At $10 per page, this information can be extremely affordable.

CONTRIBUTOR NAME: Brenda Reeb

AFFILIATION: University of Rochester

PROBLEM NUMBER 26: RESEARCH HARRAH'S ENTERTAINMENT, INC.'S FUTURE OUTLOOK AND STRATEGIC DIRECTIONS

RESEARCH BACKGROUND: Julia, an accountant within the firm, is auditing a client in the gaming industry and wants to compare the client's level of risk with one of its major competitors. She asks you to obtain two to three examples of recent investment banking analyst reports for Harrah's Entertainment. The reports need to be timely, preferably within the last year or better yet within the last six months. You have obtained analyst reports for Julia before and she understands that you can purchase just the discreet pages that you need and so she gives you the discretion to select the content. If you have any questions about which information to select, you will e-mail Julia the report Table of Contents for her to review.

RESEARCH STRATEGY EMPLOYED: Since investment banking analyst reports are rarely available for free on the Web, you turn directly to Investext, one of the firm's subscription-based electronic databases. This is the largest aggregator of investment banking analyst reports, and one of the best resources for this type of information;

reports date back to 1982 and, more importantly, new reports are added daily.

Investext's search engine allows for quick company report access by entering the company name or ticker symbol. You prefer to use the ticker symbol because it is guaranteed to retrieve all the relevant company reports. You do not know the symbol off hand but Investext's search page includes an easy symbol look-up option. Typing in the name Harrah and clicking the Look Up link returns the ticker HET. Entering HET in the ticker symbol box displays all the reports on Harrah's, sorted in reverse chronological order.

Since Julia is looking for substantive discussion about Harrah's risk and strategic directions, you know you can pass right over the shorter reports. While not an exact science, it is a good rule-of-thumb that reports greater than approximately seven pages contain more in-depth discussion. The larger the report, the more detailed analyst commentary and financial analysis.

Scanning the list of reports, you eye a 15-page report called *Harrah's Entertainment, Inc.: 2003 Outlook Still Challenging, Buy for the Long Term* written by Deutsche Bank Securities two months ago. Clicking on the link to the title displays a detailed Table of Contents that includes both text-based analysis and financial and other types of tabular data. From the descriptions of each page, you have no problem determining which information is relevant to Julia's request. You click on the box next to five pages, select the View button to confirm the pages and the total cost ($10 per page), and then click on the button to download. Within a short time you have the five pages saved in .pdf. You also print out the Table of Contents just in case Julia decides she is interested in some additional information from the report. Returning to the list of reports, you repeat the process, identifying two more reports, each by different brokerage houses.

RESEARCH RESULTS: All three reports contained excellent analysis of Harrah's current and future risk and strategic directions. The Deutsche Bank report included a detailed commentary on the company's future based on its geographic diversity and strategic use of technology:

- p. 1: "We continue to believe longer-term value investors could be well rewarded, given the company's high returns on invested capital, strong management team, powerful brand equity and industry-leading technological capabilities."

- p. 3: "We think 2003 is likely to be a challenging year for Harrah's although the company's geographic diversity will continue to cushion soft results in some markets."
- p. 5: "The company plans to roll out an improved version of Total Rewards in 2003, which allow players to bank rewards. The company estimates each incremental 1% increase in the capture rate on players' gaming budgets contributes an incremental $70 million in revenues, or an incremental $0.10 per share."
- p. 11: "Harrah's credit statistics remain healthy, as leverage (debt-to-EBITDA) and EBITDA-to-interest were 3.5x and 4.6x respectively. Harrah's has roughly $1.35 million of debt outstanding under its revolving credit facility and commercial papers. We estimate that the company has approximately $350.0 million of borrowing capacity."

In addition to Investext, there are other electronic databases that contain analyst reports, including Factiva, LexisNexis, OneSource, and Morningstar. Each has different options for purchasing reports, such as "all-you-can-eat," flat rate, or pay-as-you-go. Be sure to ask the sales rep about all of the possible purchasing options and select the one that best fits your need for this type of information. Other issues to consider when subscribing to analyst reports:

- Is there an embargo period imposed on the release of the documents? If you need reports as soon as they are released by the brokers, you will want to subscribe to a service that does not delay release for several months.
- Do you require viewing the report in .pdf, which will approximate the original format, or will a text-based output suffice?

CONTRIBUTOR NAME: Kim Whalen

AFFILIATION: Emory University

USEFUL TIPS

- If paying additional fees for the analyst report is simply not an option, consider suggesting alternatives: Factiva's Company Quick Search page usually returns useful comparison reports from Media General Financial Services; search for Fair Disclosure transcripts using Factiva's search template to locate the text of morning calls between analysts and company management (sn=fair disclosure and hd=company name) or look for articles that contain CEO interviews or profiles (hd=company name or ceo name and hd=interview or profile). If you already subscribe to Factiva, all of these will likely be part of your subscription.

- Search newspapers and trade magazines for additional strategic information. A search combing keywords such as "risk," "outlook," "strategic," "future," or "strategy" can lead to useful and insightful company intelligence. Try combining these words with the names of some of the top brokerage houses (for example, Merrill Lynch, Goldman Sachs) and you might even locate some articles that glean key information from their reports.
- Though a long shot, check the company Web site for an analyst report. Some companies do post analyst reports.

PROBLEM NUMBER 27: LOCATE BIOGRAPHICAL INFORMATION ON THE TOP OFFICERS AND DIRECTORS OF WEGMAN'S FOOD MARKETS, INC.

RESEARCH BACKGROUND: Wegman's is a prospective client of your consulting company. Members of your company will meet with Wegman's top staff and directors for the first time in about a week and consultants at your company want all the biographical information that you can find on the top officers and directors. You have been provided with a list of all the names. Since the many efforts to engage the client have finally resulted in a face-to-face meeting, you are given the go-ahead to make an investment in the information needed for the research, with a spending cap of around $200.

RESEARCH STRATEGY EMPLOYED: There are really two information requirements you need to address. The first is to locate biographical information on Wegman's officers and directors. The second is the "who knows who" game, identifying what boards, committees, or organizations the officers and directors belong to where there might be a connection to someone in your organization.

Turning to the biographical-gathering portion, the first question you need to answer is whether Wegman's is public or private. The answer will give clear signals about where to look and how much information you can expect to find. Public companies almost always publish substantially more biographical information on management and directors than private companies. If Wegman's is public, you are certain of locating employment history and board membership information in its proxy statement and 10-K. As it turns out, Wegman's is a private, regional company in the Northeast. This eliminates the option of turning to SEC filings and assures you that you will have to work a bit harder to find biographical backgrounders, and the results will likely be uneven.

Company Web sites are often used as public relations tools, and as such may provide some interesting insights about how the organization wants to be perceived by employees and customers. A visit to the Wegman's Web site, however, reveals surprisingly thin information. On the About Us page, only two officers are even identified on the site, the CEO and the president. Photos are provided, but no significant biographical information is revealed. Reading the History section you learn that Wegman's is a family-run business and that both officers have worked for the company their entire lives, but the partners preparing for the meeting probably already know that.

Your options for locating information on this private company are now limited to a few standard research tools: *Standard & Poor's Register* (the Executives and Directors Volume) and the Dun & Bradstreet Million Dollar Database. These two reference tools are useful for filling in information about age, education, work history, board, and civic activities. There is no guarantee that the names will be included in these resources, and a check of both only turns up a few of the officers in D&B's Million Dollar Database. Even though Wegman's is a private company, its officers and directors might sit on public boards. You search each of the names using Thomson Research's SEC database (formerly Compact D/SEC). Unfortunately, there are no matches.

The last step is to run the names through newspapers and trade journals, using an electronic database such as Factiva or Lexis-Nexis. Search industry trade journals in case the company has been included in one of the many popular lists of private companies, such as Inc. or Forbes, or one created by a retail industry association or trade magazine. For private companies, it is especially important to tap local and regional newspapers, since these are often the richest repositories of information on private companies. Since Wegman's is located in Rochester, New York, you use Factiva's Source Browser function to target upstate New York newspapers. The results are encouraging, yielding information about Wegman's interest in philanthropic activities and sports events; the company sponsors the Buffalo Bills training camp and hosts an annual LPGA tournament. You also read out about the Wegman family's strong support of local private schools. Note that when conducting keyword searches for individual names, you should be careful to accommodate variations in the name, such as nicknames or middle names or initials. Look to the database's advanced search functions to learn how to effectively search for names.

RESEARCH RESULTS: Gathering together all the information you have found, you create a simple spreadsheet listing for each officer and director. In particular, you categorize Boards, Civic Activities, Sports, and Fraternal Organizations. You e-mail the spreadsheet along with the articles to the project partners, copying the Marketing Department and alerting it to the contact information in the spreadsheet. It will be the Marketing Department's job to try and fill in the "who knows who" part of the request. The department has a master database that contains the names, clients, and affiliations of each of the organization's professional staff. Hopefully, running the names of the Wegman's officers and director through the database, along with names of each of their affiliated boards and activities, will yield something.

CONTRIBUTOR NAME: Brenda Reeb
AFFILIATION: University of Rochester

USEFUL TIPS

* Explore all press releases, About Us, and About Our Company links in a company's site. Biographical information or trivial details about executives could be found in any of these sections and all must be reviewed.
* Create a simple spreadsheet to capture and organize biographical information as it is located.
* Company directories are commonly available in public libraries. Consider a quick trip to the closest library if your company lacks a directory source.

PROBLEM NUMBER 28: IDENTIFY ALL OF THE CORPORATE BOARDS OF WHICH MARTHA STEWART IS A MEMBER

RESEARCH BACKGROUND: A partner has asked you to identify the corporate boards on which Martha Stewart currently sits or was a member during 2002. She is working on a proposal to a client that she has been trying to engage for over a year. You learned that the client is very impressed with Ms. Stewart's business acumen and you are hoping that you might establish some networking contacts via her board assignments.

RESEARCH STRATEGY EMPLOYED: U.S. public companies disclose their board of directors information in their annual 10-K filings and proxy statements (DEF14A filings). Because of the need to conduct a keyword search (since you do not know which boards she currently sits on, you can not hone in on any particular company filings), you use a subscription-based filings service, LIVEDGAR. You log on to LIVEDGAR and select the Full Text Search option and enter the following search statement: martha w/2 stewart w/30 board w/2 director*; you also limit the time-frame to January 1, 2001–January 1, 2003, to catch companies that observe a fiscal vs. calendar year.

It is common (and recommended) practice to use a proximity connector between a person's first and last name to accommodate middle names or initials. Since it is impossible to anticipate if an individual's full, formal name or a shortened version is used, the proximity connector acts as a "catch all." The returned filings include both the 10-K and proxy statement, which is exactly what you would have expected since the information is typically repro-duced in both documents. Using the "keywords in context" option, you scan the documents to verify that they are disclosing Martha Stewart as a member of the company's board of directors rather than someone else who works for Martha Stewart Living Omnime-dia or who has other Martha Stewart connections. Remember, the portion of the filings that identify board members also typically includes biographical background, including work-related history. You cannot assume that even though they contain your keywords, the context matches your information query!

SUMMARY OF SOLUTION: A partner asked you to identify the corpo-rate boards on which Martha Stewart was a member in 2002. You performed a free-text search in LIVEDGAR and found that Martha Stewart sat on two corporate boards during that year—Revlon Inc. and Martha Stewart Living Omnimedia. If you subscribed to other electronic research databases containing SEC filings, such as LexisNexis, Mergent Online, or Thomson Research, you could have run a similar search using any of these products, all with successful results.

If you had been given absolutely no budget for conducting this research, could you have located the answer to the question using free sources? The answer is yes, probably. First, check Martha Stewart's company Web site. Since it is a public company, it very likely has the 10-K or even proxy statement posted on the site (look for the "Investor Relations" section). Better yet, it might have the officers and their bios posted in a section on "Management." Martha's bio should include the names of all of the boards that she sat on. If her Web site did not include this information, you could use a free EDGAR site, such as SEC (*http://www.sec.gov*) or SEC Info (*http://www.secinfo.com*), access the 10-K and proxy statements for 2002 and either use a hyperlinked Table of Contents of the Edit/Find features on the Menu bar to jump to the relevant sections.

That said, there is a chance that you might miss some important information by relying on these filings. Why? What if Ms. Stewart had joined a company's board after her company's 10-K or proxy statement was filed with the SEC? What if the information on her Web site was not updated to reflect any change in her board activity? The bottom line is that you have to do the best you can with the budget constraints you are given, but it is still important to be aware of the possible pitfalls and communicate them to the requestor so that he or she can make an informed decision about the potential consequences of missing information.

CONTRIBUTOR NAME: Jan Rivers

AFFILIATION: Dorsey & Whitney LLP

USEFUL TIPS

- SEC filing resources, such as LIVEDGAR or 10k Wizard, only include public companies. You will not find information about private company boards.
- Boards of directors members are also listed in a company's 10-K filing or annual report to shareholders. Sometimes the 10-K will refer readers to the company's annual report or proxy statement rather than reproduce the actual list of members. Sometimes, the annual report is attached to a company's 10-K's Exhibit 13. 10-Ks with an attached annual report exhibit frequently are labeled as 10-K405 filings.
- Although very infrequent, it is possible that a person whose name appears on a proxy statement as a candidate for a company's board may not have been approved by shareholder vote. You can verify this by looking at the company's subsequent 10-Q, 10-K or annual report to verify if the person was actually elected to the board. In general, this step is not necessary.

• Standard & Poor's Register in print and electronic format also contains this type of information, but it may not be current enough to reflect recently elected members to the board.

PROBLEM NUMBER 29: HOW MUCH DID THE CEO OF SUN MICROSYSTEMS MAKE LAST YEAR? WHAT BENEFITS AND PERKS WERE INCLUDED IN HIS CONTRACT?

RESEARCH BACKGROUND: Lisa's boss, Tom, is making a humorous speech to a community group later this week and he wants to draw a quick comparison between himself (CEO of a small software company) and the CEO of Sun Microsystems. Tom has a small discretionary budget line for community service. Lisa needs to keep the total cost below $50.

RESEARCH STRATEGY EMPLOYED: Lisa knows that publicly traded companies like Sun must file executive compensation information with the SEC every year. Today most government agencies provide information via the Web, and the SEC is no exception. SEC filings since 1993 are available on the SEC home page. Detailed information pertaining to management compensation is contained in the filing popularly referred to as the proxy statement. Lisa uses a popular search engine, Google, to quickly locate the URL for the SEC home page (*http://www.sec.gov*).

Fortunately, Sun Microsystems is a unique and straightforward company name so it is easy to locate filings for the correct company. Lisa queries the SEC site for Sun Microsystems and retrieves a list of all the filings. A tricky detail to note is that proxy statements are officially called Form DEF-14A. The filings are all available in both HTML and text; Lisa selects the HTML version because it contains hyperlinked internal document navigation. Proxies typically run more than 40 pages in length and using internal document navigation saves time digging through the lengthy document. Clicking on the link to the most recent report displays a page with rather unattractive formatting and series of links to different documents. Caught a bit off-guard and unsure which link to select, Lisa decides to approach this systematically and begins by clicking on the link to Document 1. She is in luck! (The other choices contain signature files or exhibit files which are common addendums to the proxy statement but are irrelevant to these particular questions.)

Scrolling down to access the hyperlinked Table of Contents, Lisa scans the document sections and clicks on the link to Executive Compensation. Almost immediately she finds a table containing all of the information she needs—the compensation of the top five Sun executives: Scott G. McNeally is listed first, with his CEO title confirmed. His salary is a mere $100,000 for 2002, with a bonus of $487,500. Other compensation is listed at $59,964, which is footnoted as personal use of corporate aircraft. According to the Long Term Compensation section, he received $3,500,200 in stock options, a significant amount and more than the other four executives.

Lisa was expecting a salary figure of several million dollars, and she realizes that the stock options package is where this value is located, not in McNeally's base salary of $100,000. Unwilling to take the time to calculate the stock options, Lisa shifts her approach to this research problem and "guesses" that the total value of McNeally's package has probably already been calculated and published in the business press.

Her company subscribes to Factiva, so she runs the following keyword search in the free text box: "mcneally and sun and salary"; almost immediately she finds a short article published in *USA Today* on October 1, 2002, that reports McNeally's total package is valued at more than $87 million. The article mentions the $100,000 base salary, bonuses, even the personal use of corporate aircraft, and it briefly explains how the stock options bring the value to $87 million. Lisa prints the article and returns to the proxy to print pages 21–22 which include the compensation chart and footnotes. She delivers both to her boss' inbox within 25 minutes of beginning her search.

SUMMARY OF SOLUTION: Lisa's prior knowledge of SEC filings saved her a great deal of time solving this research problem. While it is somewhat common knowledge that public companies file compensation information with the SEC, it is less known that the information is located in the proxy filing, or that very important bit of information about the official name of the filing. The SEC home page contains a link to Descriptions of SEC forms; however this section is less than fully descriptive and does not even connect the executive compensation information with the proxy. Many people assume that the information will be found in the 10-K because it details the company's financial picture. Fortunately, the 10-K will likely contain a reference to the proxy as the source of the detailed compensation information.

While there are many options for locating SEC filings, both on the free and fee-based databases, relying on the free Web to locate press is highly problematic: running a search in Google for: "mcneally sun compensation salary" results in near misses. Another approach, using Sun's own home page, proves not much more helpful. There is a link to the proxy statement and a hopeful link to company press releases, but no revealing article was to be found. Perhaps not totally unexpected since companies often "select" the news they chose to post on their Web sites. While management salaries are not necessarily bad news, recent scandals surrounding executive take-home pay has made this a rather hot button and therefore companies are not inclined to voluntarily provide the level of user-friendly details Lisa found in the *USA Today* article. You are ensured of better and quicker results using subscription-based services, such as Factiva and LexisNexis, both of which allow for targeted keyword searches.

CONTRIBUTOR NAME: Brenda Reeb
AFFILIATION: University of Rochester

USEFUL TIPS

- Use a free search engine, such as Google (*http://www.google.com*), to quickly locate the SEC home page. Simply entering the keywords: "sec filing" pushes out links to several excellent. The free sites frequently modify their Web design so it is worth checking periodically to see if they offer features or improvements in searching or ways to document results such as printing select pages or e-mailing documents.
- When confronted with complex information in the "official source," look to the business news for friendlier, often interpretative, summaries. Give both pieces of information, primary and secondary, to the client.
- Customize what you deliver to the client to suit its needs. If the client really only needs to see some discreet information and does not need an entire document, send the information in a format that will best suit its needs and time constraints. Printing out a 40-plus-page document—and having to scan it—when all you needed were a few pages, may undercut the effort and resourcefulness it took for you to locate the information.

PROBLEM NUMBER 30: RESEARCHING THE BACKGROUND OF A PUBLIC COMPANY CEO

RESEARCH BACKGROUND: The head of the Corporate Finance group left you a voice-mail this morning requesting that you gather some articles "profiling" Scott McNeally, the CEO of Sun Microsystems. He is preparing for a meeting that will take place in two days and needs the articles by the end of today.

RESEARCH STRATEGY EMPLOYED: Gathering a "profile" on McNeally could mean a lot of different things, such as understanding his views on the future of Sun or the technology industry in general, or learning more about the success of his company and his leadership style. McNeally is an extremely visible CEO, and so you decide to start the research by turning to Sun's Web site. The Executive Perspective section contains a huge number of articles about McNeally. Some are internally generated press releases; many are articles from external business, finance, and news sources, such as *Forbes* and the *Washington Post*, while others are the transcripts of speeches that McNeally has made at technology conferences and on college campuses. He appears to be a very popular speaker! The articles offer a tremendous amount of insight into this man, his technology vision for the future, and his personal opinions about a range of subjects.

The results are so good that you are tempted to stop there but you don't want to limit the research to looking at his company's Web site. Besides, it was not too hard to guess that Sun would likely only post articles that viewed its CEO in a favorable light. It was time to dig up some alternate viewpoints.

Logging on to Factiva, you try two different search approaches. You are interested in reading an investment analyst report on Sun, but are hesitant to spend a lot of money purchasing individual reports since you already have so much good information on McNeally. Factiva's Company Profiles always includes at least one analyst report, so you click on the link to that section of the database and access a very substantive and interesting report by Lehman Brothers. Most of the report views McNeally in a favorable light, but there are some interesting passages that reflect on a few of his "visions" which failed to materialize. You save the report in .pdf.

The second approach is to conduct a keyword search in the Factiva database. Your strategy takes into consideration the following: McNeally is an unusual name, so you can probably get away with just searching on the last name, combined with Sun. There are going to be a great many occurrences of his name in the press so you need to use search functions which will narrow down the field to the most substantive discussions. Based on that, you decide to run two different searches:

- hlp=(mcneally and (interview or profile or future or outlook)) and sun and wc>900
- hlp=mcneally and (gartner or yankee or forrester or idc or Jupiter) and (outlook or predict$ or forecast$ or future)

The first search will retrieve substantive articles (word count of greater than 900 words) that mention McNeally and are labeled either interview or profile in the headline and/or lead paragraph. The second search looks for mention of McNeally by one of the larger IT market research analysts. You run both searches, scan the results, and locate about a dozen articles that were not posted on Sun's Web site, several of which provide a different "slant" on McNeally. All together, you have saved about 20 articles. While this is generally more than a requestor might want, you feel confident, based on your discussion with Sally and Mary, that the project team will want to read all of them in full text.

SUMMARY OF SOLUTION: There are several good strategy insights to be gleaned from this assignment:

- Requests for "profiles," whether it is for a company or individual, should always raise a red flag. Exactly what is the requestor really looking for? Make sure to clarify the context and the intent for gathering the information before you invest time and money. Profile requests can be lengthy and expensive; you want to make sure you get it right the first time.
- Always check the CEO's company Web site. Don't assume that it will only contain the obvious information.
- When using a large electronic database, such as Factiva, develop a search strategy that allows you to hone in exactly what you are looking for. Take advantage of the database's advanced search techniques, such as limiting words to the headline or lead paragraph and focusing on larger articles, in order to yield the best results.

CONTRIBUTOR NAME: Brenda Reeb

AFFILIATION: University of Rochester

USEFUL TIPS

- When looking for articles which report on a high-profile individual, search for the following keywords in the headline and/or lead paragraph: "profile, interview, outlook, forecast, future."
- When the individual's name is unusual, just search for the last name. When you must also use the first name, take into consideration nicknames, middle name or initial, and use advanced search strategies to accommodate these variations.

PROBLEM NUMBER 31: HOW WILL "CORPORATE GOVERNANCE" PROPOSED LEGISLATION POTENTIALLY IMPACT ACCOUNTING STANDARDS?

RESEARCH BACKGROUND: You are a staff accountant at a regional accounting firm. You were asked by your boss to lead a discussion on corporate governance and its potential impact on the accounting industry during the company's next staff meeting. Your boss has asked that you only use free sources for this assignment.

RESEARCH STRATEGY EMPLOYED: You believe that both the AICPA Web site and the SEC Web site would cover this topic since you have been monitoring the news regarding distressed public companies and potential new government regulation.

Featured on the AICPA's home page (*http://www.aicpa.org*) is a section called Spotlight Area, which contains links to discussion on hot issues. The first reference is to Sarbanes-Oxley Act/PCAOB Implementation Central. You click on the link and find a goldmine of information: links to the proposed legislation and related SEC documents and AICPA featured articles and discussion on the topic and its impact on the industry. Examples include: "How the Sarbanes-Oxley Act of 2002 impacts the Accounting Profession" and "Summary of the Sarbanes-Oxley Act." You also decide to check the SEC site (*http://www.sec.gov*) directly, in case there is some additional, useful information that was not linked to from AICPA site. A link to Auditor Independence on the home page leads you to some additional information.

To draw on some alternate viewpoints for your presentation, you try to find additional information by conducting a search using Google (*http://www.google.com*); you use the following keyword strategy "corporate governance." Scanning the results you immediately notice a link to the title Encycogov—The Encyclopedia about Corporate Governance. Intrigued, you go to the site. The topic "What Is Corporate Governance" takes you to several definitions of the phrase from some different sources. Following are a few of them:

- "Corporate governance is the system by which business corporations are directed and controlled. The corporate governance structure specifies the distribution of rights and responsibilities among different participants in the corporation, such as, the board, managers, shareholders and other stakeholders, and spells out the rules and procedures for making decisions on corporate affairs. By doing this, it also provides the structure through which the company objectives are set, and the means of attaining those objectives and monitoring performance."— OECD April 1999.
- "Corporate governance—which can be defined narrowly as the relationship of a company to its shareholders or, more broadly, as its relationship to society . . . ."—from an article in *Financial Times* [1997].
- "Corporate governance is about promoting corporate fairness, transparency and accountability."—J. Wolfensohn, president of the World Bank, as quoted by an article in *Financial Times*, June 21, 1999.

Returning to the results of your Google search, you also decided to read a speech by Alan Greenspan on March 26, 2002. While very interesting, you would still like to find more information on the recent legislation so you "tweak" your search strategy and add the term "legislation" and rerun the search. The new approach yielded several new sources of information: LeBoeuf, Lamb, Greene & MacRae LLP, a large law firm (*http://www. llgm.com*) posted an article, "President Signs Corporate Governance and Accounting Reform: Overview and analysis of Sarbanes-Oxley Act," and Piercy, Bowler, Taylor & Kern, an accounting firm, (*http://www.pbtk.com/new/accounting*) linked you to "Landmark Legislation Address Corporate Governance, Accountability." After reviewing all of the sources you have gathered, you believe that you have the material you need to prepare for your presentation.

RESEARCH RESULTS: The Public Company Accounting Reform and Investor Protection (Sarbanes-Oxley) Act of 2002 was signed into law by the president in July 2002. Intending to rebuild investor confidence, the act covers, among other things, corporate ethics and responsibility, financial disclosures, fraud, audit committees, audit oversight, and auditor independence. The act has been characterized as the most sweeping congressional lawmaking ever in the field of corporate governance. The following are excerpts from the article: "How the Sarbanes-Oxley Act of 2002 Impacts the Accounting Profession" from *http://www.aicpa.org:*

- *"How the Sarbanes-Oxley Act of 2002 Impacts the Accounting Profession.* On July 30, 2002, President Bush signed into law the Sarbanes-Oxley Act of 2002. The Act—which applies in general to publicly held companies and their audit firms—dramatically affects the accounting profession and impacts not just the largest accounting firms, but any CPA actively working as an auditor of, or for, a publicly traded company." *Some* of the basic implications of the Act for accountants are summarized below.

- "Public Company Accounting Oversight Board. Moving to a different private sector regulatory structure, a new Public Company Accounting Oversight Board (the Board) will be appointed and overseen by the SEC. The Board, made up of five full-time members, will oversee and investigate the audits and auditors of public companies, and sanction both firms and individuals for violations of laws, regulations and rules."

- "Board Composition. Two of the five Board members must be or must have been CPAs. The remaining three must not be and cannot have been CPAs. The Chair may be held by one of the CPA members, but he or she must not have practiced accounting during the five years preceding his/her appointment."

- "Standard Setting. The Board will issue standards or adopt standards set by other groups or organizations, for audit firm quality controls for the audits of public companies. These standards include: auditing and related attestation, quality control, ethics, independence and 'other standards necessary to protect the public interest.' The Board has the authority to set and enforce audit and quality control standards for public company audits."

- *"Investigative and Disciplinary Authority.* The Board is empowered to regularly inspect registered accounting firms' operations and will investigate potential violations of securities laws, standards, competency and conduct. Sanctions may be imposed for non-cooperation, violations, or failure to supervise a partner or employee in a registered accounting firm. These include revocation or suspension of an accounting firm's registration, prohibition from auditing public companies, and imposition of civil penalties. During investigations, the Board can require testimony or document production from the registered accounting firm, or request information from relevant persons outside the firm. Investigations can be referred to the SEC, or with the SEC's approval, to the Department of Justice, state attorneys general or state boards of accountancy under certain circumstances."

Source: *http://www.aicpa.org*, "How the Sarbanes-Oxley Act of 2002 Impacts the Accounting Profession," 2002. Go to the AICPA Web site to review the entire article. Copyright © 2002 by the American Institute of Certified Public Accountants, Inc. Reprinted with the permission of the publisher.

CONTRIBUTOR NAME: Michelle Hartstrom
AFFILIATION: Columbia Financial Advisors, Inc.

USEFUL TIPS

- Bookmark these Web sites for future use: *http://www.aicpa.org*, *http://www.encycogov.com*, *http://www.federalreserve.com*, and *http://www.sec.gov*.

PROBLEM NUMBER 32: HOW DOES THE UNITED KINGDOM'S ACCOUNTING STANDARDS COMPARE WITH U.S. GENERALLY ACCEPTED ACCOUNTING PRINCIPLES?

RESEARCH BACKGROUND: A staff accountant has asked you to review the differences between U.S. Generally Accepted Accounting Principles (GAAP) and England's accounting standards. He would like you to supply him with a side-by-side comparison, if one is available, or tell him where he can obtain this information online. He is about to take on a new audit client who has a strong presence in the United Kingdom. This is his first international client and he wants to make sure that he is prepared to follow the correct disclosure requirements. You can spend up to $200 on this request and he would like the information by the end of the week.

RESEARCH STRATEGY EMPLOYED: Most countries follow both their own accounting standards as well as international accounting standards set forth by the International Accounting Standards Board (IASB). You will first need to locate the accounting standards used in England and then determine how these standards compare with U.S. GAAP. To do this, you decide to consult the *Aspen-Miller European Accounting Guide*. The *Aspen-Miller Guides* are a well-recognized standard in the industry, providing timely and relevant contextual discussion of both U.S. and international accounting standards. Published annually, the editions are still available in print but they are also now available via several electronic databases, such as CCH Tax Network and LexisNexis. These are so frequently used that you subscribe to the *U.S. GAAP Guide* for your print library each year. Unfortunately, you do not have the print version of the *European Guide*, but your subscription to LexisNexis will provide you with quick access in lieu of using the print.

In LexisNexis the Aspen-Miller Guides are located in the Legal Library; clicking on Area of Law by Topic, choosing Accounting, then Miller, displays links to each of the individual titles; you click on the link to the Aspen-Miller European Accounting Guide. A hyperlinked detailed Table of Contents makes it easy to browse the sections and quickly locate the one on the United Kingdom. Quickly browsing the section, you learn that the United Kingdom utilizes both UK GAAP and International Accounting Standards requirements. Unfortunately, there is no side-by-side comparison available. In addition, you are concerned that the information may be dated since the edition of the Miller Guide in LexisNexis is from 1999.

You download the section anyway, and rethink your strategy. Fortunately, the Aspen-Miller Guide mentioned the Institute of Chartered Accountants in England and Wales and included the URL to its Web site (*http://www.icaew.co.uk*). Taking the cue, you access the site and, with a little bit of exploration, find a page containing links to information about the standards used in England and Wales. Following a link to GAAP, you discover a full-text survey of the national accounting rules in 62 countries that contains an overview of the differences between local written rules and the International Accounting Standards. A 2002 update to the study, "GAAP Convergence 2002," is available on the site and it includes both the United Kingdom and the United States.

Additional links on the site lead you to a comparative guide published by PricewaterhouseCoopers of the IAS, U.S. GAAP, and UK GAAP. This guide is from 2001 and is downloadable in .pdf format. Another link is to KPMG's "Global Accounting UK, IAS and US Compared," the comparison and summary of which are downloadable for free in .pdf from KPMG UK's Web site (*http://www.kpmg.co.uk/kpmg/uk/IMAGE/compUS_2000.pdf*). There is also a reference to a print publication, *Ernst & Young's UK/US GAAP Comparison*, containing more than 720 pages of topic-by-topic, side-by-side comparisons. Additional links on the home page include additional UK accounting-related information, such as sources for International Accounting Standards, commentaries, and summaries of Financial Reporting Standards (FRS), sources for Statements of Standard Accounting Practice (SSAPs) and Statements of Recommended Practice (SORPs), and more.

SUMMARY OF SOLUTION: The *Aspen-Miller GAAP* series of guides is an excellent starting place for understanding GAAP, both U.S. and international. Just as the United States has its own standard-setting boards, the Institute of Chartered Accountants plays a similar role for the European countries, and turning to its site was a logical approach. It yielded excellent free information and included citations to some print resources that might be a valuable contribution to your collection, especially if your firm is going to take on more international clients.

CONTRIBUTOR NAME: Jan Rivers

AFFILIATION: Dorsey & Whitney LLP

USEFUL TIPS

- Some countries' accounting standards are referred to as GAAP, such as UK GAAP or German GAAP; however, not all countries use this term.
- A country's main accounting association is frequently a good resource for information about its accounting principles and standards. Some information may be fee-based, however, or for members only.
- Major international accounting firm Web sites are also good resources of information and publications on accounting topics. Expect to find both free and for-pay publications.

PROBLEM NUMBER 33: DETERMINE PUBLIC COMPANY MARKET SHARE FOR THE BIG FOUR ACCOUNTING FIRMS IN THE SOUTHEAST

RESEARCH BACKGROUND: The director of marketing is working on a promotional piece for some of your firm's biggest clients in the Southeast region and he is hoping to include a graphic which indicates that your firm has the largest percentage of market share for auditing public companies in the Southeastern states. He would like you to create a spreadsheet that would support this.

RESEARCH STRATEGY EMPLOYED: Right away you know that a product called SEC (formerly Compact D/SEC) by Thomson Research is the best database to use. It only includes U.S. public parent companies and you can query on the name of the auditor and also output the information into an Excel spreadsheet. All the other necessary search criteria can be easily accommodated using the search interface.

Before running the search, you call the director to verify the search criteria and to discuss what fields to display in the spreadsheet. First you need to know how he was defining the Southeast. He clarified that the states were: Alabama, Florida, Georgia, Kentucky, Louisiana, Mississippi, North Carolina, and South Carolina. You also asked if he wanted to limit the companies by any additional criteria such as sales or industry. His response was no, he wanted to search as broadly as possible to come up with the largest possible number of companies.

With a clear understanding of the search criteria and the output data elements, you log onto Thomson and connect to the SEC application. The search interface is very flexible and allows for maximum customization and manipulation of data. You select Geographic Area/State Code and select each of the required states. You then select More Search Options, Auditor, Auditor Name, and select each of the Big Four firms. When you click the Enter button, the database combines the two criteria, and the result is a total of 971 public companies in the Southeast that are audited by one of the Big Four firms.

Now that you have the returned results, you need to create the report. Clicking on Display and User Defined Reports, you select the data elements to appear in a spreadsheet: Company Name, State, Sales, Industry, and Auditor Name. You save the report in .csv format and five minutes later you are viewing the results in Excel, which you forward to the marketing director via e-mail.

RESEARCH RESULTS: The marketing director was thrilled when he opened the spreadsheet, sorted by Auditor, and calculated the results. Your firm ranked #1, with 42 percent of the market share for your region. Resorting the data by Industry, he also saw that the firm ranked #1 in the Financial Institutions and Textiles industries. The rankings by auditor and industry would both make excellent graphics for the marketing piece he was developing. In addition, he forwarded the data reported for each industry to the office's managing partner for use in the spring when they begin developing target company sales lists. The industries in which the company ranked #2–#4 were potential targets for the partners heading those industry teams.

SUMMARY OF RESULTS: There are very few databases that can be used for gathering auditor market share data, and when targeting public companies, none is as facile as Thomson Research's SEC. The only other alternative is Dun & Bradstreet's Million Dollar Database, but the search engine is awkward and the output very problematic; you can only download 100 records at a time and you cannot select to view only the data elements that you need. It takes much longer to download the results into Excel and then you must take the time to delete the cells you do not want.

CONTRIBUTOR NAME: Susan M. Klopper
AFFILIATION: Goizueta Business Library

USEFUL TIPS

- When evaluating company databases, such as Thomson Research's SEC or Dun's Million Dollar Database, carefully consider your specific applications for the data and then verify if the options for selecting search criteria and output data elements fit your need. The combination of these factors is just as important, if not more, than the content contained within the database. If the content is on point, but you cannot access, manipulate, or output it in a way that will meet your information needs, its cost-to-value ratio is considerably altered.

PROBLEM NUMBER 34: WHO WERE THE AUDITORS FOR MICROSOFT, IBM, AND GEORGIA PACIFIC IN 2000 AND WHAT WERE THEY PAID?

RESEARCH BACKGROUND: A risk management partner has asked you to locate the names of the auditors and the fees they generated in 2000 for attest work performed for Microsoft, IBM, and Georgia Pacific. He is working on a proposal to each of the companies, hoping to successfully bid to become their new auditor. You can spend up to $200 on this request, but given the potential size of these engagements, you are authorized to spend more if absolutely necessary. Since time is of the essence, and the partner has confidence in your research skills, you are given an additional discretionary spending budget of $500.

RESEARCH STRATEGY EMPLOYED: The SEC approved a new rule on November 15, 2000, mandating that all public companies must disclose the amount of audit fees they pay their auditors in their proxy statements. This rule was made effective for proxies filed beginning with February 5, 2001.

You start with the SEC's Web site (*http://www.sec.gov*) and click on the Search for Company Filings link under Filings & Forms (EDGAR). This takes you to the SEC's EDGAR database of company filings. Once on the EDGAR search page, you enter one of the company names in the search box. You can only search for one company at a time. Running this search results in a list of all its filings sorted in reverse chronological order. Note that you should only enter the main portion of the company name. Never search for company endings, such as corporation, corp. co, and company. These are typically entered inconsistently across databases and searching for these will likely result in poor search results.

Let's start with Microsoft. The returned results list contains hundreds of filings. Fortunately, there is a "Filing Type" box located on the upper-right corner of the results page that allows you to limit the results by document type. Since you know that auditor fees are a required disclosure in proxy statements, you enter that filing's "official" name, DEF 14A. You MUST enter a space between the DEF and the 14A for the search to work. Proxy statements are DEF 14A filings, officially called Definitive Notice & Proxy Statement. If you do not know the "official" name of the filing, go to the SEC's home page. It has a link to Descriptions to SEC Forms that contains very useful information about filing names and purpose.

Now that the filings have been pruned down to just proxy statements, you can quickly hone in on the filings for 2000 and 2001. Microsoft's filing schedule is tricky because it operates on a fiscal financial, not a calendar year. Therefore, its financial year crosses over more than one calendar year. Since Microsoft's 2000 proxy preceded the February 5, 2001, SEC start date for audit fee disclosures, it did not contain any audit fee information. It does, however, state that Microsoft's auditor for fiscal year 2000 was Deloitte Touche. The following year's proxy statement, filed in October 2001, does contain the audit fee data that the partner requested.

You print out the relevant sections of both proxy statements for the risk management partner and repeat the same search steps for IBM and Georgia Pacific. For IBM you will have to enter the complete company name, International Business Machines, to retrieve its filings. Both IBM and Georgia Pacific have calendar financial years, so you decide to retrieve the audit fee data for both 2000 and 2001 for both companies to more closely approximate what was available for Microsoft. Once again, you print out the relevant sections for both companies, and since it will only take a few minutes and will save the partner time, you quickly input the requested data into a table and include that in the e-mail you send him with the search results.

RESEARCH RESULTS: If Microsoft had a calendar year end of December 31, its proxy statement for 2000 would have been filed in March or April of 2001, past the SEC's effective date requiring full disclosure of audit fee data. However, since it observed a fiscal year end instead, the proxy statement was filed in September 2000 and did not include the requested information. However, it did state that Deloitte Touche was Microsoft's auditor. The proxy statement for fiscal 2001, filed in October 2001, states Microsoft paid Deloitte $4,742,000 in audit fees for fiscal 2001.

In 2000, IBM paid PricewaterhouseCoopers $12.2 million in audit fees and Georgia Pacific's audit fees paid to Arthur Andersen LLP were $1,975,000.

CONTRIBUTOR NAME: Jan Rivers
AFFILIATION: Dorsey & Whitney LLP

USEFUL TIPS

- Audit fees were not required to be disclosed to the public until February 5, 2001, and so information previous to that date may not be available.
- When using SEC filing databases that allow for keyword searching, such as LexisNexis, LIVEDGAR, or 10k Wizard, searching for the phrase "audit fees" within proxy statements will usually lead you to that relevant disclosure within the filing.
- When searching by company name in an SEC database (or other types of databases), you may be required to enter the company's "legal" name (for example, International Business Machines for IBM) to access good results.

- Remember that companies may operate on fiscal vs. calendar years. You can generally "glean" this intelligence by looking at the filing date for the 10-K.

PROBLEM NUMBER 35: FIND SALARY INFORMATION FOR FINANCIAL ANALYSIS PROFESSIONALS IN THE SOUTHEAST

RESEARCH BACKGROUND: You are a financial analysis manager currently employed at a private company in Atlanta, Georgia. You have several years of experience in this position and you were recently offered a position in Charlotte, North Carolina. You decide to evaluate the market salaries for both regions. This is a personal research project and you decide to keep the costs to a minimum.

RESEARCH STRATEGY EMPLOYED: This is your first attempt at a market comparison and you decide to begin by using Google to get a feel for the resources that might be available via the Web. You look for potential sites by typing in some search terms. You also consult a few of your colleagues and they suggest a site called *http://www.salary.com*. In addition, you go to Google and type "southeast region and accounting salaries." After reviewing the sites listed, you decide to check the following listings: *http:// www.recruitersworld.com*, *http://www.jobsinthemoney.com*, and *http:// www.careerbuilder.com*.

Starting with the home page of *http://www.recruitersworld.com*, you select the option for compensation surveys. Scanning the site and clicking on the link to Accounting, Finance and Engineering surveys, you realize that the data, although appearing to be right on point, is based on a Midwest sample and is for purchase only. You decide to move on in hopes of locating some free data that you can use. Next, clicking on the link to *http://www.jobsinthemoney.com*, you investigate the options under View Financial Salary Guides. You notice one option is Cost of Living. This could be very useful in comparing relative salary levels since employers often apply a cost of living adjustment to salaries depending in which city an employee is located. Clicking on Cost of Living, the next screen asks you to select From State and To State. You select Georgia and North Carolina. Next you type in your current salary and city and the city you to which you are relocating. It also asks you if you are planning to own or rent, and you look at both choices. The results indicate that if you make $100,000 in Atlanta, you will need to make approximately $85,000 in Charlotte if you own your home. If you rerun the data assuming that you will rent in Charlotte, the results indicate your new salary will have to match your current Atlanta compensation. That represents a significant difference and is useful information for negotiating purposes.

Pleased with the data that this provided, you continue on, clicking on the link to Finance and Accounting located at the top of the page beneath the heading for Links to Financial Salary Tables. This link takes you to data gathered by Creative Financial Staffing (CFS). The data presents some national salary levels for various accounting and finance positions by years of experience and includes cost of living adjustments. For example, the salary guide for 2001 indicates a controller made $93,250 on a national average. This data would be adjusted by a factor of 102.3 percent for Atlanta and 98.3 percent for Charlotte. All very useful information.

Still interested in obtaining more comparative data, you proceed to the next site from Google, *http://www.careerbuilder.com.* You click the tab Advice & Resources and under a link to Career Resources, you click on Salary Information. There are several options of salary and cost of living data available; selecting Salary Expert, you choose the job title of "Financial Analysis Manager" and your location of "Atlanta, Georgia." According to the data, the median salary for this position is approximately $70,000 and the median total compensation is $86,000. You repeat this information for Charlotte, North Carolina. The median salary for this position is approximately $72,000 and the median total compensation is $88,000.

Recalling that your colleagues had recommended another site, you turn your attention to *http://www.salary.com.* Clicking on Personal Edition, selecting Financial Services, the location of Atlanta, Georgia, you then chose the job description for Financial Analysis Manager. A very helpful option allows you to verify the job description to ensure that it is an accurate match. Clicking on the tab of Create Basic Salary Report tells you that the median base salary is approximately $76,000; if you include bonuses (another negotiating tactic!), the median income is raised to $81,000. One nice feature of this site is the presentation of three tabs of data: salary, bonuses, and benefits. Each page presents income broken out by 25th percentile, median, and 75th percentile. The benefit data presents the median data broken out in the detail of total compensation. Running a comparison of this data tells you that the median salary for a financial analysis manager in Charlotte is $75,000, and an approximate total salary of $80,000 if you include bonuses.

At this same Web site you click on a link for Cost of Living Wizard located on the left frame. You enter your current salary and your current living and work locations and the proposed living and work locations. Next you select Calculate. The data reported tells you that the cost of living is 1.6 percent lower in Charlotte and employers typically pay 1.2 percent lower in Charlotte, compared to Atlanta. The report indicates that you may receive a slight pickup in disposable income by moving to Charlotte if you are compensated in this manner. The options of selecting both the cities in which you live and work allow for greater accuracy in estimating the appropriate cost of living adjustment.

Although you are satisfied with your search results, you decide to take the search one step further and you go the Web site for Robert Half/Accountemps (*http://www.rhii.com*). Coincidently, you had worked on an engagement that involved helping the client's HR department set salary ranges for its internal accounting department and you recall that this was a valuable source of data. However, you could not remember if the information was available for free. Well, it was! This company publishes an annual Salary Guide that contains both national and regional salaries for a range of accounting and finance-related positions, and the regional data includes data adjusted for local variances. The guide is available for free on the Web site, and in fact, both Atlanta and Charlotte are included in the local variances section of the report. Looking over the data provides you with one more validation that all of the data you have gathered is relatively consistent and reliable.

RESEARCH RESULTS: Based on the research, you were able to locate the relative cost of living adjustments appropriate for Atlanta, Georgia, and Charlotte, North Carolina. You were also able to determine the appropriate compensation levels for these locations based on a detailed job description. According to *http://www. salary.com*, the median income (salary and bonuses) of a financial analysis manager in Atlanta is $81,000; the median income for the same position in Charlotte is $80,000. The cost of living in Charlotte is 1.6 percent less than Atlanta and employers generally pay 1.2 percent less than Atlanta. You now feel that you have enough sound, comparative data to develop a reasonable strategy for negotiating the salary for your new job offer.

CONTRIBUTOR NAME: Michelle Hartstrom

AFFILIATION: Columbia Financial Advisors, Inc.

USEFUL TIPS

* The resources available at *http://www.careerbuilder.com* go far beyond salary information. There is a great deal of job search and career advice available under the tab Advice & Resources.
* If you belong to any professional organizations, check their Web sites for salary survey data. The Institute of Management Accountants conducts an annual salary survey that is available to members free of charge. Its Web site is *http://www.imanet.org*.

PROBLEM NUMBER 36: WHAT IS THE CERTIFICATION PROCESS FOR A MANAGEMENT ACCOUNTANT?

RESEARCH BACKGROUND: You have successfully worked as a CPA for several years. You have a new boss who is impressed with your skills and who encourages you to pursue further educational opportunities, specifically identifying management accounting as a specialization that would complement your current level of experience. Given the current economy and challenges facing the accounting industry, you decide that pursuing additional specialization might be a useful hedge in the current economy. Your boss asks you to investigate the certification process and come back to her with information about the requirements and any related expenses. Understanding that most of the certifications are sponsored by an industry association, you assume that the process of investigating the certification process will be free.

RESEARCH STRATEGY EMPLOYED: You have several colleagues who are certified in management accounting and so you put a call into one to find out the sponsoring association. He gets back to you shortly and identifies the Institute of Management Accountants (IMA), and gives you the URL as well, *http://www.imanet.org*. If you had not had a colleague to contact, you could call for the name of the association; you might also have called or visited the Web site for the AICPA. As the sponsoring association for CPAs, the AICPA is also very knowledgeable about related industry certifications.

Turning to the IMA's Web site, you see links directly on the home page to two certificates: Certified Management Accountant (CMA) and Certified in Financial Management (CFM). Clicking on the link to CMA, you find a great deal of information posted on the site, including details about the requirements and procedures for both earning and maintaining certification. You print out the information that you will need for your meeting with your boss and prepare to begin the process of earning the CMA certification.

RESEARCH RESULTS: Reviewing the CMA page, you learn that you must pass a series of four tests, satisfy a work experience requirement, join the IMA, and comply with the standard of ethical conduct. In addition, there are a series of educational credentials that must be met with either a bachelor's degree, CPA credentials, or by attaining a certain score on the GMAT test. Fortunately, your CPA credential satisfies the education requirements and allows you to waive one of the four required tests. The tests are offered daily in most major U.S. cities. Once the initial certification is obtained, you will be required to meet annual continuing education requirements to maintain the certification.

Typically, associations take ownership for sponsoring association certifications and continuing education requirements. The AICPA is the association responsible for the designation of Certified Public Accountant, and there are a series of additional specializations in the accounting and financial industry that allows the CPA and other qualified applicants to expand on their competencies and expertise. Associations are excellent sources of industry-related information and early on, they became one of the pioneers of tapping into the power of the Internet for communication and information sharing purposes. Within a short time, you are able to locate all the information needed about the career path, requirements to sit for the exam, exam process itself, including costs, and requirements beyond the exam for maintaining the certification. You even submit an e-mail request for the application packet to be mailed to your work address.

CONTRIBUTOR NAME: Brenda Reeb
AFFILIATION: University of Rochester

USEFUL TIPS

* Associations are an excellent source of industry-related information, and sponsoring an industry-specific certification and continuing education opportunities are just a few of many ways that they distribute and promote competencies and knowledge to both members and nonmembers. Virtually all substantive associations have a Web site and most are extremely generous about the amount of information they make available on their site.

- If you are not sure what the name or URL for a particular association is, there are several strategies you can try to identify it:
  - Type the keywords describing the industry combined with the word association in the browser address bar: management accounting association.
  - Yahoo! maintains an excellent list of association names as part of its search engine.
  - Visit a local public or academic library to use the reference book *Encyclopedia of Associations*. This excellent series of volumes contains descriptive information about U.S. local, regional, national and international associations and interest groups. Most descriptions now include a URL and all will include a phone number.

4

Accounting and Financial Research Data Source Evaluations and Reviews

In the previous three chapters we examined the context and strategies for conducting accounting and related financial research in the corporate setting. Specific sources were identified and their practical value demonstrated in a series of real-life, practical problems and scenarios. We have learned that all of these sources contain relevant content. In this chapter we examine specific data source strengths and limitations as functional research tools. The perfect collection of information may be housed in an interface that is easy to use and reasonably priced or it may be awkward and inefficient to navigate and carry a prohibitively high price tag. The combination of all of these factors—content, usability, cost—will ultimately determine their true value for your research applications.

The thirty-four detailed, critical reviews of sources of accounting and financial information contained in this chapter will help you to determine which resources best fit your organization's information needs and budget. The sources included were carefully selected based on this editor's experience conducting research, managing information budgets, and evaluating and selecting resources for an international accounting firm. A team of experienced researchers prepared the source reviews, describing each source's general content and value, as well as looking at costs, currency, comprehensiveness, and ease of use.

Given the large number of sources that are important for this research, it was impossible to include fully developed source evaluations for each of them. Realistic limits imposed on us were based on time and space constraints, the speed and frequency with which interfaces change, industry mergers, acquisitions, partnerships and bankruptcies resulting in the reengineering or demise of once-familiar products, and of course, the complex game of free vs. for-pay access.

As this volume goes to press, there are already several products that have announced they are rolling out completely new search platforms and branding initiatives. There will undoubtedly be more changes and casualties by the time you read this material. However, this does not undermine the value that these source evaluations hold for the resource decision-making process and there are two important points to bear in mind:

- The reviews are designed as general guides for deciding which sources provide the needed information most effectively and economically. The applied rating system is transferable to your evaluation of any information resource.
- Don't make your decisions based solely on this chapter. Consider the contextual and strategic discussions of a large number of information sources in the introduction chapter, as well as the application for many of these in the problems and solutions, and case study chapters.

DATA SOURCE RATINGS

All of the data source reviewers were asked to rate each source on the basis of the following eight categories, using "10" as the highest rating and "1" as the lowest ("80" being a perfect score):

1. Relative cost-to-value (a "10" would be very cost-effective)
2. Relative timeliness of data
3. Relative comprehensiveness of data
4. Ease of use
5. Search options available
6. Level of support services
7. Level of training offered
8. Amount/kinds of special services offered

The editors also provided the following general rating instructions to the reviewers: "Under this section we would like you to be critical but fair, bearing in mind that no source is perfect, complete, and free. It would be most useful if you always compare this source to similar sources when answering the following questions:

- How would you rate/describe the cost in terms of other sources? Do you feel the source is cost-effective for the applications/questions/data you are using it for?
- Describe the various cost schedules and/or options as you know and use them.
- How timely is the data? How often is it updated? Is the updating partial or complete?
- How comprehensive is the data? Consider such factors as breath, depth, and completeness of coverage.
- How easy is the source to search? What do you like best about the user interface?
- What is the level and value of technical support offered? What is the cost for this?
- What type of training is offered, and how effective is it? What is the cost for this?
- Summarize and comment on a total rating you would apply to this data source using the guidelines from the rating scale above."

Many of the initial source review ratings were double-checked by editors and other contributors, but, in the end, these opinions are expressed by individuals whose professional experience with the source under review was honestly stated. A different set of reviewers might very well arrive at different conclusions, and the reader is advised to use these ratings with some caution. A broad-based survey of one thousand users of the same source would be necessary to ensure reliable quantitative results, but that more elaborate process was not feasible for this series.

The rating results for the source reviews in this chapter are shown in Tables 4-1 through 4-10, with one table for each rating category and sources ranked from high to low. A summary table showing the comparative ranking of all sources is also provided (see Table 4-2). Ratings tables for all sources reviewed in all volumes of this series are provided in Appendix C, both alphabetically by publisher and as a total ranking for all eight rating categories, from high to low.

Table 4-1. Data Source Ratings: Alphabetical by Data Source

DATA SOURCE	1. RELATIVE COST-TO-VALUE	2. RELATIVE TIMELINESS OF DATA	3. RELATIVE COMPRE-HENSIVE-NESS OF DATA	4. EASE OF USE	5. SEARCH OPTIONS AVAILABLE	6. LEVEL OF SUPPORT SERVICES	7. LEVEL OF TRAINING OFFERED	8. AMOUNT/ KINDS OF SPECIAL SERVICES OFFERED	TOTAL
10k Wizard	9	10	10	10	10	10	5	9	73
ABI/Inform	6	10	7	10	10	8	8	10	69
Accounting & Tax Database	5	8	8	4	6	7	7	7	52
AICPA	8	9	8	7	6	7	5	3	53
Bloomberg Professional	8	10	9	6	10	10	10	9	72
Budget and Economic Outlook	10	10	10	10	5	5	5	5	60
Bureau of Labor Statistics	10	10	10	6	8	8	7	8	67
Business Wire	5	10	5	7	5	5	5	5	47
CCH Tax Research Network	7	9	8	10	10	9	8	8	69
D&B Key Business Ratios (KBR) on the Web	6	7	8	7	6	7	3	6	50
D&B Million Dollar Database	5	7	8	9	7	7	3	5	51
Dialog	8	9	9	7	10	10	9	8	70
Disclosure Database	7	8	9	9	7	7	5	7	59
Economic Indicators	7	8	6	5	3	4	5	5	43
EIU ViewsWire	8	9	9	10	9	9	9	8	71
Factiva	9	10	10	8	7	6	6	9	65

Table 4-1. Data Source Ratings: Alphabetical by Data Source (cont.)

DATA SOURCE	1. RELATIVE COST-TO-VALUE	2. RELATIVE TIMELINESS OF DATA	3. RELATIVE COMPREHENSIVENESS OF DATA	4. EASE OF USE	5. SEARCH OPTIONS AVAILABLE	6. LEVEL OF SUPPORT SERVICES	7. LEVEL OF TRAINING OFFERED	8. AMOUNT/KINDS OF SPECIAL SERVICES OFFERED	TOTAL
FactSet	7	10	10	7	5	8	8	8	63
Federal Reserve Board	10	10	8	10	10	6	5	10	69
Financial Accounting Research System (FARS)	9	8	9	6	7	4	4	5	52
Financial Accounting Standards Board (FASB)	10	10	8	10	5	8	5	3	59
Financial Forecast Center	10	10	8	10	5	8	5	8	64
Internal Revenue Service: The Digital Daily	10	10	10	8	8	8	5	8	67
International Accounting Standards Board	9	9	8	10	6	7	5	3	57
Investext	7	7	8	6	8	7	6	7	56
LexisNexis	8	9	8	7	8	8	7	7	62
LIVEDGAR	9	9	9	8	9	8	9	9	70
Mergent Online	6	9	9	8	7	8	9	6	62
Morningstar	10	10	10	9	9	8	9	9	74
RMA's Annual Statement Studies	10	8	6	9	4	7	3	7	54

Table 4-1. Data Source Ratings: Alphabetical by Data Source (cont.)

DATA SOURCE	1. RELATIVE COST-TO-VALUE	2. RELATIVE TIMELINESS OF DATA	3. RELATIVE COMPREHENSIVENESS OF DATA	4. EASE OF USE	5. SEARCH OPTIONS AVAILABLE	6. LEVEL OF SUPPORT SERVICES	7. LEVEL OF TRAINING OFFERED	8. AMOUNT/KINDS OF SPECIAL SERVICES OFFERED	TOTAL
Standard & Poor's NetAdvantage	8	10	8	7	8	7	6	8	62
The Wall Street Transcript	8	10	8	9	9	8	8	10	70
Thomson Research	5	10	10	7	8	6	5	8	59
U.S. Securities and Exchange Commission	10	10	8	9	5	6	2	2	52
Yahoo! Finance	9	10	9	9	9	5	5	6	62

Note: Reviewers were asked to rate each research data source on the basis of a "10" being the highest, most complimentary, rating and "1" being the lowest or least complimentary. A perfect score would be "80."

Table 4-2. Data Source Ratings: Ranked by Overall Rating

DATA SOURCE	1. RELATIVE COST-TO-VALUE	2. RELATIVE TIMELINESS OF DATA	3. RELATIVE COMPRE-HENSIVE-NESS OF DATA	4. EASE OF USE	5. SEARCH OPTIONS AVAILABLE	6. LEVEL OF SUPPORT SERVICES	7. LEVEL OF TRAINING OFFERED	8. AMOUNT/ KINDS OF SPECIAL SERVICES OFFERED	TOTAL
Morningstar	10	10	10	9	9	8	9	9	74
10k Wizard	9	10	10	10	10	10	5	9	73
Bloomberg Professional	8	10	9	6	10	10	10	9	72
EIU ViewsWire	8	9	9	10	9	9	9	8	71
Dialog	8	9	9	7	10	10	9	8	70
LIVEDGAR	9	9	9	8	9	8	9	9	70
The Wall Street Transcript	8	10	8	9	9	8	8	10	70
ABI/Inform	6	10	7	10	10	8	8	10	69
CCH Tax Research Network	7	9	8	10	10	9	8	8	69
Federal Reserve Board	10	10	8	10	10	6	5	10	69
Bureau of Labor Statistics	10	10	10	6	8	8	7	8	67
Internal Revenue Service: The Digital Daily	10	10	10	8	8	8	5	8	67
Factiva	9	10	10	8	7	6	6	9	65
Financial Forecast Center	10	10	8	10	5	8	5	8	64
FactSet	7	10	10	7	5	8	8	8	63
LexisNexis	8	9	8	7	8	8	7	7	62
Mergent Online	6	9	9	8	7	8	9	6	62

Table 4-2. Data Source Ratings: Ranked by Overall Rating (cont.)

DATA SOURCE	1. RELATIVE COST-TO-VALUE	2. RELATIVE TIMELINESS OF DATA	3. RELATIVE COMPREHENSIVENESS OF DATA	4. EASE OF USE	5. SEARCH OPTIONS AVAILABLE	6. LEVEL OF SUPPORT SERVICES	7. LEVEL OF TRAINING OFFERED	8. AMOUNT/KINDS OF SPECIAL SERVICES OFFERED	TOTAL
Standard & Poor's NetAdvantage	8	10	8	7	8	7	6	8	62
Yahoo! Finance	9	10	9	9	9	5	5	6	62
Budget and Economic Outlook	10	10	10	10	5	5	5	5	60
Disclosure Database	7	8	9	9	7	7	5	7	59
Financial Accounting Standards Board (FASB)	10	10	8	10	5	8	5	3	59
Thomson Research	5	10	10	7	8	6	5	8	59
International Accounting Standards Board	9	9	8	10	6	7	5	3	57
Investext	7	7	8	6	8	7	6	7	56
RMA's Annual Statement Studies	10	8	6	9	4	7	3	7	54
AICPA	8	9	8	7	6	7	5	3	53
Accounting & Tax Database	5	8	8	4	6	7	7	7	52
Financial Accounting Research System (FARS)	9	8	9	6	7	4	4	5	52
U.S. Securities and Exchange Commission	10	10	8	9	5	6	2	2	52

Table 4-2. Data Source Ratings: Ranked by Overall Rating (cont.)

DATA SOURCE	1. RELATIVE COST-TO-VALUE	2. RELATIVE TIMELINESS OF DATA	3. RELATIVE COMPREHENSIVENESS OF DATA	4. EASE OF USE	5. SEARCH OPTIONS AVAILABLE	6. LEVEL OF SUPPORT SERVICES	7. LEVEL OF TRAINING OFFERED	8. AMOUNT/KINDS OF SPECIAL SERVICES OFFERED	TOTAL
D&B Million Dollar Database	5	7	8	9	7	7	3	5	51
D&B Key Business Ratios (KBR) on the Web	6	7	8	7	6	7	3	6	50
Business Wire	5	10	5	7	5	5	5	5	47
Economic Indicators	7	8	6	5	3	4	5	5	43

Note: Reviewers were asked to rate each research data source on the basis of a "10" being the highest, most complimentary, rating and "1" being the lowest or least complimentary. A perfect score would be "80."

DATA SOURCE RATINGS:
RANKED BY INDIVIDUAL CRITERIA

Table 4-3. Ranked by Relative Cost-to-Value

DATA SOURCE	I. RELATIVE COST-TO-VALUE	TOTAL
Morningstar	10	74
Federal Reserve Board	10	69
Bureau of Labor Statistics	10	67
Internal Revenue Service: The Digital Daily	10	67
Financial Forecast Center	10	64
Budget and Economic Outlook	10	60
Financial Accounting Standards Board (FASB)	10	59
RMA's Annual Statement Studies	10	54
U.S. Securities and Exchange Commission	10	52
10k Wizard	9	73
LIVEDGAR	9	70
Factiva	9	65
Yahoo! Finance	9	62
International Accounting Standards Board	9	57
Financial Accounting Research System (FARS)	9	52
Bloomberg Professional	8	72
EIU ViewsWire	8	71
Dialog	8	70
The Wall Street Transcript	8	70
LexisNexis	8	62
Standard & Poor's NetAdvantage	8	62
AICPA	8	53
CCH Tax Research Network	7	69
FactSet	7	63
Disclosure Database	7	59
Investext	7	56
Economic Indicators	7	43
ABI/Inform	6	69
Mergent Online	6	62
D&B Key Business Ratios (KBR) on the Web	6	50
Thomson Research	5	59
Accounting & Tax Database	5	52
D&B Million Dollar Database	5	51
Business Wire	5	47

Note: Reviewers were asked to rate each research data source on the basis of a "10" being the highest, most complimentary, rating and "1" being the lowest or least complimentary. A perfect score would be "80."

Table 4-4. Ranked by Relative Timeliness of Data

DATA SOURCE	2. RELATIVE TIMELINESS OF DATA	TOTAL
Morningstar	10	74
10k Wizard	10	73
Bloomberg Professional	10	72
The Wall Street Transcript	10	70
ABI/Inform	10	69
Federal Reserve Board	10	69
Bureau of Labor Statistics	10	67
Internal Revenue Service: The Digital Daily	10	67
Factiva	10	65
Financial Forecast Center	10	64
FactSet	10	63
Standard & Poor's NetAdvantage	10	62
Yahoo! Finance	10	62
Budget and Economic Outlook	10	60
Financial Accounting Standards Board (FASB)	10	59
Thomson Research	10	59
U.S. Securities and Exchange Commission	10	52
Business Wire	10	47
EIU ViewsWire	9	71
Dialog	9	70
LIVEDGAR	9	70
CCH Tax Research Network	9	69
LexisNexis	9	62
Mergent Online	9	62
International Accounting Standards Board	9	57
AICPA	9	53
Disclosure Database	8	59
RMA's Annual Statement Studies	8	54
Accounting & Tax Database	8	52
Financial Accounting Research System (FARS)	8	52
Economic Indicators	8	43
Investext	7	56
D&B Million Dollar Database	7	51
D&B Key Business Ratios (KBR) on the Web	7	50

Note: Reviewers were asked to rate each research data source on the basis of a "10" being the highest, most complimentary, rating and "1" being the lowest or least complimentary. A perfect score would be "80."

Table 4-5. Ranked by Relative Comprehensiveness of Data

DATA SOURCE	3. RELATIVE COMPREHENSIVENESS OF DATA	TOTAL
Morningstar	10	74
10k Wizard	10	73
Bureau of Labor Statistics	10	67
Internal Revenue Service: The Digital Daily	10	67
Factiva	10	65
FactSet	10	63
Budget and Economic Outlook	10	60
Thomson Research	10	59
Bloomberg Professional	9	72
EIU ViewsWire	9	71
Dialog	9	70
LIVEDGAR	9	70
Mergent Online	9	62
Yahoo! Finance	9	62
Disclosure Database	9	59
Financial Accounting Research System (FARS)	9	52
The Wall Street Transcript	8	70
CCH Tax Research Network	8	69
Federal Reserve Board	8	69
Financial Forecast Center	8	64
LexisNexis	8	62
Standard & Poor's NetAdvantage	8	62
Financial Accounting Standards Board (FASB)	8	59
International Accounting Standards Board	8	57
Investext	8	56
AICPA	8	53
Accounting & Tax Database	8	52
U.S. Securities and Exchange Commission	8	52
D&B Million Dollar Database	8	51
D&B Key Business Ratios (KBR) on the Web	8	50
ABI/Inform	7	69
RMA's Annual Statement Studies	6	54
Economic Indicators	6	43
Business Wire	5	47

Note: Reviewers were asked to rate each research data source on the basis of a "10" being the highest, most complimentary, rating and "1" being the lowest or least complimentary. A perfect score would be "80."

Table 4-6. Ranked by Ease of Use

DATA SOURCE	4. EASE OF USE	TOTAL
10k Wizard	10	73
EIU ViewsWire	10	71
ABI/Inform	10	69
CCH Tax Research Network	10	69
Federal Reserve Board	10	69
Financial Forecast Center	10	64
Budget and Economic Outlook	10	60
Financial Accounting Standards Board (FASB)	10	59
International Accounting Standards Board	10	57
Morningstar	9	74
The Wall Street Transcript	9	70
Yahoo! Finance	9	62
Disclosure Database	9	59
RMA's Annual Statement Studies	9	54
Securities and Exchange Commission	9	52
D&B Million Dollar Database	9	51
LIVEDGAR	8	70
Internal Revenue Service: The Digital Daily	8	67
Factiva	8	65
Mergent Online	8	62
Dialog	7	70
FactSet	7	63
LexisNexis	7	62
Standard & Poor's NetAdvantage	7	62
Thomson Research	7	59
AICPA	7	53
D&B Key Business Ratios (KBR) on the Web	7	50
Business Wire	7	47
Bloomberg Professional	6	72
Bureau of Labor Statistics	6	67
Investext	6	56
Financial Accounting Research System (FARS)	6	52
Economic Indicators	5	43
Accounting & Tax Database	4	52

Note: Reviewers were asked to rate each research data source on the basis of a "10" being the highest, most complimentary, rating and "1" being the lowest or least complimentary. A perfect score would be "80."

Table 4-7. Ranked by Search Options Available

DATA SOURCE	5. SEARCH OPTIONS AVAILABLE	TOTAL
10k Wizard	10	73
Bloomberg Professional	10	72
Dialog	10	70
ABI/Inform	10	69
CCH Tax Research Network	10	69
Federal Reserve Board	10	69
Morningstar	9	74
EIU ViewsWire	9	71
LIVEDGAR	9	70
The Wall Street Transcript	9	70
Yahoo! Finance	9	62
Bureau of Labor Statistics	8	67
Internal Revenue Service: The Digital Daily	8	67
LexisNexis	8	62
Standard & Poor's NetAdvantage	8	62
Thomson Research	8	59
Investext	8	56
Factiva	7	65
Mergent Online	7	62
Disclosure Database	7	59
Financial Accounting Research System (FARS)	7	52
D&B Million Dollar Database	7	51
International Accounting Standards Board	6	57
AICPA	6	53
Accounting & Tax Database	6	52
D&B Key Business Ratios (KBR) on the Web	6	50
Financial Forecast Center	5	64
FactSet	5	63
Budget and Economic Outlook	5	60
Financial Accounting Standards Board (FASB)	5	59
Securities and Exchange Commission	5	52
Business Wire	5	47
RMA's Annual Statement Studies	4	54
Economic Indicators	3	43

Note: Reviewers were asked to rate each research data source on the basis of a "10" being the highest, most complimentary, rating and "1" being the lowest or least complimentary. A perfect score would be "80."

Table 4-8. Ranked by Level of Support Services

DATA SOURCE	6. LEVEL OF SUPPORT SERVICES	TOTAL
10k Wizard	10	73
Bloomberg Professional	10	72
Dialog	10	70
EIU ViewsWire	9	71
CCH Tax Research Network	9	69
Morningstar	8	74
LIVEDGAR	8	70
The Wall Street Transcript	8	70
ABI/Inform	8	69
Bureau of Labor Statistics	8	67
Internal Revenue Service: The Digital Daily	8	67
Financial Forecast Center	8	64
FactSet	8	63
LexisNexis	8	62
Mergent Online	8	62
Financial Accounting Standards Board (FASB)	8	59
Standard & Poor's NetAdvantage	7	62
Disclosure Database	7	59
International Accounting Standards Board	7	57
Investext	7	56
RMA's Annual Statement Studies	7	54
AICPA	7	53
Accounting & Tax Database	7	52
D&B Million Dollar Database	7	51
D&B Key Business Ratios (KBR) on the Web	7	50
Federal Reserve Board	6	69
Factiva	6	65
Thomson Research	6	59
U.S. Securities and Exchange Commission	6	52
Yahoo! Finance	5	62
Budget and Economic Outlook	5	60
Business Wire	5	47
Financial Accounting Research System (FARS)	4	52
Economic Indicators	4	43

Note: Reviewers were asked to rate each research data source on the basis of a "10" being the highest, most complimentary, rating and "1" being the lowest or least complimentary. A perfect score would be "80."

Table 4-9. Ranked by Level of Training Offered

DATA SOURCE	7. LEVEL OF TRAINING OFFERED	TOTAL
Bloomberg Professional	10	72
Morningstar	9	74
EIU ViewsWire	9	71
Dialog	9	70
LIVEDGAR	9	70
Mergent Online	9	62
The Wall Street Transcript	8	70
ABI/Inform	8	69
CCH Tax Research Network	8	69
FactSet	8	63
Bureau of Labor Statistics	7	67
LexisNexis	7	62
Accounting & Tax Database	7	52
Factiva	6	65
Standard & Poor's NetAdvantage	6	62
Investext	6	56
10k Wizard	5	73
Federal Reserve Board	5	69
Internal Revenue Service: The Digital Daily	5	67
Financial Forecast Center	5	64
Yahoo! Finance	5	62
Budget and Economic Outlook	5	60
Disclosure Database	5	59
Financial Accounting Standards Board (FASB)	5	59
Thomson Research	5	59
International Accounting Standards Board	5	57
AICPA	5	53
Business Wire	5	47
Economic Indicators	5	43
Financial Accounting Research System (FARS)	4	52
RMA's Annual Statement Studies	3	54
D&B Million Dollar Database	3	51
D&B Key Business Ratios (KBR) on the Web	3	50
U.S. Securities and Exchange Commission	2	52

Note: Reviewers were asked to rate each research data source on the basis of a "10" being the highest, most complimentary, rating and "1" being the lowest or least complimentary. A perfect score would be "80."

Table 4-10. Ranked by Amount/Kinds of Special Services Offered

DATA SOURCE	8. AMOUNT/KINDS OF SPECIAL SERVICES OFFERED	TOTAL
The Wall Street Transcript	10	70
ABI/Inform	10	69
Federal Reserve Board	10	69
Morningstar	9	74
10k Wizard	9	73
Bloomberg Professional	9	72
LIVEDGAR	9	70
Factiva	9	65
EIU ViewsWire	8	71
Dialog	8	70
CCH Tax Research Network	8	69
Bureau of Labor Statistics	8	67
Internal Revenue Service: The Digital Daily	8	67
Financial Forecast Center	8	64
FactSet	8	63
Standard & Poor's NetAdvantage	8	62
Thomson Research	8	59
LexisNexis	7	62
Disclosure Database	7	59
Investext	7	56
RMA's Annual Statement Studies	7	54
Accounting & Tax Database	7	52
Mergent Online	6	62
Yahoo! Finance	6	62
D&B Key Business Ratios (KBR) on the Web	6	50
Budget and Economic Outlook	5	60
Financial Accounting Research System (FARS)	5	52
D&B Million Dollar Database	5	51
Business Wire	5	47
Economic Indicators	5	43
Financial Accounting Standards Board (FASB)	3	59
International Accounting Standards Board	3	57
AICPA	3	53
U.S. Securities and Exchange Commission	2	52

Note: Reviewers were asked to rate each research data source on the basis of a "10" being the highest, most complimentary, rating and "1" being the lowest or least complimentary. A perfect score would be "80."

DEVELOPMENT OF THE REVIEWS

The review process was undertaken in full cooperation with the data source publishers. The publishers were all invited to participate in the project, and each publisher who accepted this invitation provided a password so that a reviewer could access the source. A few publishers did not respond, and hence there are some obvious and regrettable omissions. All publishers were asked to read and comment on the review of their data source, so the responsibility for any errors or misstatements is shared by both sides of the review process.

All of the source reviews were prepared by experienced database searchers drawing on their experience and training as information professionals and/or financial professionals. (Contributors' biographies appear in Appendix D.) Each review follows a standard format that includes a description of the source, an overview of the source content, and an evaluation of the content and its use. Most of the reviews conclude with search tips helpful for researching that particular source. Although you will need to evaluate the reviews in terms of your own needs and capabilities, these business data source evaluations should help as you sort through the most important information resources available to corporate accounting and financial researchers.

ARRANGEMENT OF THE REVIEWS

The business source reviews contained in this chapter have been grouped into eight categories, following the same general organization of content used in Chapters One and Three. Many of the sources could fit into several of these. To locate a particular source, consult the source review listing in the Table of Contents. In addition, some of the evaluations were drawn from other volumes in this series. As a result they may be written with a focus on a specific business research application other than accounting or finance. However, it should be noted that business research often requires a "blurring" of the lines that distinguish the many types of research (for example, company, industry, financial) and so there may well be value for you in learning more about applications for these products than just those relating to the subject of this volume.

The Big Three Database Aggregators

The three most important online information research services and database aggregators are, without question, Dialog, Factiva, and LexisNexis. They are the supercenters of online research, and it would be difficult to conduct thorough secondary research without resorting to one of these three excellent services at some point.

While there is a fair amount of content duplication across the "Big Three," each also contains some unique information. Each one offers a variety of interfaces to satisfy the needs of the novice, as well as the experienced researcher, and they all are populated with rich collections of full-text and data sources.

In terms of business content, Dialog, Factiva, and LexisNexis are somewhat comparable. However, as it relates to the specific focus of this volume, LexisNexis and Factiva are the clear winners for accounting and related financial information. If you could only have access to one, I would have to recommend LexisNexis, primarily because of its ability to allow financial disclosure searching and its deep archived collection of full-text Securities and Exchange Commission (SEC) filings and annual reports. Search features, such as Focus and keyword in context (KWIC) display in the Cite view, add a high level of efficiency to the search and scan process. I think that Factiva has a slight edge over LexisNexis for its current news and wire stories, but not enough to present any risk of missing important information. In the ideal world, I would recommend subscribing to both.

Following is a comparison of Dialog, Factiva, and LexisNexis' strengths as broad-based business aggregators.

Table 4-11 presents a quick summary comparison of the three services that was prepared by contributor Hal P. Kirkwood, Jr.:

Table 4-11. Comparison A of Dialog, Factiva, and LexisNexis

DATABASE FEATURES	DATABASE NAMES		
	DIALOG	FACTIVA	LEXISNEXIS
General Content	Breadth of coverage across humanities, sciences, and social sciences	General news and newswires (national and international) and business information	Accounting, tax, and case law information and general news
Business Content Strength	Market research reports, country reports, full-text business publications and company financials	Current and historic market data, full-text *Wall Street Journal*, and international business coverage	Accounting resources and publications, tax law, and company financials
Pricing	Subscription with search charges or pay per view	Standard fee based on usage and a fee based on number of users	Subscription and pay-per-view
URL	*http://www. dialogweb.com*	*http://www.factiva.com*	*http://www.nexis.com*

Another contributor, Meryl Brodsky, provided a different comparison of the "Big Three," as shown in Table 4-12.

Table 4-12. Comparison B of Dialog, Factiva, and LexisNexis

DATABASE FEATURES	DATABASE NAMES		
	DIALOG	FACTIVA	LEXISNEXIS
Content	Excellent	Very good	Very good
Searchability	Good	Excellent	Good
Support	Excellent	Good	Excellent
Price	Good	Very good	Very good
Unique Features	Amazing breadth and depth of content	Excellent search interface, very customizable	Legal, accounting, tax content
Unique Problems	Myriad of products and pricing models is mystifying	Online help, phone help, and classes could all be better	Search screens look similar, and there is so much content, selecting sources is difficult

Pricing and cost comparisons between the three are more difficult to construct; all three have a number of pricing options, each of which differs from any known standard. Meryl Brodsky also provided the following price comparison summaries:

DIALOG. In addition to DialogClassic, which is expensive, other Dialog products include DialogSelect (with two pricing options, DialogSelect and Open Access) and DialogWeb. Dialog also offers DialogPRO and Dialog1. For people who need only occasional access to Dialog, the Open Access program is best. You do not have to subscribe, and the interface is menu driven, so it is not hard to use. As with many menu-driven systems, the interface is a little chunky. This means that if you know what you are looking for, it can be difficult to make the menus find what you want in the database you want to search in. For those searchers used to using more sophisticated search techniques, going to a menu-driven system is almost like trying to speak English in a foreign country. English can be understood, but you are not sure it's going to work, and it is inelegant at best. Charges are based on output and there are no connect time costs. The per-record price is about 25 percent higher in Open Access than in DialogSelect (for subscribers). That means articles cost roughly $4 for most industry publications, and $3.40 for newspaper articles.

FACTIVA. Factiva offers several pricing models, including a subscription for up to five users at $1,000 per month. There is no pay-per-article plan for Factiva right now. Factiva has recently rolled out a plan where, for an annual subscription fee of $69, you will be able to search Factiva.com for free, and pay $2.95 per article. Other content, such as company profiles, investment and analysts' reports, and corporate credit reports, will likely cost between $5 and $15.

LEXISNEXIS: LexisNexis offers pricing models ranging from the all-you-can-eat variety (annual subscription or $250/week for news, business, and financial information or less for just one of the three) to document fees, which range from $3 for news articles to $12 for legal documents.

All three sources provide options to serve the needs of small businesses or the occasional business researcher. The source chosen may have more to do with content needs and frequency of use than with price. Dialog (DialogClassic) covers the most subject areas and offers the greatest variety of search options, from forms-based research to sophisticated search software capabilities not available in the other online services. Dialog also includes science and technology and academic journal databases that do not appear elsewhere.

For obtaining a few specific articles, the best choice may be Factiva because it offers a low-priced per-article fee and free searching through a simple search interface, with more advanced search tools when needed.

LexisNexis would be the most appropriate source for an occasional need for in-depth research or legal materials. The daily and weekly passes offer good value, particularly if several research projects are batched and run at once. There are a couple of sources in LexisNexis not readily available elsewhere, including the Market Share Reporter, which would have significant value to a market and industry researcher.

Accounting Standards

The sources evaluated in this section include a balance of subscription-based databases and free Web sites providing either primary or secondary accounting information. The Financial Accounting Standards Board's (FASB) Financial Accounting Research System (FARS) and CCH's Tax Research Network's Accounting and Auditing Library each contain full-text collections of technical accounting standards. A newer source, not included in this section, but well worth looking at, is Aspen's Accounting Research Manager (see the contact information in Chapter One, Appendix 3). Aspen purchased this product in 2002 from Arthur Andersen and it contains the full text of both technical standards and secondary analysis accessible on a well-designed Internet platform at a very reasonable price.

The information-packed Web sites for the FASB, American Institute of Certified Public Accountants (AICPA), SEC, and International Accounting Standards Board (IASB) are well designed for keeping track of current and forthcoming issues. Evaluations of two important sources of secondary analysis of accounting standards, ABI/Inform and the Accounting & Tax Database, provide comparisons for this level of information. An evaluation of the IRS's Web site, Internal Revenue Service: The Digital Daily, although not mentioned elsewhere, is also included. Typical of many government Web sites, it is an excellent source of the full text of the agency's rulings and releases but it can be challenging to find what you are looking for. This site is a very useful source for the occasional client-posed, tax-related question. When comparing electronic sources of accounting technical standards, you should also plan to take a look at another source from the AICPA, reSOURCE: Accounting & Auditing Literature Web-based product. Although we were unable to provide a review in this volume, we would be negligent if we did not include this in the suite of resources you should evaluate. AICPA reSOURCE contains the AICPA's Professional Standards, Technical Practice Aids, Accounting and Auditing Guides and Risk Alerts, and Accounting Trends and Techniques. You can also purchase a combination subscription that includes the full text of FASB's authoritative pronouncements. While the interface can be a bit awkward to navigate and the search engine is not as fine-tuned as some of the other services that are available, the addition of electronic access to the Accounting Trends and Techniques is very useful.

Financial Disclosures

This section focuses on reviews of the few sources, such as Thomson Research and LIVEDGAR, that allow for the level of targeted SEC filing searching that is so important to accounting research. While there are many EDGAR Web sites on the market, only a very few are sophisticated enough to meet the technical research needs of accounting professionals. An evaluation of LexisNexis, the other database well suited for financial disclosure research, is included in section one of this chapter.

Business Ratios

Both RMA's Annual Statements Studies, and Dun & Bradstreet (D&B) Key Business Ratios (KBR) on the Web, the two most frequently referenced sources of aggregate business ratios, are evaluated in this section. Mergent Online, useful for locating individual companies and creating comparative ratio analysis across specified companies, is also reviewed.

Financial Market Data

Access to financial market data runs the gamut from free Web sites to high-end, real-time and analytical interactive platforms. Reviews included in this section demonstrate the value, strengths, and limitations of the entire spectrum. The first sources, Yahoo!

Finance and Morningstar, combine access to free and low-end pricing content. Bloomberg Professional and FactSet represent extremely expensive and sophisticated data systems.

Economic Data

All but the last source discussed in this section are free, and most are either government Web sites or reference government data. The Federal Reserve Board, Economic Indicators, and Bureau of Labor Statistics provide access to historic and current economic data. The Congressional Budget Office's Budget and Economic Outlook is one of the few sources of forecasted data. The versatile Financial Forecast Center site contains historic, current, and forecasted data. EIU ViewsWire, a subscription-based service, specializes in international data, with strengths in country economic forecasts.

Corporate Strategic and Operational Intelligence

The four sources selected for this section are representational of different focus points for gleaning important information about corporate internal and external issues, challenges, and risks. Investext gives us the investment banking perspective; *The Wall Street Transcript* includes insightful CEO interviews; the Management, Discussion & Analysis section found in 10k Wizard's SEC filing Web site assesses an organization's financial position and future outlook; and the *Business Wire* database, accessible through electronic aggregators, such as Dialog, Factiva, and LexisNexis, contains company press releases. Fair Disclosure transcripts, searchable in Factiva (reviewed in section one), tell the corporate story through dialogs between corporate management and financial analysts.

Competitive Intelligence

All three company directories reviewed in this section are useful for generating target prospecting lists for an organization's internal marketing department, and for determining an auditor's market share. D&B Million Dollar Database and Standard & Poor's Register, accessible through its NetAdvantage platform, include both public and private companies; Thomson's Disclosure Database only targets public parent companies.

DIALOG

ALTERNATE/PREVIOUS DATA SOURCE NAMES: DialogClassic, DialogWeb, Dialog1, DialogPRO, DialogSelect, Dialog Open Access

SERVICE/PORTAL NAME: *http://www.dialog.com*

SOURCE DESCRIPTION: Dialog is a leading worldwide provider of online information services that contain an impressive amount of information on an extensive variety of subjects. Dialog users can precisely retrieve data from more than 1.4 billion unique records, via the Internet or through delivery to enterprise intranets. Searchable content includes articles and reports from thousands of real-time news feeds, newspapers, broadcast transcripts, and trade publications, plus research reports and analyst notes providing support for financial decision making. Content also includes in-depth repositories of scientific and technical data, patents, trademarks, and other intellectual property data. Information professionals and end users at business, professional, and government organizations in more than one hundred countries prize Dialog services for their depth and breadth of content, precision searching, and speed. This online information is offered through five product lines: Dialog, Dialog Profound, Dialog DataStar, NewsEdge, and Intelligence Data. The interfaces discussed in this review fall under the Dialog brand of services.

Dialog was formed as a commercial venture in 1972, originating from a project at Lockheed Corporation that dates back to the early 1960s. Today, Dialog is considered to be "the pioneer of online information services." It has developed and evolved through numerous iterations and owners, including Knight Ridder, MAID plc, and currently The Thomson Corporation. Web-based options include Dialog1, DialogClassic, DialogPRO, DialogSelect, and DialogWeb. Other interfaces include Dialog Company Profiles, Dialog NewsRoom, DialogLink for Windows, Dialog OnDisc, and Dialog thru Telnet. Dialog is also available in a selection of intranet options, including Dialog@Site and Dialog for Lotus Notes. Detailed information on these products can be found at *http://www.dialog.com/products/productline/dialog.shtml*.

Following is a detailed look at the five Dialog content options: DialogClassic, DialogWeb, DialogSelect, Dialog1, and DialogPRO.

1. **DialogClassic** is a Web interface to the command-line version of Dialog. Command-line access provides the most flexibility and control during a search. DialogClassic is text based for fast

access, and images are available from the patent and trade-mark databases. DialogClassic requires the most user knowledge of the search options and format types of Dialog, and the sparse interface makes it necessary to also have a fairly thorough knowledge of the content of the Dialog databases. It is necessary to use the command language and the indexes specific to the selected database to create carefully crafted searches in the DialogClassic interface. This method of access is geared for the knowledgeable information professional who desires speed and precise control of the search to retrieve information.

2. **DialogWeb** provides a straightforward, graphical Web-based interface accessing the entire content of the Dialog service. It provides both a Guided Search and a Command Search option.

The Guided Search option allows the user to select from a menu of categories and subcategories until arriving at the Dynamic Search screen. The Dynamic Search screen presents the user with the option of searching simultaneously all of the relevant databases attached to that subcategory, or of selecting an individual database for information retrieval (see Figures 4-1–4-3).

Figure 4-1. DialogWeb Guided Search Interface, First Screen

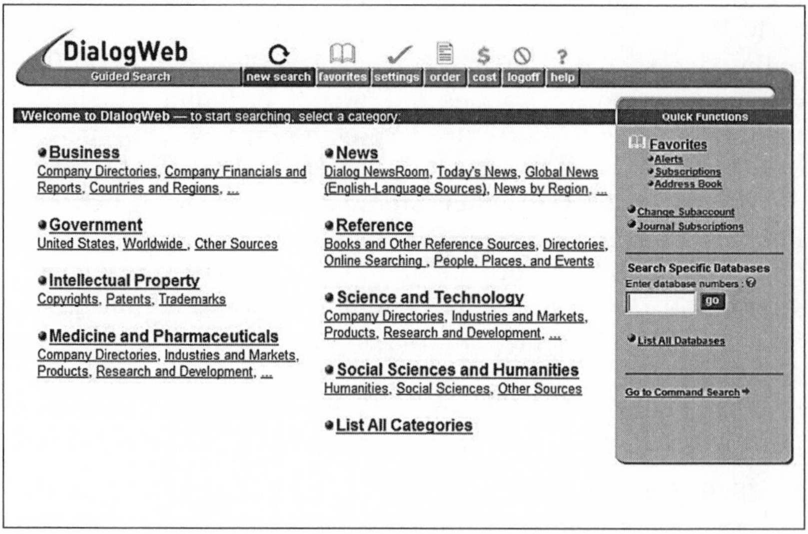

2003® Dialog, a Thomson business, *http://www.dialog.com*. Reprinted with permission of the publisher.

Figure 4-2. DialogWeb Guided Search Interface, Second Screen

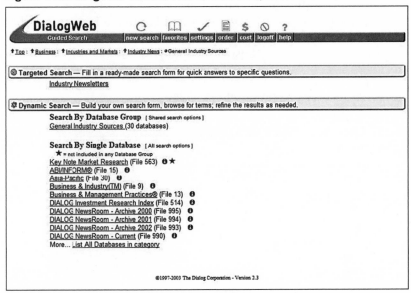

2003® Dialog, a Thomson business, *http://www.dialog.com*. Reprinted with permission of the publisher.

Figure 4-3. DialogWeb Guided Search Interface, Dynamic Search Screen

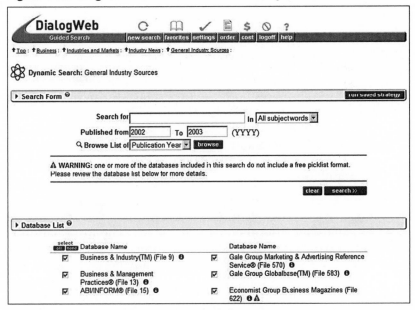

2003® Dialog, a Thomson business, *http://www.dialog.com*. Reprinted with permission of the publisher.

The Command Search option in DialogWeb provides the same flexibility and control as the DialogClassic version. Knowledge of the Dialog command language is necessary for effective searching, and database selection is facilitated by a browsable list of databases (see Figure 4-4).

Figure 4-4. DialogWeb Command Search Interface

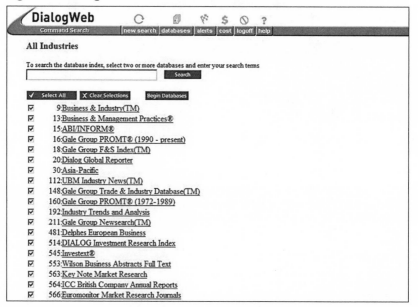

2003® Dialog, a Thomson business, *http://www.dialog.com*. Reprinted with permission of the publisher.

DialogWeb serves both the experienced searcher and the novice/intermediate searcher by providing the two search options. The browsable category menus facilitate database selection for expert and novice alike. Command Language searching is another option. This interface will serve a varied user population.

3. **DialogSelect** is a cross between DialogWeb and Dialog1, providing a Web-accessible interface to approximately three hundred databases from the main Dialog list. The information is organized into vertical categories to direct the user toward the desired content. Knowledge of the command language is not necessary, but searching is not as easy as in Dialog1. However, there is a fair amount of flexibility in creating a search, including proximity and Boolean (AND, OR, NOT) operators. There are a number of accessible fields that can be searched as well.

4. **Dialog1** is a simple interface to approximately 150 databases of Dialog content. The information is presented in Channels (see Figure 4-5) in a question-based format, leading the user through several menus and submenus until a search screen is provided that offers a clear search function, with preselected databases and appropriate content (see Figure 4-6). The search page often contains internal or hidden search parameters, created by information professionals, to facilitate the delivery of better results.

   Dialog1 removes the agony of determining which of the nine hundred files should be searched to fill an information need. It provides access to a select subset and is geared for novice and infrequent users. It lacks flexibility in its search capabilities, but this is to be expected with a beginner audience as the target market.

Figure 4-5. Dialog I Interface, Channels screen

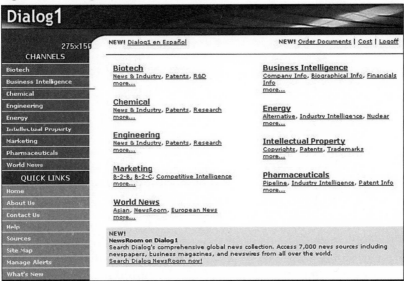

2003® Dialog, a Thomson business, *http://www.dialog.com*. Reprinted with permission of the publisher.

Figure 4-6. Dialog1 Interface, Search Screen

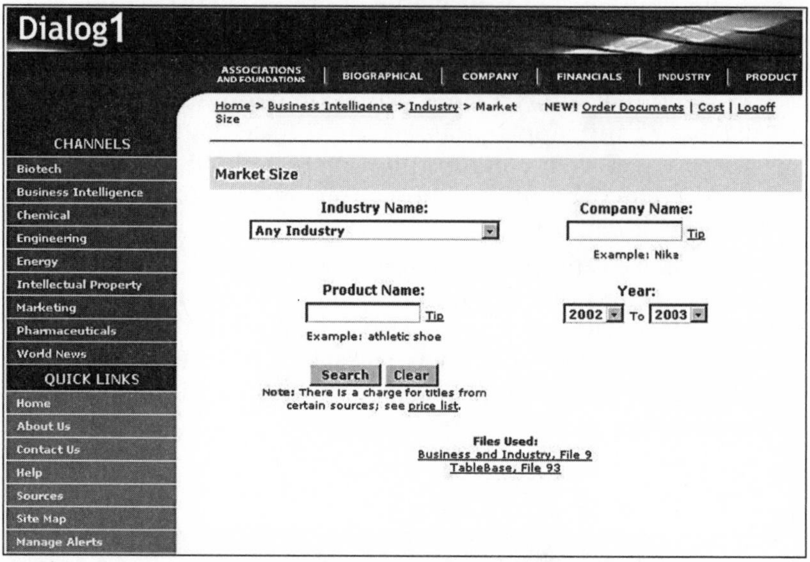

2003® Dialog, a Thomson business, *http://www.dialog.com*. Reprinted with permission of the publisher.

5. **DialogPRO** is similar to Dialog1 in that it provides access to a subset of the Dialog databases divided into Channels. This option is geared for small business owners (the "PRO" in "DialogPRO" stands for "Predictable Research Online"). Subscribers can select which channels are most relevant to their situation and pay a tiered flat fee for access. The whole content of Dialog is available on a transactional, as-needed basis. This option is particularly useful for infrequent users interested in controlling costs and in need of access to only a portion of the Dialog databases.

PRICING: The most complicated aspect of Dialog is the many pricing issues and options. Dialog charges both by connect time and by file format, and these charges are different across all of the databases. The charges range from $30 an hour for PsycInfo, with full abstracts costing $0.80 each, to $300 an hour for PharmaProjects, with full reports costing $13.40 each. Pricing for most databases falls between $80 and $300 an hour. Charges are also accrued for each User ID at the following rates:

United States and United Kingdom	1–5 User IDs	U.S.$14.00/month/User ID
Rest of the world	1–5 User IDs	U.S.$20.00/month/User ID

Dialog also offers a DialUnit charge rate, where the user is charged for the amount of system resources used during a given search session. With this option, searches that are more complex cost more money. The user can choose which method of charging is used within an account. The DialUnit charges span from $1.00 to $28.50 (for example, the DialUnit rate for PsycInfo is $3.50, and the rate for PharmaProjects is $28.50). These charges apply to DialogClassic, DialogWeb, and DialogSelect.

DialogSelect access is also available through Dialog Open Access, which is a pay-per-view option using a credit card. Dialog Open Access does not require a subscription fee, and it does not accrue any connect time or DialUnit charges. It is strictly pay-per-view for each document. Charges per document are 20 percent more than what is listed on the standard price list for the databases. Its interface is similar to the DialogSelect version.

Dialog1 is geared for less experienced users, so it does not accrue any connect time or DialUnit charges. There is a subscription fee and standard document charges. DialogPRO has a flat-fee pricing structure, with Primary, Plus, and Premier levels that provide increasing levels of access. The price points depend on the topic area and range from $60 a month to $500 a month. Several excellent articles have been written on this topic; see the "Source Reviews" section below.

Source Content: The information available through Dialog products and services consists of over nine hundred databases of content. These databases contain information on business, government, intellectual property, medicine and pharmaceuticals, news, science and technology, social sciences and humanities, and reference information. The information comes from journal and news articles, chemical abstracts, company financials, trade and country data, demographic information, government information, reference materials, intellectual property documents, and science, social science, and humanities data.

Among the Dialog databases are the following:

- Adis Clinical Trials Insight
- Brands and Their Companies
- Datamonitor Market Research
- EIU Country Analysis

- M&A Filings
- *Polymer Online*
- *San Francisco Chronicle*
- World Textiles
- Xinhua News

Some insight into the scope of the content can be obtained by viewing the subject menu for the Bluesheets:

- Business—Business & Industry
- Business—Business Statistics
- Business—International Directories & Company Financials
- Business—Product Information
- Business—U.S. Directories & Company Financials
- Social Science & Humanities
- Law & Government
- Multidisciplinary—Books
- Multidisciplinary—General
- Multidisciplinary—Reference
- News—U.S. Newspapers Fulltext
- News—Worldwide News
- Patents, Trademarks, Copyrights
- Science—Agriculture & Nutrition
- Science—Chemistry
- Science—Computer Technology
- Science—Energy & Environment
- Science—Medicine & Biosciences
- Science—Pharmaceuticals
- Science—Science & Technology

As this list illustrates, the depth and breadth of content offered in Dialog is unparalleled. Other resources that come close in size and scope within certain subjects would be LexisNexis and Factiva. However, neither of these can match the Dialog holdings across the humanities, sciences, and social sciences.

HELP AND SUPPORTING INFORMATION. Dialog provides access to a substantial amount of supporting documentation for its massive quantity of information. Specifically, each of the nine hundred databases has a unique Bluesheet that provides detailed information on the database's content, date coverage, update frequency, and source of information (See Figure 4-7). In addition to this descriptive data, the Bluesheet provides possible search tips, a sample record, and a list of the basic and additional indexes for each database. These Bluesheets are available at no cost online through the Dialog Web site (*http://library.dialog.com/bluesheets*).

Figure 4-7. Sample Dialog Bluesheet

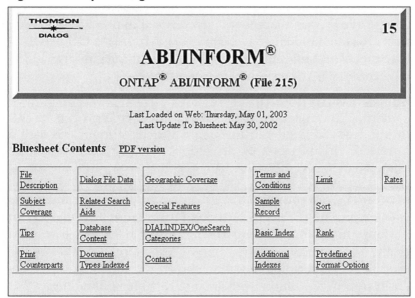

Each Bluesheet includes specific information on the available retrieval format types. Each database has this menu of formats, with its own pricing structure. 2003® Dialog, a Thomson business, *http://www.dialog.com*. Reprinted with permission of the publisher.

SEARCH AIDS. In addition to the Bluesheets, Dialog provides other search aids and documentation to assist users. These aids include general information on the Dialog service, details on search support, a manual that details how to effectively search Dialog, and several other comparison tools and quick reference resources. Also available are several database-specific search aids that provide greater detail on the indexing and classification systems of many databases. Examples include Business & Industry Concept Terms, Definitions Used in Dun & Bradstreet, and GEOREF Geographic Coordinates Fields. These specific search aids can be found online at the Dialog Web site (*http://support.dialog.com/ searchaids/dialog/#aids*).

DIALINDEX AND ONTAP FILES. Two additional features within Dialog designed to help users learn and use the database are the DIALINDEX and the ONTAP files. DIALINDEX (*http:// support.dialog.com/searchaids/dialog/pocketguide/finding_tools.shtml*) allows the searcher to send a query across multiple databases. The results returned are a total number of potentially relevant hits found within each database. Thus, the searcher can rank the databases to determine which have the most content for their search. A list of Supercategories is available so that similar databases can be searched simultaneously.

The ONTAP files are small-sized versions of a select group of major database files. These versions do not accrue any connect time or file format charges and can be used to practice searching with the command language. There are thirty-eight ONTAP database files. This tool is highly recommended for beginners wishing to become more accustomed to using Dialog.

SOURCE EVALUATION: Dialog contains a tremendous amount of content, spanning every major subject category. It provides access to hundreds of databases through a variety of interfaces with a variety of pricing formats. Its scope, breadth, and depth are unmatched by any other database aggregator or portal service.

I recommend looking carefully at the content and pricing structure before you subscribe to Dialog, to determine if it meets your organization's needs. Although its breadth may make it an obvious choice for most any situation, it may be excessive (and costly) for some information needs. Also, carefully evaluate the interfaces to determine how much power you and other researchers in your organization need and are capable of handling.

I would recommend Dialog for researchers interested in having a broad array of sources at their disposal. Because there is connect-time charging for several of the Dialog interfaces, it may be important to carefully consider who the primary users will be and how experienced they are in information seeking. Keep in mind that a benefit of this clear pricing is that it makes it very easy to track costs and bill clients.

The Dialog Web site contains a large amount of useful information about the databases, pricing options, and support tools and should be perused before you make any final decision on acquiring this database.

SOURCE VALUE RATING: All of the data source reviewers were asked to rate each source on the basis of the following eight categories, using "10" as the highest rating and "1" as the lowest ("80" being a perfect score):

I. Relative cost-to-value:	8
2. Relative timeliness of data:	9
3. Relative comprehensiveness of data:	9
4. Ease of use:	7
5. Search options available:	10
6. Level of support services:	10
7. Level of training offered:	9
8. Amount/kinds of special services offered:	8
Total Rating:	70

SOURCE REVIEWS: This is only a selection of the articles available on Dialog and its services and pricing schemes:

Bates, M. E. "Dialog Pricing Redux: Deja Vu All Over Again." *Searcher* 10, no. 3 (March 2002): 36–49.

——."Dialog's Connect Time Pricing." *Online* 26, no. 2 (March/April 2002): 88.

——."Dialog One." *EContent* 23, no. 5 (October/November 2000): 96.

——."Dialog's Dialunits: There Is a Great Disturbance in the Force." *Searcher* 7, no. 7 (July/August 1999): 52–57.

Hurst, J. A. "DialogWeb under the Microscope: Facts & Stats." *EContent* 23, no. 3 (June/July 2000): 35–38.

O'Leary, M. "Dialog keeps end-user-searching edge." *Information Today* Vol.18:8 (September 2001): 15-6.

——."DialogSelect Opens Access to Premium Business Content." *Link-Up* 18, no. 3 (May/June 2001): 9–10.

Quint, B. E. "DialogPRO Brings Flat-Fee Subscriptions to Low-End Small-Business Market." *Information Today* 19, no. 4 (April 2002): 78, 80.

CONTRIBUTOR NAME: Hal P. Kirkwood, Jr./Meryl Brodsky
AFFILIATION: Purdue University/Consultant

USEFUL TIPS

- Read the Bluesheet prior to using any database.
- Use DialIndex to help determine which databases will be useful.
- Utilize both in-house and Dialog-supplied training options for your users to ensure effective and cost-conscious use of the databases.

FACTIVA

ALTERNATE/PREVIOUS DATA SOURCE NAMES: Dow Jones Interactive, Reuters Business Briefing, Dow Jones News/Retrieval

SERVICE/PORTAL NAME: *http://www.factiva.com*

SOURCE DESCRIPTION: Factiva is a joint venture, formed in 1999 by Dow Jones & Co. and The Reuters Group. Its flagship product, Factiva.com, is the successor online service to Dow Jones Interactive (formerly Dow Jones News/Retrieval) and Reuters Business Briefing, both of which were known for their focus on international information sources. Factiva.com now includes almost all of the content of both of its predecessors, along with capabilities and services not previously available.

Factiva contains four basic tabs: Search, Track, News Pages, and Companies/Markets, each of which is described in the Source Content section below. The heart of Factiva is its collection of nearly eight thousand publications in twenty-two languages from 118 countries, and its emphasis on acquiring content directly from publishers whenever possible. This enables the company to ensure that the updates are added as soon as they are available, and that the coverage of individual publications is as comprehensive as it is feasible. Factiva data includes current news, archived articles, company data, investment analyst reports, market data, historical stock price performance, and company financials.

Factiva content includes ten basic categories of business information:

1. Local and regional newspapers, including exclusive access to the *Wall Street Journal*
2. Trade publications
3. Business newswires, including exclusive access to the Dow Jones & Reuters newswires
4. Press release wires
5. Media transcripts
6. Selected news photos
7. Investment analyst reports

8. Country and regional profiles
9. Company profiles
10. Historical and intraday market data

The Search function includes expanded content from eleven thousand Web sites in twenty-two languages, all judged to be of particular interest to business searchers. These sites pertain primarily to companies, newspapers, industry publications, government agencies, and trade associations. Areas within these sites are crawled at least daily, if appropriate, to retrieve and index content that is not otherwise available on Factiva ("crawling" is the process employed to find and index Web sites). The Search function also includes pictures from Reuters and Knight Ridder, with over four thousand images added weekly. Selected content is available in PDF format, and articles can be displayed and saved in rich text format (RTF) as well as in HTML and plain text.

Factiva has recently developed an indexing process called Factiva Intelligent Indexing, which assigns company, industry, regional, and subject codes consistently across all content in its Search and Track areas. These codes are based on international indexing standards, such as NAICS (North American Industry Classification System) and ISO (International Organization for Standardization), and include up to five levels of hierarchy. For example, a search on the industry term *Computers* would automatically include all the more granular terms within the Computer industry hierarchy.

The advantages of Intelligent Indexing are that you can search non-English content by using the Intelligent Indexing terms in the language you wish to use. Indexing terms are consistently applied across all content providers, and you can limit your search to a specific geographic region, to articles about a particular company—even if the name is misspelled (for example, it will find "DuPont" or " Du Pont"), or even to type of document (editorial, interview, or an overview of industry trends).

PRICING: Factiva offers several basic pricing structures, including flat-fee access and pay-as-you-go, transaction-based pricing. Since flat-fee subscriptions start at $1,000 a month, low-volume searchers will probably want to use the Individual Subscription option, which offers articles at $2.95 each with an annual fee of $69. Note that individual subscribers do not have access to the News Pages or Companies/Markets areas of Factiva.

Source Content: Factiva offers four basic navigational tabs: Search, Track, News Pages, and Companies/Markets. (Note that News Page and Companies/Markets tabs are not available to Individual Subscription users.) Below is a detailed commentary on the content of each tab:

1. **Search** provides access to eight thousand publications and content from eleven thousand business-related Web sites. Factiva supports both free-text searching and searches with the Factiva Intelligent Indexing codes.

   Although most researchers will use the free-text search box to construct their search, Factiva supports full Boolean logic, including the following terms:

   - AND
   - OR
   - NOT
   - ADJ**n**—Two terms in this order, within **n** words of each other
   - NEAR**n**—Two terms within **n** words of each other, in either order
   - SAME—Two words in the same paragraph
   - ATLEAST**n**—Frequency operator used to specify the minimum number of times (**n**) the search word(s) must appear in the text

   There are a relatively small number of words that cannot be routinely searched for in Factiva. These include *and, or, not, same, near,* and *date.* However, even these words can be searched for if enclosed in quotation marks. The search phrase *"to be or not to be"*—consisting entirely of words that are unsearchable in most online services—is a valid search in Factiva.

   Researchers can also limit the search by field; these include Headline, Lead Paragraph, Author, Word Count, Date, Publication Title, Language, and Intelligent Indexing term. Most of the field restrictions can be indicated through pull-down boxes, with an option to add a custom list of fields from a collection of thirty specialized indexing fields. The Factiva Intelligent Indexing terms are searchable through the links at the top of the Advanced Search page. Clicking on Company, Industry, Region, or Subject opens a new window to display the options available, as illustrated in Figure 4-8.

   Each of the hierarchical categories that appears can be expanded by clicking the **Plus icon**. The default selection of sources to search is All Content, but sources can be specified by clicking the **Source Browser** link on the main search page, which allows the user to build a custom source list by selecting publications organized by title, industry, region, type, or language. Source lists can be saved for later use or selected for one-time searching. See Figure 4-9 for an example of the Publication Type Source Browser.

Figure 4-8. Factiva Search Option, Intelligent Indexing Search by Industry

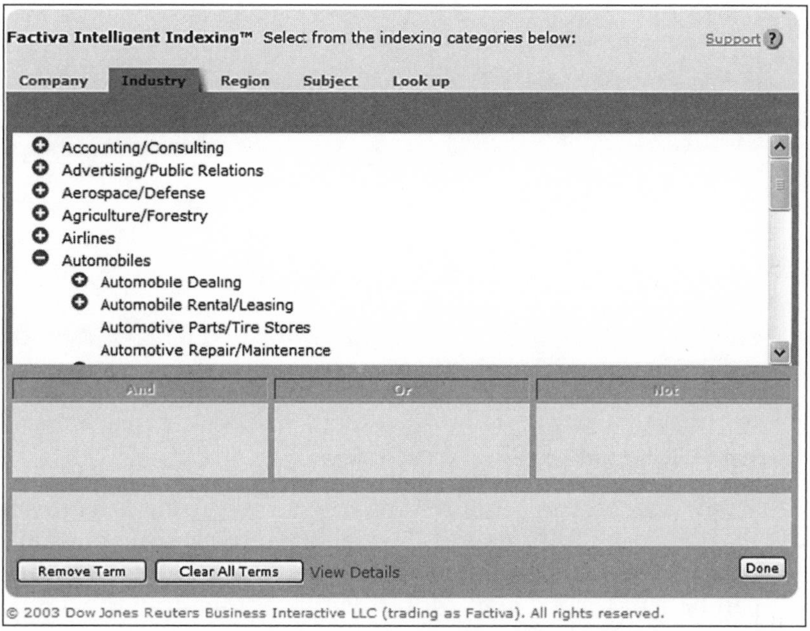

© 2003 Dow Jones Reuters Business Interactive LLC (Trading as Factiva). All rights reserved. Reprinted with permission of the publisher.

After a search has been executed, the default search results screen displays the complete citation, word count, and lead sentence. Articles can then be displayed in full or in one of several other formats, and the researcher can also create customized display formats. The results can be viewed and saved in rich text format as well as plain text, they can be e-mailed to the researcher or a third party, or they can be placed in the "Briefcase," which stores up to one hundred documents for thirty days.

Figure 4-9. Publication Type Source Browser in Factiva

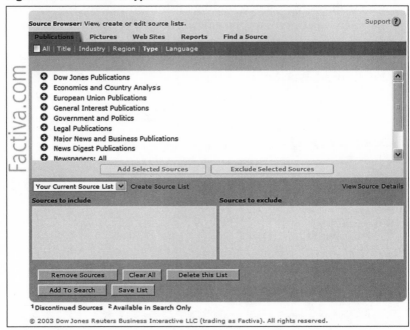

© 2003 Dow Jones Reuters Business Interactive LLC (Trading as Factiva). All rights reserved. Reprinted with permission of the publisher.

2. **Track** is an alerting tool that monitors news from close to six thousand publications and 750 Web sites. Track works continuously; the results can be viewed in the Track Folders, or they can be sent to an e-mail address, either throughout the day as articles are added or aggregated into a single e-mail once or twice a day. The search logic is similar to that of Search; both free-text searching and queries using Intelligent Indexing are supported. An interesting feature of the Track option is the ability to set the relevance level of the retrieved items to high, medium, or any degree of relevance. The relevance level score is based on the number of terms in the search query and how many of the terms appear in a document. The score also reflects the number of times a specific term appears in a document and the word count of the document. Searchers can use the relevance level setting to restrict the Track Folder to only articles that are directly about a particular topic or to expand the Folder to any articles that mention a topic or company, even just in passing.

3. **News Page** provides access to several content areas of Factiva from a single screen. The default Factiva Pages include the top news from up to ten major news sources, based on the subscriber's region; key stock market indices; and Editor's Links to Web sites of topical interest (see Figure 4-10). Note that with the pull-down menu at the upper left of the screen, the Factiva Pages can be customized by geographic region and by industry category.

Figure 4-10. Factiva's News Page Option

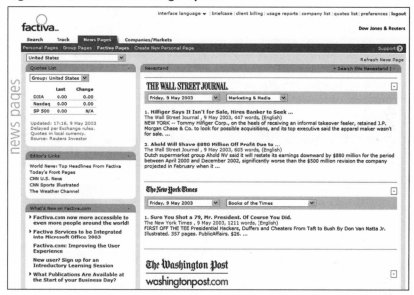

© 2003 Dow Jones Reuters Business Interactive LLC (Trading as Factiva). All rights reserved. Reprinted with permission of the publisher.

Other types of News Pages include Group News, set up by an organization's administrator to provide customized current news for selected groups of users with the organization, and Personal News, which subscribers can set up individually to display the sources and sections from publications they want to monitor.

4. **Companies/Markets** provides access to detailed information on companies in seventy-two countries. The Companies/Markets area consists of five categories of content:

1. Financial data for 42,500 companies worldwide
2. 36.5 million Dun & Bradstreet records, with links to full Dun & Bradstreet reports

3. 30,000 investment analyst reports in PDF format
4. Stock quotes, often going back twenty-five years, on publicly traded securities
5. Company profiles, snapshots, and news

Subscribers can use the Companies/Markets area to build a list of companies that meet specific criteria, create charts of stocks, funds, and market indices, view investment reports on companies or industries of interest, and build customized company profiles. The Company Quick Search feature, shown below for Johnson & Johnson (see Figure 4-11), is particularly useful when one needs to pull together content from a number of sources and areas within Factiva.

Figure 4-11. Factiva's Company Quick Search Feature

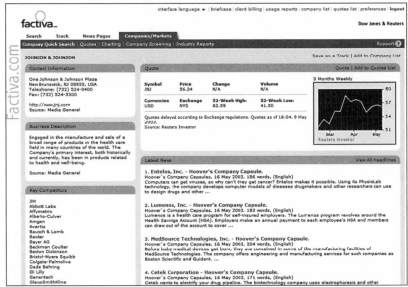

© 2003 Dow Jones Reuters Business Interactive LLC (Trading as Factiva). All rights reserved. Reprinted with permission of the publisher.

SOURCE EVALUATION: Factiva's strength lies in its focus on business and industry information sources and in its global content. It offers a powerful and flexible search interface, advanced search features, deep archives of content, and intuitive tools for pulling information together from a variety of sources. Keep in mind that because of its focus on business information, Factiva is *not* a one-stop source for researchers who also need access to scientific-technical, medical, or legal information.

Factiva has recently made some significant improvements to its service. One such improvement is the box on the Search screen that allows users to exclude republished news (which is so common in newswire data sources) and other types of articles. Intelligent Indexing is also an improvement over what Dow Jones had before, but it can be frustrating for professional researchers. Another limitation is that when one is using the More Like This function, it is not clear which indexing terms the system is keying on. The Help functionality could also be beefed up. When clicking on the question mark in the upper-right corner, you go to a very generalized Help menu and must scroll through to find what you need. Often you must go to the more detailed written guides on the Factiva site.

Through its partnership with Reuters and SunGard (Tradeline), Factiva has taken the integration of market data and business news to a new level, allowing users to see the direct effect of company news and announcements on stock price. Factiva subscribers can drag a mouse over the performance line or bars in a company's historical stock chart to see headlines that link to stories describing the cause in the rise or fall in stock price.

Factiva's user interfaces are both feature rich and intuitive. Many of the default settings can be customized through the Preferences screen, which further enhances the usability of the interfaces. The user interfaces are available in nine languages. Factiva offers several technical support and customer service options, available through Factiva's Membership Circle by clicking the Support icon. Support and service options include:

- A knowledge base of frequently asked questions, under the Find Answers tab
- Ask-A-Question via e-mail, with responses within one hour, during business hours
- Call-Me 24x7, through which a customer service representative calls the subscriber with an answer within ten minutes of an e-mail request, Monday through Friday, or within one hour during weekends and holidays. (This is not available to Knowledge Tier customers.)

Flat-fee subscribers can also call a toll-free number for live customer service and technical support. User documentation, case studies, reports, and white papers are also available online (*http://www.factiva.com/collateral*). Some of these documents are available in multiple languages, including French, German, Italian, Spanish, and Japanese. In addition, Factiva offers free self-directed lessons and product tours, and online and face-to-face training sessions throughout the world. The schedules for these sessions are listed online (*http://www.factiva.com/learning*).

SOURCE VALUE RATING: All of the data source reviewers were asked to rate each source on the basis of the following eight categories, using "10" as the highest rating and "1" as the lowest ("80" being a perfect score):

1. Relative cost-to-value:	9
2. Relative timeliness of data:	10
3. Relative comprehensiveness of data:	10
4. Ease of use:	8
5. Search options available:	7
6. Level of support services:	6
7. Level of training offered:	6
8. Amount/kinds of special services offered:	9
Total Rating:	65

SOURCE REVIEWS: Factiva is one of *KM World Magazine*'s "Top 100 Companies in Knowledge Management" and part of *EContent Magazine*'s "Top 100 content companies to watch." Factiva is also recognized as a winner of the 2002 Software & Information Industry Association's Codie Awards in the Best Online Business, Corporate or Professional Information category. Other reviews include:

Hane, Paula. "Serious About Customer Service." *Information Today* 20, no. 3 (March 1, 2003). Interview with Clare Hart, CEO of Factiva.com, in which she discusses the company's products and plans, as well as trends in the information industry.

O'Leary, Mick. "Factiva.com: The New Dow Jones/Reuters Synthesis." *EContent* 24, no. 5 (July 2001). This in-depth article discusses the formation of Factiva.com and introduces the major Factiva.com modules.

Wood, Anthony. "Factiva: The Way We Search Now." *Business Information Searcher* 11, no. 3/4 (February 2002). Extensive review of Factiva's search module, its standard and advanced user interfaces, and output options.

CONTRIBUTOR NAME: Mary Ellen Bates/Meryl Brodsky
AFFILIATION: Bates Information Services, Inc./ Consultant

USEFUL TIPS

- You can save frequently run searches by clicking the Save Search icon at the bottom of the Search screen.
- How-to-use guides are available from the Factiva Web site (*http://www.factiva.com/collateral/download_brchr.asp?node=learning2*). You must have Acrobat Reader software to access them.
- In the Search area, there is a pull-down menu that allows you to sort results by date (either chronological or reverse chronological) or by relevance. Another pull-down menu allows you to select the format of the results. Using these display functions can save time.
- Factiva.com offers a number of preferences that can be set by the user, including the default search interface and date and language restrictions, and the format of search results. The Preferences link is in the top-right corner of the main Factiva.com screen.

LEXISNEXIS

ALTERNATE/PREVIOUS DATA SOURCE NAMES: LexisNexis at lexis. com, LexisNexis at nexis.com, LexisNexis by Credit Card, LN Academic, Anti-Money Laundering Solutions, Authority On Demand, Automated Forms, BNA Mergers & Acquisitions, Collection Solutions, LN Company Analyzer, LN Congressional, Corporate Legal, Courtlink eAccess, Courtlink eFile, LN Document Solutions, LN Environmental, LN Europe Web Product, Get & Print, Gov Periodicals Index, Primary Sources in U.S. History, Insurance Solutions, Intranet Solutions, LN for Law Schools, Law Enforcement Solutions, lexisONE, Mealey's Online, PeopleWise.net, Pranywhere, PowerInvoice, requester, Risk Management Solutions, Scholastic Edition, LN State Capital, LN Statistical, LN Development Pro, Web Publisher, Butterworths LexisNexis Direct, LexisNexis Martindale-Hubbell

SERVICE/PORTAL NAME: *http://www.lexisnexis.com,*
http://www.lexisone.com

SOURCE DESCRIPTION: LexisNexis serves a broad spectrum of the legal, business, government, financial, and academic communities, providing access to current and historic materials in the areas of law, science/medicine, finance, news, international news, and public records from more than thirty-one thousand database sources. The majority of the material in LexisNexis is full text, even in the older files.

LexisNexis is best known as one of the two great sources of legal information; Westlaw is the other. It's practically a given that LexisNexis and/or Westlaw can be found in almost every law office in the country. Lawyers and others who need to research and prepare legal materials use LexisNexis, in part, because it allows users to "Shepardize" legal articles—that is, to research cases and the cases that are cited in those cases. Shepardizing is citation research that leads back to the original case in which the legal matter was first reported. This process is invaluable for gaining perspective, and lawyers depend on it to understand the legal ground they are covering. As a legal research tool, LexisNexis is excellent. Because it serves as a one-stop shop for lawyers, it has also evolved into an excellent news, tax, and accounting source.

The Lexis side of the service, begun in 1973 in Dayton, Ohio, by Mead Data Central, is one of the two major U.S. sources of case law, statutes, and administrative and regulatory information at the state and federal levels. International law also is covered. The material is organized into libraries, allowing for either geographic or subject-oriented lists of possible sources to be viewed. At about the same time, Mead Data Central began offering the National Automated Accounting Research Service (NAARS), a tax database from the American Institute of Certified Public Accountants. This file has been superceded by a number of other tax materials available from a variety of sources.

Over the years, Lexis has added many new features and options. A number of purchases and alliances have added many titles previously available only in print editions to the list of offerings available on Lexis. In a departure from the traditional Lexis subscription-based approach, a more flexible option is now available, the lexisONE service (*http://www.lexisone.com*), which is priced by the day, week, or month for the individual or small firm. Also, the acquisition of CourtLink Corporation allows customers to electronically file legal documents and access and monitor court records. This option is of use to the business community, as well as to attorneys, as will be seen in the discussion of public records below.

Nexis was introduced in 1980, offering several magazines and newspapers, as well as the Reuters and Associated Press newswires. Several years later the New York Times Information Service and its INFOBANK library were added to Nexis, which remains the only place to search the full-text of the *New York Times* back to 1980. Also added during this period was the LEXPAT service, with more than 650,000 patents issued since January 1, 1975. Over the years, a software package made patent drawing sheets available in the first and largest commercial online database of image files—five million in number.

In the two decades since its inception, Nexis has evolved into a comprehensive collection of U.S. and international business information sources in several languages that includes current and archived news, newspapers, broadcast transcripts from major networks, wire services, magazines, and trade journals. In 1994, Mead Data Central was acquired by Reed Elsevier plc, an Anglo-Dutch Company, which changed the company's name to LexisNexis . The LexisNexis Group is now the global legal and information division of Reed Elsevier. New alliances have since been made that add both depth and breadth to the LexisNexis list of offerings.

For example, a real-time, dial-up service for Securities and Exchange Commission electronic EDGAR filings was made available through the new EDGAR Interactive Service. Also in the 1990s, LexisNexis formed a strategic alliance with the National Fraud Center (NFC) to collaborate in the development and delivery of fraud prevention, investigation, and recovery solutions worldwide. This approach has continued, as specialized applications have been developed for a number of segments of the business world. Taking advantage of technological advances, LexisNexis released its full-blown Web product for business professionals, LexisNexis Universe, in 1998. This product combined the functionality found in traditional dial-up access with some of the new bells and whistles that have since become the norm for Internet users.

With the new millenium, LexisNexis announced "a family of knowledge solutions to help customers transform information into business-critical knowledge to drive better decisions." LexisNexis Web Publisher, LexisNexis Intranet Publisher, LexisNexis Custom User Interface, and LexisNexis Portal Integration allow corporations and government agencies to combine local content with relevant services that are part of their LexisNexis subscription.

As part of its global branding initiative, LexisNexis introduced the new corporate Web site at *http://www.LexisNexis.com*. The new site gives customers a view of all the company's products and services offered for sale in the United States, with drop-down menus for browsing by industry, occupation, task, or featured products.

LexisNexis offers two different types of searching: "term and connector" and "natural language." The term and connector method employs keyword searching separated by the Boolean connectors AND, OR, and WITHIN. In natural language searching, searches are entered in plain English without using Boolean connectors. The natural language search in LexisNexis ranks the search results according to relevance, something that really sets the source apart from its peers. To add synonyms, word variations, and other terms or phrases to the search statement, you simply click Suggest Words and Concepts for Entered Terms on the natural language search screen.

No matter which search method you choose, conducting a search on LexisNexis requires first selecting a source, and then entering the search statement. The source selection menu and the search interface look similar, so this part can be confusing. As an alternative, you can use the Guided Search Forms, in which sources are preidentified. Or you can use Command Searching, which is designed for people familiar with the database structure. Command Searching is covered in the LexisNexis training.

After signing on to either Lexis or Nexis, the user is taken to a screen that can be customized or personalized in a number of ways, either by the user or with the assistance of the company's local representative. In addition, a number of standardized home pages have been developed for particular types of users.

To meet the needs of different types of users or search requests, several approaches are presented for searching under the following categories:

- *Quick Search.* Allows simple searches across a combination of file types simultaneously and presents results.
- *Subject Directory.* Searches on one of thirty-four categories of subject headings for current articles on more than twelve hundred topics.
- *Power Search.* Searches the full text of three billion documents in more than thirty-one thousand individual publications or large groups of sources. Allows more sophisticated search strategy construction using Boolean logic, date limitations, and so on.

- *Personal News and Shared News.* Provides regular updates about specific topics of interest to your organization, delivered via e-mail or published on your intranet.

The example shown in Figure 4-12 is customized for use by a business power searcher. The **Personal News** link on the left side of the page leads to search results for search strategies created by the user to monitor topics of choice. These can be created using either keywords or phrases, or an actual search strategy such as *john w/3 jones.* The latter would return hot-linked citations to articles than mention "john" within three words of "jones"—in any order. If this strategy retrieves too many irrelevant articles, narrower construction of search phrases is possible. **Real Time News** functions in the same way. This link uses search terms or strategies created by the user to retrieve articles from the newswires, which are updated at least hourly.

The center section of the power search page is where the actual search is constructed. The Source to Search box for this searcher's page offers two options: All Services/Less Investext, as shown in the figure, and Public Records. The next box contains a drop-down list of the user's favorite sources, to be searched in the typical search request. As shown, the list may be expanded or changed easily by clicking on one of the two buttons provided for this purpose, Find More Sources and Edit My Sources. Examples and hints are provided underneath the next box, where the actual search strategy is entered.

Experienced searchers or those with a complex research problem will probably take advantage of one or more of the various options available for this purpose. But Nexis has added another invaluable tool to this page—the index tool. When one enters a search term, such as *derivatives,* four broad categories and six company names using the word appear in the index box, with buttons that will add them to the search strategy constructed previously. When the user clicks on the categories returned, definitions and possible broader search terms are displayed. This tool may not be needed for every search, but it is bound to be helpful when dealing with unfamiliar terms or when too few articles are retrieved using other search strategies.

The Search Forms box on the right side of the screen provides search forms for individual items in the list of sources chosen by the researcher. This approach is useful when the search should be limited to a specific source.

Figure 4-12. Power Search Page on LexisNexis

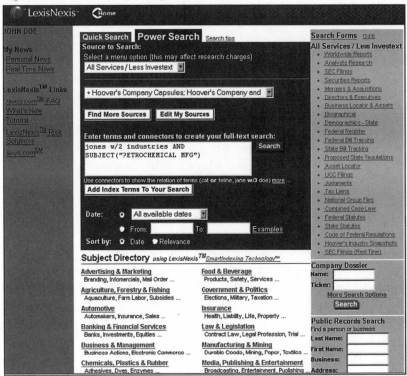

LexisNexis is a trademark of Reed Elsevier Properties, Inc. Reprinted with the permission of LexisNexis.

The remaining areas of the business research power search page include Company Dossier, Public Records Search, Market Information, and Subject Directory. The Company Dossier tool locates companies by name or ticker symbol. Additional search options will identify companies by location, industry, size, or financial status. The amount of information retrieved will vary depending on whether the company is publicly or privately held. A sample search on a major U.S. corporation, for example, yields a lengthy report consisting of information from Hoover's Company Capsules, a summary of yearly financials and detailed financials from Disclosure, stock quotations and charts, a listing of officers and directors, parent-subsidiary information, key competitors, and recent news articles mentioning the company.

Another useful link accessible in the Company Dossier section offers a Company Compare option. Up to four additional companies may be compared to the company being searched. Balance sheet, income statement, and ratio information will be reported for companies that are listed on one of the U.S. stock exchanges in the currency that the company reports to the SEC.

For company research outside of the United States, Nexis offers group files, such as All International Company Reports, All Europe Company Information, and All Asia & Pacific Rim Company Information. Additional possibilities for locating foreign companies include a long list of country-specific or international directory files.

Examining industries is another common business research application. A link on the home page points to a group file called INDNWS, which retrieves industry-oriented articles from among the publications in the Nexis collection. Nexis also offers Responsive Database Service's TableBase, a database specializing exclusively in tabular data. TableBase includes data on companies, industries, products, and demographics from over one thousand sources, including RDS's Business & Industry database, privately published statistical annuals, trade associations, government agencies, nonprofit research groups, and industry reports prepared by investment research groups. Figure 4-13 shows a table retrieved with TableBase from a detailed article on packaging strategies.

Figure 4-13. Sample of the TableBase Feature on LexisNexis

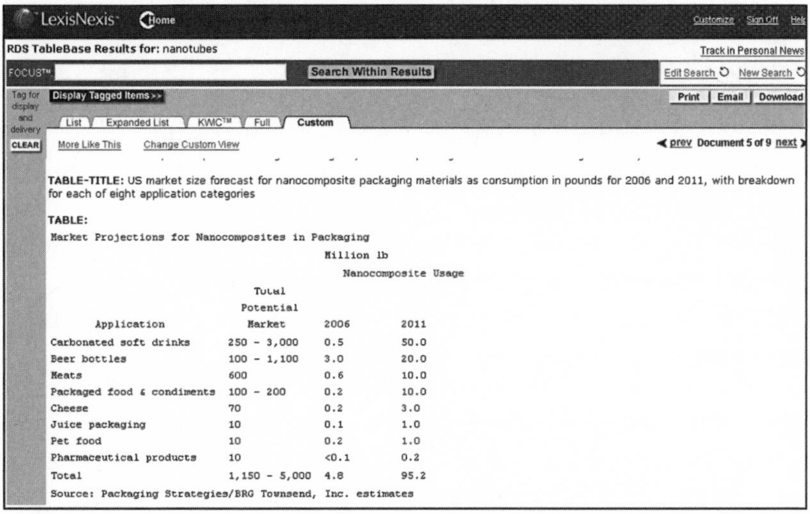

TABLE-TITLE: US market size forecast for nanocomposite packaging materials as consumption in pounds for 2006 and 2011, with breakdown for each of eight application categories

TABLE:

Market Projections for Nanocomposites in Packaging

Application	Tutal Potential Market	Million lb Nanocomposite Usage 2006	2011
Carbonated soft drinks	250 - 3,000	0.5	50.0
Beer bottles	100 - 1,100	3.0	20.0
Meats	600	0.6	10.0
Packaged food & condiments	100 - 200	0.2	10.0
Cheese	70	0.2	3.0
Juice packaging	10	0.1	1.0
Pet food	10	0.2	1.0
Pharmaceutical products	10	<0.1	0.2
Total	1,150 - 5,000	4.8	95.2

Source: Packaging Strategies/BRG Townsend, Inc. estimates

LexisNexis is a trademark of Reed Elsevier Properties, Inc. Reprinted with the permission of LexisNexis.

TableBase is used for researching topics such as market share, company and brand rankings, industry and product forecasts, production and consumption statistics, imports and exports, usage and capacity, number of users/outlets, trends, and much more.

LexisNexis also offers a large quantity of non-U.S. data. Country reports are available from several highly respected sources, and searching for non-U.S. news and information may be expedited by using categories such as Americas (Non-U.S.), Asia & Pacific Rim, Europe, and Middle East & Africa.

Public records provide a wealth of information for the business researcher looking for information about companies or individuals. Real and personal property records, business and person locators, civil and criminal court filings, secretary of state records (including corporate charters), liens, judgments, UCC filings, jury verdicts and settlements, professional licenses, and bankruptcy filings are included among the record types found in LexisNexis, representing counties and states from across the United States. Information found within these documents can be used to locate a company or person's current address, uncover hidden assets or associations, discover legal entanglements, and more.

In Figure 4-14, a search for *Jones Industries* was entered in the Public Records search box of the Power Search page. The search turned up companies with this name, or variations thereof, in eight states. It revealed that incorporation records for Jones Industries exist in Connecticut, Arizona, Idaho, Florida, California, Georgia, and Indiana. By examining one of these records and noting the Corporate Charter ID number, your company could contact the secretary of state to order a copy of that charter and gain valuable information not available publicly elsewhere. Assumed or fictitious name filings also appear for several states. In Texas, Jones Industries is apparently not incorporated with the secretary of state, but the assumed name record provides the name and address of the party registered to use that business name.

The handy Public Records Search feature lets you perform a quick Public Records search in the LexisNexis EZFIND combined person-location file and the ALLBIZ file, which provides business and corporation information. Several other public record types are included in the list of links on the right side of the business searcher home page. Figure 4-15 shows the search screen available for Commercial Code (UCC) filings, which provide evidence of debt in the form of loans or leases.

Figure 4-14. LexisNexis Supports Public Record Searching with Numerous Options

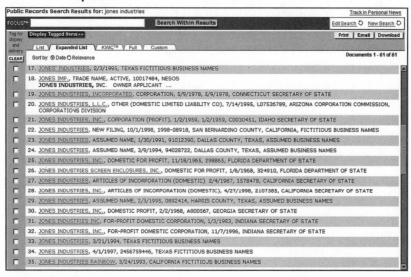

LexisNexis is a trademark of Reed Elsevier Properties, Inc. Reprinted with the permission of LexisNexis.

Figure 4-15. UCC Filings Are Searchable on LexisNexis

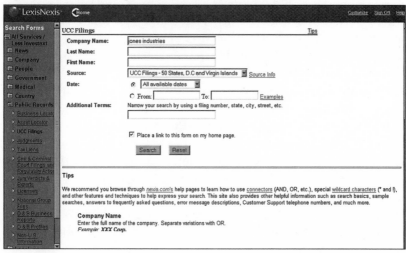

LexisNexis is a trademark of Reed Elsevier Properties, Inc. Reprinted with the permission of LexisNexis.

Additional links provide access to similar search forms for the Asset Locator, Uniform Judgments, and Tax Liens.

Most large companies find that it is important to keep up with new federal legislation or in the state(s) where they do business. New laws that may affect taxation, environmental issues, and many other matters can have a significant impact on a company's ability to do business profitably. LexisNexis offers both Federal Bill Tracking and State Bill Tracking databases for this purpose. Additional links on the business researcher's home page provide access to the full text of federal or state bills and to the *Federal Register* and Proposed State Bills.

PRICING: Cost is an important factor to consider when performing online research. LexisNexis has supplemented its original monthly subscription-based approach by adding a number of new purchasing options. Large companies, law firms, or academic institutions would likely prefer the flat-rate subscription that is negotiated based on the number of users, typical amount of searching per month, and other factors. Small firms or individual users may purchase short-term packages, say for one day or one week, and download as much as they want during the lifetime of the package. For $75 per day or $250 per week, a searcher could plan a concentrated period of search activity. This could be a very cost-effective way to use LexisNexis when needed.

Another approach provides "pay-as-you-go" access. In this case prices can vary from $1 for a public record to $12 per document for company or financial information. Certain files may not be included in these package deals, but if these files are required, it may be possible to make special arrangements through Customer Service. Spokespeople for LexisNexis stress the flexibility in their purchase plans. Complete descriptions of these nonsubscription pricing plans and lists of files or titles available under either of the plans can be viewed by clicking on the link entitled **Nonsubscribers: Pay as you go!** which is found in the upper-left corner of the main LexisNexis home page (*http://www.lexisnexis.com*).

SOURCE EVALUATION: The fact that LexisNexis offers many business-related databases in full text has facilitated the development of the new products described previously. When combined with the wide range of subject matter available, the availability of full text may mean that the user can complete a major business research project with one-stop shopping at *http://www.lexisnexis.com.*

Customer Support via telephone has always been both friendly and high quality in this reviewer's experience. Support personnel, divided into Lexis and Nexis categories, are obviously knowledgeable about their databases. On more than one occasion a support person has tried various searches for the caller, discussed what was found, and then provided the exact search strategy that was successful. Free training may be arranged telephonically through a link at *http://www.lexisnexis.com.* The session lasts for about one hour and can be customized according to interests and level of expertise.

SOURCE VALUE RATING: All of the data source reviewers were asked to rate each source on the basis of the following eight categories, using "10" as the highest rating and "1" as the lowest ("80" being a perfect score):

1. Relative cost-to-value:	8
2. Relative timeliness of data:	9
3. Relative comprehensiveness of data:	8
4. Ease of use:	7
5. Search options available:	8
6. Level of support services:	8
7. Level of training offered:	7
8. Amount/kinds of special services offered:	7
Total Rating:	62

SOURCE REVIEWS:

Bates, Mary Ellen. "Can Small Businesses Go Online?" *Searcher* (January 2003): 16. Dialog, LexisNexis, Factiva, and Northern Light are compared, mostly in terms of "by-the-drink" prices.

"Choosing a Journal Database Provider: Current Options for Searching Journal Databases Online." *The Information Advisor* 15, no. 4 (April 2003). Reviews current vendor options for searching key databases of trade and journal articles.

Christiani, Linnea. "Meeting the New Challenges at West and LexisNexis." *Searcher* 10, no. 5 (May 1, 2002): 68. Interviews with the chief technology officers at West and LexisNexis.

Gordon, Stacey L. "What's New on Westlaw, LexisNexis, Versus-Law, and Loislaw." *Legal Information Alert* 21, no. 10

(November 1, 2002): 1. Updates, including content and technological enhancements to the user interface.

Hurst, Jill Ann, and David M. Oldenkamp. "LexisNexis Statistical Universe,Web Wise Ways." *Searcher* 6, no. 10 (June 1, 2002): 18. Detailed review of what is now called LexisNexis Statistical.

Lawrence, Stephanie. "Natural Selection Is the Key to Software Evolution, Consult on All Proposed Changes and a Successful Program Can Be Updated to Appeal to Less Sophisticated New Users Without Alienating Savvy Old Hands." *Information World Review* (December 1, 2002): 26. Discussion of the evolution of software at LexisNexis. The author is a product manager at LexisNexis Butterworths Tolley.

Matesic, Maura. "International News Sources." Chapter *Courier*, Summer 2001 <*http://www.sla.org/chapter/ctor/ courier/v38/v38n4a4.htm*>. Discusses international news searching on Factiva's Dow Jones Interactive, LexisNexis, and free Internet news Web sites in terms of search engine, content, and delivery method.

Russell, Roger. "LexisNexis Targets Small to Midsized CPA Firms." *Accounting Today* 16, no. 4 (February 25, 2002): 22. Discusses how small and medium-sized accounting firms can use LexisNexis.

CONTRIBUTOR NAME: Helen P. Burwell/Meryl Brodsky
AFFILIATION: Burwell Enterprises/Consultant

USEFUL TIPS

- Look for group files that cover all sources on LexisNexis that cover your topic.
- Add links to your LexisNexis home page for sources that you use frequently. Watch for a box on the search screen that says "Place a link to this form on my home page."
- Try customizing your LexisNexis home page. This saves time in the long run.
- The pay-as-you-go option allows you to conduct a search or view headlines for no charge. Users pay only for the complete text of articles that they view.
- The pay-by-the-day (or week) option allows unlimited access to specific subsets of the LexisNexis database (and its documents) at a set price.

FINANCIAL ACCOUNTING RESEARCH SYSTEM (FARS)

ALTERNATIVE/PREVIOUS DATA SOURCE NAMES: FASB (Financial Accounting Standards Board) Current Text, Original Pronouncements, EITF Abstracts

SOURCE DESCRIPTION: The FASB's Financial Accounting Research System (FARS) (*http://www.fasb.org/fars*) is a CD-ROM product that contains the complete current and historic authoritative accounting standards for businesses. While all of the contents are also available for purchase in print, it provides quick access for the retrieval and output of specific pronouncements, as well as the ability to search across this important body of accounting literature. This product can be regarded as a tool-of-the-trade for the accountant or anyone needing to access accounting technical standards.

SOURCE CONTENT: FARS contains the following information:

- **Original Pronouncements.** FASB and AICPA pronouncements (including totally superseded pronouncements): FASB Statements, Interpretations, Technical Bulletins, and Concepts Statements; ARBs 43-51; APB Opinions and Statements; and AICPA Accounting Interpretations and Terminology Bulletins
- **Current Text.** Integration of financial accounting and reporting standards arranged by topic. Contains General Standards, Industry Standards, and Current Text sections that have been totally superseded but are still applicable due to a delayed effective date
- **EITF Abstracts.** Full text of each abstract for every issue discussed by the FASB's Emerging Issues Task Force since its inception in 1984. Also includes EITF topical index
- **Implementation Guides.** Q&As from FASB Special Reports and other published implementation guidance, including a special implementation aid for statements 133, 137, and 138, *Derivative Instruments and Hedging Activities*
- **Comprehensive Topical Index.** References linked to appropriate sections of all the included publications

The content included in FARS is very comprehensive, including the text of all the financial accounting technical standards, even those that have been totally superceded. However, it does not include all of the FASB's print publications series; among the series not included are *Discussion Memoranda, Invitations to Comment,* and *Exposure Drafts.* These titles can be ordered in print directly from the FASB Store link located on the Web site.

The content is presented in Folio Views, a search interface that is very popular in legal research. Information can be accessed using four approaches:

- **Table of Contents** that links to the appropriate document or text in the document
- **Topical index references** that link to the corresponding text
- **Predefined query templates** that facilitate the most commonly used search queries
- **User-defined queries** that allow you to customize your searches

Results from any approach may be printed or downloaded immediately, or they may be tagged for later batch printing or downloading.

FARS is relatively timely with new disks issues six times a year to reflect the issuance of new FASB documents. Regularly checking the FASB Web site for new and forthcoming releases will enable the searcher to catch any new documents released in-between receiving the six updates.

SOURCE EVALUATION: FARS is a relatively easy product to browse and search although someone new to the Folio Views interface will want to begin by using the FARS Reference Guide. The guide also contains links to the excellent Folio Views Help. Telephone and e-mail technical support is available from FASB, and the FARS Web site contains a useful series of technical FAQs. Product-specific training is not available.

FARS is priced very reasonably and, to its credit, in line with the cost of purchasing the print editions of the content. A single-user license for FARS costs $585 for the first year and $520 for succeeding years. A license for network access to the product costs $585 for the first user and $518 for each added user; renewal prices are $520 and $456, respectively. A subscription to the print sources that include all the titles on FARS would cost $662.

The FARS Web site includes a link to a small subset of the content that can be easily downloaded. The demo is free and is very useful for giving the prospective user a good idea of the Folio Views search experience.

For anyone regularly needing to access or search FASB accounting technical standards, FARS presents an extremely reasonable product. Its simple search interface and conservative pricing model make this a product that should be seriously considered by anyone regularly needing to access this content.

SOURCE VALUE RATING: All of the data source reviewers were asked to rate each source on the basis of the following eight categories, using "10" as the highest rating and "1" as the lowest ("80" being a perfect score):

1. Relative cost-to-value:	9
2. Relative timeliness of data:	8
3. Relative comprehensiveness of data:	9
4. Ease of use:	6
5. Search options available:	7
6. Level of support services:	4
7. Level of training offered:	4
8. Amount/kinds of special services offered:	5
Total Rating:	52

CONTRIBUTOR NAME: Naomi Clifford
AFFILIATION: Consultant

USEFUL TIPS

- The novice user is strongly urged to carefully review the FARS Reference Guide to familiarize himself/herself with the features of the product.

CCH TAX RESEARCH NETWORK

SERVICE/PORTAL NAME: *http://tax.cchgroup.com*

SOURCE DESCRIPTION: CCH, as part of a larger collection of tax-specific databases, also includes a library focused on accounting and auditing research materials. CCH has partnered with Aspen to provide access to its excellent series of industry newsletters and many of the popular Miller Guides. The Miller Guides provide concise explanations of accounting and auditing standards and have long been a standard reference source for researching U.S. and international authoritative accounting standards. Interestingly, CCH's own publication, *U.S. Master GAAP Guide*, is not included in this library, although it is available in several of the tax libraries.

Access to the CCH Tax Research Network is divided into a series of subject tabs representing different "libraries" or "collections" of related content. These tabs are Accounting and Auditing, plus a series which are tax-focused: Federal, State, Financial &

Estate, Special Entities, Pension & Payroll, International, Perform Plus II, and CCH Client Relate. Each tab contains its own collection of sources, although some titles are reproduced in multiple tabs and CCH's search option allows for selecting content across tabs for keyword searching. CCH offers very flexible purchasing plans, providing the customer with many options for purchasing discreet titles. In other words, you can pay for just the content that is important to your information needs.

SOURCE CONTENT: The Accounting and Auditing library is divided into two main sections:

- **News and Developments**. This section contains access to the full text of a number of industry newsletters. One of these, the *Public Accounting Report*, often referenced as PAR, is the premier newsletter for profiling and ranking the top first and second tier accounting firms and tracking and examining industry trends and their impact on firm engagements and practice. Full-text, cover-to-cover access to this important publication is very limited, and so having such complete access to it via CCH's interface is a real plus for this product. Several of the other Aspen newsletters, in particular, *CPA Marketing Report, CPA Personnel Report,* and *CPA Managing Partner Report,* provide important guidance for successful strategies important to client engagement work and the running of a competitive accounting firm. All of the newsletters can be searched in full text and downloaded in .pdf.
- **Miller Libraries**. The remaining six subsections contain the Miller Guides: GAAP, Governmental, GAAS, Engagement, Not-for-Profit, and International. The GAAP section contains the *Miller GAAP Guide,* the oldest and most widely used of the series. It also contains the very important *Miller GAAP Financial Disclosure Statement Manual.* The latter publication, a competitor to the *AICPA's Accounting Trends and Techniques,* contains more than nine hundred examples of realistic sample footnote disclosures in the preparation of financial statements and a financial statement disclosure checklist of required and recommended GAAP disclosures currently in use. The *Miller GAAP Guide,* like the other guides in the series, provides contextual guidance for application of standards, cross-references to related authoritative standards, and when appropriate, information about policies, procedures, and reviews.

SOURCE EVALUATION: The Miller Guides are available on other electronic databases, such as LexisNexis, but there might be several advantages for the researcher to consider when evaluating access to the content via CCH vs. LexisNexis or other interfaces:

- **Excellent browsing and search options.** CCH's interface presents an impressive combination of ease of use with a powerful search engine that allows for full Boolean keyword searching. CCH also enables quick browsing from the Table of Contents down to the section and discreet document level, and you can even combine browsing with keyword searching. You always have the option of searching across all the subscribed to sources, one discreet source, or any combination of individual sources.
- **Access to important tax research resources.** If your research needs also require that you access certain tax information, another benefit of subscribing to the CCH Tax Research Network is access to its excellent and reputable collection of tax sources.
- **Ability to search across library content.** CCH's powerful search interface enables the user to easily select sources from across multiple tabs for efficient and comprehensive searching.
- **Keeplist.** As you locate documents that you want to output, CCH's Keeplist function enables you to painlessly "save" the document in a folder, which you customize for particular projects. This feature allows you to efficiently tag documents for later output without having to interrupt your workflow to print or save documents while in the research process.
- **Path.** CCH maintains an ongoing audit trail of your search strategy and returned documents, providing important information both for the client's work papers and for the manager who may be checking the work.

CCH also provides excellent documentation that includes lots of useful tips and strategies for effectively using its interface. All the documentation is available directly on the Web site and be either "looked up" while online or printed for later reference.

As a publisher of important tax content, CCH's Tax Research Network has been known for setting the standard of creating a tax search interface that approximates the research methodology favored by most tax practitioners. The addition of the popular Miller Guides is a real perk. CCH's Accounting and Auditing library is very reasonably priced. However, since the *Miller GAAP Guides* are also available on other interfaces, the researcher will want to consider the following to best determine the cost-to-value:

- Is electronic access to the content important for the researcher and his or her clients? Would purchasing a few titles in print suffice?
- Is the researcher already subscribing to an electronic database that contains the Miller Guides?
- If so, does the interface provide access to the content in a manner which suits the information needs and time constraints of the searcher?
- Is the researcher already subscribing to some CCH's tax content, and if so, would the cost to add the additional content be relatively small?

Source Value Rating: All of the data source reviewers were asked to rate each source on the basis of the following eight categories, using "10" as the highest rating and "1" as the lowest ("80" being a perfect score):

1. Relative cost-to-value:	7
2. Relative timeliness of data:	9
3. Relative comprehensiveness of data:	8
4. Ease of use:	10
5. Search options available:	10
6. Level of support services:	9
7. Level of training offered:	8
8. Amount/kinds of special services offered:	8
Total Rating:	69

Contributor Name: Susan M. Klopper
Affiliation: Goizueta Business Library

USEFUL TIPS

- Although this is an extremely easy product to use, it would be useful to print out the documentation, available through the HELP button at the top of the page, in order to ensure that you take advantage of all the excellent search, save, and output options.

FINANCIAL ACCOUNTING STANDARDS BOARD (FASB)

ALTERNATIVE/PREVIOUS DATA SOURCE NAMES: FASB

SERVICE/PORTAL NAME: *http://www.fasb.org*

SOURCE DESCRIPTION: The FASB is responsible for issuing authoritative accounting standards. Its information resources and its Web site are highly important for anyone needing to conduct accounting research and to monitor significant events relating to the accounting industry. Both of these objectives can be well accommodated using this Web site.

SOURCE CONTENT: FASB does not make available (for free) on its Web site the text of all of its standards. Rather, it provides summaries and selected full text of "recent" releases and excellent summaries, cross-references, and status updates of a significant number of pronouncements. Clearly labeled links on the left of the screen together with additionally informative "bubble-overs," make it extremely easy to navigate to the desired content. Key links include: **Recent Additions, Action Alerts, Exposure Drafts, EITF, Staff Positions, Derivatives, International, BRRP, Articles & Reports, and FAS Summaries**. The site also includes links to **Governmental Accounting Standards Board (GASB)** and **International Accounting Standards (IAS)** information. Anyone needing to monitor recently released and forthcoming documents and read about hot accounting issues should regularly click on the **News Center** link at the top of the page to track substantive announcements.

Additionally useful content is the **FASB Store** which provides extremely detailed descriptive information about print and electronic publications including **FASB Facts**, containing good explanations of who FASB is, its responsibilities and documents, and **Technical Inquiry**, a series of FAQs which provide guidance on contacting FASB for technical information.

SOURCE EVALUATION: This Web site is extremely well designed. It is uncluttered and easy on the eyes. The navigational links on the left frame are clearly labeled and clicking on them takes you to substantive and well-explained information. All reports are well documented with clear citations that include information on any updates. Pages often contain information about the date that the information was posted on the site, an all too unfamiliar, but much needed, level of information on most Web sites. The site does have a search engine that only accepts basic keyword searching but, when tested, the results were surprisingly good. There is also a search option on each page for searching across just that content.

Although the majority of FASB's documents are not available for free on the site, its summaries are effective for helping the researcher glean some basic information and identify some key sources, all of which can be ordered online. The FASB site contains enough information to satisfy the casual information requestor and yet provide the serious researcher with critical information for moving ahead with his or her research efforts.

SOURCE VALUE RATING: All of the data source reviewers were asked to rate each source on the basis of the following eight categories, using "10" as the highest rating and "1" as the lowest ("80" being a perfect score):

1. Relative cost-to-value:	10
2. Relative timeliness of data:	10
3. Relative comprehensiveness of data:	8
4. Ease of use:	10
5. Search options available:	5
6. Level of support services:	8
7. Level of training offered:	5
8. Amount/kinds of special services offered:	3
Total Rating:	59

CONTRIBUTOR NAME: Susan M. Klopper
AFFILIATION: Goizueta Business Library

USEFUL TIPS

• If you are unfamiliar with the FASB, click on the link to FASB Facts to read very useful information about the FASB, its purpose, internal structure, and publications.
• The link to Contact FASB provides very useful information about individuals on the FASB staff to contact about specific accounting issues.

AMERICAN INSTITUTE OF CERTIFIED PUBLIC ACCOUNTANTS (AICPA)

ALTERNATIVE/PREVIOUS DATA SOURCE NAMES: American Institute of Certified Public Accountants

SERVICE/PORTAL NAME: *http://www.aicpa.org*

SOURCE DESCRIPTION: The AICPA is the national, professional organization of CPAs, with more than 330,000 members in business and industry, public practice, government, and education. It sets auditing standards for private U.S. companies and ethical standards for the accounting profession.

SOURCE CONTENT: Like the FASB Web site, the AICPA does not provide free full-text access to the majority of its standards, although important, recently released documents might be available for a short period of time. It does a very good job of posting information about recently released and forthcoming pronouncements and important accounting issues that the AICPA staff is focusing on, as well as current lobbying initiatives.

For the researcher needing to identify auditing and accounting standards, the primary links are (1) Audit & Attest Standards; (2) Technical Activities and Publications and Accounting Standards; and (3) Technical Documents. To track current professional news, issues, and events, visit the CPA News Center and the Spotlight sections on the home page. To keep up with professional publications, in particular, the *Journal of Accountancy*, click on the link to Online Newsletters. If you are a CPA and do not have access to accounting information, you might want to click on the link to Accounting Library of the University of Mississippi. Several years ago, when the AICPA downsized its physical library collection, it donated the majority of its print collection to the University of Mississippi, which now offers excellent information access and library loan options to CPAs. One of its best features is the link to CPA Links, which contains one of the best collections of recommended professional links.

For those needing to take the CPA Exam or pursue earning continuing education credits, look at the CPA Exam and State News & Info sections.

The link to AICPA Store provides access to descriptions and online purchasing of the AICPA's large number of print and electronic products.

SOURCE EVALUATION: The AICPA's home page is very busy looking and at first glance it can be difficult to hone in on the most important content. Part of this confusion is caused by the fact that the AICPA provides information targeted at different audiences. Although it sometimes falls short of not providing enough information, it will be very beneficial for the researcher needing to identify documents and to keep abreast of recently released documents and forthcoming releases.

It has a very decent search engine that includes some advanced options, such as the ability to search targeted sections of the Web site. If you are unfamiliar with the AICPA, click on the link to About the AICPA to learn more about its roles and standards-setting responsibilities. Contact AICPA contains useful phone numbers for contacting the right group to discuss a technical standards issue.

Although I wish the site was a bit less cluttered with links and text, the AICPA's Web site contains information which is critical to anyone conducting accounting research and needing to monitor accounting news and significant events. Once you become familiar with the sections that are most relevant to your needs, it becomes quicker to navigate.

SOURCE VALUE RATING: All of the data source reviewers were asked to rate each source on the basis of the following eight categories, using "10" as the highest rating and "1" as the lowest ("80" being a perfect score):

1. Relative cost-to-value:	8
2. Relative timeliness of data:	9
3. Relative comprehensiveness of data:	8
4. Ease of use:	7
5. Search options available:	6
6. Level of support services:	7
7. Level of training offered:	5
8. Amount/kinds of special services offered:	3
Total Rating:	53

CONTRIBUTOR NAME: Susan M. Klopper

AFFILIATION: Goizueta Business Library

USEFUL TIPS

- If you are unfamiliar with the AICPA, click on the link to About the AICPA to read useful information about the AICPA, its purpose, internal structure, and publications.
- The link to Contact AICPA provides useful information about individuals on the AICPA staff to contact about specific accounting issues.

U.S. SECURITIES AND EXCHANGE COMMISSION (SEC)

ALTERNATE/PREVIOUS DATA SOURCE NAME: SEC

SERVICE/PORTAL NAME: *http://www.sec.gov*

SOURCE DESCRIPTION: The role of the SEC is to protect investors and to maintain the integrity of the securities markets. It acts like a watchdog over public companies, as well as accounting and investment banking professionals, to ensure that appropriate disclosure regarding public corporate financial information is achieved. For the professional accounting community, the SEC site is most useful for its links to legislation, rules and interpretations, and "pressure points" relating to accounting governance, monitoring, and litigation. EDGAR SEC filings can also be accessed via the Web site, although its interface is inferior to several other free EDGAR sites currently available on the marketplace, such as SEC Info (*http://www.secinfo.com*) and EdgarScan (*http://edgarscan.pwcglobal.com/servlets/edgarscan*). This review will focus on the non-EDGAR content found on the SEC Web site.

SOURCE CONTENT: The SEC home page is neatly divided into broad categories that clearly guide you to relevant content:

- **Information for Accountants** offers a menu of links to virtually all of the information that relates to the accounting profession, including legislation, SEC rules and enforcement releases, speeches, hot issues, links to related associations, and more.
- **Financial Reporting Information Center** contains links to recent SEC actions, regulatory pronouncements, speeches, testimony, and other financial-reporting investor information.
- **SEC Corporate Finance** contains links to information coming from the Division of Corporate Finance, which is focused on making sure that investors have the information they need to make informed investment decisions. This page includes links to Current Accounting and Disclosure Issues and International Financial Reporting and Disclosure Issues.

- **Key Telephone Numbers and Email Addresses** provides links to useful contacts.
- **FAQs** provide useful answers that are highly relevant to financial questions about the SEC documents.
- **News & Press Statements** links you to recent press releases, news digests, public statements and more.

SOURCE EVALUATION: Virtually all of the content found on this Web site is critical to the accounting professional and anyone concerned with conducting research in the area or staying abreast of current events and hot issues. The Web site is relatively well designed and organized into logical sections. In most cases the full text of recently released documents is available on the site; historical documents are much less consistently available and, in fact, it is difficult to predict what older documents might be found here. From the research perspective, it would be nice if the SEC would consistently make more of the historical documents available via the Web site or at a minimum include comprehensive citations or abstracts. As it currently stands, the researcher will still need to subscribe to subscription-based electronic databases, such as LexisNexis or print loose-leaf services, such as CCH's SEC Reporter, to be ensured of complete historical and current content.

SOURCE VALUE RATING: All of the data source reviewers were asked to rate each source on the basis of the following eight categories, using "10" as the highest rating and "1" as the lowest ("80" being a perfect score):

1. Relative cost-to-value:	10
2. Relative timeliness of data:	10
3. Relative comprehensiveness of data:	8
4. Ease of use:	9
5. Search options available:	5
6. Level of support services:	6
7. Level of training offered:	2
8. Amount/kinds of special services offered:	2
Total Rating:	52

CONTRIBUTOR NAME: Brenda Reeb
AFFILIATION: University of Rochester

INTERNATIONAL ACCOUNTING
STANDARDS BOARD (IASB)

ALTERNATIVE/PREVIOUS DATA SOURCE NAMES: IASB

SERVICE/PORTAL NAME: *http://www.iasb.org.uk*

SOURCE DESCRIPTION: The IASB is responsible for setting a single set of global accounting standards. It functions in close collaboration with the FASB, AICPA, and SEC to achieve convergence of accounting standards around the world. Its Web site is the official site for information about its standards, announcements of current and forthcoming releases, and important industry news.

SOURCE CONTENT: The Web site is neatly divided into a few discreet and important sections, all accessible via tabs located at the top of the page. The **Standards** section contains brief descriptions and in many cases summaries of its accounting standards. It also contains excellent information about current and forthcoming projects. **IASB Around the World** contains critical information about the applications of global IAS standards in specific countries. An A–Z directory allows you to click on a specific company to learn if it has its own standards and/or has adopted global accounting standards. **News** contains global news about IASB and related efforts to work toward creating and adopting global standards.

SOURCE EVALUATION: The IASB Web site is efficiently designed and very easy to navigate. A few quick clicks get you to the information that you are looking for. Like the FASB and AICPA Web sites, it is the place to learn about new standards and to monitor industry news. Like these sites, it makes useful summaries of its accounting standards available on the free site, but very little full text. You can subscribe to all its content electronically and view descriptions of, and order, its publications online.

A search engine allows you to conduct simple keyword searches across the Web site. This is truly an international Web site. Although all of the IASB documents are published in English, many of the country-specific documents are in the language of the originating country.

SOURCE VALUE RATING: All of the data source reviewers were asked to rate each source on the basis of the following eight categories, using "10" as the highest rating and "1" as the lowest ("80" being a perfect score):

1. Relative cost-to-value:	9
2. Relative timeliness of data:	9
3. Relative comprehensiveness of data:	8
4. Ease of use:	10
5. Search options available:	6
6. Level of support services:	7
7. Level of training offered:	5
8. Amount/kinds of special services offered:	3
Total Rating:	57

CONTRIBUTOR NAME: Susan M. Klopper
AFFILIATION: Goizueta Business Library

USEFUL TIPS

• If you are unfamiliar with the IASB, click on the link to About Us to read very useful information about the IASB, its purpose, internal structure, and publications.

INTERNAL REVENUE SERVICE: THE DIGITAL DAILY

SERVICE/PORTAL NAME: *http://www.irs.ustreas.gov*

SOURCE DESCRIPTION: The IRS's Web site contains a wealth of information, primarily focused on providing the taxpayer with the various forms and schedules they need to address tax filing issues. While it does not contain very much of the type of "technical" information that an accountant or tax specialist would need, there are some applications which will benefit both accountants and their clients.

SOURCE CONTENT: Three content areas that are most applicable to the accountant are as follows:

• **Forms and Publications** (*http://www.irs.gov/formspubs/index. html*). This section contains all the tax forms and instructions, IRS Publications, IRS Notices, and links to state tax forms. All documents are available in .pdf and will look exactly like the copies you receive from the IRS or from local banks. Forms and publications are available beginning with 1992. Of this type of information, the IRS Publications and IRS Notices are the most frequently used by accountants. The forms and publications are well organized on this page, with several different access points, including alphabetically, by date, and by topic.

- **Tax Information for Businesses** (*http://www.irs.gov/businesses/ index.html*). This section contains some of the technical releases from the IRS that are frequently referenced by accountants and tax specialists including:
  - Market Segment Specialization Program (MSSPs). Audit guides which contain examination techniques, common and unique industry issues, business practices, industry terminology, and other information to assist examiners in performing examinations. A market segment may be an industry, a profession, or an issue.
  - Coordinated Issue Papers. Although not official IRS pronouncements, these papers are important for providing a sense of the IRS's thinking on complex and significant industry-wide issues. One of their main functions is to provide guidance to field examiners to ensure uniform application of the law.
- **How to Contact Us** (*http://www.irs.gov/contact/index.html*). This page contains a wealth of information about how the IRS is organized, from the national down to the regional office and who and how to contact agents as needed. Clicking on Contact My Local Office (*http://www.irs.gov/localcontacts/index.html*) takes you directly to all the contacts for your state.
- **Publication 78, Cumulative List of Organizations**. This is the online version of the print publication used to identify if an organization is exempt from federal taxation, and if so, to determine how much of its contributions are tax deductible. Unfortunately, it is extremely difficult to navigate your way to this content from anywhere on the Web site. The best way to link to this page is to type "publication 78" in "Search IRS Web Site" box.

The IRS Web site also contains important technical IRS documents such as revenue rulings, revenue procedures, field service advice (FSAs) and private letter rulings. Again, to locate these you have to use the search box. Limit your search to simple keywords, such as "revenue rulings," "revenue procedures," "letter rulings," "field service advice." Trying to search on the topic of the ruling is highly problematic. Certainly this access should not be relied on by anyone who regularly needs to access or search these documents but for the infrequent lookup, it is worth a try. Remember that the entire collection of these documents will not be available so that the researcher risks missing important information if access is limited to this site. The Web site also contains an excellent site map and search options both for forms and publications and keywords.

SOURCE EVALUATION: For locating forms or instructions, or IRS publications, the IRS site is well designed and easily navigated with clearly defined links, search options, FAQs and a well-designed site map. Document availability for download into .pdf provides the user with the content in the original format. This Web site proves very useful both for the tax or accounting professional, the casual or experienced user, and the client.

SOURCE VALUE RATING: All of the data source reviewers were asked to rate each source on the basis of the following eight categories, using "10" as the highest rating and "1" as the lowest ("80" being a perfect score):

1. Relative cost-to-value:	10
2. Relative timeliness of data:	10
3. Relative comprehensiveness of data:	10
4. Ease of use:	8
5. Search options available:	8
6. Level of support services:	8
7. Level of training offered:	5
8. Amount/kinds of special services offered:	8
Total Rating:	67

CONTRIBUTOR NAME: Brenda Reeb
AFFILIATION: University of Rochester

ABI/INFORM

SERVICE/PORTAL NAME: *http://www.proquest.com;*
http://www.il.proquest.com

SOURCE DESCRIPTION: ABI/Inform began in 1971 when three graduate students at Portland State University were charged with designing a system that would improve corporate access to business literature. Inspired by the information service developed at a local power company and with contributions from a University of Wisconsin database project called Inform, the students succeeded in developing their system. After graduation they founded a small company that merged their new brand, ABI (Abstracted Business Information) with the Wisconsin database name, Inform, and

ABI/Inform was born. The product generated minimal interest and profits until a Kentucky newspaper owner purchased it in 1973 and made the file available in Dialog. Initially, documents were in abstract-only form. But full-text records were added in 1991, making the product a forerunner among document delivery services for full-text information. After a bitter family argument, the Kentucky media giants sold ABI/Inform to UMI (University Microfilms) in 1986.

ABI/Inform supplies journal articles and abstracts of articles that contain business and management content. The database covers 1,116 periodicals (including a small number of business newspapers such as Barron's), of which 65 percent provide their articles in full text. ABI is known for providing more extensive archival information than its competitors; some retrospective articles date back to 1971. The average date span covers the past ten years.

ABI/Inform targets all environments that depend on business information—academic, corporate, and public. Because the service provides prolific amounts of business literature and can be expensive (depending on the institution size, number of users, and subscription details), most subscribers are larger, research-oriented organizations. Broad topical coverage includes business conditions and trends, management techniques, corporate strategies, and industry information on both a domestic and global level.

Aside from the ProQuest portal, ABI/Inform content may be accessed through any of the following products: Dialog (*http://www.dialog.com*), Ovid/Silverplatter (*http://www.ovid.com*), OCLC/FirstSearch (*http://www.oclc.org*), and the corporate version of LexisNexis (*http://www.lexis-nexis.com*).

ABI/Inform contains one of the best collections of accounting and financial journals, and has traditionally been one of the best sources to turn to for secondary discussions and analysis of accounting standards. Subscribing to this database via the ProQuest portal offers the advantage of displaying most of the articles in .pdf, but it is expensive and therefore may not be an option for many organizations. ABI's collection of articles is also available on Dialog. If you need to regularly search back more than five years for accounting issues, you may want to explore Dialog's pay-as-you-go pricing options. For articles published in the past five years and moving forward, many of the journals have now been added to the other business aggregators, such as Factiva and LexisNexis.

PRICING: An annual subscription to ABI/Inform ranges from $6,000 to approximately $75,000.

SOURCE CONTENT: This section describes the content and related features of ABI/Inform under the following five categories:

1. **Origin of Information**. ABI/Inform does not create its content; rather, it gathers content created by others and provides the search engine and indexing that allows the information to be searchable. Journal aggregators, such as ABI/Inform, are evaluated on both the volume and quality of the incorporated publications and the effectiveness of the search engine.

2. **Navigation**. Six features are presented on the top horizontal navigation bar: Collections, Search Methods, Topic Finder, Browse Lists, Results & Marked List, and Search Guide. The key to searching ABI/Inform lies in understanding how to successfully use the search tools. The Search Methods button is the researcher's primary instrument. From Search Methods, the researcher has five different options, allowing for a range of searching styles—from "quick and dirty" searching in the Basic module to precision level in the Guided module.

3. **Search Methods**. The Basic search contains four drop boxes and three check-box options for fine-tuning a search. The search box allows for keyword searching of an article. The user is guided to fill in the box with a word, words, or specific phrase. The user next specifies a date range by choosing Current (1999–Present), Backfile (1986–1998), or Deep Backfile (Prior to 1986); the default is Current. For Publication Type, the user is prompted to choose All, Periodicals, or Newspapers; the default is All. Identifying whether the keywords should search just the citations and abstracts or the entire article text is the next step; the default is Citations and Abstracts. The searcher can further limit the results by clicking on a check box to turn on three different options: show results with full-text availability only, show articles from peer-reviewed publications only, and a more unusual limiter, or show total number of articles. Most journal aggregators automatically provide the total number of hits somewhere on the results pages. It is unusual that ABI/Inform does not. The searcher may turn on this feature by clicking a box.

   For the researcher requiring more defined searching options, there are advantages to using the other four search tools. The Guided search is geared toward precision searching. Whereas the basic engine is useful for "free searching"— looking for general research ideas—Guided search is best for the user with a citation in–hand: someone who already knows the article title or author. This tool allows for limiting by Article Type. For example, it is possible to narrow a search to editorials, cover stories, or interviews. Customizing the search to a specific company or geographic area is also possible.

The Advanced Word search page is arranged with the basic search interfaces on the top half and the Search Guide as the bottom half. It presents a method of searching various codes, a thesaurus, a hierarchical map of terms, and other tools that will encourage the user to choose search terms based on the way the indexing has been set up. The idea is to show how the categories and subcategories of subjects are arranged, so that the user will understand the logic and make better keyword and subject choices and hence receive better search results. Two features show how to search ABI/Inform using code numbers instead of words. Guides that offer information on connection operators (AND, NOT, etc.), stop words (ignored words such as "a," "the," etc.), and truncation techniques are also included.

Natural Language allows the user to search ABI/Inform in a conversational style. That is, you can ask the database a question, much as in the Internet-based search engine Ask Jeeves (*http://www.askjeeves.com*). The results list shows red graphic "stars" next to each article to indicate relevance.

With the Publication search tool, the researcher types the title of the desired journal into a search box. If the journal is part of the ABI/Inform database, a page of links appears, each link representing a volume/issue. When the user clicks on a link, the table of contents and list of articles for that particular volume are displayed. The user cannot perform a keyword search of a particular volume in this search module, but such a keyword search for a particular journal can be done in the Guided Search mode.

4. **Highlights of Other Web Features**. The Topic Finder offers an alternative to the "keywords-and-search-box" style of article searching. With Topic Finder, a hierarchy of hyperlinked business-related topics and subtopics are presented. The interface initially shows six main topic areas: Business & Industry, Computers & Internet, Economics & Trade, Environment, Government & Law, and Social Issues & Policy. When the user clicks on one of these, another group of hyperlinked subtopics appear. After clicking on a subtopic, the user gets a selection of article links to choose from.

Browse Lists offers a straight list of A–Z terms that are a combination of subjects, people, places, and companies. Under each term is a link prompting the user to use the View Articles link. Many of the terms also have a Narrow by Related Terms link. The user may either click hyperlinked alphabetical letters or enter a word in the search box to navigate through the list of terms.

The Results and Marked List button offers three features: Marked List & Durable Links, Results List, and Recent Searches. Marked List & Durable Links is a tool for managing saved articles. This section presents the user with the check-marked "favorite" articles that were selected. The user has the option of saving the durable link to the article by clicking the Export button. The user may then cut and paste the link as a URL into a browser and the article will be available for perusal for one month. Printing the article is also an option. Whether an article contains the abstract or full text of an article is indicated by icons of a camera or a sheet of paper, respectively. The words "abstract" and "full text" do not appear. This might be confusing to a researcher who doesn't understand the icons.

Also of note is a new tool called ProQuest SiteBuilder. This tool makes ABI/Inform articles available on third-party Web sites. Results List and Recent Searches are the article list result page of the latest search and a list of all the current session's executed search strings.

5. **Special Services and Competitor Comparison.** In addition to offering ProQuest SiteBuilder, ABI/Inform has other changes in the works. ABI/Inform's Archive Database is a recent addition, offering historical back-file content of twenty-five business periodicals, with coverage dates beginning in the early twentieth century. The back file includes image access, which allows viewing of advertisements from decades past. One of the newer features is the integration of Hoover's company profiles, although I was unable to access these from my portal.

A simple search of ABI and its main competitor, Business Source Premier, indicates a significant difference in the number and relevance of article results. Using the basic-level search option in Business Source Premier and ABI/Inform, I executed a search for the phrase *small business* among all articles published in 2002. I received 35 results using ABI/Inform and 116 using Business Source Premier. ABI/Inform results are more exact, according to the company's literature, because the articles are indexed with a high level of detail. This style of indexing, combined with an effective controlled vocabulary, culminates in what ABI brands "relevance bias." ABI/Inform indexes some unique fields, such as article type, geographic name, classification code, personal name, headnote, and document column head.

SOURCE EVALUATION: If your organization is interested in purchasing the "Rolls Royce" of business journal databases, ABI/Inform is the database for you. ABI/Inform offers precision searching, daily data updates, superior technical service, useful archival content, and tools, such as the ProQuest SiteBuilder, that respond to the changing technological needs of its customers. The tools are arranged logically under main buttons, allowing the user to quickly identify the location of features.

Depending upon the type of institution and needs of its users, all environments may not need the high-powered features of ABI/Inform. ABI offers superior indexing and a search engine with more options than its competitors, but it comes at a price. A general cost analysis for a mid-to-large-sized academic institution suggests that an annual subscription price of ABI/Inform costs 35–45 percent more than a similar contract with EBSCO's Business Source Premier. Aside from being more economical, Business Source Premier offers a less complicated interface and easier-to-use, albeit less effective, search tools. In addition, it provides access to more full-text journals: 2,800 compared with ABI/Inform's 1,116. Keep in mind that "more" might not always mean "better." Looking through a specific crop of the best business journals could make for a better search pool than choosing from a larger unrefined group of irrelevant journals.

SOURCE VALUE RATING: All of the data source reviewers were asked to rate each source on the basis of the following eight categories, using "10" as the highest rating and "1" as the lowest ("80" being a perfect score):

1. Relative cost-to-value:	6
2. Relative timeliness of data:	10
3. Relative comprehensiveness of data:	7
4. Ease of use:	10
5. Search options available:	10
6. Level of support services:	8
7. Level of training offered:	8
8. Amount/kinds of special services offered:	10
Total Rating:	69

SOURCE REVIEWS:

Chapman, K. "Full-Text Database Support for Scholarly Research in Finance." *Journal of Business & Finance Librarianship* 7 (2002): 35–44. Compares three business journal databases—ABI/Inform, Business Source Premier, and General BusinessFile—to determine the quality of finance coverage in the content. ABI/Inform is the writer's pick, providing the most comprehensive coverage with 76 percent of the articles, 35.9 percent of which are full text.

O'Leary, Mick. "Big Databases Pose Big Questions." *Online* May 25, 2001: 82–86. Comparison and review of "mega databases" created by Gale Group, ProQuest, EBSCO, and LexisNexis. This article argues that quantity does not guarantee quality. The author writes about "jumbo-sized" databases that are too big and costly. The source mentions ABI's focus on archived information.

CONTRIBUTOR NAME: Jen Venable/Patricia A. Watkins

AFFILIATION: Purdue University/Thunderbird School of International Management

USEFUL TIPS

- Use the Basic search module when executing keyword and subject searches.
- Use the Guided search module when you know the publication title, author, or article title.
- Use the Publication search module when you are interested in browsing a particular journal volume.

ACCOUNTING & TAX DATABASE

ALTERNATE/PREVIOUS DATA SOURCE NAMES: Accounting & Tax Index, Accountant's Index Supplement

SERVICE/PORTAL NAME: *http://www.dialog.com*

SOURCE DESCRIPTION: Accounting & Tax Database provides citations, abstracts, and selected full text of articles focused on the accounting and tax industry and profession, as well as to the related subject areas of financial management, compensation, consulting, and the financial services industry. The database is available only on Dialog or directly from the publisher, ProQuest. The database contains articles from approximately 1,000 English language journals and while the focus is on U.S. publications, a small number of the journals are published in the U.K., Canada, and Australia.

One of the unique features of this database is the inclusion of citations and abstracts to books, conference proceedings, speeches, and pamphlets for the time periods between 1971 and 1999. Unfortunately, when the publication was purchased by UMI in the late 1990s, the publication content was restricted to journals. The database is based in part on the AICPA's *Accountant's Index* and the *Accountant's Index Supplement*, which were published from 1921–1999, and are outstanding reference tools that reflected the robust collection housed in the AICPA's library. A print index to citations derived from this database is available by subscription.

Today, the Accounting & Tax Database is maintained as Dialog File 485 and is available via *http://www.dialog.com* as part of Dialog's substantial repository of more than six hundred databases rich in content related to business and multiple other disciplines. Dialog offers its users a choice of several different search engines, allowing users with different levels of experience to tap into a rich range of business information.

SOURCE CONTENT: The Accounting & Tax Database supports in-depth research in accounting and auditing issues, practices and standards, developments in tax law, regulation and compliance, and the impact of those developments on business and industry as a whole. It provides detailed insight into the activities of the professional services industry, its practitioners, practices, and responses to changing conditions.

Database records contain complete bibliographic citations (that is, title, author, source, date, and a brief abstract and subject descriptors) for journal articles appearing in approximately 1,000 journals covering accounting, taxation, business, management, and financial industries. Only about 40 percent of the articles found in the database include the full text. Approximately 15 percent of the magazines included in the Accounting & Tax Database are unique to this file and are not as comprehensively indexed in any other Dialog database. The database provides timely access to its content: searches performed mid-month include articles published as recently as seven days into the same month.

There is no one database that competes directly with Accounting & Tax Database with its large collection of sources and such extensive coverage of the accounting and professional services industries. Dialog databases ABI/Inform (File 15) and Gale Group Trade & Industry Database (File 148) include many of the same sources and parts of these latter two databases are available in Factiva and LexisNexis. However, with approximately 15 percent of the journals included in the Accounting & Tax Database unique to this database collection, it stands out as a resource that should not be ignored by those needing to conduct extremely comprehensive accounting research.

Accounting & Tax Database can be searched using one of three Dialog user interfaces. DialogSelect and DialogWeb are the most user-friendly, both providing useful forms which nicely guide the user through the search process. The third interface, DialogClassic Web, is a command-driven interface most often used by experienced online searchers; it is most effectively used after extensive training.

Search results are displayed by title in reverse chronological order. All or select records may be chosen for displaying, printing or downloading in HTML or text formats. Select full-text records retrieved from searches conducted using DialogSelect can also be retrieved in .pdf or text-and-graphics versions of the document.

SOURCE EVALUATION: The cost of searching this database can be variable, highly unpredictable, and confusing. Those interested in using Dialog are strongly encouraged to spend time with a Dialog representative to fully understand the choices and potential impact on one's pocketbook before using this product. A bill from Dialog is comprised of two costs: a base charge for use of the system; and if use of the system yields results that are displayed, printed, or downloaded, additional charges for each item displayed, printed, or downloaded. The user must select one of two options that cover the base system use charge, Connect-Hour or Dial-Units. Connect-Hour pricing is based on a predefined hourly rate set for each Dialog file and the user is charged a pro-rated fee based on the amount of time he or she is online. The name of the game here is to be extremely knowledgeable about the database content and the topic at hand so that the search can be conducted as quickly as possible. Dial-Unit pricing is based not so much on time spent online but rather on what system resources are required to fulfill the request. For example, displaying a record requires very few system resources. However, removing duplicates from a list of results requires many more system resources and so will be more expensive. A novice searcher is likely to achieve the most cost-effective pricing by choosing Dial-Unit pricing since this option does not penalize one for the process of conducting multiple searches until the best results are achieved.

In addition to its two pricing options, Dialog also applies charges for outputting (displaying, printing, downloading) search results. For File 485 the charge to output a full-text article is $3.55/article, with a range of lesser charges for viewing smaller portions of the article. Lastly, Dialog also imposes a monthly service fee based on the number of passwords issued to the organization; the fee for 1–4 passwords is $14/month per password, $1/month per password for 6–100 passwords, and the fee is waived entirely if more than 100 passwords are assigned to an organization. While Dialog does have a credit card pay-as-you-go-option, called DialogSelect Open Access, File 485 is not included in this purchasing plan at this time.

If the user needs the full text of articles that are not available in this format in File 485, Dialog does provide a document delivery service at additional cost. Base cost for the delivery service is $12 service fee plus an article purchase charge (averages $15–$25 per article) and shipping costs. Most documents are shipped within 2–5 business days, based on the delivery method specified by the purchaser. The Dialog service also supports an alerting function that allows the searcher to create and save a search strategy and be alerted when matching new articles appear in the database. The cost of this feature ranges from $6.40–$10.00 per update.

While both DialogWeb and DialogSelect provide effective search interfaces, DialogWeb is preferable because it allows the user more guided flexibility in structuring the search.

Dialog's technical support and training is outstanding. A very large amount of information is available at no cost from the Dialog.com home page, including database specific product information, the "Bluesheets," database specific search aids, access software, such as DialogLink, FAQ's, online tutorials and courses, Quick Tours, and free practice searching, and much more. The Web site also provides current information about classroom training schedules for which reasonable fees are charged.

Calling either technical or customer support results in a relatively quick connection with knowledgeable and courteous support staff, and the cost of this support is included in the service fees.

The bottom line is that those needing to conduct accounting research should carefully evaluate the added value of tapping into some of the unique sources included in the Accounting & Tax Database and the challenges of unpredictable cost against other electronic databases providing very similar information. One recommended strategy would be to request a free trial to Accounting & Tax Database and run a particular search against this database and compare the results with the same search using Factiva, Lexis-Nexis, ABI/Inform, or other databases to which you subscribe.

The Accounting & Tax Database is unique in its focus on the accounting industry and related disciplines, but the increased availability of a large percent of its content in other electronic databases, combined with Dialog's irregular pricing structure, opens the window to successfully substituting other databases for very similar results.

The relative cost-to-value rating below is based on the perspective of the more casual searcher who can adequately substitute another electronic database for searching accounting articles. For the more serious searcher of accounting content, the cost-to-value is higher.

SOURCE VALUE RATING: All of the data source reviewers were asked to rate each source on the basis of the following eight categories, using "10" as the highest rating and "1" as the lowest ("80" being a perfect score):

1. Relative cost-to-value:	5
2. Relative timeliness of data:	8
3. Relative comprehensiveness of data:	8
4. Ease of use:	4
5. Search options available:	6
6. Level of support services:	7
7. Level of training offered:	7
8. Amount/kinds of special services offered:	7
Total Rating:	52

CONTRIBUTOR NAME: Naomi Clifford
AFFILIATION: Consultant

USEFUL TIPS

- It is strongly recommended that a new user or one needing a refresher download several excellent documents, all available for free in .pdf from the Dialog.com Web site: Dialog Pocket Guide, Dialog Search Summary Quick Reference, Successful Searching on Dialog, and the Accounting & Tax Database Bluesheet.

THOMSON RESEARCH

ALTERNATE/PREVIOUS DATA SOURCE NAMES: Disclosure Global Access, G.A Pro, Disclosure's Compact D/SEC, Worldscope, Laser D, Piranha, Investext, Research Bank Web, Industry Insider, I/B/E/S, Business & Industry, Business & Management Practices, TableBase, Extel Cards, MarkIntel, First Call Meeting Notes, and UK Regulatory News Service

SERVICE/PORTAL NAME: *http://research.thomsonib.com*

SOURCE DESCRIPTION: Thomson Research provides access to financial data from U.S. and foreign exchange filings, news/periodical articles on companies and industries, and investment and marketing reports. Marketing research reports are listed and available only on a pay-as-you-use basis; all the other data and reports are available in full-text format.

The major strength of this huge dataset of over 6 million documents, including 3.2 million research reports from twelve different databases, is its coverage of full-text financial filings (SEC filings and equivalent foreign filings) and its reports built from the data in these filings. In addition, it integrates information from Investext, MarkIntel, I/B/E/S, and periodical articles to provide more comprehensive information on companies and industries.

Much of the data is presented in image format, including color annual reports, prospectuses, and circulars. Thomson Extel cards are presented in both HTML and PDF formats. SEC EDGAR filings are in HTML. This database is designed for research professionals and analysts at investment banks and at law, accounting, and consulting firms. It is used in corporations and university libraries. Researchers familiar with corporate research will recognize Thomson Research as the newest reiteration of Global Access.

The product available to academic libraries differs somewhat from that available to commercial/corporate libraries. Academic subscribers will see little difference between Global Access and Thomson Research except that the latter offers color and faster downloading of Adobe files. Commercial subscribers benefit from the integration of the research reports and periodical articles into the product. The periodical indexing/abstracting/full-text databases are also omitted from the academic version.

The history of this database goes back to the 1970s, when Disclosure produced microfiche copies of annual reports and SEC filings (10-Ks, 10-Qs, proxies, prospectuses) for U.S. publicly owned companies. Many corporate and academic business libraries stopped building print collections of these reports and began relying on Disclosure's microfiche at that time. About 1986 Disclosure designed a PC-based product that dramatically changed corporate research by extracting the most important financial and text data in the filings and placing it in a searchable database called Compact Disclosure (later named Compact D/SEC and Compact D/Worldscope.) This product was so innovative that it was actually introduced before most librarians had access to departmental PCs, let alone desktop PCs; users were still using dumb terminals to do online searches. Compact Disclosure revolutionized corporate research, and every major business library quickly adopted it as a basic database subscription.

In 1988 Disclosure introduced Laser D, a CD-ROM product with full-text filings that caused another major change in corporation research. Soon after Disclosure was purchased by Primark, which took another step in the development of computer-based corporate research when it launched Piranha, integrating financial databases into a single delivery platform. Searchers could screen for specific companies and produce tables of the results. In addition they could integrate their own data into the tables or use any of the portfolios of predesigned reports available. All this could then be analyzed in spreadsheet software, such as Microsoft Excel.

In mid-2000 Thomson acquired Primark Corporation and then rolled out Piranha Web, a Web-based program that allowed searching and screening across Primark's financial databases. Thomson Research was the natural next step in the development of corporate research products. Thomson Analytics is the replacement for Piranha. Subscribers can purchase either or both files. (This review is focused on Thomson Research, not Thomson Analytics.)

PRICING: Thomson Research is a high-priced research tool. Pricing is based on which database subfiles the customer chooses to buy, and commercial/corporate subscribers will pay between $55,000 and $60,000 annually. If the price seems high compared to expected usage, there is an option to pay as you go. To subscribe this way, a corporation would pay $2,500 for access and then pay for each report as needed. A 20 percent discount on reports is included with the access fee. Academic library subscription prices are between $30,000 and $42,000 annually, depending on the number of simultaneous users and full-time enrollment figures for the school. IP filtering is available for academic subscriptions. There is an additional subscription fee for Thomson Analytics.

SOURCE CONTENT: For each company the following seven types of data are available: Content Profile, Filings, Overview Reports, Research, News, Ownership, Financials, and Stock Graph, which are described below:

1. **Content Profile** provides an outline and extensive list of documents available on the company, with hotlinks to each report. As soon as users log into Thomson Research, they are dropped into the Content Profile of Thomson Corp. as a sample company and to show the type of the data available. To change the company listed, one can do a Quick Company Search via a window on the far left. From there searchers can link to Filings, Insider Analytics, Price and Earnings Data, Overview Reports, Research Reports, Spreadsheet Financials, and News.

Figure 4-16. Sample Filings Hotlinks in Thomson Research

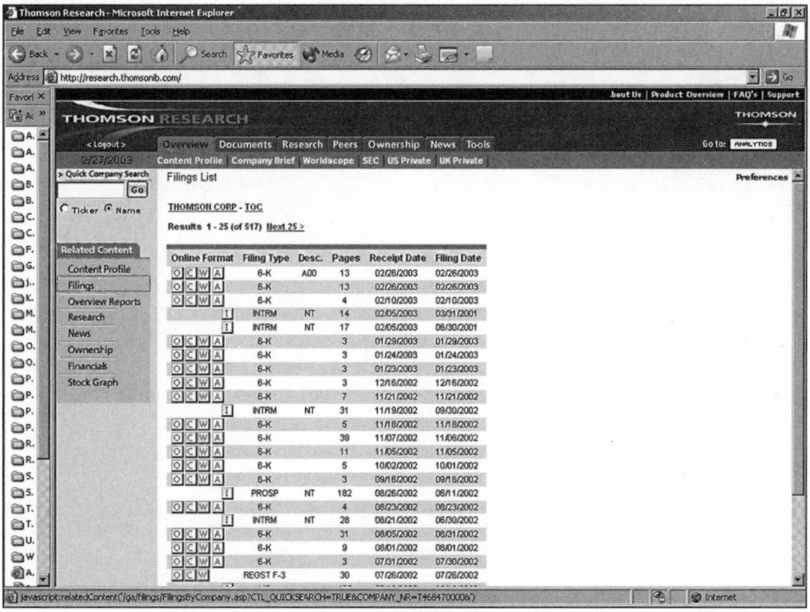

Reprinted with the permission of Thomson Financial Networks.

2. **Filings** includes hotlinks to Registrations, Annual Reports, 10-Ks, 10-Qs, Circulars, Interim Financials, Prospectuses, 20-F filings, and so on, as well as an indexing of paper reports back to 1968. These documents are the source for financial data for investors. The annual report, the company's report sent to investors, is written for the nonprofessional. It can be used to see the style or corporate culture of a company, but it also has detailed and audited financial data.

3. **Overview Reports** in Thomson Research are Extel, World-scope, SEC Reports, Price and Earnings Data, and Dun & Bradstreet Reports. These are all reports generated from the data in the financial filings, or I/B/I/S, with data in each report selected to target specific information needs. For example, the Worldscope Reports provide financial tear-sheets, peer analysis, and industry reports. The SEC Reports provide annual or quarterly financials, ratios, and lists of directors and subsidiaries. Price and Earnings Data give consensus earnings, a tearsheet of detailed earnings, current stock quotes, and daily, weekly, and monthly stock graphs.

Figure 4-17. The Overview Reports Option in Thomson Research

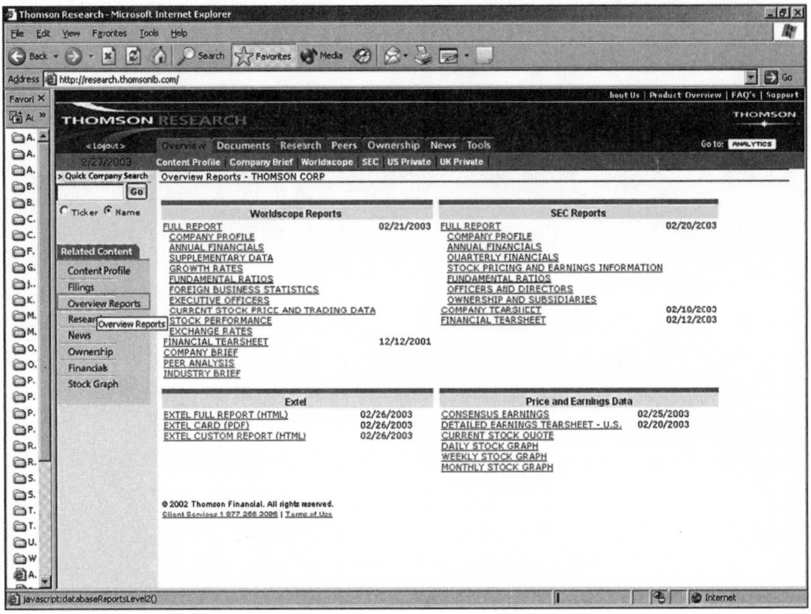

Reprinted with the permission of Thomson Financial Networks.

4. **News** links users to the articles indexed in Business & Industry, Business and Management Practices, and TableBase. The first two databases are standard periodical index/abstracting/full-text tools. TableBase is somewhat unique in that it indexes and provides full text of the tables and charts inside of articles, making it easy to locate such things as market shares and rankings of companies.

5. **Research** reports include the Morning Meeting Notes, Inves-text Research Reports, Industry Insider, and MarkIntel Reports. Investext reports are from brokerage analysts and give

lengthy advisory reports for investors on companies and industries. The Industry Insider database provides trade association reports, which are available on a pay-as-you-go basis (the full text is not included without charge with a basic subscription). MarkIntel reports are from investment banks, brokerage houses, market research firms, and trade associations and can be used for market research and topics such as company market share, industry trends, forecasts, and new product/new service markets.

6. **Ownership** provides access to information in newswires and the 3, 4, 5, or 144 filings on insider ownership (these are filings that 10 percent owners and others with inside information, such as members of the board, relatives, and so on, must make with the SEC every time they offer to sell, sell, or buy shares).

7. **Financials** provide preformatted tables of financial data from the current or historic 10-Ks, 10-Qs, or proxy filings.

8. **Stock Graph** provides graphs of a stock's activity.

Searching the databases is done via the tabs at the top of the screen: Overview, Documents, Research, Peers, Ownership, and News. These tabs expand out into further choices; for example, Overview expands into Company Brief, Worldscope, SEC, Peers, US Private, and UK Private. Each of these brings up a different search screen with a custom-built search template to match that database. For example, the Company Brief search screen provides search choices by company name, ticker or CUSIP (Committee for Uniform Securities Identification Procedures) code, and SIC (Standard Industrial Classification) code. The Worldscope and SEC search screens provide additional search parameters such as fiscal year, net income, total assets, net sales, market capitalization, and P/E (price over earnings) ratio. Results of searches can be sorted by company name, ticker, exchange, state, and country.

The other search buttons also provide extended search options. Of note is the EDGAR Free Text option, which allows searching for any word within EDGAR documents. By searching within the Ownership tab, you can retrieve ownership information from newswires or 3, 4, 5, or 144 filings. The Holdings Common search button will retrieve a table of insiders with the position, transaction date, direct holdings, indirect holdings, total common holdings, and the holding source. Searching in the Peer section brings up a "Price Performance – 36 months" chart and a "1 Yr Sales Growth" chart for the major competitors of a company. It also retrieves a table of peer companies, including sales, net income, total assets, total liabilities, and various key ratios for competitors. Searches can also retrieve Industry Briefs with similar information.

Search functions are one of the strengths of the Thomson Research database. Simple and quick searches by company names and advanced searches are both available, and searches can be saved. Printing and downloading capacities are available, in image format, HTML, and page prints. Preformatted reports, full-text filings, and templates for selected data make printing and downloading easy. Adobe files download three times faster than they did in Global Access. ARS reports and other reports and graphs can be printed in color. Charts can be easily downloaded into Microsoft spreadsheets. Currently the downloading function for charts works best in Netscape. (See Useful Tips below.)

SOURCE EVALUATION: Overall, Thomson Research is a welcome expansion of Global Access, which has been recognized as a major research tool for finance and investment professionals. The data is very timely and updated daily. It covers all companies filing with the SEC (about twelve thousand) and a large number of international companies (about sixteen thousand), and it allows researchers to search for companies and analyze the data in spreadsheet form. For the commercial/corporate subscriber, Thomson Research integrates additional research reports and articles into the company research process. For the academic subscriber, it provides one major enhancement: faster downloading of image files. It is an essential database for anyone doing corporate research.

Mergent Online is a major, but less expensive, competitor to Thomson Research. Like Thomson Research, it provides full-text ARSs and SEC filings. Other competitors are Factiva and Hoover's. Mergent is the only competitor that approaches the screening features of Thomson Research. Even though we have all these choices in our library, our researchers still demand Thomson Research.

The arrangement of the databases in Thomson Research is generally logical and useful. However, I find that first-time users are confused by the fact that the program opens with a sample company. This seems to be the only database we have that does this when users are expecting a blank search template. It is also confusing that the names on the search tabs that run across the top of the screen seem to parallel some, but not all, of the Related Content buttons in the left window, which bring up a list of the documents available for the specific company. The response time is irritatingly slow, and the help screens do not tell you anything you could not have figured out from the screen. Expanded help is available under Help – View More Help, but this is hard to find.

SOURCE VALUE RATING: All of the data source reviewers were asked to rate each source on the basis of the following eight categories, using "10" as the highest rating and "1" as the lowest ("80" being a perfect score):

1. Relative cost-to-value:	5
2. Relative timeliness of data:	10
3. Relative comprehensiveness of data:	10
4. Ease of use:	7
5. Search options available:	8
6. Level of support services:	6
7. Level of training offered:	5
8. Amount/kinds of special services offered:	8
Total Rating:	59

SOURCE REVIEWS:

Quint, Barbara. "Thomson Financial Launches *Thomson Research." Information Today* 19, no. 9 (October 2002): 1, 30.

CONTRIBUTOR NAME: Judith M. Nixon/Patricia A. Watkins
AFFILIATION: Purdue University/Thunderbird School of International Management

USEFUL TIPS

- Thomson Research works best with Internet Explorer.
- Image comprehension software, which speeds up the downloading of image files, needs to be set up. To do this, log on as Administrator and set preferences for Image Compression Software.
- Downloading of spreadsheets in Thomson Research works best with Netscape. IE users will need to set their browser to open separate windows. To do this open Windows Explorer and go to Tools/Folder Options/File Types. Then choose Microsoft Excel Worksheet, click on the Advance button, and uncheck Browser in Same Window.

LIVEDGAR

ALTERNATE/PREVIOUS DATA SOURCE NAMES: GSIonline, Global Securities Information

SERVICE/PORTAL NAME: *http://www.gsionline.com*

SOURCE DESCRIPTION: Global Securities Information's LIVEDGAR contains corporate SEC filing information for U.S. public companies, as well as for non-U.S. companies whose stock is traded on U.S. exchanges. The database also contains SEC compliance information in the form of releases, rules and rulings, corporate finance and mergers and acquisitions data, and news and alerts.

LIVEDGAR is useful for obtaining a company's 10-K filing, for example, but is really targeted to people doing in-depth corporate securities research or who are looking for comparative data on companies. The product provides a variety of options for locating targeted information, as well as preformatted searches contained in its Topical Research Library.

Figure 4-18. Main Menu Screen for LIVEDGAR

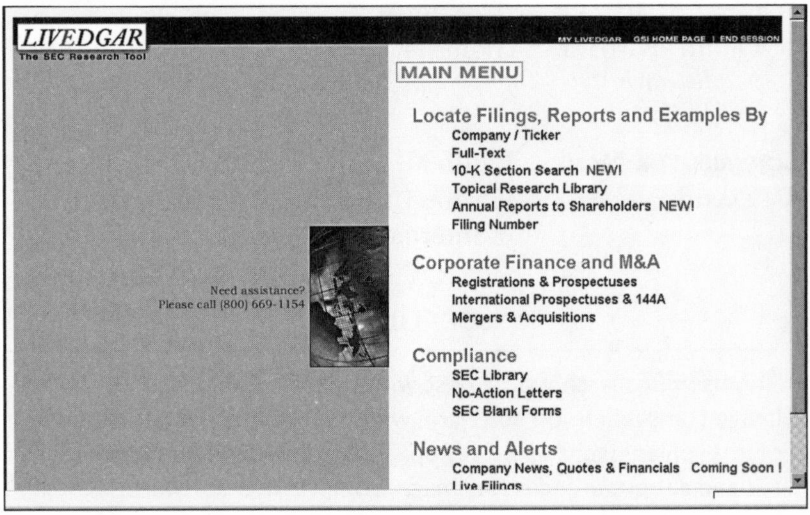

Source: Global Securities Information, Inc. Reprinted with permission.

PRICING: Subscribers are charged a monthly fee based on number of users per institution. There is also a "pay-as-you-go" feature: each time a user logs on, the account is charged $10. The account is also charged $1.75 for each minute the user stays on LIVEDGAR. (Source: *http://www.gsionline.com* Web site).

SOURCE CONTENT: This review summarizes the following five content areas within LIVEDGAR:

- **Corporate Filings**. Users are able to search company filings via a variety of options, including company ticker symbol, full-text keyword searching, 10-K section search limiting a search to specific areas of the 10-K filing, Topical Research Library, annual reports to shareholders and filing number. The Topical Research Library consists of hundreds of preconstructed searches, listed alphabetically by topic. Users select and run these preconstructed searches. If necessary, the searches are also editable if there are additional criteria needed to add, such as date restrictions. The Topical Research Library can also be accessed by subject category, such as Tax/Accounting or Intellectual Property, as well as browsed alphabetically. Filings can be e-mailed or downloaded in .pdf, .rtf, write, or text format. Annual reports to shareholders are in .pdf format.

- **Corporate Finance and M&A**. Registration Filings and Prospectuses can be searched in this section via customized search templates. International prospectuses and 144A filings are also included. This area also includes lists of the most recent original and final initial public offerings (IPOs). The lists are in reverse chronological order and can be used to generate Transaction Data Reports to be exported into Excel format. These reports contain data elements the user selects from a large checklist of options and contain comparative information for the IPO deals listed in this section. This same functionality can be found in the International Prospectuses and 144A section of this LIVEDGAR category. Rankings League Tables are also available in the Corporate Finance and M&A section; however, they are not available in the International Prospectuses and 144A area.

- **The League Tables**. These tables rank the top 25 Registrations and Prospectuses for specific time periods by Issuer Counsel, Target Counsel, or Lead Underwriters or the top 25 Mergers & Acquisitions for specific time periods by Target Counsel, Target Financial Advisor, Acquiror Counsel, or Acquiror Financial Advisor. Tables include Rank, Law Firm or Underwriter Firm or Financial Advisor name, number of deals, and total transaction values for the time period selected (for example, last 90 days, year to date, and so on). The Mergers and Acquisitions database is also searchable via custom templates with a wide variety of available search criteria. Users can search for comparable deals or comparable events, as well as obtain a list of most recent additions.

Figure 4-19. M&A Screen from LIVEDGAR

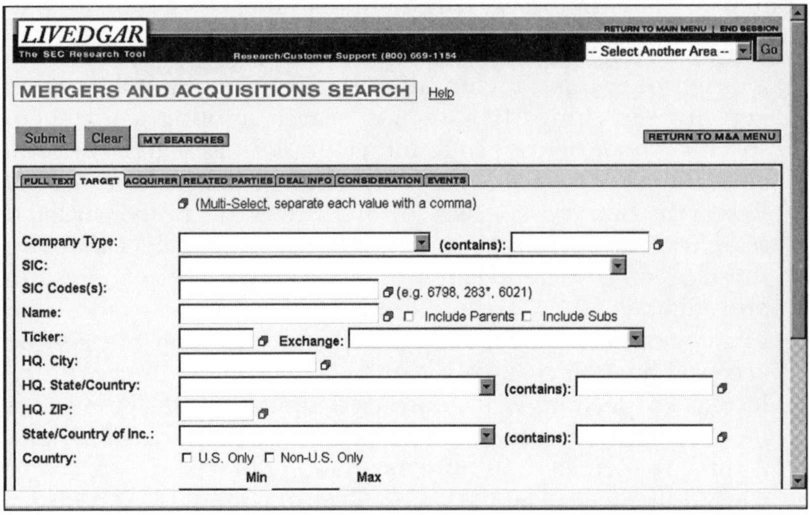

Source: Global Securities Information, Inc. Reprinted with permission.

- **Compliance.** You can search the following via the SEC Library contained in this section: regulatory actions, staff interpretations, news and public statements, litigation information from the SEC (including proposed and final rules), administrative proceedings and litigation releases, speeches and testimony, exemptive orders, and staff accounting bulletins. All are searchable via a custom template (see Figure 4-20). A No-Action Letter Database is also contained in the Compliance section and is keyword searchable. Blank SEC forms are contained within Compliance as well.
- **News and Alerts.** The Live Filings area lists SEC filings in reverse chronological order as soon as they are filed with the SEC. You can also set up alerts in this area by company name, ticker symbol, or full-text. Full-text alerts run across all Edgar documents, No-Action Letters, and foreign SEC filings in the LIVEDGAR database. Alerts run daily and results are sent via e-mail to you.

SOURCE EVALUATION: LIVEDGAR is a cost-effective source for corporate filings or SEC-related research. It is easy to use and offers a broad range of search alternatives, broad categories, and other means of targeting information. It is a richer resource than the SEC's Web site, Securities Mosaic, or other EDGAR resources. The log-in fee plus per minute charge is cheaper than obtaining the same information via LexisNexis, Westlaw, or Dialog. Multiple documents can be downloaded simultaneously in .pdf format. Searchers using keywords can elect to see their keywords in con-

Figure 4-20. SEC Library Search Screen from LIVEDGAR

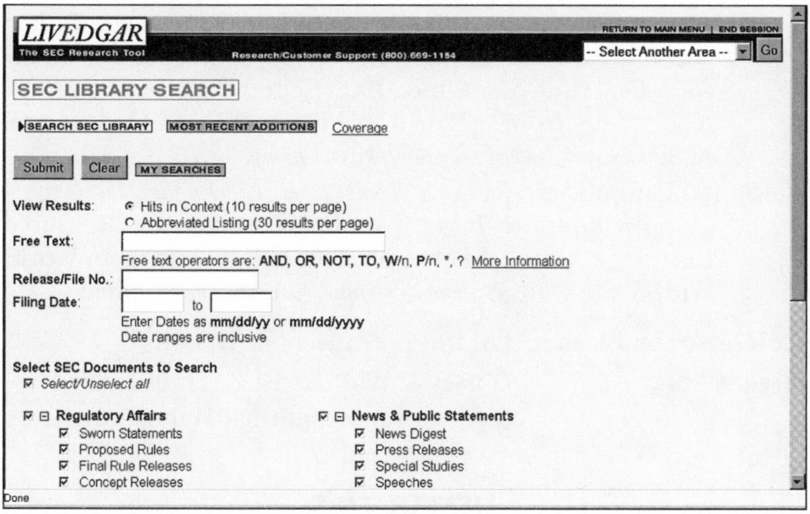

Source: Global Securities Information, Inc. Reprinted with permission.

text. Users can also elect to obtain portions of the SEC filing; another option not always available in free EDGAR resources. Frequently run searches can be saved under My Searches. Additionally, both online help and toll-free telephone help options are available.

SOURCE VALUE RATING: All of the data source reviewers were asked to rate each source on the basis of the following eight categories, using "10" as the highest rating and "1" as the lowest ("80" being a perfect score):

1. Relative cost-to-value:	9
2. Relative timeliness of data:	9
3. Relative comprehensiveness of data:	9
4. Ease of use:	8
5. Search options available:	9
6. Level of support services:	8
7. Level of training offered:	9
8. Amount/kinds of special services offered:	9
Total Rating:	70

SOURCE REVIEWS:

Kassel, Amelia. *Disclosure, the SEC, and LiveEdgar: Some Musings and Elucidations.* [online] New Jersey: Information Today Inc., Searcher Magazine, 1999 [cited 3 February 2003]. Available from World Wide Web: (*http://www. infotoday.com/searcher/jul99/kassel.htm*).

Story, Laura. *New Research Tools from LiveEdgar: Customized Research and Web Pages.* [online] Law Library Resource Exchange, [cited 3 February 2003]. Available from World Wide Web: (*http://www.llrx.com/features/livedgar.htm*).

CONTRIBUTOR NAME: Jan Rivers/Patricia A. Watkins
AFFILIATION: Dorsey & Whitney LLP/Thunderbird School of International Management

USEFUL TIPS

- The results from the pre-formatted searches may be too general in some instances. You may have to edit or further customize the pre-formatted searches from the Topical Research Library in order to retrieve more relevant information.
- Remember LIVEDGAR only covers U.S. public companies and foreign companies that file with the Securities & Exchange Commission. Private companies are not included and will not be represented in any "top company" lists or tables. This is especially important to remember when utilizing the Ranking League Tables tool.
- You may have to click on "View" multiple times before you are able to view the entire filing.
- Rather than printing individual documents, you may select documents to be saved to your work list for downloading and printing later.

RMA' S ANNUAL STATEMENT STUDIES

ALTERNATE/PREVIOUS DATA SOURCE NAMES: Annual Statement Studies Financial Ratio Benchmarks

SERVICE/PORTAL NAME: *http://www.rmahq.org*

SOURCE DESCRIPTION: The Risk Management Association's (RMA) classic print publication, *Annual Statement Studies,* now called *Annual Statement Studies Financial Ratio Benchmarks,* is one of just a small handful of resources that provide business ratio and industry norm data across a number of industries. The hardcopy of this and Dun's *Industry Norms and Key Business Ratios* have been a staple resource for anyone regularly conducting accounting and financial-related research. A few years ago, RMA began to make its important data series available electronically via CD-ROM and the Internet, which allows you to download it to your hard drive; there is currently no interactive Web-based access. This review focuses on the CD-ROM version of this product.

SOURCE CONTENT: The financial and ratio data in *Financial Ratio Benchmarks* is derived from more than 150,000 financial statements drawn from small and medium-size businesses, (with company identification suppressed). Beginning with the 2002–2003 edition of *Annual Statement Studies,* RMA expanded the industry data traditionally available in the print version to include average probability of default estimates, cash flow measures, and change in financial position information categorized for more than 450 industries. Industry Default Probabilities and Cash Flow Measures integrates the power of Moody's RiskCalc for private companies and the Statement Studies data to provide distribution statistics on one- and five-year probability of default estimates by industry, adding substantial value to the critical data. The data is updated annually.

For the purposes of this evaluation, the reviewer used the data from Financial Ratio Benchmarks. The data is organized by four-digit SIC codes, and within each code by five-year history, by asset range (7) and sales range (6). There are 600-plus industries included. Search options are by SIC code, NAICS code, or industry name. Starting with the 2003–2004 data, the industries will be identified by NAICS codes with reference to the corresponding SIC codes.

Each SIC code can be viewed by asset or sales breakdown or by the five-year history. Each of the views may be printed or downloaded in comma-delimited format; however, all three cannot be combined into a single report. A single line of the common-size industry norm data may be displayed or printed as a line, bar, pie, or mark graph and a "Profile" features allows for some output customization.

For researchers needing only to focus on business activity in a discreet geographic region, data can be purchased by region: Northeast, Southeast, Ohio Valley, Texas and the lower Mississippi, the Upper Midwest, or the West and Southwest. The data also can be purchased by individual SIC code. Data can be downloaded to a hard drive and put in an Excel or Access file for further analysis.

SOURCE EVALUATION: RMA's products offer the searcher an excellent balance of relatively comprehensive data at reasonable cost combined with a history of providing consistently reliable data. The data is easily accessed, primarily by SIC or NAICS code or industry name, which is consistent with the way it is usually requested. There is some flexibility in displaying data but some limitations in what you can download (for example, one view per industry). Overall the product is very easy to install and use and technical support is available at an 800 number. The Help available on the CD-ROM is written for someone who is a bit more experienced using the data. However, there is excellent information available free on the RMA Web site (*http://www.rmahq.com*). A detailed Definition of Ratios replicates the explanation found in the beginning of the print edition and fully explains how the ratios are calculated. An FAQ document also provides some additional information about the focus of the products.

All of the content is extremely reasonably priced. *Annual Statement Studies: Financial Ratio Benchmarks* and *Annual Statement Studies: Industry Default Probabilities* print editions and CD-ROM versions are each priced at $145, with the Ratio regional data available for $79 per region. Both sets of data can be purchased for a bundled price of $259. Discreet SIC code data is available online for $60 per code.

There are three main competitors in the marketplace for industry ratio data: RMA, Dun & Bradstreet, and Integra. RMA's content is by far the most reasonably priced with D&B's priced at the extreme other end of the spectrum. Integra's data is priced closer to RMA. When considering which to purchase, you will want to take into account cost, number and range of industries covered, and ability to access and manipulate the data to meet your needs. Given RMA's excellent reputation, history of quality data, reasonable price structure, and demonstrated focus on expanding its content, both in format and data, it would be difficult to justify not investing in RMA for this type of information.

SOURCE VALUE RATING: All of the data source reviewers were asked to rate each source on the basis of the following eight categories, using "10" as the highest rating and "1" as the lowest ("80" being a perfect score):

1. Relative cost-to-value:	10
2. Relative timeliness of data:	8
3. Relative comprehensiveness of data:	6
4. Ease of use:	9
5. Search options available:	4
6. Level of support services:	7
7. Level of training offered:	3
8. Amount/kinds of special services offered:	7
Total Rating:	54

CONTRIBUTOR NAME: Naomi Clifford
AFFILIATION: Consultant

USEFUL TIPS

- A new user of RMA's content should print Definition of Ratios, available for free on the Web site (*http://www.rmahq.com/ann_studies/ratiodef_frb.html*) in order to understand both the computation and interpretation of the data.

D&B KEY BUSINESS RATIOS (KBR) ON THE WEB

ALTERNATE/PREVIOUS DATA SOURCE NAMES: Key Business Ratios, KBR, Industry Norms and Key Business Ratios

SERVICE/PORTAL NAME: *http://kbr.dnd.com*

SOURCE DESCRIPTION: D&B's Key Business Ratios (KBR) on the Web contains financial ratios—critical information that is available only on a few electronic databases. The data in KBR is collected from company financial statements residing in D&B's master company database. Fourteen financial ratios are categorized into the three main areas used for business performance audits: solvency, efficiency, and profitability. The data can be used for locating aggregate comparative data across like companies or it can be customized to enable the searcher to compare an individual company's financial statements with its industry business ratios. The database incorporates the Business Ratios section of D&B's annual print publication, *Industry Norms and Key Business Ratios,* long considered a standard publication in the industry.

SOURCE CONTENT: For users unfamiliar with how D&B's business ratios are calculated or how to use them for business performance valuation applications, helpful information is provided by three links on the KBR home page: Understanding Financial Statements, What Are Key Business Ratios, and 14 Key Business Ratios Used by D&B. These links are accessible without having to log on. In addition, once you have logged on to KBR, clicking on the Help button provides access to three other important information documents, each listed under the headings **Ratios: Calculating Ratios**, **Displaying Ratios**, and **Performing a Comparative Analysis**. As good as these documents are, the same cannot be said about the Help function in general. While not necessarily a difficult database to use, KBR does include some functions that are far from intuitive. Users will need to invest a bit of "play" time in figuring out how to navigate this product and take advantage of its functionality. A call to D&B's Customer Service at the start might be a wise investment in time.

Data on KBR is available for companies falling into 800 lines of business (those with two-digit SIC codes) and covering several thousand four-digit SIC codes. All 14 ratios are organized by industry, year, and company size. There are six Solvency Ratios: Quick, Current, Current Liabilities to Net Worth, Current Liabilities to Inventory, Total Liabilities to Net Worth, and Fixed Assets to Net Worth; five Efficiency Ratios: Collection Period, Sales to Inventory, Assets to Sales, Sales to Net Working Capital, and Accounts Payable to Sales; and three Profitability Ratios: Return on Sales, Return on Assets, and Return on Net Worth.

Once the user logs on, the opening screen displays the first page of Solvency Ratios, sorted by SIC code. There are corresponding tabs for Efficiency and Productivity. All the data can be searched and/or resorted by Line of Business, Year, and Asset Range (see Figure 4-21).

Figure 4-21. Solvency Ratios in KBR

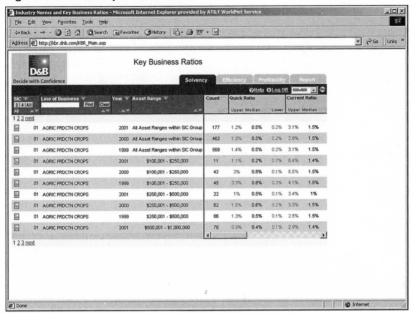

Reprinted with the permission of Dun & Bradstreet, Inc.

Once the desired dataset is displayed, the ratios for the set can be viewed in a series of ten lines of business or SIC codes at a time. Output, however, is limited to one "selection" at a time. To print or download the ratio set for a line, the user clicks the icon to the far left of the line. This produces a formatted report for that line, which can be printed or downloaded in comma-delimited format.

A particularly valuable feature of the database allows users to compare, one at a time, a company (or companies) for which they have financial statements, with the financial performance of its industry peers. To do so, select the appropriate SIC code or line of business from KBR, and format that report. Click on the **Report** tab, then select the **My Financials** tab (see Figure 4-22) and enter the requested data. This generates a report that shows the subject company's ratios against the industry ratios. This is an extremely useful feature of this database, but it is also very awkward to use.

Figure 4-22. Comparing Ratios in KBR

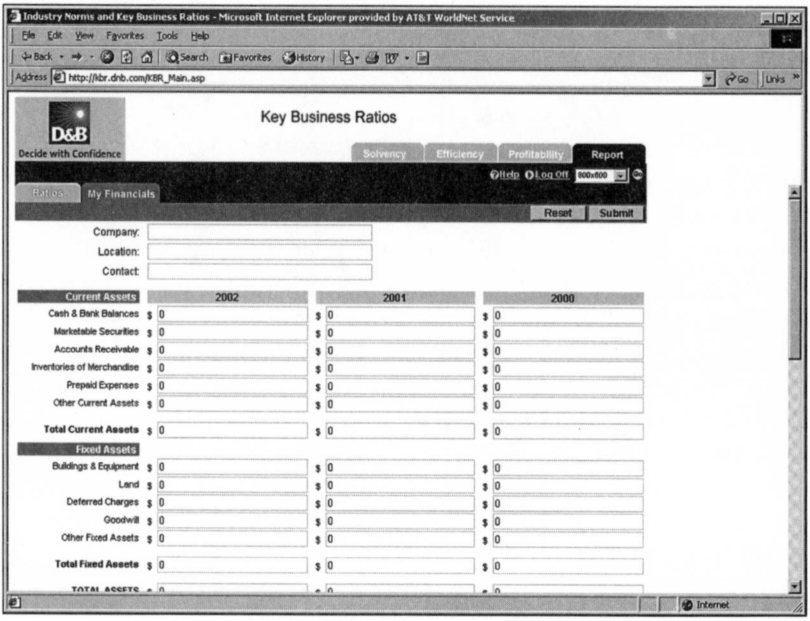

Reprinted with the permission of Dun & Bradstreet, Inc.

SOURCE EVALUATION: There are really just a few sources, print or electronic, that provide business ratio data: D&B's KBR, RMA's *Annual Statement Studies*, and *Integra Industry Norms*. Each gathers its data from slightly different sources and provides slightly different functionality for accessing and manipulating the data. Each is also priced quite differently, with KBR at the high end of the range. KBR data is available only by direct subscription with D&B, and it is priced on a cost-per-seat model. The cost for a one-year subscription to a single year's worth of ratio data for one user is $8,400; the same dataset accessible to ten users costs $23,661. The cost of a one-year subscription to three year's worth of ratio data for one user is $15,750; the same dataset accessible to ten users is priced at $44,364. If a researcher needed to use the data for a period of less than one year, D&B appears to be open to prorating the cost.

KBR contains excellent, difficult-to-find information even though the data is unimaginatively and somewhat awkwardly organized for querying. The interface can be slow and clunky, and the online help is extremely limited and not particularly intuitive, which might cause problems for someone unfamiliar with using business ratios and working with spreadsheets. KBR permits the exporting of data into Excel but, again, the process is clumsy and can be confusing. The data is moderately timely; in mid-winter

2003 the most recent data comes from 2001 financial statements. This matches the timeliness of the data in both RMA and Integra Industry Norms. D&B data is updated twice a year.

KBR's great strengths are the value of the information and the ability to perform comparative analyses using one's own data. Technical and customer support are included in the cost of the subscription. Its weaknesses are its flat-footed design, slow processing speed, limitations on output, and high cost. I recommend that anyone needing to access business ratios perform sound due diligence: evaluate the print edition of D&B's *Industry Norms and Key Business Ratios* and evaluate both the print and electronic versions of RMA's *Annual Statement Studies*. Consider cost and your need to access the data electronically vs. looking it up in print. In short, both the cost and the value are high, but there are very few alternatives. Thus, a slightly higher than mid-weight rating is assigned below.

SOURCE VALUE RATING: All of the data source reviewers were asked to rate each source on the basis of the following eight categories, using "10" as the highest rating and "1" as the lowest ("80" being a perfect score):

1. Relative cost-to-value:	6
2. Relative timeliness of data:	7
3. Relative comprehensiveness of data:	8
4. Ease of use:	7
5. Search options available:	6
6. Level of support services:	7
7. Level of training offered:	3
8. Amount/kinds of special services offered:	6
Total Rating:	50

CONTRIBUTOR NAME: Naomi Clifford
AFFILIATION: Consultant

USEFUL TIPS

- New users should review the guides to understanding financial statements, business ratios, and D&B's use of ratios, accessible from the KBR home page and in Help.
- Carefully evaluate this product against its print version and its main competitor before making a purchasing decision. Both vendors provide valuable and reliable data.

MERGENT ONLINE

ALTERNATE/PREVIOUS DATA SOURCE NAMES: Previously FISonline

SERVICE/PORTAL NAME: *http://www.mergentonline.com*

SOURCE DESCRIPTION: Mergent Online, a database of domestic and international company information, is available solely through the Web site at *http://www.mergentonline.com*. Mergent Online is the successor to FISonline, originally published by Financial Information Services (FIS), a division of Moody's Investor Services. In 1998, Mergent Incorporated acquired FIS from Moody's and expanded and enhanced the database, making Mergent Online a powerful source of company information. The database includes fifteen years of detailed quarterly and annual financial reports and is an invaluable tool for competitive intelligence, industry analysis, prospecting, and market research.

SOURCE CONTENT: Content in Mergent Online consists of financial data, detailed business descriptions, and company histories. The content comes mainly from the published financial reports of public companies. Unlike its predecessor, FISonline, Mergent Online does not carry Moody's Corporate Bond. It does, however, present a summary of long-term debt outstanding for each company. This is a strength of this database, as many other online company information resources do not list a company's debt issues. Information is exportable into Microsoft Word, Excel, or Adobe Acrobat (PDF).

Mergent Online is ideal for comparing a company to its competitors, industry, or market. The database makes it easy to create custom reports that compare financial data and ratios that could be used for, among other things, SWOT (strength-weakness-threat-opportunity) analysis. Mergent Online also allows a researcher to track trends within a company or industry.

Mergent stands out among the company profile competition in several ways, providing (1) fifteen years of quarterly financials, as compared to ten for most other sources, (2) offering more choices for financial data—as reported, preliminary, and restated, and (3) long-term debt details.

A basic subscription to Mergent Online contains U.S. Company Data and International Company Data. There are several optional add-on modules, including Dun & Bradstreet's Million Dollar Directory Plus, data on institutional holdings, insider trading data, and annual reports (not summaries, but the actual reports sent to stockholders). Two recent additions are Equity Portraits and Corporate Bond Portraits. Equity Portraits combine financial reports with price, volume, and performance ratios to present a seamless picture for investment analysis. Corporate Bond Portraits present detailed information and comparative analysis on over fifty-five thousand debt issues. New features include full-color annual reports and six preformatted report layouts.

SOURCE EVALUATION: Mergent Online is an improvement over its predecessor, FISonline. The increased date range (fifteen years), debt coverage, and expanded search criteria combine to make Mergent a force to be reckoned with in the online company information industry. The database is updated continually, whenever company reports are filed with the SEC. (Mergent provides real-time EDGAR filings.) Content is drawn from quarterly and annual reports from both U.S. and international companies. The depth of data reported by Mergent is excellent, presenting all financial data items from the above-mentioned reports.

Mergent is searchable by a wide variety of criteria, including financial ratios, geography, and industry classification. This is a welcome improvement over FISonline, and one hopes that future updates will include even more search parameters. Mergent Online is easy to search and features point-and-click creation of custom reports that compare a company against its competitors—a very useful feature in company research. Mergent Online is also speedy, retrieving and presenting documents in a matter of seconds (assuming the user has a high-speed Internet connection).

Both training and technical support are provided without charge during normal business hours. The database is highly reliable and is rarely down for maintenance. Mergent provides printed quick-start guides for the service, and help is also available online.

SOURCE VALUE RATING: All of the data source reviewers were asked to rate each source on the basis of the following eight categories, using "10" as the highest rating and "1" as the lowest ("80" being a perfect score):

1. Relative cost-to-value:	6
2. Relative timeliness of data:	9
3. Relative comprehensiveness of data:	9
4. Ease of use:	8
5. Search options available:	7
6. Level of support services:	8
7. Level of training offered:	9
8. Amount/kinds of special services offered:	6
Total Rating:	62

CONTRIBUTOR NAME: Wes Edens/Patricia A. Watkins
AFFILIATION: Thunderbird School of International Management

USEFUL TIPS

- Click on the square icon next to a company name to add it to a list for later comparison in a standard or custom report.
- Check out the six predefined report formats before creating your own.

YAHOO! FINANCE

ALTERNATE/PREVIOUS DATA SOURCE NAMES: *http://biz.yahoo.com*

SERVICE/PORTAL NAME: *http://finance.yahoo.com*

SOURCE DESCRIPTION: Yahoo! Finance offers a wealth of investment research information for the United States and worldwide financial markets and is one of the best free portal sites for investment research. The ease of navigation and comprehensive coverage of U.S. and worldwide markets is unmatched by the competition.

This product is targeted to business researchers and independent investors, from novice to professional. Additional subscription packages can enhance the basic Yahoo! Finance by offering to include real-time quotes, premium real-time news, and advanced stock screening options through other portals, such as Smart-Money Select.

SOURCE CONTENT: This summary will review four key offerings of Yahoo! Finance: Stock Research, Financial News, Industry Research, and International Coverage.

1. **Stock Research**: Yahoo! Finance contains all the necessary tools for stock research, including information on company earnings, analyst research, company report, mutual funds, financial calendars, research tools, bonds, and options. The stock screening function (see Figure 4-23) is particularly user-friendly and speedy. Search for stocks by selecting from industry or financial index membership, share and/or performance data, valuation ratios, and analyst estimates. Narrowing your searches requires you to return and modify your initial search. Analyst reports are available to purchase directly through Yahoo! Finance. In addition, Yahoo! Finance offers an analyst performance center that rates the analysts using data analysis generated from StarMine.com. The resulting score represents the return performance of an analyst's recommendations relative to his peers.

2. **Financial News**: The financial news section of Yahoo! Finance is simple and straightforward. Recent news is posted near the top of the section, while individual news sources are listed in a left-hand, vertical navigation bar. A news search function is also available. News alerts can be created that search for defined keywords, breaking news, or news updates, and these alerts can be forwarded to any e-mail address or mobile device.

Figure 4-23. Yahoo! Finance Stock Screener Search Results

Report Screener | Stock Screener | Bond Screener | Fund Screener

Stock Screener Search Results (Showing 1 to 20 of 24)   As of 17-Mar-2003

New Screen

Display for this screen: Performance[current] [View]

Symbol	Company ▲	Return %	Beta	More Info
ABRX	Able Laboratories Inc	91.42	1.241	Quote, Chart, News, Profile, Reports, Research, SEC, Msgs, Insider, Financials
APPI.OB	Advanced Plant Pharmaceuticals Inc	83.33	1.561	Quote, News, Profile, Reports, SEC, Insider, Financials
AMLN	Amylin Pharmaceuticals Inc	30.70	0.163	Quote, Chart, News, Profile, Reports, Research, SEC, Msgs, Insider, Financials, Analyst Ratings
ANIK	Anika Therapeutics Inc	41.12	1.468	Quote, Chart, News, Profile, Reports, SEC, Msgs, Insider, Financials
BSTE	Biosite Inc	47.63	1.262	Quote, Chart, News, Profile, Reports, Research, SEC, Msgs, Insider, Financials, Analyst Ratings
CNCT	Connetics Corp	65.55	1.347	Quote, Chart, News, Profile, Reports, Research, SEC, Msgs, Insider, Financials
ESPR	Esperion Therapeutics Inc	76.67	0.206	Quote, Chart, News, Profile, Reports, Research, SEC, Msgs, Insider, Financials, Analyst Ratings
FLML	Flamel Technologies SA	136.04	1.273	Quote, Chart, News, Profile, Reports, Msgs, Insider
HITK	Hi-Tech Pharmacal Inc	125.13	0.12	Quote, Chart, News, Profile, Reports, SEC, Insider, Financials
ISPH	Inspire Pharmaceuticals Inc	559.17	1.905	Quote, Chart, News, Profile, Reports, Research, SEC, Msgs, Insider, Financials, Analyst Ratings
IHTC.OB	Integrated Health Technologies Inc	268.85	0.076	Quote, Chart, News, Profile, Reports, Insider
LCI	Lannett Co Inc	280.30	1.931	Quote, Chart, News, Profile, Reports, Msgs, Insider
LCAR.OB	Lescarden Ltd	100.00	2.206	Quote, Chart, News, Profile, Reports, SEC, Insider, Financials
MYL	Mylan Laboratories Inc	30.43	0.573	Quote, Chart, News, Profile, Reports, Research, SEC, Msgs, Insider, Financials, Analyst Ratings
NAII	Natural Alternatives International Inc	87.22	0.713	Quote, Chart, News, Profile, Reports, SEC, Msgs, Insider, Financials
NTII	Neurobiological Technologies Inc	40.04	2.083	Quote, Chart, News, Profile, Reports, Research, SEC, Msgs, Insider, Financials
ONXX	Onyx Pharmaceuticals Inc	50.10	1.871	Quote, Chart, News, Profile, Reports, Research, SEC, Msgs, Insider, Financials, Analyst Ratings
PRX	Pharmaceutical Resources Inc	82.17	1.103	Quote, Chart, News, Profile, Reports, Research, SEC, Msgs, Insider, Financials, Analyst Ratings
PROA	Polymer Research Corp of America	69.33	-0.075	Quote, Chart, News, Profile, Reports, SEC, Insider, Financials
QGLY	Quigley Corp	50.65	1.355	Quote, Chart, News, Profile, Reports, SEC, Msgs, Insider, Financials

Next 4

Want more in-depth screening? Try SmartMoney Select's Stock Screener. Free 2-week trial!

© SmartMoney 2003

Reproduced with permission of Yahoo! Inc. © 2003 by Yahoo! Inc. YAHOO! and the YAHOO! logo are trademarks of Yahoo! Inc.

3. **Industry Research**: Yahoo! Finance has 17 industry categories that summarize relevant industry news, press releases, industry research, market performance, industry calendar events, and top companies within the industry. Industry Calendar events can be added to your Yahoo! account, with an e-mail notification option to remind you to attend. The Industry Buzz section is particularly insightful. It highlights the most actively read news articles, most active message boards, and most unusually active message boards for the industry. Think of it as the "What's Hot" section of Yahoo! Finance.

4. **International Coverage**: Yahoo! Finance is very strong in international business coverage from two different perspectives. First, most major international markets have local language versions of Yahoo! Finance that cover the same type of information available in the U.S. Second, international news coverage of AP and Reuters articles is available by region or country. Yahoo! has partnered with CountryWatch.com to provide country fact sheets that include a basic country overview, economic performance, balance of payments, energy, environment, and agriculture (see Figure 4-24).

Figure 4-24. Yahoo! Finance International Country News and Fact Sheets

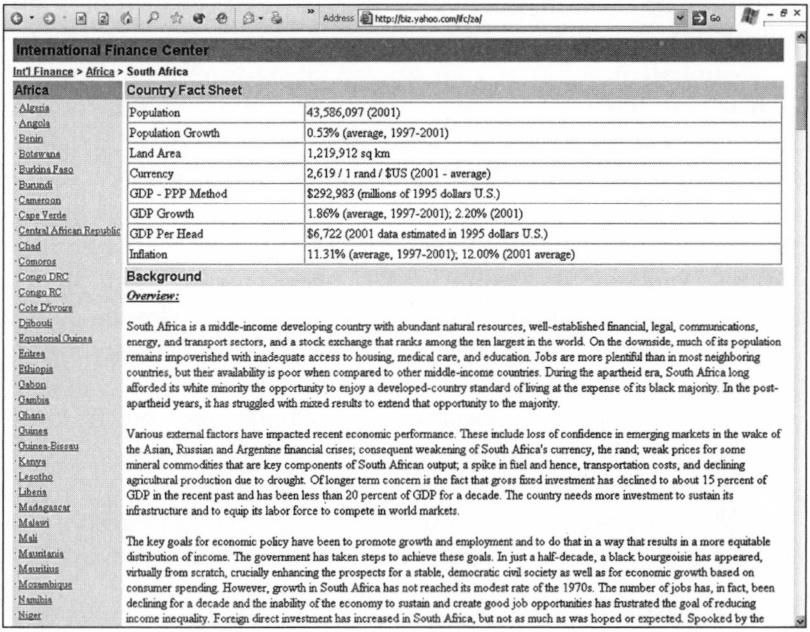

Address http://biz.yahoo.com/ifc/za/

International Finance Center

Int'l Finance > Africa > South Africa

Africa

Algeria · Angola · Benin · Botswana · Burkina Faso · Burundi · Cameroon · Cape Verde · Central African Republic · Chad · Comoros · Congo DRC · Congo RC · Cote D'ivoire · Djibouti · Equatorial Guinea · Eritrea · Ethiopia · Gabon · Gambia · Ghana · Guinea · Guinea-Bissau · Kenya · Lesotho · Liberia · Madagascar · Malawi · Mali · Mauritania · Mauritius · Mozambique · Namibia · Niger

Country Fact Sheet

Population	43,586,097 (2001)
Population Growth	0.53% (average, 1997-2001)
Land Area	1,219,912 sq km
Currency	2,619 / 1 rand / $US (2001 - average)
GDP - PPP Method	$292,983 (millions of 1995 dollars U.S.)
GDP Growth	1.86% (average, 1997-2001); 2.20% (2001)
GDP Per Head	$6,722 (2001 data estimated in 1995 dollars U.S.)
Inflation	11.31% (average, 1997-2001); 12.00% (2001 average)

Background

Overview:

South Africa is a middle-income developing country with abundant natural resources, well-established financial, legal, communications, energy, and transport sectors, and a stock exchange that ranks among the ten largest in the world. On the downside, much of its population remains impoverished with inadequate access to housing, medical care, and education. Jobs are more plentiful than in most neighboring countries, but their availability is poor when compared to other middle-income countries. During the apartheid era, South Africa long afforded its white minority the opportunity to enjoy a developed-country standard of living at the expense of its black majority. In the post-apartheid years, it has struggled with mixed results to extend that opportunity to the majority.

Various external factors have impacted recent economic performance. These include loss of confidence in emerging markets in the wake of the Asian, Russian and Argentine financial crises; consequent weakening of South Africa's currency, the rand; weak prices for some mineral commodities that are key components of South African output; a spike in fuel and hence, transportation costs, and declining agricultural production due to drought. Of longer term concern is the fact that gross fixed investment has declined to about 15 percent of GDP in the recent past and has been less than 20 percent of GDP for a decade. The country needs more investment to sustain its infrastructure and to equip its labor force to compete in world markets.

The key goals for economic policy have been to promote growth and employment and to do that in a way that results in a more equitable distribution of income. The government has taken steps to achieve these goals. In just a half-decade, a black bourgeoisie has appeared, virtually from scratch, crucially enhancing the prospects for a stable, democratic civil society as well as for economic growth based on consumer spending. However, growth in South Africa has not reached its modest rate of the 1970s. The number of jobs has, in fact, been declining for a decade and the inability of the economy to sustain and create good job opportunities has frustrated the goal of reducing income inequality. Foreign direct investment has increased in South Africa, but not as much as was hoped or expected. Spooked by the

Source: CountryWatch. *http://www.countrywatch.com.*
Reproduced with permission of Yahoo! Inc. © 2003 by Yahoo! Inc. YAHOO! and the YAHOO! logo are trademarks of Yahoo! Inc.

Source Evaluation: Yahoo! is best known for its one-stop shopping structure, and the same features and functionality extend to their financial portal. It is the premier financial portal for data that is generally considered freely available and contains typical financial market data, such as delayed quotes, historical quotes, portfolio tracking (unlimited number of portfolios with two hundred symbols each), SEC filings, exchange rates, and brokerage recommendations. It has a very strong financial news component, with coverage from Reuters, AP, S&P, Business Wire, Internet Wire, PrimeZone, and PR Newswire. News is also supported by strong editorial content from The Motley Fool, TheStreet.com, Individual Investor, ISDEX and the Online Investor. Typical of Yahoo! is the very strong coverage of worldwide affairs, particularly foreign financial markets, foreign and domestic news, and quotes. Foreign Yahoo! Finance sites are available in the native language.

Yahoo! Finance differs from much of the competition in that the entire site has text-based navigation and hence compatibility with different operating systems and Web browsers is exceptional.

The search functionality is quick, responsive, and almost always fruitful. Financial message boards and stock chat rooms are extremely well executed.

Optional, premium services are available from Yahoo! Finance, such as real-time quotes that cost $9.95/month. Real-time portfolio tracking requires Java and is only supported by Windows 95/98/NT/2000/ME. Other platforms are self-supported. A premium news service provided by TheStreet.com is available in two packages ranging from $99.95 to $149.95 per year (monthly options available). Premium market research can be purchased directly through Yahoo!, including free abstract viewing and a unique "thumbnail image" view of the all other pages to determine their content.

Unfortunately, free portals need to make revenue from all those page views and, therefore, advertising is present on most Yahoo! Finance pages. Basic product training and support is limited to online FAQ help and e-mail support that is fairly responsive to general inquiries, and very responsive for premium services.

SOURCE VALUE RATING: All of the data source reviewers were asked to rate each source on the basis of the following eight categories, using "10" as the highest rating and "1" as the lowest ("80" being a perfect score):

1. Relative cost-to-value:	9
2. Relative timeliness of data:	10
3. Relative comprehensiveness of data:	9
4. Ease of use:	9
5. Search options available:	9
6. Level of support services:	5
7. Level of training offered:	5
8. Amount/kinds of special services offered:	6
Total Rating:	62

CONTRIBUTOR NAME: Matthew J. McBride
AFFILIATION: Information Consultant

USEFUL TIPS

- Review the information sources and content providers used on Yahoo! Finance at *http://help.yahoo.com/help/us/fin/fin-06.html*.
- Register for a free Yahoo! account to take advantage of portfolio tracking and other optional Yahoo! services.
- Check out and keep track of the latest buzz and hottest news articles viewed in your industry at *http://biz.yahoo.com/ic/jumps/buzz.html*.

MORNINGSTAR

PREVIOUS DATA SOURCE NAMES: Morningstar.net.

SERVICE/PORTAL NAME: *http://www.morningstar.com*

SOURCE DESCRIPTION: Morningstar, Inc. is a private global investment research firm, based in Chicago, which offers "print, software and Web-based products and services for individual investors, professional financial advisors, and institutions" (from the Web page of Morningstar.com).

The material covered includes information and data analysis capabilities for stocks, mutual funds (including exchange-traded and closed-end funds) and variable annuity accounts. At this time the company follows and analyzes approximately 100,000 company securities. Two of the most well-known features of Morningstar are the "star rating," which ranks both funds and stocks with a one to five star rating, and the Style Box which designates the category of the fund being investigated.

Morningstar.com also has international partnerships with services for Asia, Australia and New Zealand, Canada, Europe (U.K., France, Italy, Spain, Germany and the Netherlands), Finland, Japan, Korea, Norway, and Sweden. Contact information for these services is available from the Morningstar Web page.

The Morningstar service began with a print publication in 1984—*The Mutual Fund Sourcebook*—and then expanded to include more print publications, including the weekly *Morningstar Mutual Funds,* which became one of the most requested products in public libraries. Morningstar rapidly increased its distribution, first with CD-ROM and then Internet products, to become a leading provider of investment information and tools.

Pricing: Individual subscription rates are (this information is taken from the Web site):

$11.95 per month; $109 for 1 year or $189 for 2 years; and a free 2 week trial is offered. For institutional and corporation licensing information check *http://www.morningstar.com/Cover/AboutUs.html.*

Source Content: After logging in to this service using the ID and password, the user is presented immediately with a very full screen with index information listed to the left, portfolio information to the right, and analyst reports and ratings in the center. Eight tabs along the top of the screen link to a personally created portfolio, stocks, mutual fund, and exchange-traded fund information, as well as markets, tools, personal finance, and discussion forums. Premium service only features are designated with a + sign. The content of each tab is summarized below:

- **Portfolio tab**. The user can create 25 Quick Portfolios and 25 Transaction Portfolios. The Quick Portfolio is most useful for keeping track of a list of securities or funds while the Transaction Portfolio enables the user to track buys, sells, splits, and dividends and analyze both current positions and historic transactions through tools such as Portfolio X-Rays.

- **Stocks tab**. Enter a stock symbol in the search box to generate a "Quicktake" report. This includes the company snapshot with a price and volume interactive graph to create comparisons against companies or indexes, and performance and valuation figures, analyst reports and notes, 5 years of restated financials, fund owners and insider trading. At any point in the report a new stock can be added to a portfolio. At the main stock page one can also check on analyst stock picks by industry sector. The definitions page, linked at the bottom of each report screen, will show all the definitions for the corresponding "Quicktake" report.

- **Funds tab**. This allows the user to enter a fund symbol in the search box to generate a "Quicktake" report. This includes key statistics, performance history, sector breakdown, analyst reports, Morningstar ratings, volatility, and management details. Funds can be added to a portfolio.

- **Exchange-Traded Funds tab**. "Quicktake" reports, ratings, and analysis are provided.

- **Market tab**. This includes stock and fund category news, Morningstar indexes, market results, and top Dow Jones news.

- **Tools tab**. These tools include a Premium Fund Screener and Premium Stock Screener allowing the user to screen hundreds of data points to obtain results, that can be saved as a watch list. Other tools include Stock Quickrank that will reveal which stocks have the highest earnings growth rates or best returns in their sector and the Fund Quickrank that will provide a list of the funds with the highest returns or lowest risk in their category. To build a portfolio one can use the Asset Allocator and then use the Portfolio Analyzer to check on a target mix. Another useful tool is the Risk Analyzer that will determine how much the portfolio might lose in a bear market and which holdings contribute most to overall risk and how adjustments might reduce risk.

- **Personal Finance tab**. This includes many tutorials and guides.
- **Discusstab**. This provides the user with a list of all the discussion forums supported by Morningstar.

Morningstar.com is a well-planned site that provides quotes, learning resources, tools for analysis, and forums for discussion. Some of the features are free, after registration, but to use all the capabilities provided one must subscribe, for a relatively small fee, to Morningstar Premium.

SOURCE EVALUATION: The range of search features and tools for analysis make it easy for even the novice to find quickly the needed material and perform portfolio analysis. The investment Tools compliment the wealth of information provided in the Quicktakes. For investment tracking Morningstar.com is an outstanding resource.

SOURCE VALUE RATING: All of the data source reviewers were asked to rate each source on the basis of the following eight categories, using "10" as the highest rating and "1" as the lowest ("80" being a perfect score):

1. Relative cost-to-value:	10
2. Relative timeliness of data:	10
3. Relative comprehensiveness of data:	10
4. Ease of use:	9
5. Search options available:	9
6. Level of support services:	8
7. Level of training offered:	9
8. Amount/kinds of special services offered:	9
Total Rating:	74

CONTRIBUTOR NAME: Rita W. Moss

AFFILIATION: University of North Carolina–Chapel Hill

USEFUL TIPS

- Help section contains guides and "ask the professor" for answers to questions not already listed.
- Online investment seminars are available.
- Before signing up for the Premium service, check out the free information at *http://www.morningstar.com*.

BLOOMBERG PROFESSIONAL

ALTERNATE/PREVIOUS DATA SOURCE NAMES: Some information, such as current news and information on stock indexes, is free at *http://www.bloomberg.com*.

SERVICE/PORTAL NAME: Bloomberg L.P.

SOURCE DESCRIPTION: Bloomberg Professional service combines in a single platform, data, analytics, electronic trading and processing tools, multimedia reports, and e-mail. The service is available 24/7, 365 days a year, with a help response that takes only minutes. Online help manuals are comprehensive.

Bloomberg Professional is very much directed at the financial services industry and provides clients with information that includes real-time and historical price data, economic statistics, financial, political and business news, analysis of companies, and descriptions of companies from various sources, including Hoover's. Bloomberg News generates more than four thousand news stories daily and is also the main content provider for the entire family of Bloomberg media. The Professional service combines a wealth of information with the ability to use real-time tools to analyze the data.

PRICING: $1,285 per month per workstation (multiple system clients); $1,640 per month per workstation (single system clients).

SOURCE CONTENT: When logged on, two side-by-side screens open automatically and the user can toggle between them by using the Panel key (on the number pad). Different information can be displayed on the screens for comparison purposes or for in-depth research. Bloomberg uses a menu-driven and function-key system that takes time to learn and use properly. Keys are color-coded for ease of use as follows:

- **Red keys** are used to log on and log off.
- **Green keys** are used for System Navigation through the results screens.

- **Blue keys** are used for Panel Navigation.
- **Yellow keys** denote Market Sectors.

Listed below are the main keys, the functions they control, and the information that can be accessed. < > denotes a key to hit.

- **GREEN** Keys (navigation or action keys):
  GO: activates all commands (like the enter key)
  MENU: goes back one command (rather than one page)
  LAST <GO>: gives last eight commands used
  PAGE UP/PAGE DOWN: move between pages (number of pages is at upper left)
  HELP: online help (or hit key twice to contact support services)
  GRAB <GO>: to e-mail a graph or chart
- **YELLOW** Keys (link to information on market sectors):
  GOVT: Displays list of bonds that match a ticker symbol, coupon, and/or maturity that you select. Includes U.S. government bonds (such as T Bonds) and international bonds
  CORP: Use for finding corporate debt, corporate bond prices, and yields by company
  MTGE: Mortgage-backed security pass-throughs
  M-MKT: Includes programs that contain specific issue information. The securities include U.S. government bonds, Treasury Bills, and commercial paper.
  MUNI: Information about bonds issued by municipalities in the United States
  PFD: Covers both public and private securities offered mostly by the United States and United Kingdom. Types include fixed rate issues, zero coupon issues, floating rate notes, variable rate issues, convertible, and warranties
  EQUITY: Displays actual trades and information on ADRs (American Depository Receipts), mutual funds, rights, stocks, warrants, and options. U.S. equity data goes back to 1980
  CMDTY: The commodities menu has all exchange listed futures and options contracts of underlying financial and physical products and spot rates
  INDEX: World financial markets and economic indices
  CRNCY: Spots, futures, and options on over one hundred currencies

Bloomberg Professional includes information on 202,000 equity securities in 110 countries and 97,000 companies listed on 82 exchanges; 406,000 corporate bonds, 12,500 government bonds, 8,800 preferreds, 149,000 mortgages, and 3,050,000 municipal bonds; and 47,000 funds covering 60 countries. Added to this are the more than 4,000 news stories generated each day.

SOURCE EVALUATION: This is an excellent resource that is especially useful for finance professionals. The learning curve is steep, but once mastered, the ability to monitor risk and exposure, utilize pricing models and evaluate long- and short-term performance is invaluable. Within just one sector—EQUITY—one can obtain the ticker symbol, get news on the company, analyze the financials, retrieve electronic filings, get stock prices (in eight forms, including tables and graphs), and then compare companies or compare a company with an index. At first the amount of information can prove overwhelming, but practice in manipulating the screens and keys make this a very reliable and extremely useful investment information resource.

SOURCE VALUE RATING: All of the data source reviewers were asked to rate each source on the basis of the following eight categories, using "10" as the highest rating and "1" as the lowest ("80" being a perfect score):

1. Relative cost-to-value:	8
2. Relative timeliness of data:	10
3. Relative comprehensiveness of data:	9
4. Ease of use:	6
5. Search options available:	10
6. Level of support services:	10
7. Level of training offered:	10
8. Amount/kinds of special services offered:	9
Total Rating:	72

CONTRIBUTOR NAME: Rita W. Moss/Patricia A. Watkins
AFFILIATION: Walter Royal Library, University of North Carolina–Chapel Hill/Thunderbird School of International Management

USEFUL TIPS

- Take plenty of time to get to know the features of the database.
- If possible, take advantage of the on-site training sessions offered by the company.
- Use the help section freely—both the online manuals and the 24/7 assistance.
- Screens can be customized by each user.

FACTSET

SERVICE/PORTAL NAME: *http://www.factset.com*

SOURCE DESCRIPTION: Founded in 1978, FactSet has become a leading aggregator of almost all types of financial data. Given its high costs, however, it is often found only in the leading financial services firms. FactSet continues to offer one of the largest selections of financial information products in a single source. It provides clients, primarily institutional investors, with access to more than 200 databases from about 50 specialty financial service content providers. In addition, FactSet often offers access to multiple overlapping sources, thus providing parallel financial data solutions of significant choice and veracity.

FactSet tools offer superior search and screening functions, which allow users to combine a variety of data sources and customize data analysis and retrieval. FactSet also offers a broad range of customization and excellent data download features, which allow users to save their work in a variety of formats and models. FactSet has built an impressive base of clients through an emphasis on service and consulting. It offers training, dedicated telephone and account consultants, and 24-hour customer service. FactSet is targeted to the financial markets and therefore requires at least a basic understanding of financial services terminology to use.

PRICING: The average subscription is approximately $240,000 a year according to the most recent FactSet Annual Report (2002). According to a Hoover's Company Capsule on this public company, subscribers pay FactSet a fixed fee for access to the service. The fee is payable in cash or in the form of commissions on securities transactions (when clients make a trade, a clearing broker directs the commission to FactSet).

SOURCE CONTENT: While FactSet offers a wealth of real-time and quantitative data, this review focuses on its major researcher-focused sources of Company/Financial Analysis, Economic Analysis, and Fixed Income Analysis:

- **Company/Financial Analysis.** FactSet's extensive collection of company and financial data allows an individual to perform a complete analysis of tens of thousands of companies and mutual funds collecting information from leading sources, such as Barra, Compustat, Extel, Lipper, and Multex. Also, FactSet probably has the most comprehensive set of international company data. An additional strength here is the exceptional depth of company and mutual fund charting data, with a fairly flexible search interface.

- **Economic Analysis.** FactSet is an excellent source for preformatted country and regional reports, which aggregate data from several of the leading sources of international, regional, and country information, including DRI-WEFA, the IMF, MSCI, and the OECD. In addition, FactSet also offer's significant macroeconomic data from the Conference Board.

- **Fixed Income Analysis.** FactSet has great domestic and international bond databases, valuations models, and bond calculators. Sources potentially available on FactSet include First Call Bond, LJS, Moody's, and fixed income indexes from JP Morgan, Lehman Brothers, and Merrill Lynch. FactSet, is always my first source for hard-to-find yield curves and bond pricing data.

SOURCE EVALUATION: FactSet is simply a great aggregator of financial information. However, with the average annual subscription at approximately $240,000 (according to the most recent FactSet Annual Report, 2002), it is very hard to justify its value in most general business research settings. Setting aside the issue of cost, FactSet is an excellent product. It offers the option of easy-to-use preformatted reports, while also allowing the more sophisticated user the ability to build complex screens and reports. FactSet company reports are a strong starting point for combining market data with financials, thus allowing the user to build charts that combine stock pricing, industry fundamentals, and company news and events in relatively short order. Additionally, the reporting functions allow a user to build presentations in a variety of formats quickly and with little post-download manipulation.

FactSet offers solid, in-person training programs and a very good telephone support line. FactSet's support team is available 24 hours a day, 7 days a week. Throughout the year, FactSet also holds training seminars in cities around the world at no additional cost to its clients. Its online help is fairly limited, however, and it is not a product that is suggested to the novice user. FactSet does offer very good Web-based training sessions.

SOURCE VALUE RATING: All of the data source reviewers were asked to rate each source on the basis of the following eight categories, using "10" as the highest rating and "1" as the lowest ("80" being a perfect score):

1. Relative cost-to-value:	7
2. Relative timeliness of data:	10
3. Relative comprehensiveness of data:	10
4. Ease of use:	7
5. Search options available:	5
6. Level of support services:	8
7. Level of training offered:	8
8. Amount/kinds of special services offered:	8
Total Rating:	63

SOURCE REVIEWS:

"It's hard to beat Network effect: Even in a down economy, some outfits continue to thrive because users' habits, routines, or technologies center on their products." *Business Week Online.* Personal Investing column, March 3, 2003. (Factiva database search @ *http://www.factiva.com*).

CONTRIBUTOR NAME: William S. Marriott/Patricia A. Watkins
AFFILIATION: Marriott Research and Recruitment/ Thunderbird School of International Management

USEFUL TIPS

- Take the time to attend training, it is worth it and offers some very good search examples. Also, find time to attend various remote access Web-based training modules. These are a convenient way to review databases you may not have access to and explore more complex elements of search and screening functions.
- When building charts, try not to overcomplicate the perimeters. The easier the chart is to read the more likely the recipient will actually view it.

FEDERAL RESERVE BOARD

SERVICE/PORTAL NAME: *http://www.federalreserve.gov/releases*

SOURCE DESCRIPTION: The Federal Reserve is the central bank for the United States. It serves to stabilize the U.S. banking industry through regulation and policy, and provides financial services to the federal government, financial institutions, and individuals. The Federal Reserve Board publishes key economic and financial data, as well as an analysis of the U.S. economy and the banking industry.

SOURCE CONTENT: Data from the Federal Reserve site that are most frequently requested by accountants can be found in two primary releases:

- **Foreign Exchange Rates**. Daily and Weekly (H.10), Monthly (G.5), and Annually (G.5A).
- **Selected Interest Rates**. Daily and Weekly (H.15), Monthly (G.13). Release G.13 was discontinued in January 2002 and now all data reported on a daily, weekly, monthly, and annual basis are published in Release H.15. Information reported in the Selected Interest Rates releases includes prime rate; federal funds, commercial paper; and 1-, 2-, 3-, 5-, 7-, 10-, 20-, and 30-year Treasuries.

Both the exchange rates and selected interest rate data are available historically, with different beginning dates depending on the item. In most cases, however, the data are available for at least 30 years and for many data series, often longer. Clicking on the link to Historical Data for each release displays a table with links to all the data (daily, weekly, monthly, annually) for each of the items contained in a particular release. The data are available to download in .pdf and all of the tabular data can be copied and pasted into Excel.

In addition to the data posted on the Federal Reserve Board's home site, there is also a large range of data available on the sites of the Federal Reserve's 12 district and regional banks. While these sites focus primarily on state or regional data, many also take a data series available in the Federal Reserve's releases and expand it, sometimes providing more historical data and/or providing links to download the data into Excel. Going to *http://www.federalreserve. gov/otherfrb.htm* displays a U.S. map with links to each regional or district bank. One of the best of these sites is the St. Louis Federal Reserve Bank, *http://www.stlouisfed.org/fred2.*

SOURCE EVALUATION: The Federal Reserve Web sites are all fairly easy to navigate and packed full of information. The quick access to this free valuable content on the Web is extremely important to supporting the accountant's information needs. The sites offer well-organized FAQ sections as well.

SOURCE VALUE RATING: All of the data source reviewers were asked to rate each source on the basis of the following eight categories, using "10" as the highest rating and "1" as the lowest ("80" being a perfect score):

1. Relative cost-to-value:	10
2. Relative timeliness of data:	10
3. Relative comprehensiveness of data:	8
4. Ease of use:	10
5. Search options available:	10
6. Level of support services:	6
7. Level of training offered:	5
8. Amount/kinds of special services offered:	10
Total Rating:	69

CONTRIBUTOR NAME: Brenda Reeb
AFFILIATION: University of Rochester

ECONOMIC INDICATORS

SERVICE/PORTAL NAME: *http://www.access.gpo.gov/congress/ cong002.html*

SOURCE DESCRIPTION: Economic Indicators is a free monthly time-series of data collected from various governmental agencies and nongovernmental organizations to provide the United States Congress and the White House a bellwether of the United States' economy. Published online since 1995, Economic Indicators tracks a variety of economic statistics that illustrate U.S. productivity, business and employment climate, financial markets, and federal income and spending.

SOURCE CONTENT: Economic Indicators is organized into seven areas of coverage:

- **Total Output, Income, and Spending** is a collection of gross domestic product and income, and expenditure data on businesses, farms, and individuals.

- **Employment, Unemployment, and Wages** tracks unemployment, worker productivity, and employment compensation trends.
- **Production and Business Activity** covers new construction, industrial productivity, and business inventories.
- **Prices** provides information on consumer, farm, and producer prices and provides a basic measurement of inflation.
- **Money, Credit, and Security Markets** delivers information on business and consumer credit, the U.S. stock and bond markets, commercial banking rates, and interest rates.
- **Federal Finance** measures federal income and debt and is the starting point to find federal deficit statistics.
- **International Statistics** tracks international trade and industrial production numbers of larger non-U.S. countries. It is an easily accessible point of departure for tracking trade deficits.

SOURCE EVALUATION: The Economic Indicators Web site provides a very simple front page with a wealth of free data. While the simplistic Boolean search engine is exceptionally limited, the browse function is recommended, given the uniformity of the data provided on a monthly basis.

The strength of the Economic Indicators has always been its unique aggregation of data from a variety of sources into a simple regularly updated collection. Economic Indicators is always a good starting point for governmental information because it provides sources for all its information, which can often be backtracked to find data and industry experts. While the limitations of the search interface have already been noted, it should also be said that the help functions at this Web site are limited and several e-mails to the Web site administrator went unanswered.

The Economic Indicators site has added a hotlink, "Additional Instructions for Searching Databases," which leads the user to a GPO Access Web site, *http://www.access.gpo.gov/su_docs/help/hints/searching.html*) where additional "General Searching Instructions" are listed.

Source Value Rating: All of the data source reviewers were asked to rate each source on the basis of the following eight categories, using "10" as the highest rating and "1" as the lowest ("80" being a perfect score):

1. Relative cost-to-value:	7
2. Relative timeliness of data:	8
3. Relative comprehensiveness of data:	6
4. Ease of use:	5
5. Search options available:	3
6. Level of support services:	4
7. Level of training offered:	5
8. Amount/kinds of special services offered:	5
Total Rating:	43

Contributor Name: William. S. Marriott/Patricia A. Watkins
Affiliation: Marriott Research and Recruitment/ Thunderbird School of International Management

BUREAU OF LABOR STATISTICS

Alternate/Previous Data Source Names: Department of Labor, Bureau of Labor Statistics

Service/Portal Name: *http://www.bls.gov*

Source Description: According to its Web page, "The Bureau of Labor Statistics (BLS) is the principal fact-finding agency for the U.S. (United States) Federal Government in the broad field of labor economics and statistics. The BLS is an independent national statistical agency that collects, processes, analyzes, and disseminates essential statistical data to the American public, the U.S. Congress, other Federal agencies, State and local governments, business, and labor. The BLS also serves as a statistical resource to the Department of Labor."

Bureau of Labor Statistics data satisfy a number of criteria, including relevance to current social and economic issues, timeliness, accuracy, and impartiality in both subject matter and presentation. The indicators provided by the BLS, including the Consumer Price Index (CPI) and the Producer Price Index (PPI) are among the major measurements of inflation.

PRICING: No cost; free Web site.

SOURCE CONTENT: As is usual with government Web sites, the BLS site includes an almost overwhelming amount of information. This summary will deal with the main areas displayed and the information contained within these areas.

- **Inflation and Consumer Spending**. The main information sources in this area are the CPI, a CPI calculator, the consumer expenditure survey, the PPI, and Import/Export Price Indexes. All data is available in table format, and customized tables can be formed. Large files can be transferred using file transfer protocol (FTP). But for most users the customized tables supply the needed information.

- **Wages, Earnings, and Benefits**. Includes information on wages by area and occupation, earnings by industry, employee benefits, and costs, state and county wages, national compensation data, and statistics on the collective bargaining area. As in all areas of the site, users can customize tables by using the Detailed Statistics section.

- **Productivity**. Includes productivity and costs and international wage comparisons.

- **International**. Includes Import/Export Price Indexes and imports and exports searchable by Harmonized Classification systems and SITC (Standard International Trade Classifications) number.

- **Employment and Unemployment**. Lists occupational and demographic characteristics of the labor force, as well as injury and fatalities data by national, state, and local geography.

- **At a Glance Tables**. Includes data for the past six months, in table format, for the main indicators: Unemployment Rate, Change in Payroll Employment, Average Hourly Earnings, Consumer Price Index, Producer Price Index, U.S. Import Price Index, Employment Cost Index, and the Productivity Index. A link is provided to annual data for ten years in table or graph format. The data is also available at the region or state level.

- **Publications and Research Papers**. Includes occupation and career guides, but perhaps most useful, it links to the online full-text edition of the *Monthly Labor Review*.

- **BLS Information Offices & Other Statistical Sites**. These sections provide links to regional offices that provide contact information, as well as links to other federal statistical sites.
- **Other Sections**. Other sections include statistical information on Industries, Business Costs, Geography, Safety and Health, Occupations, and Demographics. The latest index numbers are displayed in the center of the page, as are questions from users of the site.

SOURCE EVALUATION: Although the sheer amount of information on this site can be overwhelming, the information is presented in a logical manner. Some information, such as the CPI, is available in more than one section and so is easily found. The At a Glance Tables section satisfies most information needs, and the ability to customize other tables is invaluable. There is also a search box, an excellent A–Z index, and a glossary. Maneuverability within the sections is not impossible, but it is much easier to return to the BLS home page (a link is available on each screen) to begin a new search.

SOURCE VALUE RATING: All of the data source reviewers were asked to rate each source on the basis of the following eight categories, using "10" as the highest rating and "1" as the lowest ("80" being a perfect score):

1. Relative cost-to-value:	10
2. Relative timeliness of data:	10
3. Relative comprehensiveness of data:	10
4. Ease of use:	6
5. Search options available:	8
6. Level of support services:	8
7. Level of training offered:	7
8. Amount/kinds of special services offered:	8
Total Rating:	67

SOURCE REVIEWS:

"Webwatch" [column]. *Library Journal* 123, no. 18 (November 1, 1998): 28. "Data tables download quickly and print easily. Labor demographic data with links to the full reports will be found at Economy at a Glance, Surveys and Programs, and Publications and Research Papers. Bottom Line: This site offers timely information on labor and financial demographics—a narrower mandate than the Census site."

CONTRIBUTOR NAME: Rita W. Moss/Patricia A. Watkins
AFFILIATION: University of North Carolina–Chapel Hill/Thunderbird School of International Management

USEFUL TIPS

- Spend time clicking on all the data and tools.
- Make use of the e-mail alerting service for new statistical releases.
- By clicking on the Detailed Statistics area in each section, one can easily customize tables.

BUDGET AND ECONOMIC OUTLOOK

SERVICE/PORTAL NAME: *http://www.cbo.gov*

SOURCE DESCRIPTION: The Budget and Economic Outlook, published by the Congressional Budget Office (CBO), is the CBO's official report on the state of the federal budget and the economy. It is published in response to a requirement from Congress that the CBO submit periodic reports about fiscal policy and to provide baseline projections of the federal budget. It is published in January each year with an update issues in the summer, usually in August. The Outlook is an invaluable free source for expert commentary and projections on the federal budget, as well as the overall economy. There is a link to the Outlook located directly on the CBO home page; you can also locate it and other CBO reports by clicking on the Publications tab at the top of the page. Access via the Publications tab displays a chronological list of all of CBO's reports back to 1997.

SOURCE CONTENT: The Budget and Economic Outlook contains an overwhelming amount of financial and economic data. The section that will be of importance to the accountant is "The Economic Outlook." This section contains estimates, forecasts, and projected annual averages extended to ten years and includes: CDP, Inflation, three-month Treasury bills, and ten-year Treasury bills. Most data is presented both in tabular and graphic form. This is one of the very few places where you can locate projections for inflation, an information need that is very common to accountants. The fact that the projections are carried out so far and are so easily accessible via the free Web makes this an extremely valuable resource to know about. The reports are available for downloading in HTML, .pdf, and Word and certain tables are also tagged for downloading into Excel.

SOURCE EVALUATION: The CBO's Budget and Economic Outlook is an important information resource and should be included in anyone's arsenal of sources that provide forecasts of key economic data. The CBO's Web site is easy to navigate and since this is one of its primary reports, it is quickly accessible from the home page. It's available for downloading in multiple formats and the availability of historical reports makes it both efficient and effective for the researcher.

SOURCE VALUE RATING: All of the data source reviewers were asked to rate each source on the basis of the following eight categories, using "10" as the highest rating and "1" as the lowest ("80" being a perfect score):

1. Relative cost-to-value:	10
2. Relative timeliness of data:	10
3. Relative comprehensiveness of data:	10
4. Ease of use:	10
5. Search options available:	5
6. Level of support services:	5
7. Level of training offered:	5
8. Amount/kinds of special services offered:	5
Total Rating:	60

CONTRIBUTOR NAME: Brenda Reeb
AFFILIATION: University of Rochester

FINANCIAL FORECAST CENTER

SERVICE/PORTAL NAME: *http://www.forecasting.org*

SOURCE DESCRIPTION: The Financial Forcast Center is a free Web site (with a separate subscription-based election) that contains a wealth of financial and economic data. Although the name implies that it is forecasting focused, it contains historical and current data as well.

SOURCE CONTENT: The content is divided into four primary sections. The sections and the information contained in them are as follows:

- **Stock Indexes**. Dow Jones Industrials, S&P 500, Nikkei 25, and Russell 2000
- **Money Rates**. Prime Interest Rate, Federal Funds, 30-Year Mortgage Interest, Three-Month LIBOR, and One-Year T-Bill
- **Exchange Rates**. Yen, Euro, Canadian Dollar, British Pound, Australian Dollar, and Peso
- **Economic Indicators**. CPI and Inflation, Housing Starts, Unemployment, Gold and Oil Prices

You can get to a section by either clicking on the link at the top of the page or the left frame. When you select a specific data type, such as CPI & Inflation, the display is forecasted data. You need to scroll down to the bottom of the page to locate the links to historical data. While you can locate forecasted information for all of the data included on the site, those requiring data that is forecasted beyond approximately six months will need to subscribe to the service. A $30 annual subscription fee will provide you with regular feeds of forecasted data going out 18 months to 10 years.

Historical data is available for free for all the included data elements and in most cases the data is available both as a table and graph. While The Forecasting Center does perform its own forecasts (information on the site explains the source and methodology), it pulls the historic data from the originating source and is often available dating back five to eight decades. For example, the CPI Index is available dating back to 1946 and the Bureau of Labor Statistics is identified as the data source. Although the data is not formatted for downloading into a spreadsheet, you can easily copy and paste the data into Excel.

Ever wondered what the Dow Jones Industrial Average was in 1922 or which companies made it up? Click on the link to Research located at the top of the page to find the answers to these and some other useful financial information. Additional links to Forecasts and Data at the top of the page provide access to some additional layers of information.

SOURCE EVALUATION: The Financial Forecast Center Web site is a gem and a real find for anyone asked to locate key financial and economic data. And for $30 a year, it is not too difficult to justify subscribing to the forecasted data as well. Click on the link to Help at the top of the page for access to a simple search engine, glossary, site map, and FAQs. The site is easy to navigate and the simple organization of the content makes it easy to find exactly what you need.

SOURCE VALUE RATING: All of the data source reviewers were asked to rate each source on the basis of the following eight categories, using "10" as the highest rating and "1" as the lowest ("80" being a perfect score):

1. Relative cost-to-value:	10
2. Relative timeliness of data:	10
3. Relative comprehensiveness of data:	8
4. Ease of use:	10
5. Search options available:	5
6. Level of support services:	8
7. Level of training offered:	5
8. Amount/kinds of special services offered:	8
Total Rating:	64

CONTRIBUTOR NAME: Susan M. Klopper
AFFILIATION: Goizueta Business Library

USEFUL TIPS

- The Financial Forecast Center does an excellent job of sourcing its historical data. As with any source, whether it be print or electronic, make sure that any data that is going to be relied on for decision-making purposes is valid. One way to do this is to look for sourcing to publishers and agencies that are reputable and reliable.

EIU VIEWSWIRE

SERVICE/PORTAL NAME: *http://www.viewswire.com*

SOURCE DESCRIPTION: The Economist Intelligence Unit's (EIU) ViewsWire provides business intelligence for 195 countries. The product is targeted at busy corporate executives, business researchers, and investors. ViewsWire is a distillation of the larger Economist database of political and economic news, background, and analysis.

The EIU has been gathering and analyzing political and economic information for decades. The company is well known for publishing the weekly magazine the *Economist*, but it is also the publisher of other, less well-known periodicals, including the *Journal of Commerce*. Since 1997, the EIU has offered a large variety of reports on the Web. The EIU as a whole is a large and potentially intimidating resource, but it provides data extending back many years. ViewsWire bundles together the most relevant parts of EIU and presents them in an easy-to-navigate format. ViewsWire is a current awareness service, briefing decision makers with insightful and authoritative analysis, as well as news.

PRICING: ViewsWire is available by annual subscription, with pricing based on the number of users and the number of geographic regions selected (see Table 4-13).

Table 4-13. Global Network Pricing for EIU ViewsWire

NUMBER OF USERS	ANNUAL SUBSCRIPTION COST
Up to 5	$11,950
Up to 10	$16,400
Up to 25	$21,850
Up to 50	$27,300
Up to 100	$32,750
More than 100	Call for pricing information

Subscriptions for individual regions are available at lower prices.

SOURCE CONTENT: ViewsWire is organized by country and by channel. Users can choose a country and then a channel, or vice versa. Channels include Politics, Economics, Business, Finance, and Regulations. An additional channel, EIU RiskWire, provides risk ratings for 60 of the 195 countries.

The content of ViewsWire is drawn from both the EIU database and from strategic alliances with organizations such as the British Broadcasting Corporation (BBC), the World Bank, the *Financial*

Times, China Online, and the Organisation for Economic Cooperation and Development (OECD). Because ViewsWire incorporates articles from business publications, it provides stronger company and industry coverage than does the traditional EIU database. ViewsWire's main strength, however, as with EIU, lies in political and economic analysis.

Information is presented in the form of articles, tables, and graphs. Data may be downloaded in Excel format, and articles and tables may be reformatted into a printer-friendly format with a single click. ViewsWire features a powerful internal search engine, and the entire database can be searched by keyword. Limiters including country, industry, channel, category, date, and source can be used to narrow the search.

ViewsWire provides country-specific information to support organizational decision making. This database stands out above other services in two important aspects: First, it is produced by the authoritative Economist Intelligence Unit. Second, ViewsWire adds a tremendous amount of value with its insightful analysis and forecasts.

SOURCE EVALUATION: ViewsWire takes the most useful parts of a large, relatively expensive database (EIU) and distills them into a concise, powerful service. ViewsWire cuts through the clutter to the information needed by busy managers. For many organizations it is a reasonable alternative to a full EIU subscription. The various parts of ViewsWire are updated at different times. Analysis of major news events is presented within forty-eight hours, and ViewsWire provides daily updates for some items, such as stock indices and currency exchange rates.

There are many sources of country information on the Web (Country Commercial Guides from the U.S. Department of Commerce, for example), but ViewsWire takes country information an extra step and provides five-year forecasts of the data items covered. Business planners can therefore use ViewsWire as a tool to reduce uncertainty. The interface is intuitive and very easy to use. A special feature of ViewsWire is an e-mail alerting service based upon the interest profile set up by the user.

Technical support is included free of charge and is available during normal working hours. ViewsWire is well designed and straightforward to use, and training is available at no charge. Phone assistance is available during business hours, and account managers can provide face-to-face assistance when they are in the customer's geographic area. ViewsWire is unmatched in its concise, timely, and authoritative reporting.

SOURCE VALUE RATING: All of the data source reviewers were asked to rate each source on the basis of the following eight categories, using "10" as the highest rating and "1" as the lowest ("80" being a perfect score):

1. Relative cost-to-value:	8
2. Relative timeliness of data:	9
3. Relative comprehensiveness of data:	9
4. Ease of use:	10
5. Search options available:	9
6. Level of support services:	9
7. Level of training offered:	9
8. Amount/kinds of special services offered:	8
Total Rating:	71

SOURCE REVIEWS:

O'Leary, Mick. "ViewsWire Bundles Best of EIU." *Information Today* 16, no. 7 (July/August 1999): 11–12. O'Leary gives a favorable review and notes that navigating the Web site is straightforward. He writes that ViewsWire's strength lies not so much in the news it provides, but in the analysis of that news.

CONTRIBUTOR NAME: Wes Edens/Patricia A. Watkins
AFFILIATION: Thunderbird School of International Management

USEFUL TIPS

- Use British spelling when searching. For example, use "labour" instead of "labor."
- Use the advanced search feature to limit your searches to your country of interest.

INVESTEXT

SERVICE/PORTAL NAME: Thomson Research (*http://research.thomsonib.com*)

SOURCE DESCRIPTION: Since the early 1980s, Investext has been the largest database of company and industry analysis available. Collected from many of the world's leading investment, consulting, and market research firms, Investext provides an exceptional source for detailed company, industry, and geographic data, in-depth analysis, and forecasts.

The product is considered a basic resource for business and investment research. Though often used to access equity research information for its detailed company analysis and forecasts, Investext provides ready entry to industry analysis that can often deliver a depth and breadth of information unavailable elsewhere. Investext on Thomson Research is a combination of four major research resources: Investext, MarkIntel, Industry Insider, and a new Morning Meeting Notes database.

PRICING: Pricing for Investext through Thomson Research is variable, but costs as much as $2,000 can occur for multiple company/industry searches. Dialog pricing, too, is variable, and depends on the amount of time spent searching, the articles and format for reports and articles, and the Dialog interface chosen (i.e., DialogClassic, DialogWeb).

SOURCE CONTENT: This summary will review the key offerings of Investext on Thomson Research (*http://research.thomsonib.com*) in four content collections: Investment Research, Market Research, Trade Research Association, and Morning Meeting Notes as follows:

1. **Investment Research**. The main and traditional Investext database is a collection of millions of reports from more than six hundred leading investment and brokerage firms. Written by many of the financial services industry's leading analysts, reports found on Investext provide company, industry, geographic current data, and financial forecasts for more than sixty thousand domestic and international companies. Although high priced, Investext is often a solid starting point for gathering primary and secondary company research and analysis.

2. **Market Research**. Also known separately as MarkIntel, Market Research provides access to primary research and statistics from more than 145 of the leading independent market research organizations, such as the Yankee Group, Datamonitor, IDC, and the Gartner Group. Although similar to investment research reports in format, market research reports are almost exclusively market- or industry-focused, and often provide current and forecast statistics in greater depth than other research resources.

3. **Trade Research Association**. Also known as Industry Insider, Trade Research Association is a smaller compilation of research from a variety of key professional and trade associations that generally track their industries for the benefit of their members. Research provided is usually from a collection of sources, both primary and secondary, and often contains industry insights not found in other publications.

4. **Morning Meeting Notes**. A collection of research notes released from the major brokerage houses, Morning Meeting Notes are excellent sources to track a company or industry that is undergoing rapid change. Updated daily, these briefings also track macroeconomic changes and commentary from many of the leading equity and fixed income analysts on global and American markets.

SOURCE EVALUATION: Investext is an invaluable business research resource. Although costly, it provides an unsurpassed collection of millions of research reports from more than a thousand research-driven investment, consulting, and market research firms. Often a mandatory resource in the financial community, Investext is an excellent "first source" for large industry and market studies and is an exceptional point of access to leading analysts. The key limitation of Investext is the lack of "real-time" updating of reports. Most reports can take weeks to become available because of limitations imposed by their providers. Additionally, although the cost per page is reasonable given its value, the cost of whole reports is still too high, especially given the lower-cost options available elsewhere.

The arrangement of Investext's full search screen on Thomson Research follows a standard pattern: Company or Ticker, Industry (by name, SIC, or NAICS codes), Region (geographic), Title & Free-Text Searching (FT search available only since 1999), Date, Contributor (corporate), Author, Collection, Report Number, and Date (see Figure 4-25). This organization is fairly straightforward and intuitive for the beginning searcher. Additionally, the look-up functions provide solid search-refinement tools. Help windows are available and fairly solid, although the help function lacks true interactivity with a user's level in search and retrieval. Additionally, the Show Criteria window on the initial search page and on the results page is exceptionally useful for editing searches on the fly. The best feature about the database, however, is the ability to customize almost all search and display settings, which allows each user to deliver a highly tailored research product.

The only real flaw I found is that the static Support tab available on the upper right-hand corner of every page lists only the phone numbers and e-mails of regional technical support. This link would be more useful if it were to refer the user to the available Help files.

Figure 4-25. Thomson Research Full Search Screen

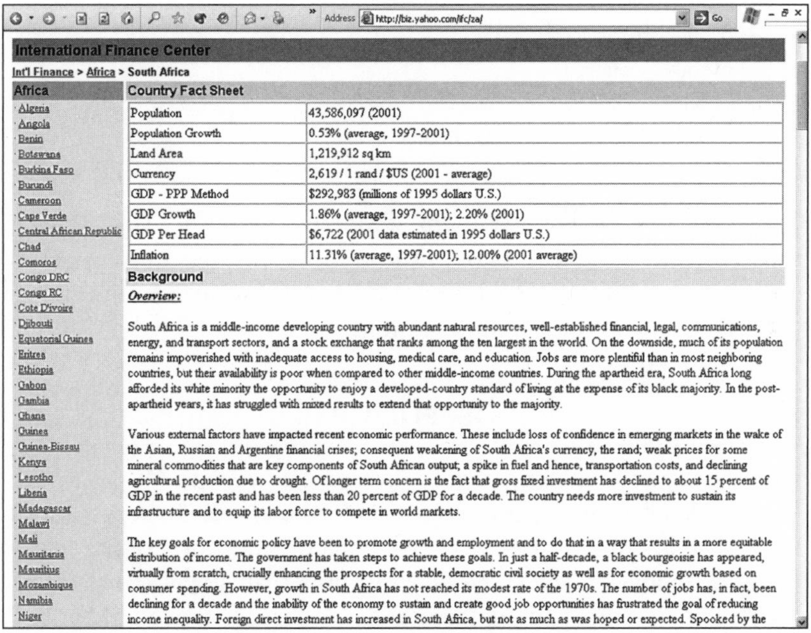

Reprinted with the permission of Thomson Financial Networks.

For first-time users, Thomson Research offers a simple Company search page that allows for searches by Company Name, Ticker, and Industry (by Industry name, SIC, or NAICS codes). This is a fine initial search engine for pulling industry and company reports. However, it lacks the ability to limit a search by anything other than the above indexing and is not recommended for anyone other than the most inexperienced researcher.

SOURCE VALUE RATING: All of the data source reviewers were asked to rate each source on the basis of the following eight categories, using "10" as the highest rating and "1" as the lowest ("80" being a perfect score):

1. Relative cost-to-value:	7
2. Relative timeliness of data:	7
3. Relative comprehensiveness of data:	8
4. Ease of use:	6
5. Search options available:	8
6. Level of support services:	7
7. Level of training offered:	6
8. Amount/kinds of special services offered:	7
Total Rating:	56

CONTRIBUTOR NAME: William S. Marriott/Patricia A. Watkins
AFFILIATION: Marriott Research and Recruitment/ Thunderbird School of International Management

USEFUL TIPS

- Always try to complement your Investext usage with Multex, which provides full analyst research reports for hundreds if not thousands less than Investext. However, keep in mind that Investext provides superior indexing and is the only resource that allows you to view tables of contents and purchase only the pages you need of analyst reports. Additionally, both Multex and Investext have significant overlap, but each does offer its own exclusive sources.
- Unless you are looking for specific research notes, ignore any report fewer than five pages long (>5), especially during earnings report season. These are often only a regurgitation of a company's press release, which can be found for free or for little cost.
- Excellent industry and company reports are often available when an analyst initiates coverage. Try to look for these, as they often provide incredibly detailed studies of, and methods for, evaluating companies, industries, and geographies.
- Stay away from Corporate Technology Information reports and older reports from Market Guide. They provide no original forecasts, just a restatement of earnings reports with basic financial ratios and other information available from alternative, less expensive sources.

THE WALL STREET TRANSCRIPT

ALTERNATE/PREVIOUS DATA SOURCE NAMES: TWST, TWST Online

SERVICE/PORTAL NAME: *http://www.twst.com*

SOURCE DESCRIPTION: Published in print since 1963 and available online since 1997, *The Wall Street Transcript (TWST)* provides the full transcripts of corporate conferences and interviews with corporate leaders and Wall Street professionals, including money managers and research analysts. The Focus Series, which allows users to choose coverage of one industry sector, and a European edition were added in 1999. Seven industry sectors are covered in the Focus Series: technology, health care, consumer, industry/services, financial services, natural resources, and investing strategies.

TWST aims to assist investors in making investment decisions. Subscribers include individual and institutional investors, money managers, brokers, and researchers, both academic and professional. *TWST* is also available through online services Multex and First Call.

PRICING: *TWST* services can be accessed in a variety of ways and within a variety of budgets. Researchers can purchase individual issues, trial subscriptions, as well as quarterly or yearly subscriptions, with cost ranging anywhere from $100 to over $2,000.

The cost for full access to all interviews in all sectors might be a bit high for individual and academic subscribers, but is reasonable for corporate entities at $2,290 annually or $630 per quarter. The limited Focus Series subscriptions or individual issues may be more appropriate and affordable for individuals at $495 per year and $195 for a thirteen-week trial subscription. Site licenses are available for multiple users in a corporate or institutional environment, and networking is possible. Site licenses are priced according to the number of simultaneous users.

SOURCE CONTENT: *TWST* is unique in that the content is provided in interview form. Some interviews include in-depth reviews of industries with stock recommendations for that industry, others comprise confidential analyst surveys regarding company performance in a specific sectors. There are interviews with money managers who provide investment strategies and evaluation advice, research analysts discussing their particular areas of expertise, and CEOs revealing investment-related details of their companies.

As shown in the Table 4-14, *TWST* is arranged in seven broad industry sectors, with subsectors/industries for each.

Table 4-14. Industry Sectors and Subsectors in *TWST*

SECTOR NAME	SUBSECTORS
Technology	Internet, Software, Services
	Telecommunications
	Computers and Electronics
Health Care	Drugs and Biotech
	Health Care Services
Consumer	Media
	Retail
	Leisure
	Consumer Products
Industry/Services	Manufacturing/Engineering
	Services
Financial Services	Banks/Brokers
	Insurance
	Real Estate/REITs
Natural Resources	Chemicals
	Mining and Minerals
	Oil and Gas
Investing Strategies	Money Manager Interviews

Nonsubscribers may preview articles, but a subscription log-in is required to access the full interview transcript, in HTML or PDF format. The interviews may be printed, saved to disk or desktop, or e-mailed for later viewing.

The interface provides basic and advanced search options (see Figures 4-26 and 4-27). The basic search searches the current issue using a simple keyword search (see Figure 4-28). The basic search box is present at the top of every screen. The advanced search option allows the user to search the current issue or *TWST* archives. In the advanced search, the user may specify date range, type of interview (money manager, analyst, and so forth), industry sector, title of interview or document number (if known), and company ticker symbol. Any or all of these search fields may be utilized to focus the advanced search. In addition to defined fields, a text search (by keyword) may be added as well.

Figure 4-26. Basic Search Screen for *The Wall Street Transcript*

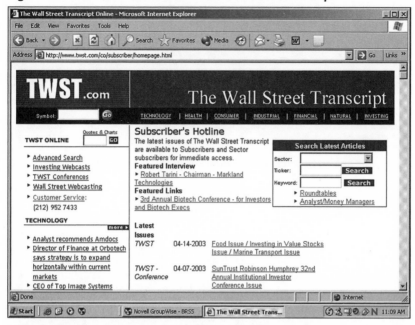

Reprinted with the permission of *The Wall Street Transcript.*

Figure 4-27. Advanced Search Screen for *The Wall Street Transcript*

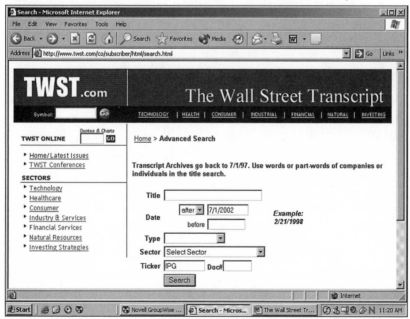

Reprinted with the permission of *The Wall Street Transcript.*

Figure 4-28. Sample Results Page of a Basic Search in *The Wall Street Transcript*

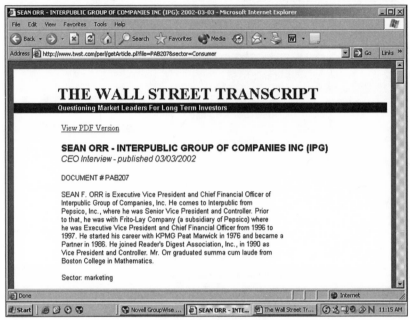

Reprinted with the permission of *The Wall Street Transcript.*

SOURCE EVALUATION: It is difficult to compare *TWST* to similar products because I know of no other source that provides quality interviews from the same professional sources. The combination of CEO interviews and researcher/analyst interviews provides a balanced approach to company and industry information. The *TWST* Web site is well organized, and both the basic and advanced search options are intuitive and easy to use. This product would be useful for individual and professional investors as well as academic and professional researchers.

SOURCE VALUE RATING: All of the data source reviewers were asked to rate each source on the basis of the following eight categories, using "10" as the highest rating and "1" as the lowest ("80" being a perfect score):

1. Relative cost-to-value:	8
2. Relative timeliness of data:	10
3. Relative comprehensiveness of data:	8
4. Ease of use:	9
5. Search options available:	9
6. Level of support services:	8
7. Level of training offered:	8
8. Amount/kinds of special services offered:	10
Total Rating:	70

CONTRIBUTOR NAME: Polly D. Boruff-Jones/Patricia A. Watkins
AFFILIATION: IUPUI University Library/Thunderbird School of International Management

USEFUL TIPS

* *TWST* uses the Excite for Web Servers search engine; search documentation is available through a link on the Text Search screen within the Advanced Search feature. The documentation includes basic and advanced query tips and an explanation of the use of Boolean operators.

10K WIZARD

SERVICE/PORTAL NAME: *http://www.10kwizard.com*

SOURCE DESCRIPTION: 10k Wizard was formed in April 1999 by Martin Zacarias, a Harvard Business School graduate and financial analyst, and Kee Kimbrell, a game software developer. Recognizing the need for expanded coverage of and advanced search capabilities for the Securities and Exchange Commission (SEC) database, together the two developed proprietary software to search through the vast amount of information available to the public via the SEC's EDGAR (Electronic Data Gathering, Analysis, and Retrieval) system. Not only can the user search by company name or ticker with 10k Wizard, but the Power Search feature also allows one to search the whole document for individual words or word phrases and to use Boolean operators (AND, OR, NOT). Search returns display complete company files or specified sections. There are several additional modules, including Alert Streaming, Portfolio Wizard, IR Wizard, and Global Reports, as well as Fundamental Financials, which offers 140 data points taken from the income statement, balance sheet, and cash flow statement and then displayed in annual, quarterly, and trailing twelve-month views.

PRICING: Base price is $150 per year, $25 per month, or $50 per quarter. For pricing information on additional modules contact 10k Wizard at *http://www.10kwizard.com.*

SOURCE CONTENT: 10k Wizard is the name given to the basic package offered on this Web site. Tabs along the top of the page link the user to seven different search mechanisms or search areas: Basic, Advanced, Exhibits, Corporate Actions, Profiles, Annual Reports, and Financials (this is an optional upgrade). Basic searching is free and open to all. Any of the other search options, including financials, requires a subscription. One can search free in the Basic mode, but document retrieval requires a subscription. All the other search areas require a subscription before access.

In the Basic mode one can search by company name, ticker, CIK, words, and industry and limit by type of form group and dates. The advanced search adds the ability to drill down as far as ZIP code or area code in searching and to limit by specific form and fiscal year end. The Exhibits section allows one to search by the entire group or within specific exhibits. This is particularly helpful when you need to quickly find information not included in the forms, such as agreements with other groups. Corporate Action is the section for tracking resignations, acquisitions, changes in control, and bankruptcies. The Profile section will provide some descriptive material, a list of the latest filings, and links to filings by companies in the same industry group—here 10k Wizard is linking to a company's competitors. The Annual Report section supports searching, at this time, for fifty-six countries. Although annual reports are searchable, there is an added cost to purchase them.

There are five add-on modules or sections:

1. **Insider Trading**. In this section one can search either EDGAR or non-EDGAR filings. Searching is available by company name, ticker, word, or search form number. One can limit by date range. It is simple to choose a date and form type and retrieve names of the people who bought, sold, or exercised an option on those days.

2. **Fundamental Financials**. This is an added optional module that enables comparisons across companies. Comparisons can be obtained for seven years of annual data, sixteen quarters, or a trailing twelve months. Ratios are provided annually and quarterly. Data is taken from income statements, balance sheets, and cash flow information in the various SEC documents. Coverage is provided for companies listed on the NYSE, AMEX, NASDAQ, and OTC.

3. **Alert Service**. An added module, this provides streaming service, to the desktop, for an alert list set up by the user. Each alert is linked to the full-text filing.

4. **Portfolio Wizard**. This service tracks large listings of financial and news resources and is most suited to analysts, brokers, and institutions with large holdings. It is integrated into a company's Web site, and the interface can be customized. This is an added module.

5. **IR Wizard**. This tool enables a company to integrate its SEC filings onto the company Web site, where they can be accessed by customers and investors. This is an added module.

SOURCE EVALUATION: Overall, 10k Wizard is a solid corporate resource that enables the user to save time in finding needed company financial information. The range of search features makes it easy for even the novice to quickly find the needed material. Even the basic search feature is a big improvement on the EDGAR database, which allows a search for information in the headers only. The added modules give the option of amalgamating more features, but the basic database is by itself a reliable and useful resource.

SOURCE VALUE RATING: All of the data source reviewers were asked to rate each source on the basis of the following eight categories, using "10" as the highest rating and "1" as the lowest ("80" being a perfect score):

1. Relative cost-to-value:	9
2. Relative timeliness of data:	10
3. Relative comprehensiveness of data:	10
4. Ease of use:	10
5. Search options available:	10
6. Level of support services:	10
7. Level of training offered:	5
8. Amount/kinds of special services offered:	9
Total Rating:	73

SOURCE REVIEWS: This Web site was nominated for a Webby Award in 2002 (*http://www.webbyawards.com/main/webby_awards/nominees. html#finance*).

Hoover's Company Capsules, via Factiva database search. "M10K Wizard Technology, LLC–Hoover's Company Capsule." May 10, 2002. "Need a little magic to sort through SEC filings? 10K Wizard Technology provides free online access to Securities and Exchange Commission filings (more than 70 types of documents), as well as powerful searching and parsing tools to sort through the information. Users can search by company name, ticker, SIC code, industry type, or keyword, and registered users can receive e-mail alerts of new filings. 10K Wizard also uses its technology to power the SEC portions of Web sites, including Hoover's [publisher of this profile]."

CONTRIBUTOR NAME: Rita W. Moss/Patricia A. Watkins
AFFILIATION: University of North Carolina–Chapel Hill/Thunderbird School of International Management

BUSINESS WIRE

SERVICE/PORTAL NAME: *http://www.dialogweb.com.* Database numbers 610 (March 1999 to current) and 810 (historical 1986–February 1999)

SOURCE DESCRIPTION: *Business Wire* contains the full text of news releases issued by approximately 14,000 corporations, universities, research institutes, hospitals, and other organizations. Primary focus is on U.S. industries and organizations, although some information on international events is included. News releases received by *Business Wire* are updated continuously in the *Business Wire* database.

PRICING: *Business Wire* is available from Dialog (Files 610, 810).

Cost per DialUnit: $1.00
Cost per minute: $0.58
Format 9: $2.95

Business Wire is also a portion of the Business Dateline database from ProQuest Information and Learning.

SOURCE CONTENT: *Business Wire* content is fairly homogenous consisting of press releases and announcements from corporations, nonprofits, and other organizations. News covering all industries and business topics is covered, including:

- Computers
- Banking
- Entertainment
- Sports
- Aviation
- Oil
- New Products

- Financial results
- Stock offerings
- Mergers
- Personnel changes
- Company news
- Feature stories

In DialogWeb, *Business Wire* is found in Files 610 and 810. File 610 is the current data starting in March 1999, while File 810 is an archival database from 1986 to February 1999.

SOURCE EVALUATION: *Business Wire* is useful for searching specific company or organization press releases. Using both files a searcher can track a corporation's events over time. Searching *Business Wire* within DialogWeb is fairly straightforward with a menu of field options to choose from, a date range option, and an article size (less than or more than 1,000 words). There is also a browse option for each of the fields. Not every field is searchable in both *Business Wire* files. Most notably, ticker symbol is searchable in the archival file but not in the current file. The narrow focus of this database makes it useful for specific corporate or timeline-type information requests. While it would be less than useful for more in-depth research, it is helpful as a current awareness tool, particularly for events affecting public companies. Material can be printed, e-mailed, faxed, FTP'ed, or sent postal mail (USPS)—each for a charge.

SOURCE VALUE RATING: All of the data source reviewers were asked to rate each source on the basis of the following eight categories, using "10" as the highest rating and "1" as the lowest ("80" being a perfect score):

1. Relative cost-to-value:	5
2. Relative timeliness of data:	10
3. Relative comprehensiveness of data:	5
4. Ease of use:	7
5. Search options available:	5
6. Level of support services:	5
7. Level of training offered:	5
8. Amount/kinds of special services offered:	5
Total Rating:	47

CONTRIBUTOR NAME: Hal P. Kirkwood, Jr./Patricia A. Watkins
AFFILIATION: Purdue University/Thunderbird School of International Management

USEFUL TIPS

* Remember that the content is company and organization press releases.
* Search options between the two Dialog files are not consistent.

D&B MILLION DOLLAR DATABASE

ALTERNATE/PREVIOUS DATA SOURCE NAME: MDDI, Million Dollar Database–Internet, North American Million Dollar Database, Million Dollar Directory

SERVICE/PORTAL NAME: *http://www.dnbmdd.com/mddi*

SOURCE DESCRIPTION: D&B's Million Dollar Database is the Web-based interface for one of the best known and most heavily used general business directories. It contains summary descriptive data on 1.45 million U.S. and 165,000 Canadian public and private companies, including parent, subsidiary, division, and branch locations. The database provides the researcher with baseline knowledge of the size, location, executives, and market focus for each company. D&B's Million Dollar Database supports company identification, general marketing and sales prospecting, auditor market share analysis, and corporate family definition.

Selection criteria for the companies included in the database are as follows:

* $1,000,000 in sales, OR
* 20 or more employees, OR
* Branches with 50 or more employees

D&B's Million Dollar Database is available from Dun & Bradstreet only by subscription and is priced on a cost-per-seat model. The full retail cost for D&B's Million Dollar Database is $12,000 a year for the first user. The cost per user declines as the number of users increases, so that a subscription for 24 users would cost approximately $45,000 a year.

SOURCE CONTENT: The following information is included for each company in the database: name, D-U-N-S number, complete address, telephone, sales (actual or estimated), short business description, SIC codes (D&B developed an expanded version of the four- digit SIC system which further refines the line of business down to eight digits), URL, number of employees (local and total), parent/subsidiaries, public or private status, ticker symbol (U.S. public only), banking and accounting firm relationship, and executive names and brief executive work history. Public U.S. companies also contain a link to SEC filings.

The company data contained in D&B's Million Dollar Database comes from three main sources: D&B's internal staff, the Internet, and D&B business partners. Incoming data is subjected to extensive validation procedures and D&B's Million Dollar Database is refreshed and updated every 60 days.

A user can connect with the D&B Million Dollar Database from the home page by using the site map, selecting Analysis and Research, and clicking on the Million Dollar Directory Suite link. The alternative approach is to type in the URL (*http://www.dnbmdd.com/mddi*). The home page contains links to FAQs, What's New, Last Update, Information Quality, which has useful definitions for using the linking feature effectively, and a short, interesting D&B history.

The Search Option Menu provides two choices for accessing the content:

- Three highly structured Quick Search options, each of which lead the user through the construction of a search by name or stock symbol, industry size and/or geography, or executive by name, company title and/or biography.
- An Advanced Search option which allows the user to construct a search using any combination of the 30 elements available for searching.

Search results in D&B's Million Dollar Database can be printed or exported. Exported results can be saved in comma-delimited format for ease of importing the data into Excel. Both the print and export options restrict the number of records that can be output at any one time to one hundred. Search results of more than one hundred companies require resetting the range and repeating the output steps for each range of one hundred. This output restriction is a standard with D&B's electronic company products and it persists in making this valuable resource less than user-friendly.

D&B's Million Dollar Database supports basic company identification, but remains one of the most powerful research tools for internal marketing and sales prospecting activities. It can be used to identify potential targets by geography, size, industry, and important biographical intelligence on executives. Existing business relationships can be leveraged with the database's capacity to define the customer's entire company family and, of particular interest to accounting and financial institutions, it is one of the very few business directories that provides accountant and banking relationships. While extremely valuable information, the data is often incomplete for private companies. Another excellent company database, Standard & Poor's Register of Corporations also contains this same information, but the Register covers approximately 100,000 companies vs. the 1.6 million companies found in D&B's Million Dollar Database

D&B's linking feature, which supports identification of complete corporate families, is a high mark of the product. Researchers tasked with tracing family connections will find this function invaluable for marketing or conflict checking. Another excellent company database, National Register's Directory of Corporate Affiliations, also tracks corporate hierarchy, but its database is limited to approximately 114,000 companies.

SOURCE EVALUATION: D&B's Million Dollar Database is well organized with lots of content options and there is no question that it is a valuable company resource. Its vast collection of public and private companies, relative ease of searching, and unique linking capability render it one of the most desirable databases for gathering company information. Its strengths, like many other D&B information products, are its comprehensive coverage of a defined set of businesses, the presence of difficult-to-find data (for example, accounting and banking relationships), useful search functionality, and corporate family linking. Its limitations are lingering data quality issues although D&B has greatly improved on its data integrity, limitations on output, and high cost.

The search interface is relatively easy to use: The Quick Search options are effectively designed and an experienced searcher will have no difficulty navigating Advanced Search. It is strongly recommended that searchers take the time to read the section on Information Quality, available from the home page, to understand how D&B defines and uses the words "branch," "subsidiary," "parent," "division," and "headquarters" so that they take full advantage of the family linking functionality. Technical support and customer search support are available as part of the basic subscription package. There is no formal training available, although customer support can be used for that purpose informally. If formal training is desired, it will need to be organized by the sales representative.

Cost-to-value for any high-cost source is a decision that can really only be made by the buyer. If the content matches the researcher's need, if the hard-to-find information is extremely important, and if the database will be heavily used, then the cost-to-value of this source is low. If all or most of those considerations are not true for the company considering subscribing, then the cost-to-value is too high and other options should be explored.

D&B licenses parts of its data to a number of information providers, including Dialog, LexisNexis, Hoover's, and One-Source. If the cost of purchasing a standalone subscription to D&B's Million Dollar Database is not negotiable and you already have access to one of these other interfaces, then you might need to consider accessing D&B's data via one of these products. Be sure to explore the answers to questions such as: How much of the complete D&B data is available using another information provider? How current is the information? Does D&B place an embargo on sharing the data? What are the search and output options? If you specifically need to access the D&B's data to create spreadsheets which display and sort by auditor, will the vendor's interface accommodate the manipulation of the database to suit this need? Do not assume that the answer is yes! Ask these questions up-front. Depending on the value of the content relative to your organization's profitability, you may determine that that cost-to-value is lower than you expected.

SOURCE VALUE RATING: All of the data source reviewers were asked to rate each source on the basis of the following eight categories, using "10" as the highest rating and "1" as the lowest ("80" being a perfect score):

1. Relative cost-to-value:*	5
2. Relative timeliness of data:	7
3. Relative comprehensiveness of data:	8
4. Ease of use:	9
5. Search options available:	7
6. Level of support services:	7
7. Level of training offered:	3
8. Amount/kinds of special services offered:	5
Total Rating:	51

*The cost is high, but so is the value—so a middle rank is assigned.

CONTRIBUTOR NAME: Naomi Clifford
AFFILIATION: Consultant

USEFUL TIPS

- The new D&B Million Dollar Database user can learn a great deal about the database by investing some time upfront and reading the extensive product information linked on the home page.
- If you already subscribe to an information provider that already contains D&B's company information, do your homework and verify if the content and the search and output functionality fits your specific information needs.

STANDARD & POOR'S NETADVANTAGE

SERVICE/PORTAL NAME: *http://www.netadvantage.standardandpoors. com/*

SOURCE DESCRIPTION: Standard & Poor's NetAdvantage is a comprehensive source of business and finance information, offering online access to popular Standard & Poor's research products, such as Industry Surveys, Stock Reports, Corporation Records, the Register of Corporations, Directors, and Executives, and *The Outlook*, among others. It is designed to meet the information needs of analysts, business researchers, librarians, management consultants, personal and professional investors, students, and educators.

SOURCE CONTENT: This summary will review the four key components of Standard & Poor's NetAdvantage: Industry Surveys, Stock Reports, *The Outlook*, and the Register of Corporations:

1. **Industry Surveys**. This feature provides in-depth financial business analysis of over fifty major U.S. industries. Analysis includes data, forecasts, and trends across industry groups. Written by Standard & Poor's equity analysts, Industry Surveys provide an in-depth look at industry trends, how the industry operates, key ratios, and statistics. Industry Surveys is a good starting point for industry analysis because it provides a "big picture" of the industry, identifies key players, comments on the growth of the industry, and lists major business issues facing the industry. Links to industry references are provided, including contact information to key industry associations.

2. **Stock Reports.** This component of NetAdvantage covers approximately five thousand public companies and closed-end funds, featuring the Standard & Poor's STARS (Stock Appreciation Ranking System), the current stock price, and a price range. A four-year stock chart, ten years of income statements, and a balance sheet are also provided. In the Stock Reports database, searches can be conducted by Company, Ticker, STARS Ranking, Fair Value Rank (Outlook), EPS Growth Rate, Dividend Yield, and P/E Ratio. Additionally, reports up to five pages in length are available for each publicly held company. These include Stock Reports (a basic summary of stock performance over the past five years and one-year trading estimates), News Headlines, Industry Outlook, and Wall Street Consensus.

3. *The Outlook.* A weekly investment advisory newsletter that identifies and analyzes trends and developments affecting stock performance, *The Outlook* identifies the sectors considered most attractive for investors, provides news that may affect the market, highlights specific companies with buy recommendations, identifies rising STARS (companies with new, higher rankings), lists companies that Standard & Poor's analysts believe will outperform the market in the next 6 to 12 months, and provides a list of Master List stock portfolios (those recommended for long-term investors). *The Outlook* is indexed, so company reviews can be accessed via general searches in Standard & Poor's NetAdvantage. Although the newsletter provides a lot of useful information, its main strength is the indexing feature because most researchers will not have time to read each issue cover to cover.

4. **Register of Corporations.** This source lists approximately one hundred thousand companies, both public and privately held. The Register of Directors and Executives provides brief biographical profiles on more than seventy thousand officers and executives. The Register of Corporations is an excellent starting place for obtaining short biographical profiles of executives, confirming the spelling of a name, identifying officers and board members and for collecting basic background information on executives.

SOURCE EVALUATION: Overall, Standard & Poor's NetAdvantage is a solid resource. It provides a wide range of business research offerings in a pleasing format. For researchers familiar with the print S&P sources, this product is particularly beneficial, offering all the benefits of an electronic resource in the format of standard paper products.

The arrangement of the NetAdvantage databases is logical, with the header frame providing the basic components of the product: Home, Search, Industry, Help, and Contact. The Navigation frame lists all the databases, with links on the left of the screen. The main application frame corresponds to the Navigation frame and provides a search screen for the database selected. In most cases radio buttons make searching a quick and logical process.

NetAdvantage is fairly intuitive to use, but the first-time user with a tight deadline could experience some frustration. NetAdvantage Help is a useful tool, with basic search techniques and instructions to maximize research efforts. The guide section includes an "Investment Glossary," "Investor's Guide," "Publication Guide," and "User's Manual." Most findings can be captured in either print or electronic files.

This product could be improved by including on the main header from some simple directional information and short explanations of what is contained in each database. Users can easily waste valuable time seeking data that doesn't exist or cycling through the product, only to find themselves back at the beginning.

SOURCE VALUE RATING: All of the data source reviewers were asked to rate each source on the basis of the following eight categories, using "10" as the highest rating and "1" as the lowest ("80" being a perfect score):

1. Relative cost-to-value:	8
2. Relative timeliness of data:	10
3. Relative comprehensiveness of data:	8
4. Ease of use:	7
5. Search options available:	8
6. Level of support services:	7
7. Level of training offered:	6
8. Amount/kinds of special services offered:	8
Total Rating:	70

CONTRIBUTOR NAME: Elena Carvajal

AFFILIATION: Ernst & Young

USEFUL TIPS

- Allow plenty of time to familiarize yourself with Standard & Poor's NetAdvantage before you need it to complete a report or meet a deadline.
- To supplement the basic company information provided in the Stock Reports section, you may want to seek additional company information elsewhere. NetAdvantage is a great starting place for company research.

DISCLOSURE DATABASE

ALTERNATE/PREVIOUS DATA SOURCE NAME: Compact D/SEC (on CD-ROM) and also part of Thomson Research

SERVICE/PORTAL NAME: Dialog (*http://www.dialog.com*)

SOURCE DESCRIPTION: Financial and directory information on publicly owned companies, including balance sheets, income statements, and some historic financial data on about 14,000 companies.

SOURCE CONTENT: All publicly owned companies (that is, those that sell shares to the public) are required by the Disclosure Act of 1934 to send their shareholders financial statements and to file annual and quarterly financial reports with the SEC. The Disclosure Database extensively mines these reports to extract information and data, including the annual report, 10-K, 10-Q, 20-F (for non-U.S. companies), proxy, prospectus, registration, and 8-K filings. The result is a huge database of records that includes detailed financial data: balance sheets, income and sales figures, financial ratios, and price earnings, just to name a few. Each record also includes the full text of the management discussion and the president's letter to shareholders from the annual reports, a list of directors and salaries of top ranking executives, SIC codes, and line of business. The auditor's report and directory information on each company is also included.

The most common search is by company name (see Figures 4-29 and 4-30). Easily and quickly done, the company name search retrieves the main company record and other records that mention the company. The display of the full record can easily be more than 15 or 20 pages long and costs $40.

Figure 4-29. The Disclosure Database Search Screen

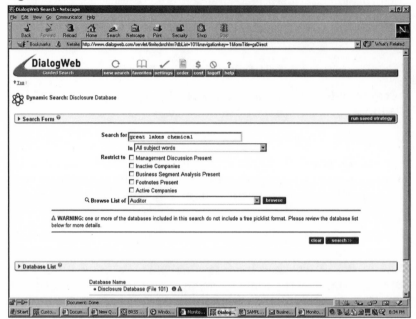

2003 ® Dialog, a Thomson business, *http://www.dialog.com*. Reprinted with the permission of Thomson Financial Networks.

The power of the Disclosure Database system is revealed when the searcher targets a specific range of companies by some financial item such as "percentage of earnings per share." Figure 4-31 illustrates a search for EPS (earnings per share) growth of between 5 percent and 6 percent. Records are then sorted by EPS, as shown in Figure 4-32.

Figure 4-30. The Disclosure Database Basic Company Search Results

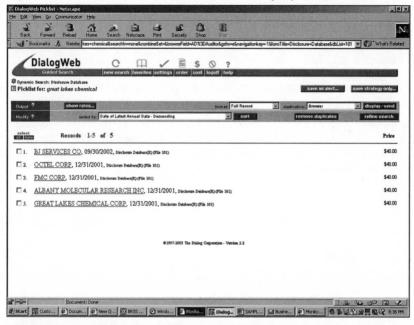

2003 ® Dialog, a Thomson business, *http://www.dialog.com*. Reprinted with the permission of Thomson Financial Networks.

Figure 4-31. Sample Search for EPS Growth in Disclosure Database

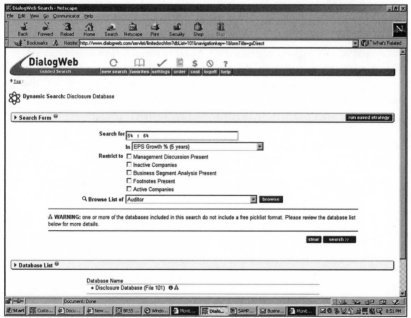

2003 ® Dialog, a Thomson business, *http://www.dialog.com*. Reprinted with the permission of Thomson Financial Networks.

Figure 4-32. Sorting of EPS Search Results by Company Using Disclosure Database

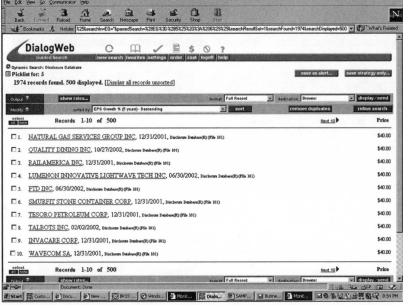

2003 ® Dialog, a Thomson business, *http://www.dialog.com*. Reprinted with the permission of Thomson Financial Networks.

SOURCE EVALUATION: A powerful database for retrieving information on publicly owned companies, Disclosure Database has long been a well-used and well-loved source for financial research because it provides a succinct summary of information from numerous and lengthy SEC documents. The Dialog search engine provides excellent search capacity to the data compiled by Disclosure. It also works very well for retrieving financials on a few companies and is quite useful for competitive research.

SOURCE VALUE RATING: All of the data source reviewers were asked to rate each source on the basis of the following eight categories, using "10" as the highest rating and "1" as the lowest ("80" being a perfect score):

1. Relative cost-to-value:	7
2. Relative timeliness of data:	8
3. Relative comprehensiveness of data:	9
4. Ease of use:	9
5. Search options available:	7
6. Level of support services:	7
7. Level of training offered:	5
8. Amount/kinds of special services offered:	7
Total Rating:	59

SOURCE REVIEWS:

"Disclosure Covers Public Companies." *Link-Up,* March/April 1992.

CONTRIBUTOR NAME: Judith M. Nixon
AFFILIATION: Purdue University

USEFUL TIPS

- When using Disclosure Database, search ranges of numeric values using quotation marks ("), the less-than sign (<), the greater-than sign (>), and the equals sign (=).
- Search financial items in real numbers, rounded down to the two left-most significant digits.
- Basic company information includes name, address, telephone, status (active, inactive), exchange, ticker, CUSIP, *Forbes* and *Fortune* numbers, and state of incorporation.
- Five-year summaries include sales, net income, and EPS.

Appendix

The source listings and source value rating surveys provided in this Appendix are, by nature, very time sensitive and will certainly be dated to some extent at publication. Here is a very brief overview of the origin of each appendix.

A. **Directory of Online Business Data Sources:** All of the data sources (databases) that are referred to in this volume and/ or other volumes in the Business Research Solutions Series are listed alphabetically by name with the name of the publisher immediately underneath. The contact information is often slanted to public relations rather than sales or support but each publisher handles outside queries in a different fashion.

B. **Directory of Online Business Data Publishers:** All of the publishers of business data sources are listed by publisher name in this directory followed by the names of the data sources (databases) that are owned and distributed by that publisher. The contact information that follows is identical to that in the first directory discussed above.

C. **Business Data Source Rating Survey:** This presentation of source ratings is in the same form as the survey in Chapter Four but has been extended to include *all* 102 business data sources covered in *all* volumes of the Business Research Solutions Series. The reader is cautioned, again, that these ratings reflect only the opinions of the contributor/reviewer and should not be viewed as the results of a large-scale national survey. Please also refer to the data source ratings section in the introduction to Chapter Four of this volume.

D. **Contributor Biographies:** The biographies of contributors to all the volumes in the Series are included to the extent that was possible. Much of the credit for the problems and solutions and the data source reviews goes to the creative group of experts.

Appendix A:
Directory of Online
Business Data Sources

10k Wizard
10k Wizard Technology LLC
Elise Soyza
Director, Marketing
elise@10kwizard.com
(214) 800-4565
1950 Stemmons Freeway,
Suite 7016
Dallas, TX 75207

ABI/Inform
ProQuest, Inc.
Tina Creguer
Marketing/Communications
Director
tina.creguer@il.proquest.com
(800) 521-0600 x3805
300 N. Zeeb Road, P.O. Box 1346
Ann Arbor, MI 48106

Accounting & Tax Database
ProQuest, Inc.
Tina Creguer
Marketing/Communications
Director
tina.creguer@il.proquest.com
(800) 521-0600 x3805
300 N. Zeeb Road, P.O. Box 1346
Ann Arbor, MI 48106

Accurint
Seisint, Inc.
Cathy Demarco
cdemarco@accurint.com
(561) 893-8008
6601 Park of Commerce
Boulevard
Boca Raton, FL 33487

Adweek
VNU eMedia
Deborah Patton
Media Relations
Dpatton@vnubusinessmedia.com
(646) 654-5755
770 Broadway, 7th Floor
New York, NY 10003

AICPA
*American Institute of Certified Public
Accountants*
Edward J. Novack
Product Marketing Director
edward.novack@CPA2Biz.com
(201) 521-5714
1211 Avenue of the Americas
New York, NY 10036

Alacra
Alacra, Inc.
Carol Ann Thomas
Marketing Manager
carolann.thomas@alacra.com
(212) 804-1541
88 Pine Street, 3rd Floor
New York, NY 10005

BigCharts
MarketWatch.com, Inc.
123 North 3rd Street
Minneapolis, MN 55401

Bloomberg Professional
Bloomberg L.P.
Leslie Van Ordsdel
Bloomberg Professional
Product Training
lvanorsdel@bloomberg.net
(212) 318-2244
499 Park Avenue
New York, NY 10022

Bondtrac
Bondtrac, Inc.
Dan Powers
President
dan.powers@bondtrac.com
(800) 555-6864
210 Park Avenue, Suite 2200
Oklahoma City, OK 73102

Brandweek
VNU eMedia
Deborah Patton
Media Relations
Dpatton@vnubusinessmedia.com
(646) 654-5755
770 Broadway, 7th Floor
New York, NY 10003

Briefing.com
Briefing.com
Cassandra Bayna
Media Relations
cbayna@briefing.com
(312) 670-4463 x232
401 N. Michigan Avenue,
Suite 1680
Chicago, IL 60611

Budget and Economic Outlook
U.S. Congressional Budget Office
William J. Gainer
Associate Director for
Management
(202) 226-2600
Ford House Office Building,
4th Floor
Second and D Streets SW
Washington, DC 20515

Bureau of Economic Analysis (BEA)
U.S. Bureau of Economic Analysis
Larry R. Moran
Media contact
LARRY.MORAN@BEA.GOV
(202) 606-9691
1441 L Street NW
Washington, DC 20230

Bureau of Labor Statistics
U.S. Bureau of Labor Statistics
Katharine G. Abraham
Commissioner
blsdata_staff@bls.gov
(202) 606-7800
2 Massachusetts Avenue, NE
Washington, DC 20212

Bureau of the Census
U.S. Census Bureau
Stephen Buckner
Media contact
stephen.l.buckner@census.gov
(301) 763.2135
U.S. Census Bureau
Washington, DC 20233

Bureau of the Public Debt online:
Treasury Bills, Notes, and Bonds
U.S. Bureau of the Public Debt
Van Zeck
Commissioner
OAdmin@bpd.treas.gov
Bureau of the Public Debt
200 3rd Street
Parkersburg, WV 26106

Business & Industry
Thomson Learning
Jennifer Bernardelli
Product Manager, Gale
Jennifer.Bernardelli@gale.com
(800) 877-4253 x1514
Gale Group
27500 Drake Road
Farmington Hills, MI 48331

Business Dateline
ProQuest, Inc.
Tina Creguer
Marketing/Communications
Director
tina.creguer@il.proquest.com
(800) 521-0600 x3805
300 N. Zeeb Road, P.O. Box 1346
Ann Arbor, MI 48106

Business Wire
Business Wire, Inc.
Sandy Malloy
Senior Information Specialist
sandy.malloy@businesswire.com
(415) 986-4422 x512
44 Montgomery Street,
39th Floor
San Francisco, CA 94104

CBS MarketWatch
MarketWatch.com, Inc.
Dan Silmore
Director, Public Relations
dsilmore@marketwatch.com
(415) 733-0534
KPIX Building
825 Battery Street, 3rd Floor
San Francisco, CA 94111

CCH Tax Research Network
CCH Incorporated
Leslie Bonacum
Media Relations
bonacuml@cch.com
(847) 267-7153
2700 Lake Cook Road
Riverwoods, IL 60015

Chilling Effects
Electronic Frontier Foundation
Wendy Seltzer
Founder
wendy@seltzer
Electronic Frontier Foundation
454 Shotwell Street
San Francisco, CA 94110

CLAIMS/U.S. Patents
IFI Claims Patent Services
Jim Brown
Customer Service
(302) 633-7200
3202 Kirkwood Highway,
Suite 203
Wilmington, DE 19808

Closed End Fund Center
Mutual Fund Educational Association
Brian M. Smith
Media contact
bsmith@cefa.com
(816) 413-8900
P.O. Box 28037
Kansas City, MO 64188

Corporate Affiliations
LexisNexis
Judi Schultz
Senior Public Relations Manager
judith.schultz@lexisnexis.com
(937) 865-7942
LexisNexis Group
P.O. Box 933
Dayton, OH 45401

Country Data
PRS Group, Inc., The
Adrian Shute
Vice President Marketing/Public
Relations
ashute@prsgroup.com
(315) 431-0511
6320 Fly Road, Suite 102,
P.O. Box 248
East Syracuse, NY 13057

CyberAlert
CyberAlert, Inc.
Joel Crosley
Director, Business Development
jcrosley@CyberAlert.com
(800) 461-7353
Foot of Broad Street
Stratford, CT 06615

D&B—Dun's Electronic Business Directory
Dun & Bradstreet, Inc.
Julie C. Hiner
Public Relations, U.S.
hinerj@dnb.com
(973) 921-5608
One Diamond Hill Road
Murray Hill, NJ 07974

D&B—Dun's Financial Records Plus
Dun & Bradstreet, Inc.
Julie C. Hiner
Public Relations, U.S.
hinerj@dnb.com
(973) 921-5608
One Diamond Hill Road
Murray Hill, NJ 07974

D&B—Dun's Market Identifiers
Dun & Bradstreet, Inc.
Julie C. Hiner
Public Relations, U.S.
hinerj@dnb.com
(973) 921-5608
One Diamond Hill Road
Murray Hill, NJ 07974

D&B Key Business Ratios (KBR) on the Web
Dun & Bradstreet, Inc.
Julie C. Hiner
Public Relations, U.S.
hinerj@dnb.com
(973) 921-5608
One Diamond Hill Road
Murray Hill, NJ 07974

D&B Million Dollar Database
Dun & Bradstreet, Inc.
Julie C. Hiner
Public Relations, U.S.
hinerj@dnb.com
(973) 921-5608
3 Sylvan Way
Parsippany, NJ 07054

DailyStocks.com
DailyStocks, Inc.
info@dailystocks.com
New York, NY 10006

Datamonitor Market Research
Datamonitor/Reuters
info@datamonitor.com
106 Baker Street
London W1M 1LA, UK

Derwent Patents Citation Index
Derwent Information
sales@derwentus.com
(703) 706-4220
14 Great Queen Street
London WC2B 5DF, UK

Dialog
Thomson Legal & Regulatory
Sandy Scherer
Director, Corporate Communications, Dialog
sandy.scherer@dialog.com
(919) 461-7354
The Dialog Corporation
11000 Regency Parkway, Suite 10
Cary, NC 27511

Disclosure Database
Thomson Financial
Kerri Shepherd
Manager, Public Relations
kerri.shepherd@tfn.com
(646) 822-2077
195 Broadway, 8th Floor
New York, NY 10007

Economic Indicators
Council of Economic Advisors
wwwadmin@gpo.gov
(888) 293-6498
Office of Electronic Information
Dissemination Services
732 N. Capitol Street
Washington, DC 20402

Economy.com
Economy.com, Inc.
Monica Mercurio
Director, Customer Service
mmercurio@economy.com
(610)241-3362
600 Willowbrook Lane
West Chester, PA 19382

EIU ViewsWire
Economist Intelligence Unit
Jisla Escoto
Senior Contract Administrator
jislaescoto@eiu.com
(212) 554-0600
111 West 57th Street
New York, NY 10019

Encyclopedia of Associations (EA)
Thomson Learning
Jennifer Bernardelli
Product Manager, Gale
Jennifer.Bernardelli@gale.com
(800) 877-4253 x1514
Gale Group
27500 Drake Road
Farmington Hills, MI 48331

EventLine
Elsevier Science B.V.
Eric Merkel-Sobotta
Director, Corporate Relations
PressOffice@elsevier.com
31 20 485-2994
P.O. Box 211
NL-1000 AE Amsterdam,
Netherlands

Experian Business Credit Profiles
Experian
Donald Girard
Public Relations Director
donald.girard@experian.com
(714) 830-5647
505 City Parkway W, 3rd Floor
Orange, CA 92868

Factiva
Factiva
Gina Giamanco
Global Public Relations
gina.giamanco@factiva.com
(609) 627-2342
105 Madison Avenue, 10th Floor
New York, NY 10016

FactSet
FactSet Data Systems, Inc.
Betsy Fischer
Media Relations
efischer@factset.com
(203) 863-1500
One Greenwich Plaza
Greenwich, CT 06830

Fastcase
Fastcase, Inc.
Edward Walters
Media Relations
ed.walters@fastcase.com
(202) 466-5920
1916 Wilson Boulevard, Suite 302
Arlington, VA 22201

Federal Reserve Board
U.S. Board of Governors, Federal Reserve System
Jennifer J. Johnson
Secretary
(202) 452-3000
20th Street and Constitution
Avenue NW
Washington, DC 20551

Financial Accounting Research System (FARS)
Financial Accounting Standards Board
Ron Guerrette
Vice President, Publishing
rpguerrette@f-a-f.org
(203) 847-0700 x237
FASB Research Systems
401 Merritt 7, P.O. Box 5116
Norwalk, CT 06856

Financial Accounting Standards Board (FASB)
Financial Accounting Standards Board
Sheryl L. Thompson
Public Relations Manager
slthompson@f-a-f.org
(203) 847-0700
401 Merritt 7, P.O. Box 5116
Norwalk, CT 06856

Financial Forecast Center
Institute of Business Forecasting
ibf@ibf.org
(516) 504-7576
P.O. Box 670159
Flushing, NY 11367

Financial Times
Financial Times Electronic Publishing
Gregory Roth
Public Relations Manager, U.S.
Gregory.Roth@ft.com
44 171 8257777
Fitzroy House
13-17 Epworth Street
London EC2A 4DL, UK

FindLaw
Thomson Legal & Regulatory
(650) 210-1900
1235 Pear Avenue, Suite 111
Mountain View, CA 94043

First Research
First Research, Inc.
Bobby Martin
bmartin@firstresearch.com
(888) 331-2275 x1

FreeEDGAR
EDGAR Online, Inc.
Jay Sears
Senior Vice President, Business & Strategy Development
sears@edgar-online.com
(203) 852-5669
50 Washington Street, 9th Floor
Norwalk, CT 06854

Gale Group Business A.R.T.S.
Thomson Learning
Jennifer Bernardelli
Product Manager, Gale
Jennifer.Bernardelli@gale.com
(800) 877-4253 x1514
Gale Group
27500 Drake Road
Farmington Hills, MI 48331

Gale Group New Product Announcements/Plus (NPA/Plus)
Thomson Learning
Jennifer Bernardelli
Product Manager, Gale
Jennifer.Bernardelli@gale.com
(800) 877-4253 x1514
Gale Group
27500 Drake Road
Farmington Hills, MI 48331

Gale Group Newsletter Database
Thomson Learning
Jennifer Bernardelli
Product Manager, Gale
Jennifer.Bernardelli@gale.com
(800) 877-4253 x1514
Gale Group
27500 Drake Road
Farmington Hills, MI 48331

Gale Group Trade & Industry Database
Thomson Learning
Jennifer Bernardelli
Product Manager, Gale
Jennifer.Bernardelli@gale.com
(800) 877-4253 x1514
Gale Group
27500 Drake Road
Farmington Hills, MI 48331

Global Insight
Global Insight, Inc.
Ken McGill
ken.mcgill@globalinsight.com
(610) 490-2644
1000 Winter Street, Suite 4300N
Waltham, MA 02451

GPO Access
Superintendent of Documents, U.S.
Government Printing Office
gpoaccess@gpo.gov
(888) 293-6498
U.S. Government Printing Office
732 North Capitol Street, NW
Washington, DC 20401

Hoover's Online
Dun & Bradstreet, Inc.
Lisa Glass
Public Relations Manager
lglass@hoovers.com
(512) 374-4662
5800 Airport Boulevard
Austin, TX 78752

INPADOC/Families and Legal Status
European Patent Office
Elena Sereix
Database Online Services
maes@epo.e-mail.com
(431) 521 26 40 51
Information Service
Schottenfeldgasse 29 Postfach 82
A-1072 Vienna, Austria

Internal Revenue Service:
The Digital Daily
Internal Revenue Service, Department
of the Treasury
Robert E. Wenzel
Commissioner
1111 Constitution Avenue NW,
Room 1552
Washington, DC 20224

International Accounting
Standards Board
International Accounting Standards
Board
Tom Seidenstein
Media contact
tseidenstein@iasb.org.uk
44 20 7246 6410
30 Cannon Street
London EC4M 6XH, UK

Investext
Thomson Financial
Kerri Shepherd
Manager, Public Relations
kerri.shepherd@tfn.com
(646) 822-2077
195 Broadway, 8th Floor
New York, NY 10007

IPO Express
EDGAR Online, Inc.
Jay Sears
Senior Vice President, Business
& Strategy Development
sears@edgar-online.com
(203) 852-5669
50 Washington Sreet, 9th Floor
Norwalk, CT 06854

IPO.com
IPO Group, Inc.
DeWayne Martin
Publisher
dmartin@ipo.com
(212) 918-4510
48 Wall Street, Suite 1100
New York, NY 10005

KnowX
ChoicePoint Asset Company
Jane Rafedie
jane.rafeedie@choicepoint.com
(404) 541-0300

Law Digest
LexisNexis
Judi Schultz
Senior Public Relations Manager
judith.schultz@lexisnexis.com
(937) 865-7942
LexisNexis Group
P.O. Box 933
Dayton, OH 45401

Lawyers.com
LexisNexis
Judi Schultz
Senior Public Relations Manager
judith.schultz@lexisnexis.com
(937) 865-7942
LexisNexis Group
P.O. Box 933
Dayton, OH 45401

Legal Information Institute (LII)
*Legal Information Institute/Cornell
Law School*
Thomas R. Bruce and
Peter W. Martin
Co-Directors
lii@lii.law.cornell.edu
Cornell Law School
Myron Taylor Hall
Ithaca, NY 14853

LexisNexis
LexisNexis
Judi Schultz
Senior Public Relations Manager
judith.schultz@lexisnexis.com
(937) 865-7942
LexisNexis Group
P.O. Box 933
Dayton, OH 45401

LexisNexis (legal)
LexisNexis
Judi Schultz
Senior Public Relations Manager
judith.schultz@lexisnexis.com
(937) 865-7942
LexisNexis Group
P.O. Box 933
Dayton, OH 45401

LexisNexis (public records)
LexisNexis
Judi Schultz
Senior Public Relations Manager
judith.schultz@lexisnexis.com
(937) 865-7942
LexisNexis Group
P.O. Box 933
Dayton, OH 45401

LexisONE
LexisNexis
Judi Schultz
Senior Public Relations Manager
judith.schultz@lexisnexis.com
(937) 865-7942
LexisNexis Group
P.O. Box 933
Dayton, OH 45401

Lipper Horizon
Reuters
Camilla Altamura
Media Relations Manager
Camilla.Altamura@lipper.
reuters.com
(877) 955-4773
3 Times Square, 17th Floor
New York, NY 10036

Litigation Stock Report
Thomson Media
Paul E. McGowan
Editor-in-Chief
pmcgowan@lsrmail.com
(804) 282-7026
P.O. Box 18322
Richmond, VA 23226

LIVEDGAR
Global Securities Information, Inc.
Bob Brooks
Marketing/Public Relations
Director
bbrooks@gsionline.com
(202) 628-1155
419 7th Street NW, Suite 300
Washington, DC 20004

LLRX.com
Law Library Resource Xchange LLC
Sabrina Pacifici
President/CEO
spacific@earthlink.net

Loislaw

Aspen Publishers
Marc Jennings
Publisher
marc.jennings@
aspenpublishers.com
(646) 728-3001 x423
1185 Avenue of the Americas
New York, NY 10036

Market Share Reporter

Thomson Learning
Jennifer Bernardelli
Product Manager, Gale
Jennifer.Bernardelli@gale.com
(800) 877-4253 x1514
Gale Group
27500 Drake Road
Farmington Hills, MI 48331

MarketResearch.com

MarketResearch.com, Inc.
Robert Granader
CEO
rgranader@marketresearch.com
(301) 468.3650 x216
11810 Parklawn Drive
Rockville, MD 20852

Markets & Industry Library on LexisNexis

LexisNexis
Judi Schultz
Senior Public Relations Manager
judith.schultz@lexisnexis.com
(937) 865-7942
LexisNexis Group
P.O. Box 933
Dayton, OH 45401

MarkMonitor

MarkMonitor, Inc.
Elisa Cooper
Director of Marketing
elisa.cooper@markmonitor.com
(208) 389-5779
12438 W. Bridge Street, Suite 100
Boise, ID 83713

Mergent Online

Mergent FIS, Inc.
Kimberly Pile
Human Resources
hr@mergent.com
(800) 342-5647
60 Madison Avenue, 6th Floor
New York, NY 10010

MindBranch

MindBranch, Inc.
Sharon Oakes
Director, Marketing
soakes@mindbranch.com
(413) 458-7673
160 Water Street
Williamstown, MA 01267

Morningstar

Morningstar, Inc.
Martha Conlon Moss
Corporate Communications
martha.moss@morningstar.com
(312) 696-6050
225 W. Wacker Drive
Chicago, IL 60606

MSN Money

Microsoft Corporation
Microsoft Corporation
One Microsoft Way
Redmond, WA 98052

Multex Fundamentals

Multex, Inc.
Samantha Topping
Media contact
stopping@multex.com
(917) 294-0329
100 William Street, 7th Floor
New York, NY 10038

National Law Library
Juri Search
Satish Sheth
President
ssheth@jurisearch.com
(877) 484-7529
4301 Windfern Road, Suite 200
Houston, TX 77041

News on LexisNexis
LexisNexis
Judi Schultz
Senior Public Relations Manager
judith.schultz@lexisnexis.com
(937) 865-7942
LexisNexis Group
P.O. Box 933
Dayton, OH 45401

OneSource
OneSource Information Services
Ed Hutchinson
Director, Public Relations
Edward_Hutchinson@
onesource.com
(978) 318-4300
300 Baker Avenue, Suite 303
Concord, MA 01742

PatentWeb
Information Holdings, Inc. (MicroPatent)
Laura Gaze
Marketing/Communications
Director
lgaze@micropatent.com
(203) 466-5055 x205
MicroPatent USA
250 Dodge Avenue
East Haven, CT 06512

PatSearch FullText
Information Holdings, Inc. (MicroPatent)
Laura Gaze
Marketing/Communications
Director
lgaze@micropatent.com
(203) 466-5055 x205
MicroPatent USA
250 Dodge Avenue
East Haven, CT 06512

Profound
Thomson Legal & Regulatory
Sandy Scherer
Director, Corporate Communica-
tions, Dialog
sandy.scherer@dialog.com
(919) 461-7354
The Dialog Corporation
11000 Regency Parkway, Suite 10
Cary, NC 27511

PROMT
Thomson Learning
Jennifer Bernardelli
Product Manager, Gale
Jennifer.Bernardelli@gale.com
(800) 877-4253 x1514
Gale Group
27500 Drake Road
Farmington Hills, MI 48331

Reuters Business Insight
Datamonitor/Reuters
info@datamonitor.com
106 Baker Street
London W1M 1LA, UK

RMA's Annual Statement Studies
Risk Management Association, The
Kathleen Beans
Public Relations Manager/
Senior Writer
kbeans@rmahq.org
(215) 446-4095
1650 Market Street, Suite 2300
Philadelphia, PA 19103

SAEGIS
Thomson Legal & Regulatory
Scott Rutherford
Senior Marketing Communica-
tions Specialist
Scott.Rutherford@t-t.com
(617) 376-7667
Thomson & Thomson
500 Victory Road
North Quincy, MA 02171

SDC Platinum

Thomson Financial
Kerri Shepherd
Manager, Public Relations
kerri.shepherd@tfn.com
(646) 822-2077
195 Broadway, 8th Floor
New York, NY 10007

SmartMoney

*Dow Jones & Company, Inc. & Hearst
Communications, Inc.*
Amy Knapp
Public Relations
aknapp@smartmoney.com
(212) 649-2765
250 W. 55th Street, 10th Floor
New York, NY 10019

Standard & Poor's NetAdvantage

McGraw-Hill
Burt Shulman
Vice President, Marketing
Services & Publishing
burt_shulman@
standardandpoors.com
(212) 438-1288
55 Water Street
New York, NY 10041

The Virtual Chase

Ballard Spahr Andrews & Ingersoll LLP
Genie Tyburski
Web Manager, The Virtual Chase
tyburski@virtualchase.com
(215) 665-8500
1735 Market Street, 51st Floor
Philadelphia, PA 19103

The Wall Street Transcript

The Wall Street Transcript
Andrew Pickup
CEO/Publisher
pickup@twst.com
(212) 952-7437
67 Wall Street, 16th Floor
New York, NY 10005

TheStreet.com

TheStreet.com
Wendy Tullo
Media contact
wendy.tullo@thestreet.com
(212) 321-5000
14 Wall Street
New York, NY 10005

Thomas Register

Thomas Publishing Company
Ruth Hurd
Publisher
RHURD@trpublication.com
(212) 290-7277
TR User Services
Five Penn Plaza, 12th floor
New York, NY 10001

**Thomas: Legislative Information on
the Internet**

Library of Congress
thomas@loc.gov
(202) 707-5000
101 Independence Avenue, SE
Washington, DC 20540

Thomson Analytics

Thomson Financial
Kerri Shepherd
Manager, Public Relations
kerri.shepherd@tfn.com
(646) 822-2077
195 Broadway, 8th Floor
New York, NY 10007

Thomson Research

Thomson Financial
Kerri Shepherd
Manager, Public Relations
kerri.shepherd@tfn.com
(646) 822-2077
195 Broadway, 8th Floor
New York, NY 10007

Trademark Applications and Registrations Retrieval (TARR)
U.S. Patent and Trademark Office
James E. Rogan
Director
usptoinfo@uspto.gov
General Information Services
Division (800) 786-9199
Crystal Plaza 3, Room 2C02
Washington, DC 20231

Trademark Electronic Search System (TESS)
U.S. Patent and Trademark Office
James E. Rogan
Director
usptoinfo@uspto.gov
(800) 786-9199
General Information Services
Division
Crystal Plaza 3, Room 2C02
Washington, DC 20231

Trademark.com
Information Holdings, Inc. (MicroPatent)
Laura Gaze
Marketing/Communications
Director
lgaze@micropatent.com
(203) 466-5055 x205
250 Dodge Avenue
East Haven, CT 06512

TRADEMARKSCAN
Thomson Legal & Regulatory
Scott Rutherford
Senior Marketing Communications Specialist
Scott.Rutherford@t-t.com
(617) 376-7667
Thomson & Thomson
500 Victory Road
North Quincy, MA 02171

U.S. Copyright Office
U.S. Copyright Office, Library of Congress
Marybeth Peters
Register of Copyrights
101 Independence Avenue, SE
Washington, DC 20559

U.S. Copyrights
Thomson Legal & Regulatory
Sandy Scherer
Director, Corporate Communications, Dialog
sandy.scherer@dialog.com
(919) 461-7354
The Dialog Corporation
11000 Regency Parkway, Suite 10
Cary, NC 27511

U.S. Patents Fulltext
Thomson Legal & Regulatory
Sandy Scherer
Director, Corporate Communications, Dialog
sandy.scherer@dialog.com
(919) 461-7354
The Dialog Corporation
11000 Regency Parkway, Suite 10
Cary, NC 27511

U.S. Securities and Exchange Commission
U.S. Securities and Exchange Commission
Harvey L. Pitt
Chairman
help@sec.gov
(202) 942-7040
Office of Investor Education and Assistance
450 Fifth Street, NW
Washington, DC 20549

USADATA

USADATA, Inc.
Dominic LeClaire
Director of Marketing
dleclaire@usadata.com
(212) 679-1411 x222
292 Madison Avenue, 3rd Floor
New York, NY 10017

USPTO

U.S. Patent and Trademark Office
James E. Rogan
Director
usptoinfo@uspto.gov
(800) 786-9199
Office of Electronic Information
Products
Crystal Plaza 3, Suite 441
Washington, DC 20231

Value Line

Value Line
David Henigson
dhenigson@valueline.com
(212) 907-1500
Institutional Services
220 E. 42nd Street
New York, NY 10017

VersusLaw

VersusLaw, Inc.
Jim Corbett
Vice President, Business
Development
jcorbett@versuslaw.com
(888) 377-8752 x3024
2613 - 151st Place NE
Redmond, WA 98052

Wall Street City ProStation

Telescan, Inc.
Dan Olson
Media contact
dan@investools.com
(281) 588-9700
5959 Corporate Drive,
Suite LL250
Houston, TX 77036

Wall Street Journal (WSJ)

Dow Jones & Company, Inc.
Aaron Bedy
aaron.bedy@dowjones.com
(609) 520-7889
P.O. Box 300
Princeton, NJ 08543

Westlaw (legal)

Thomson Legal & Regulatory
Ruth Orrick
Senior Vice President, Corporate Communications
ruth.orrick@westgroup.com
(651) 687-4099
West Group
610 Opperman Drive
Eagan, MN 55123

Westlaw (public records)

Thomson Legal & Regulatory
Ruth Orrick
Senior Vice President, Corporate Communications
ruth.orrick@westgroup.com
(651) 687-4099
West Group
610 Opperman Drive
Eagan, MN 55123

**White House Economic Statistics
Briefing Room**

White House, The
feedback@whitehouse.gov
(202) 456-1414
1600 Pennsylvania Avenue, NW
Washington, DC 20500

Yahoo! Bond Center

Yahoo! Inc.
Chris Castro
Chief Communications Officer,
Senior Vice President
(408) 349-3300
701 First Avenue
Sunnyvale, CA 94089

Yahoo! Finance

Yahoo! Inc.

Chris Castro

Chief Communications Officer,

Senior Vice President

(408) 349-3300

701 First Avenue

Sunnyvale, CA 94089

Zacks

Zacks Investment Research

support@zacks.com

(800) 767-3771

155 N. Wacker Drive

Chicago, IL 60606

Appendix B: Directory of Online Business Data Source Publishers

10k Wizard Technology LLC
10k Wizard
Elise Soyza
Director, Marketing
elise@10kwizard.com
(214) 800-4565
1950 Stemmons Freeway,
Suite 7016
Dallas, TX 75207

Alacra, Inc.
Alacra
Carol Ann Thomas
Marketing Manager
carolann.thomas@alacra.com
(212) 804-1541
88 Pine Street, 3rd Floor
New York, NY 10005

American Institute of Certified Public Accountants
AICPA
Edward J. Novack
Product Marketing Director
edward.novack@CPA2Biz.com
(201) 521-5714
1211 Avenue of the Americas
New York, NY 10036

Aspen Publishers
Loislaw
Marc Jennings
Publisher
marc.jennings@
aspenpublishers.com
(646) 728-3001 x423
1185 Avenue of the Americas
New York, NY 10036

Ballard Spahr Andrews & Ingersoll LLP
The Virtual Chase
Genie Tyburski
Web Manager, The Virtual Chase
tyburski@virtualchase.com
(215) 665-8500
1735 Market Street, 51st Floor
Philadelphia, PA 19103

Bloomberg L.P.
Bloomberg Professional
Leslie Van Ordsdel
Bloomberg Professional Product
Training
lvanorsdel@bloomberg.net
(212) 318-2244
499 Park Avenue
New York, NY 10022

Bondtrac, Inc.
Bondtrac
Dan Powers
President
dan.powers@bondtrac.com
(800) 555-6864
210 Park Avenue, Suite 2200
Oklahoma City, OK 73102

Briefing.com
Briefing.com
Cassandra Bayna
Media Relations
cbayna@briefing.com
(312) 670-4463 x232
401 N. Michigan Avenue,
Suite 1680
Chicago, IL 60611

Business Wire, Inc.
Business Wire
 Sandy Malloy
 Senior Information Specialist
 sandy.malloy@businesswire.com
 (415) 986-4422 x512
 44 Montgomery Street, 39th Floor
 San Francisco, CA 94104

CCH Incorporated
CCH Tax Research Network
 Leslie Bonacum
 Media Relations
 bonacuml@cch.com
 (847) 267-7153
 2700 Lake Cook Road
 Riverwoods, IL 60015

ChoicePoint Asset Company
KnowX
 Jane Rafedie
 jane.rafeedie@choicepoint.com
 (404) 541-0300

Council of Economic Advisors
Economic Indicators
 wwwadmin@gpo.gov
 (888) 293-6498
 Office of Electronic Information
 Dissemination Services
 732 N. Capitol Street
 Washington, DC 20402

CyberAlert, Inc.
CyberAlert
 Joel Crosley
 Director, Business Development
 jcrosley@CyberAlert.com
 (800) 461-7353
 Foot of Broad Street
 Stratford, CT 06615

DailyStocks, Inc.
DailyStocks.com
 info@dailystocks.com
 New York, NY 10006

Datamonitor/Reuters
Datamonitor Market Research
Reuters Business Insight
 info@datamonitor.com
 106 Baker Street
 London W1M 1LA, UK

Derwent Information
Derwent Patents Citation Index
 sales@derwentus.com
 (703) 706-4220
 14 Great Queen Street
 London WC2B 5DF, UK

Dow Jones & Company, Inc.
Wall Street Journal (WSJ)
 Aaron Bedy
 aaron.bedy@dowjones.com
 (609) 520-7889
 P.O. Box 300
 Princeton, NJ 08543

Dow Jones & Company, Inc. & Hearst Communications, Inc.
SmartMoney
 Amy Knapp
 Public Relations
 aknapp@smartmoney.com
 (212) 649-2765
 250 W. 55th Street, 10th Floor
 New York, NY 10019

Dun & Bradstreet, Inc.
D&B—Dun's Electronic Business Directory
D&B—Dun's Financial Records Plus
D&B—Dun's Market Identifiers
D&B Key Business Ratios (KBR) on the Web
D&B Million Dollar Database
 Julie C. Hiner
 Public Relations, U.S.
 hinerj@dnb.com
 (973) 921-5608
 3 Sylvan Way
 Parsippany, NJ 07054

Hoover's Online
Lisa Glass
Public Relations Manager
lglass@hoovers.com
(512) 374-4662
5800 Airport Boulevard
Austin, TX 78752

Economist Intelligence Unit
EIU ViewsWire
Jisla Escoto
Senior Contract Administrator
jislaescoto@eiu.com
(212) 554-0600
111 West 57th Street
New York, NY 10019

Economy.com, Inc.
Economy.com
Monica Mercurio
Director, Customer Service
mmercurio@economy.com
(610) 241-3362
600 Willowbrook Lane
West Chester, PA 19382

EDGAR Online, Inc.
FreeEDGAR
IPO Express
Jay Sears
Senior Vice President, Business
& Strategy Development
sears@edgar-online.com
(203) 852-5669
50 Washington Sreet, 9th Floor
Norwalk, CT 06854

Electronic Frontier Foundation
Chilling Effects
Wendy Seltzer
Founder
wendy@seltzer
Electronic Frontier Foundation
454 Shotwell Street
San Francisco, CA 94110

Elsevier Science B.V.
EventLine
Eric Merkel-Sobotta
Director, Corporate Relations
PressOffice@elsevier.com
31 20 485-2994
P.O. Box 211
NL-1000 AE Amsterdam,
Netherlands

European Patent Office
INPADOC/Families and Legal Status
Elena Sereix
Database Online Services
maes@epo.e-mail.com
(431) 521 26 40 51
Information Service
Schottenfeldgasse 29 Postfach 82
A-1072 Vienna, Austria

Experian
Experian Business Credit Profiles
Donald Girard
Public Relations Director
donald.girard@experian.com
(714) 830-5647
505 City Parkway W, 3rd Floor
Orange, CA 92868

Factiva
Factiva
Gina Giamanco
Global Public Relations
gina.giamanco@factiva.com
(609) 627-2342
105 Madison Avenue, 10th Floor
New York, NY 10016

FactSet Data Systems, Inc.
FactSet
Betsy Fischer
Media Relations
efischer@factset.com
(203) 863-1500
One Greenwich Plaza
Greenwich, CT 06830

Fastcase, Inc.
Fastcase
Edward Walters
Media Relations
ed.walters@fastcase.com
(202) 466-5920
1916 Wilson Boulevard,
Suite 302
Arlington, VA 22201

Financial Accounting Standards Board
*Financial Accounting Research System
(FARS)*
Ron Guerrette
Vice President, Publishing
rpguerrette@f-a-f.org
(203) 847-0700 x237
FASB Research Systems
401 Merritt 7, P.O. Box 5116
Norwalk, CT 06856
*Financial Accounting Standards
Board (FASB)*
Sheryl L. Thompson
Public Relations Manager
slthompson@f-a-f.org
(203) 847-0700
401 Merritt 7, P.O. Box 5116
Norwalk, CT 06856

Financial Times Electronic Publishing
Financial Times
Gregory Roth
Public Relations Manager, U.S.
Gregory.Roth@ft.com
44 171 8257777
Fitzroy House
13-17 Epworth Street
London EC2A 4DL, UK

First Research, Inc.
First Research
Bobby Martin
bmartin@firstresearch.com
(888) 331-2275 x1

Global Insight, Inc.
Global Insight
Ken McGill
ken.mcgill@globalinsight.com
(610) 490-2644
1000 Winter Street, Suite 4300N
Waltham, MA 02451

Global Securities Information, Inc.
LIVEDGAR
Bob Brooks
Marketing/Public Relations
Director
bbrooks@gsionline.com
(202) 628-1155
419 7th Street NW, Suite 300
Washington, DC 20004

IFI Claims Patent Services
CLAIMS/U.S. Patents
Jim Brown
Customer Service
(302) 633-7200
3202 Kirkwood Highway,
Suite 203
Wilmington, DE 19808

**Information Holdings, Inc.
(MicroPatent)**
PatentWeb
PatSearch FullText
Trademark.com
Laura Gaze
Marketing/Communications
Director
lgaze@micropatent.com
(203) 466-5055 x205
250 Dodge Avenue
East Haven, CT 06512

Institute of Business Forecasting
Financial Forecast Center
ibf@ibf.org
(516) 504-7576
P.O. Box 670159
Flushing, NY 11367

Internal Revenue Service, Department of the Treasury
Internal Revenue Service: The Digital Daily
Robert E. Wenzel
Commissioner
1111 Constitution Avenue NW,
Room 1552
Washington, DC 20224

International Accounting Standards Board
International Accounting Standards Board
Tom Seidenstein
Media contact
tseidenstein@iasb.org.uk
44 20 7246 6410
30 Cannon Street
London EC4M 6XH, UK

IPO Group, Inc.
IPO.com
DeWayne Martin
Publisher
dmartin@ipo.com
(212) 918-4510
48 Wall Street, Suite 1100
New York, NY 10005

Juri Search
National Law Library
Satish Sheth
President
ssheth@jurisearch.com
(877) 484-7529
4301 Windfern Road, Suite 200
Houston, TX 77041

Law Library Resource Xchange LLC
LLRX.com
Sabrina Pacifici
President/CEO
spacific@earthlink.net

Legal Information Institute/Cornell Law School
Legal Information Institute (LII)
Thomas R. Bruce and Peter W. Martin
Co-Directors
lii@lii.law.cornell.edu
Cornell Law School
Myron Taylor Hall
Ithaca, NY 14853

LexisNexis
Corporate Affiliations
Law Digest
Lawyers.com
LexisNexis
LexisNexis (legal)
LexisNexis (public records)
LexisONE
Markets & Industry Library on LexisNexis
News on LexisNexis
Judi Schultz
Senior Public Relations Manager
judith.schultz@lexisnexis.com
(937) 865-7942
LexisNexis Group
P.O. Box 933
Dayton, OH 45401

Library of Congress
Thomas: Legislative Information on the Internet
thomas@loc.gov
(202) 707-5000
101 Independence Avenue, SE
Washington, DC 20540

MarketResearch.com, Inc.
MarketResearch.com
Robert Granader
CEO
rgranader@marketresearch.com
(301) 468.3650 x216
11810 Parklawn Drive
Rockville, MD 20852

MarketWatch.com, Inc.
BigCharts
123 North 3rd Street
Minneapolis, MN 55401
CBS MarketWatch
Dan Silmore
Director, Public Relations
dsilmore@marketwatch.com
(415) 733-0534
KPIX Building
825 Battery Street, 3rd Floor
San Francisco, CA 94111

MarkMonitor, Inc.
MarkMonitor
Elisa Cooper
Director of Marketing
elisa.cooper@markmonitor.com
(208) 389-5779
12438 W. Bridge Street, Suite 100
Boise, ID 83713

McGraw-Hill
Standard & Poor's NetAdvantage
Burt Shulman
Vice President, Marketing Services & Publishing
burt_shulman@
standardandpoors.com
(212) 438-1288
55 Water Street
New York, NY 10041

Mergent FIS, Inc.
Mergent Online
Kimberly Pile
Human Resources
hr@mergent.com
(800) 342-5647
60 Madison Avenue, 6th Floor
New York, NY 10010

Microsoft Corporation
MSN Money
Microsoft Corporation
One Microsoft Way
Redmond, WA 98052

MindBranch, Inc.
MindBranch
Sharon Oakes
Director, Marketing
soakes@mindbranch.com
(413) 458-7673
160 Water Street
Williamstown, MA 01267

Morningstar, Inc.
Morningstar
Martha Conlon Moss
Corporate Communications
martha.moss@morningstar.com
(312) 696-6050
225 W. Wacker Drive
Chicago, IL 60606

Multex, Inc.
Multex Fundamentals
Samantha Topping
Media contact
stopping@multex.com
(917) 294-0329
100 William Street, 7th Floor
New York, NY 10038

Mutual Fund Educational Association
Closed-End Fund Center
Brian M. Smith
Media contact
bsmith@cefa.com
(816) 413-8900
P.O. Box 28037
Kansas City, MO 64188

OneSource Information Services
OneSource
Ed Hutchinson
Director, Public Relations
Edward_Hutchinson@
onesource.com
(978) 318-4300
300 Baker Avenue, Suite 303
Concord, MA 01742

ProQuest, Inc.
ABI/Inform
Accounting & Tax Database
Business Dateline
  Tina Creguer
  Marketing/Communications
  Director
  tina.creguer@il.proquest.com
  (800) 521-0600 x3805
  300 N. Zeeb Road, P.O. Box 1346
  Ann Arbor, MI 48106

PRS Group, Inc., The
Country Data
  Adrian Shute
  Vice President Marketing/Public
  Relations
  ashute@prsgroup.com
  (315) 431-0511
  6320 Fly Road, Suite 102,
  P.O. Box 248
  East Syracuse, NY 13057

Reuters
Lipper Horizon
  Camilla Altamura
  Media Relations Manager
  Camilla.Altamura@lipper.
  reuters.com
  (877) 955-4773
  3 Times Square, 17th Floor
  New York, NY 10036

Risk Management Association, The
RMA's Annual Statement Studies
  Kathleen Beans
  Public Relations Manager/
  Senior Writer
  kbeans@rmahq.org
  (215) 446-4095
  1650 Market Street, Suite 2300
  Philadelphia, PA 19103

Seisint, Inc.
Accurint
  Cathy Demarco
  cdemarco@accurint.com
  (561) 893-8008
  6601 Park of Commerce
  Boulevard
  Boca Raton, FL 33487

Superintendent of Documents, U.S. Government Printing Office
GPO Access
  gpoaccess@gpo.gov
  (888) 293-6498
  U.S. Government Printing Office
  732 North Capitol Street, NW
  Washington, DC 20401

Telescan, Inc.
Wall Street City ProStation
  Dan Olson
  Media contact
  dan@investools.com
  (281) 588-9700
  5959 Corporate Drive,
  Suite LL250
  Houston, TX 77036

The Wall Street Transcript
The Wall Street Transcript
  Andrew Pickup
  CEO/Publisher
  pickup@twst.com
  (212) 952-7437
  67 Wall Street, 16th Floor
  New York, NY 10005

TheStreet.com
TheStreet.com
  Wendy Tullo
  Media contact
  wendy.tullo@thestreet.com
  (212) 321-5000
  14 Wall Street
  New York, NY 10005

Thomas Publishing Company
Thomas Register
  Ruth Hurd
  Publisher
  RHURD@trpublication.com
  (212) 290-7277
  TR User Services
  Five Penn Plaza, 12th floor
  New York, NY 10001

Thomson Financial
Disclosure Database
Investext
SDC Platinum
Thomson Analytics
Thomson Research
  Kerri Shepherd
  Manager, Public Relations
  kerri.shepherd@tfn.com
  (646) 822-2077
  195 Broadway, 8th Floor
  New York, NY 10007

Thomson Learning
Business & Industry
Encyclopedia of Associations (EA)
Gale Group Business A.R.T.S.
Gale Group New Product Announce-
ments/Plus (NPA/Plus)
Gale Group Newsletter Database
Gale Group Trade & Industry Database
Market Share Reporter
PROMT
  Jennifer Bernardelli
  Product Manager, Gale
  Jennifer.Bernardelli@gale.com
  (800) 877-4253 x1514
  Gale Group
  27500 Drake Road
  Farmington Hills, MI 48331

Thomson Legal & Regulatory
Dialog
Profound
U.S. Copyrights
U.S. Patents Fulltext
  Sandy Scherer
  Director, Corporate Communica-
  tions, Dialog
  sandy.scherer@dialog.com
  (919) 461-7354
  The Dialog Corporation
  11000 Regency Parkway, Suite 10
  Cary, NC 27511
FindLaw
  (650) 210-1900
  1235 Pear Avenue, Suite 111
  Mountain View, CA 94043

SAEGIS
TRADEMARKSCAN
  Scott Rutherford
  Senior Marketing Communica-
  tions Specialist
  Scott.Rutherford@t-t.com
  (617) 376-7667
  Thomson & Thomson
  500 Victory Road
  North Quincy, MA 02171
Westlaw (legal)
Westlaw (public records)
  Ruth Orrick
  Senior Vice President, Corpo-
  rate Communications
  ruth.orrick@westgroup.com
  (651) 687-4099
  West Group
  610 Opperman Drive
  Eagan, MN 55123

Thomson Media
Litigation Stock Report
  Paul E. McGowan
  Editor-in-Chief
  pmcgowan@lsrmail.com
  (804) 282-7026
  P.O. Box 18322
  Richmond, VA 23226

U.S. Board of Governors, Federal Reserve System
Federal Reserve Board
  Jennifer J. Johnson
  Secretary
  (202) 452-3000
  20th Street and Constitution
  Avenue NW
  Washington, DC 20551

U.S. Bureau of Economic Analysis
Bureau of Economic Analysis (BEA)
  Larry R. Moran
  Media contact
  LARRY.MORAN@BEA.GOV
  (202) 606-9691
  1441 L Street NW
  Washington, DC 20230

U.S. Bureau of Labor Statistics
Bureau of Labor Statistics
Katharine G. Abraham
Commissioner
blsdata_staff@bls.gov
(202) 606-7800
2 Massachusetts Avenue, NE
Washington, DC 20212

U.S. Bureau of the Public Debt
Bureau of the Public Debt online:
Treasury Bills, Notes, and Bonds
Van Zeck
Commissioner
OAdmin@bpd.treas.gov
Bureau of the Public Debt
200 3rd Street
Parkersburg, WV 26106

U.S. Census Bureau
Bureau of the Census
Stephen Buckner
Media contact
stephen.l.buckner@census.gov
(301) 763.2135
U.S. Census Bureau
Washington, DC 20233

U.S. Congressional Budget Office
Budget and Economic Outlook
William J. Gainer
Associate Director for
Management
(202) 226-2600
Ford House Office Building,
4th Floor
Second and D Streets SW
Washington, DC 20515

U.S. Copyright Office, Library of Congress
U.S. Copyright Office
Marybeth Peters
Register of Copyrights
101 Independence Avenue, SE
Washington, DC 20559

U.S. Patent and Trademark Office
Trademark Applications and Registra-
tions Retrieval (TARR)
Trademark Electronic Search System
(TESS)
USPTO
James E. Rogan
Director
usptoinfo@uspto.gov
(800) 786-9199
Office of Electronic Information
Products
Crystal Plaza 3, Suite 441
Washington, DC 20231

U.S. Securities and Exchange Commission
U.S. Securities and Exchange
Commission
Harvey L. Pitt
Chairman
help@sec.gov
(202) 942-7040
Office of Investor Education and
Assistance
450 Fifth Street, NW
Washington, DC 20549

USADATA, Inc.
USADATA
Dominic LeClaire
Director of Marketing
dleclaire@usadata.com
(212) 679-1411 x222
292 Madison Avenue, 3rd Floor
New York, NY 10017

Value Line
Value Line
David Henigson
dhenigson@valueline.com
(212) 907-1500
Institutional Services
220 E. 42nd Street
New York, NY 10017

VersusLaw, Inc.
VersusLaw
Jim Corbett
Vice President, Business Development
jcorbett@versuslaw.com
(888) 377-8752 x3024
2613 - 151st Place NE
Redmond, WA 98052

VNU eMedia
Adweek
Brandweek
Deborah Patton
Media Relations
Dpatton@
vnubusinessmedia.com
(646) 654-5755
770 Broadway, 7th Floor
New York, NY 10003

White House, The
White House Economic Statistics
Briefing Room
feedback@whitehouse.gov
(202) 456-1414
1600 Pennsylvania Avenue, NW
Washington, DC 20500

Yahoo! Inc.
Yahoo! Bond Center
Yahoo! Finance
Chris Castro
Chief Communications Officer,
Senior Vice President
(408) 349-3300
701 First Avenue
Sunnyvale, CA 94089

Zacks Investment Research
Zacks
support@zacks.com
(800) 767-3771
155 N. Wacker Drive
Chicago, IL 60606

Appendix C: Business Data Source Rating Survey

Table C.1. Data Source Ratings – Alphabetical by Data Source

DATA SOURCE	1. RELATIVE COST-TO-VALUE	2. RELATIVE TIMELINESS OF DATA	3. RELATIVE COMPRE-HENSIVENESS OF DATA	4. EASE OF USE	5. SEARCH OPTIONS AVAILABLE	6. LEVEL OF SUPPORT SERVICES	7. LEVEL OF TRAINING OFFERED	8. AMOUNT/ KINDS OF SPECIAL SERVICES OFFERED	TOTAL
10k Wizard	9	10	10	10	10	10	5	9	73
ABI/Inform	6	10	7	10	10	8	8	10	69
Accounting & Tax Database	5	8	8	4	6	7	7	7	52
Accurint	10	9	7	9	9	7	9	9	69
Adweek	7	10	10	5	3	5	5	3	48
AICPA	8	9	8	7	6	7	5	3	53
Alacra	8	8	8	7	7	8	7	7	60
Bloomberg Professional	8	10	9	6	10	10	10	9	72
Bondtrac	5	10	10	10	10	10	10	10	75
Brandweek	7	10	10	5	3	5	5	3	48
Briefing.com	8	10	8	9	7	8	8	8	66
Budget and Economic Outlook	10	10	10	10	5	5	5	5	60
Bureau of Economic Analysis (BEA)	10	10	10	8	5	7	6	8	64
Bureau of Labor Statistics	10	10	10	6	8	8	7	8	67

Table C.1. Data Source Ratings – Alphabetical by Data Source (cont.)

DATA SOURCE	1. RELATIVE COST-TO-VALUE	2. RELATIVE TIMELINESS OF DATA	3. RELATIVE COMPREHENSIVENESS OF DATA	4. EASE OF USE	5. SEARCH OPTIONS AVAILABLE	6. LEVEL OF SUPPORT SERVICES	7. LEVEL OF TRAINING OFFERED	8. AMOUNT/KINDS OF SPECIAL SERVICES OFFERED	TOTAL
Bureau of the Census	10	10	10	6	7	8	8	8	67
Business & Industry	7	6	8	8	8	7	8	6	58
Business Dateline	5	9	8	9	9	8	7	6	61
Business Wire	5	10	5	7	5	5	5	5	47
CBS MarketWatch	10	9	9	9	8	8	8	8	69
CCH Tax Research Network	7	9	8	10	10	9	8	8	69
Chilling Effects	9	6	7	8	8	7	5	9	59
Corporate Affiliations	5	7	7	9	10	10	9	9	66
Country Data	10	10	10	8	8	10	6	10	72
D&B—Dun's Electronic Business Directory	7	7	6	2	9	8	8	8	55
D&B—Dun's Financial Records Plus	7	7	6	2	9	8	8	8	55
D&B—Dun's Market Identifiers	7	7	6	2	9	8	8	8	55

Table C.1. Data Source Ratings – Alphabetical by Data Source (cont.)

DATA SOURCE	1. RELATIVE COST-TO-VALUE	2. RELATIVE TIMELINESS OF DATA	3. RELATIVE COMPRE-HENSIVENESS OF DATA	4. EASE OF USE	5. SEARCH OPTIONS AVAILABLE	6. LEVEL OF SUPPORT SERVICES	7. LEVEL OF TRAINING OFFERED	8. AMOUNT/ KINDS OF SPECIAL SERVICES OFFERED	TOTAL
D&B Key Business Ratios (KBR) on the Web	6	7	8	7	6	7	3	6	50
D&B Million Dollar Database	5	7	8	9	7	7	3	5	51
Datamonitor Market Research	7	6	9	8	6	6	5	5	52
Dialog	8	9	9	7	10	10	9	8	70
Disclosure Database	7	8	9	9	7	7	5	7	59
Economic Indicators	7	8	6	5	3	4	5	5	43
Economy.com	8	10	8	9	7	8	8	8	66
EIU ViewsWire	8	9	9	10	9	9	9	8	71
Encyclopedia of Associations (EA)	9	8	8	8	9	9	5	5	61
EventLine	7	8	7	7	10	10	10	5	64
Experian Business Credit Profiles	3	8	5	6	6	7	6	9	50
Factiva	9	10	10	8	7	6	6	9	65
FactSet	7	10	10	7	5	8	8	8	63
Fastcase	7	7	6	7	8	9	5	6	55

Table C.1. Data Source Ratings – Alphabetical by Data Source (cont.)

DATA SOURCE	1. RELATIVE COST-TO-VALUE	2. RELATIVE TIMELINESS OF DATA	3. RELATIVE COMPRE-HENSIVENESS OF DATA	4. EASE OF USE	5. SEARCH OPTIONS AVAILABLE	6. LEVEL OF SUPPORT SERVICES	7. LEVEL OF TRAINING OFFERED	8. AMOUNT/ KINDS OF SPECIAL SERVICES OFFERED	TOTAL
Federal Reserve Board	10	10	8	10	10	6	5	10	69
Financial Accounting Research System (FARS)	9	8	9	6	7	4	4	5	52
Financial Accounting Standards Board (FASB)	10	10	8	10	5	8	5	3	59
Financial Forecast Center	10	10	8	10	5	8	5	8	64
Financial Times	8	10	6	7	7	2	5	5	50
FindLaw	10	8	10	7	8	2	5	7	57
First Research	5	8	8	8	5	5	5	5	49
FreeEDGAR/EDGAR Online/EDGARpro	6	9	7	6	7	8	8	6	57
Gale Group Business A.R.T.S.	7	10	7	6	6	7	8	5	56
Gale Group New Product Announcements/ Plus (NPA/Plus)	7	10	9	8	9	9	8	7	67

Table C.1. Data Source Ratings – Alphabetical by Data Source (cont.)

DATA SOURCE	1. RELATIVE COST-TO-VALUE	2. RELATIVE TIMELINESS OF DATA	3. RELATIVE COMPREHENSIVENESS OF DATA	4. EASE OF USE	5. SEARCH OPTIONS AVAILABLE	6. LEVEL OF SUPPORT SERVICES	7. LEVEL OF TRAINING OFFERED	8. AMOUNT/KINDS OF SPECIAL SERVICES OFFERED	TOTAL
Gale Group Newsletter Database	7	8	7	6	6	8	9	9	60
Gale Group Trade & Industry Database	8	9	6	8	9	4	5	5	54
GPO Access	5	7	6	6	8	1	3	6	42
Hoover's Online	9	8	7	8	6	7	6	9	60
Internal Revenue Service: The Digital Daily	10	10	10	8	8	8	5	8	67
International Accounting Standards Board	9	9	8	10	6	7	5	3	57
Investext	7	7	8	6	8	7	6	7	56
KnowX	5	7	6	8	5	5	2	4	42
Legal Information Institute (LII)	10	10	10	10	9	8	5	9	71
LexisNexis	8	9	8	7	8	8	7	7	62
LexisNexis (public records)	7	9	10	7	10	8	8	9	68
LexisONE	5	7	4	5	7	1	2	5	36
Lipper Horizon	5	10	10	6	7	8	7	8	61

Table C.I. Data Source Ratings – Alphabetical by Data Source (cont.)

DATA SOURCE	1. RELATIVE COST-TO-VALUE	2. RELATIVE TIMELINESS OF DATA	3. RELATIVE COMPRE-HENSIVENESS OF DATA	4. EASE OF USE	5. SEARCH OPTIONS AVAILABLE	6. LEVEL OF SUPPORT SERVICES	7. LEVEL OF TRAINING OFFERED	8. AMOUNT/KINDS OF SPECIAL SERVICES OFFERED	TOTAL
LIVEDGAR	9	9	9	8	9	8	9	9	70
LLRX.com	10	9	9	10	8	8	5	10	69
Loislaw	10	10	9	8	8	9	7	9	70
Market Share Reporter	10	5	10	10	10	10	8	10	73
MarketResearch.com	8	9	9	10	10	10	7	8	71
Markets & Industry Library on LexisNexis	8	10	10	7	8	10	10	10	73
MarkMonitor	10	10	10	10	9	9	9	10	77
Mergent Online	6	9	9	8	7	8	9	6	62
MindBranch	9	8	9	9	7	10	2	7	61
Morningstar	10	10	10	9	9	8	9	9	74
MSN Money	9	8	8	7	7	4	1	3	47
Multex Fundamentals	6	8	10	7	8	5	5	5	54
National Law Library	4	3	4	4	5	2	4	2	28
News on LexisNexis	8	8	7	7	8	7	6	8	59
OneSource	8	8	8	10	9	8	8	9	68
Profound	9	10	9	9	9	9	10	10	75
PROMT	8	10	7	7	7	6	6	7	58
Reuters Business Insight	7	6	7	8	5	9	9	7	58

Table C.1. Data Source Ratings – Alphabetical by Data Source (cont.)

DATA SOURCE	1. RELATIVE COST-TO-VALUE	2. RELATIVE TIMELINESS OF DATA	3. RELATIVE COMPRE-HENSIVENESS OF DATA	4. EASE OF USE	5. SEARCH OPTIONS AVAILABLE	6. LEVEL OF SUPPORT SERVICES	7. LEVEL OF TRAINING OFFERED	8. AMOUNT/KINDS OF SPECIAL SERVICES OFFERED	TOTAL
RMA's Annual Statement Studies	10	8	6	9	4	7	3	7	54
SmartMoney	7	10	8	6	7	5	5	6	54
Standard & Poor's NetAdvantage	8	10	8	7	8	7	6	8	62
The Virtual Chase	10	9	9	8	9	7	9	9	70
The Wall Street Transcript	8	10	8	9	9	8	8	10	70
TheStreet.com	9	10	9	6	8	8	8	9	67
Thomas Register	10	8	9	9	7	10	2	10	65
Thomas: Legislative Information on the Internet	10	10	10	10	10	8	5	8	71
Thomson Research	5	10	10	7	8	6	5	8	59
Trademark	10	8	9	10	8	8	5	5	63
Trademark Applications and Registrations Retrieval (TARR)									
Trademark Electronic Search System (TESS)	9	8	9	9	10	7	5	5	62

Table C.1. Data Source Ratings – Alphabetical by Data Source (cont.)

DATA SOURCE	1. RELATIVE COST-TO-VALUE	2. RELATIVE TIMELINESS OF DATA	3. RELATIVE COMPREHENSIVENESS OF DATA	4. EASE OF USE	5. SEARCH OPTIONS AVAILABLE	6. LEVEL OF SUPPORT SERVICES	7. LEVEL OF TRAINING OFFERED	8. AMOUNT/KINDS OF SPECIAL SERVICES OFFERED	TOTAL
Trademark.com	8	9	10	8	9	8	9	8	69
TRADEMARKSCAN	9	9	10	10	8	10	10	5	71
U.S. Copyright Office	9	10	9	7	7	1	5	10	58
U.S. Copyrights	10	9	9	9	8	10	10	1	66
U.S. Securities and Exchange Commission	10	10	8	9	5	6	2	2	52
USADATA	10	8	9	10	3	8	8	9	65
USPTO	10	10	10	7	9	8	7	10	71
Value Line	9	9	9	10	5	10	10	9	71
Yahoo! Finance	9	10	9	9	9	5	5	6	62
Zacks	10	9	9	10	10	5	5	10	68

Note: Reviewers were asked to rate each research data source on the basis of a "10" being the highest, most complimentary, rating and "1" being the lowest or least complimentary ("80" being a perfect score).

Table C.2. Data Source Ratings – Ranked by Overall Rating

DATA SOURCE	1. RELATIVE COST-TO-VALUE	2. RELATIVE TIMELINESS OF DATA	3. RELATIVE COMPREHENSIVENESS OF DATA	4. EASE OF USE	5. SEARCH OPTIONS AVAILABLE	6. LEVEL OF SUPPORT SERVICES	7. LEVEL OF TRAINING OFFERED	8. AMOUNT/ KINDS OF SPECIAL SERVICES OFFERED	TOTAL
MarkMonitor	10	10	10	10	9	9	9	10	77
Bondtrac	5	10	10	10	10	10	10	10	75
Profound	9	10	9	9	9	9	10	10	75
Morningstar	10	10	10	9	9	8	9	9	74
10k Wizard	9	10	10	10	10	10	5	9	73
Market Share Reporter	10	5	10	10	10	10	8	10	73
Markets & Industry Library on LexisNexis	8	10	10	7	8	10	10	10	73
Bloomberg Professional	8	10	9	6	10	10	10	9	72
Country Data	10	10	10	8	8	10	6	10	72
EIU ViewsWire	8	9	9	10	9	9	9	8	71
Legal Information Institute (LII)	10	10	10	10	9	8	5	9	71
MarketResearch.com	8	9	9	10	10	10	7	8	71
Thomas: Legislative Information on the Internet	10	10	10	10	10	8	5	8	71
TRADEMARKSCAN	9	9	10	10	8	10	10	5	71

Table C.2. Data Source Ratings – Ranked by Overall Rating (cont.)

DATA SOURCE	1. RELATIVE COST-TO-VALUE	2. RELATIVE TIMELINESS OF DATA	3. RELATIVE COMPREHENSIVENESS OF DATA	4. EASE OF USE	5. SEARCH OPTIONS AVAILABLE	6. LEVEL OF SUPPORT SERVICES	7. LEVEL OF TRAINING OFFERED	8. AMOUNT/ KINDS OF SPECIAL SERVICES OFFERED	TOTAL
USPTO	10	10	10	7	9	8	7	10	71
Value Line	9	9	9	10	5	10	10	9	71
Dialog	8	9	9	7	10	10	9	8	70
LIVEDGAR	9	9	9	8	9	8	9	9	70
Loislaw	10	10	9	8	8	9	7	9	70
The Virtual Chase	10	9	9	8	9	7	9	9	70
The Wall Street Transcript	8	10	8	9	9	8	8	10	70
ABI/Inform	6	10	7	10	10	8	8	10	69
Accurint	10	9	7	9	9	7	9	9	69
CBS MarketWatch	10	9	9	9	8	8	8	8	69
CCH Tax Research Network	7	9	8	10	10	9	8	8	69
Federal Reserve Board	10	10	8	10	10	6	5	10	69
LLRX.com	10	9	9	10	8	8	5	10	69
Trademark.com	8	9	10	8	9	8	9	8	69
LexisNexis (public records)	7	9	10	7	10	8	8	9	68
OneSource	8	8	8	10	9	8	8	9	68
Zacks	10	9	9	10	10	5	5	10	68

Table C.2. Data Source Ratings – Ranked by Overall Rating (cont.)

DATA SOURCE	1. RELATIVE COST-TO-VALUE	2. RELATIVE TIMELINESS OF DATA	3. RELATIVE COMPREHENSIVENESS OF DATA	4. EASE OF USE	5. SEARCH OPTIONS AVAILABLE	6. LEVEL OF SUPPORT SERVICES	7. LEVEL OF TRAINING OFFERED	8. AMOUNT/KINDS OF SPECIAL SERVICES OFFERED	TOTAL
Bureau of Labor Statistics	10	10	10	6	8	8	7	8	67
Bureau of the Census	10	10	10	6	7	8	8	8	67
Gale Group New Product Announcements/ Plus (NPA/Plus)	7	10	9	8	9	9	8	7	67
Internal Revenue Service: The Digital Daily	10	10	10	8	8	8	5	8	67
TheStreet.com	9	10	9	6	8	8	8	9	67
Briefing.com	8	10	8	9	7	8	8	8	66
Corporate Affiliations	5	7	7	9	10	10	9	9	66
Economy.com	8	10	8	9	7	8	8	8	66
U.S. Copyrights	10	9	9	9	8	10	10	1	66
Factiva	9	10	10	8	7	6	6	9	65
Thomas Register	10	8	9	9	7	10	2	10	65
USADATA	10	8	9	10	3	8	8	9	65
Bureau of Economic Analysis (BEA)	10	10	10	8	5	7	6	8	64

Table C.2. Data Source Ratings – Ranked by Overall Rating (cont.)

DATA SOURCE	1. RELATIVE COST-TO-VALUE	2. RELATIVE TIMELINESS OF DATA	3. RELATIVE COMPRE-HENSIVENESS OF DATA	4. EASE OF USE	5. SEARCH OPTIONS AVAILABLE	6. LEVEL OF SUPPORT SERVICES	7. LEVEL OF TRAINING OFFERED	8. AMOUNT/ KINDS OF SPECIAL SERVICES OFFERED	TOTAL
EventLine	7	8	7	7	10	10	10	5	64
Financial Forecast Center	10	10	8	10	5	8	5	8	64
FactSet	7	10	10	7	5	8	8	8	63
Trademark Applications and Registrations Retrieval (TARR)	10	8	9	10	8	8	5	5	63
LexisNexis	8	9	8	7	8	8	7	7	62
Mergent Online	6	9	9	8	7	8	9	6	62
Standard & Poor's NetAdvantage	8	10	8	7	8	7	6	8	62
Trademark Electronic Search System (TESS)	9	8	9	9	10	7	5	5	62
Yahoo! Finance	9	10	9	9	9	5	5	6	62
Business Dateline	5	9	8	9	9	8	7	6	61
Encyclopedia of Associations (EA)	9	8	8	8	9	9	5	5	61
Lipper Horizon	5	10	10	6	7	8	7	8	61
MindBranch	9	8	9	9	7	10	2	7	61
Alacra	8	8	8	7	7	8	7	7	60

Table C.2. Data Source Ratings – Ranked by Overall Rating (cont.)

DATA SOURCE	1. RELATIVE COST-TO-VALUE	2. RELATIVE TIMELINESS OF DATA	3. RELATIVE COMPREHENSIVENESS OF DATA	4. EASE OF USE	5. SEARCH OPTIONS AVAILABLE	6. LEVEL OF SUPPORT SERVICES	7. LEVEL OF TRAINING OFFERED	8. AMOUNT/KINDS OF SPECIAL SERVICES OFFERED	TOTAL
Budget and Economic Outlook	10	10	10	10	5	5	5	5	60
Gale Group Newsletter Database	7	8	7	6	6	8	9	9	60
Hoover's Online	9	8	7	8	6	7	6	9	60
Chilling Effects	9	6	7	8	8	7	5	9	59
Disclosure Database	7	8	9	9	7	7	5	7	59
Financial Accounting Standards Board (FASB)	10	10	8	10	5	8	5	3	59
News on LexisNexis	8	8	7	7	8	7	6	8	59
Thomson Research	5	10	10	7	8	6	5	8	59
Business & Industry	7	6	8	8	8	7	8	6	58
PROMT	8	10	7	7	7	6	6	7	58
Reuters Business Insight	7	6	7	8	5	9	9	7	58
U.S. Copyright Office	9	10	9	7	7	1	5	10	58
FindLaw	10	8	10	7	8	2	5	7	57
FreeEDGAR/EDGAR Online/EDGARpro	6	9	7	6	7	8	8	6	57

Table C.2. Data Source Ratings – Ranked by Overall Rating (cont.)

DATA SOURCE	1. RELATIVE COST-TO-VALUE	2. RELATIVE TIMELINESS OF DATA	3. RELATIVE COMPRE-HENSIVENESS OF DATA	4. EASE OF USE	5. SEARCH OPTIONS AVAILABLE	6. LEVEL OF SUPPORT SERVICES	7. LEVEL OF TRAINING OFFERED	8. AMOUNT/KINDS OF SPECIAL SERVICES OFFERED	TOTAL
International Accounting Standards Board	9	9	8	10	6	7	5	3	57
Gale Group Business A.R.T.S.	7	10	7	6	6	7	8	5	56
Investext	7	7	8	6	8	7	6	7	56
D&B—Dun's Electronic Business Directory	7	7	6	2	9	8	8	8	55
D&B—Dun's Financial Records Plus	7	7	6	2	9	8	8	8	55
D&B—Dun's Market Identifiers	7	7	6	2	9	8	8	8	55
Fastcase	7	7	6	7	8	9	5	6	55
Gale Group Trade & Industry Database	8	9	6	8	9	4	5	5	54
Multex Fundamentals	6	8	10	7	8	5	5	5	54
RMA's Annual Statement Studies	10	8	6	9	4	7	3	7	54
SmartMoney	7	10	8	6	7	5	5	6	54
AICPA	8	9	8	7	6	7	5	3	53

Table C.2. Data Source Ratings – Ranked by Overall Rating (cont.)

DATA SOURCE	1. RELATIVE COST-TO-VALUE	2. RELATIVE TIMELINESS OF DATA	3. RELATIVE COMPRE-HENSIVENESS OF DATA	4. EASE OF USE	5. SEARCH OPTIONS AVAILABLE	6. LEVEL OF SUPPORT SERVICES	7. LEVEL OF TRAINING OFFERED	8. AMOUNT/ KINDS OF SPECIAL SERVICES OFFERED	TOTAL
Accounting & Tax Database	5	8	8	4	6	7	7	7	52
Datamonitor Market Research	7	6	9	8	6	6	5	5	52
Financial Accounting Research System (FARS)	9	8	9	6	7	4	4	5	52
U.S. Securities and Exchange Commission	10	10	8	9	5	6	2	2	52
D&B Million Dollar Database	5	7	8	9	7	7	3	5	51
D&B Key Business Ratios (KBR) on the Web	6	7	8	7	6	7	3	6	50
Experian Business Credit Profiles	3	8	5	6	6	7	6	9	50
Financial Times	8	10	6	7	7	2	5	5	50
First Research	5	8	8	8	5	5	5	5	49
Adweek	7	10	10	5	3	5	5	3	48
Brandweek	7	10	10	5	3	5	5	3	48

Table C.2. Data Source Ratings – Ranked by Overall Rating (cont.)

DATA SOURCE	1. RELATIVE COST-TO-VALUE	2. RELATIVE TIMELINESS OF DATA	3. RELATIVE COMPREHENSIVENESS OF DATA	4. EASE OF USE	5. SEARCH OPTIONS AVAILABLE	6. LEVEL OF SUPPORT SERVICES	7. LEVEL OF TRAINING OFFERED	8. AMOUNT/KINDS OF SPECIAL SERVICES OFFERED	TOTAL
Business Wire	5	10	5	7	5	5	5	5	47
MSN Money	9	8	8	7	7	4	1	3	47
Economic Indicators	7	8	6	5	3	4	5	5	43
GPO Access	5	7	6	6	8	1	3	6	42
KnowX	5	7	6	8	5	5	2	4	42
LexisONE	5	7	4	5	7	1	2	5	36
National Law Library	4	3	4	4	5	2	4	2	28

Note: Reviewers were asked to rate each research data source on the basis of a "10" being the highest, most complimentary, rating and "1" being the lowest or least complimentary ("80" being a perfect score).

Appendix D:
Contributor Biographies

Melissa Barr
Cuyahoga County Public Library

Melissa Barr is the legal resources specialist and reference librarian at the Maple Heights Regional Library, part of the Cuyahoga County Public Library system in Northeast Ohio. She serves as a building steward for the Cuyahoga County Library Union (Service Employees International Union, District 1199) and as an SEIU/1199 delegate to the Cleveland Federation of Labor. She is a member of the Ohio Regional Association of Law Libraries, the American Association of Law Libraries (AALL), and two AALL Special Interest Sections: Research Instruction & Patron Services and Legal Information Services to the Public.

Melissa earned a B.A. in English from Heidelberg College in Tiffin, Ohio (1977), a paralegal certificate from Ohio Paralegal Institute in Cleveland, Ohio (1982), and an M.L.S. from Kent State University (1997). She has also attended Baldwin Wallace College in Berea, Ohio; Central Texas College in Killeen, Texas; Bad Kreuznach, West Germany; Cuyahoga Community College in Parma, Ohio; and Cleveland State University, where her interests ranged from criminal justice to business communications, cultural anthropology, and Web page design.

After completing a tour of duty in the U.S. Army, Melissa started out in the legal field as a file clerk for a law firm and then moved on to work as a paralegal, bankruptcy liaison clerk, legal secretary, recruiting coordinator, and law library assistant. She also worked as a research assistant for a consulting company that prepared economic damage claim reports for court cases. While attending graduate school at Kent State University, Melissa was employed as the waste tracking coordinator at a hazardous waste recycling plant. She joined the Cuyahoga County Public Library staff in 1999. Melissa is the author of "Democracy in the Dark: Public Access Restrictions from Westlaw and LexisNexis," which appeared in the January 2003 edition of *Searcher: The Magazine for Database Professionals*.

Kathy Biehl
Independent Researcher

Attorney and freelance journalist Kathy Biehl is coauthor of *The Lawyer's Guide to Internet Research* (Scarecrow Press, 2000). She has reviewed online legal research resources as a columnist for LLRX.com, the Internet Legal Research Newsletter, and Pro2Net (now Smart Pros). In addition to legal and Internet writing, she has contributed more than eight hundred articles on a spectrum of general interest topics to national and regional publications. She is the winner of the 2002 Lone Star Award in magazine column writing presented by the Houston Press Club. Biehl earned a B.A. from Southern Methodist University with highest honors and a J.D. from the University of Texas School of Law with honors. She taught business law at Rice University and legal research and writing at the University of Houston Law Center. A member of the State Bar of Texas, she maintained a private law practice for nineteen years before turning to full-time research and writing.

Polly D. Boruff-Jones
IUPUI University Library

Polly Boruff-Jones is an assistant librarian at University Library on the Indiana University Purdue University Indianapolis (IUPUI) campus, where she serves as the reference team leader and business subject specialist. She received both her B.A. and M.L.S. degrees from Indiana University, Bloomington.

Ms. Boruff-Jones's primary areas of research are integration and assessment of information literacy in the business school undergraduate curriculum and management of virtual reference services in academic libraries.

Meryl Brodsky
Consultant

Meryl Brodsky is currently working as an independent consultant after working as a librarian at Ernst & Young LLP for four years and Cornell University for ten years. She has an M.B.A. from the Business School at Cornell and an M.L.S. from Southern Connecticut State University. She specializes in the financial services industry and particularly likes to analyze and compare databases. She is a member of the Special Libraries Association and the American Library Association.

Helen P. Burwell
Burwell Enterprises

Author and online expert Helen Burwell is well known for providing consulting services to the information industry and international business community. Since 1984, as president of Burwell Enterprises, Inc., she has helped corporate clients develop successful strategies for electronic retrieval of competitive intelligence information.

Ms. Burwell is editor and publisher of *The Burwell World Directory of Information Brokers,* an annual annotated directory of nearly one thousand companies that provide information retrieval and consulting. Now in its fourteenth edition, *The Burwell Directory* is widely used by business and industry for outsourcing information research. The directory is also available on the Internet at *http://www.burwellinc.com.*

Ms. Burwell holds a master's degree from Louisiana State University's School of Library and Information Science, which named her its 1996 Outstanding Alumna for her contributions to the information profession. In 1998, the Association of Independent Information Professionals, an international organization comprising information consultants, online searchers, document delivery services, and other information professionals, presented Ms. Burwell with the President's Award for outstanding service to the profession.

In recent years Ms. Burwell has been an invited guest speaker both at the European Information Brokers Meeting in Frankfurt, Germany, and at the first Asian and Pacific Rim Conference and Exhibition on Electronic Commerce in Shanghai, China. Regular speaking engagements in the United States have included national conferences and large trade shows such as the National Online Meeting, Online World, and the Society of Competitive Intelligence Professionals.

Ms. Burwell is the author of *Online Competitive Intelligence,* published by Facts On Demand Press in 1999 and 2000. The second edition will be released in January 2004.

Cindy Carlson
Fried, Frank, Harris, Shriver & Jacobson

Cindy Carlson is the electronic resources librarian for the Washington, D.C., office of the law firm of Fried, Frank, Harris, Shriver & Jacobson and has over fifteen years of experience working in libraries. She writes a monthly column, "Notes from the Technology Trenches," on electronic research, training, and legal information technology for LLRX.com, the Law Library Resource Exchange. An occasional contributor to other publications covering information research, she has also spoken at several conferences concerning Internet resources in business and legal research. She leads the Legal Research Training Focus Group of the Law Librarians' Society of the District of Columbia.

Elena Carvajal
Ernst & Young

Elena Carvajal is an information professional at Ernst & Young's Center for Business Knowledge. She has over twenty years of experience as a librarian, researcher, analyst, and communications specialist. Prior to joining Ernst & Young, Carvajal worked at EDS in a variety of roles, including research analyst for the corporate library and market analyst and industry relations/public relations specialist for the travel and transportation industry. She also served as marketing communication specialist for the Executive Communications Group at EDS.

Ms. Carvajal earned her B.A. in English and her M.L.S. from the University of North Texas. She has previously served on a number of committees and programs for the American Library Association, where her contributions include editing "COGnotes," the conference newsletter, and presenting a workshop entitled "Wrestling with the Future" at an ALA LITA Pre-Conference. She is a member of the Special Library Association.

Donna Cavallini
Kilpatrick Stockton LLP

Donna F. Cavallini has over fifteen years experience in the legal profession in a wide variety of settings, including academic and governmental and in both large and small law firms. Currently, she serves the attorneys of the law firm of Kilpatrick Stockton

LLP as manager of competitive knowledge, a position that combines the disciplines of knowledge management and competitive intelligence and focuses on the practice areas of corporate/securities, intellectual property, and technology law. Before joining the firm in 1996, Ms. Cavallini was library program administrator for the Florida Attorney General's Office, and prior to working for the state of Florida, she was solo librarian for a medium-sized firm in Tallahassee, Florida. She is a regular contributor to information professional Listservs and newsletters, including LLRX and The Virtual Chase, and she has been a speaker for professional groups both large and small. Ms. Cavallini received a B.A. in Classics from Washington University and a J.D. from St. Louis University.

Dudee Chiang
Amgen, Inc.

Dudee Chiang currently works as the library business analyst at Amgen, Inc., the world's largest biotechnology company. Prior to her current position, she worked as the database information consultant at Amgen Library, and she held various positions at the Norris Medical Library and Leavey Library at University of Southern California. She holds an M.S. degree and a certificate of advanced studies (C.A.S.) in Library and Information Science from the University of Illinois at Urbana-Champaign, and she also has a M.B.A. degree from the Pepperdine University. She is an experienced professional in information retrieval, end-user training, and resource evaluation; in recent years, she has taken on project management responsibilities for implementing technologies within the library environment, including Web and portals. She is always looking for new challenges in her work

Wes Edens
Thunderbird School of International Management

Wes Edens is on the faculty of the International Business Information Centre at Thunderbird, the American Graduate School of International Management, in Glendale, Arizona. In addition to duties as a full-time international business researcher, Wes evaluates and selects electronic resources for Thunderbird, ranked number one in the world for international business by *US News & World Report* and the *Wall Street Journal*. He holds a B.S. in

Business Administration and a M.L.S. degree, both from the University of Arizona, and is an M.B.A. candidate at Arizona State University.

Prior to coming to Thunderbird, Mr. Edens was business librarian/bibliographer for the University of North Dakota in Grand Forks. He has also worked as a reference librarian for Pima Community College in Tucson, Arizona.

Mr. Edens's publications include: "An International Information Gateway: Thunderbird's Intranet for Teaching, Learning and Research" (with Carol Hammond, Ann Tolzman, and Cate Cebrowski) in *Advances in Library Administration and Organization*, October 1997; and "World Database of Business Information Sources on the Web," a review for the November/December 1998 issue of *Business Information Alert*. In addition, he was interviewed by Mary Ellen Bates in the 2001 book, *Super Searchers Cover the World: The Online Secrets of International Business Researchers*, published by Eight Bit Books.

He is a member of the Special Libraries Association and the Arizona Libraries Association. He is married with three children and is an avid reader, stargazer, and amateur radio operator.

David Ernsthausen
Kenan-Flagler Business School

Since 1997 David Ernsthausen has been the faculty teaching and research support librarian of the University of North Carolina at Chapel Hill's Kenan-Flagler Business School. He consults with faculty and students about which resources are most likely to provide useful answers for their research. He also presents guest lectures for classes in the M.B.A. and bachelor's degree programs. Prior to 1997 he worked for seven years as a reference librarian at Wake Forest University, working mainly with the undergraduate business students and faculty. He has an M.B.A. from the Babcock Graduate School of Management at Wake Forest University and a M.L.S. degree from Indiana University.

Michelle Fennimore
Competitive Insights

Michelle Fennimore is the principal of Competitive Insights, a market research company specializing in competitive intelligence, company, and industry research. Its services range from online research and one-on-one interviews to custom-designed market research studies, including mail and telephone surveys. Ms. Fennimore's work focuses primarily on marketing and advertising issues, as well as business development and expansion. Prior to founding Competitive Insights, she spent nine years in New York City, marketing national brands for global advertising agencies including J. Walter Thompson, Saatchi & Saatchi, and Grey Advertising.

James Harrington
Fujitsu Network Communications

Jim Harrington earned his M.L.S. from the State University of New York at Buffalo. He began his career assisting libraries in the setup and implementation of a variety of automated services for both staff and end users, primarily dealing with system design and training. For the past four years, he has worked as the corporate librarian for Fujitsu Network Communications, providing library services primarily for the marketing and sales organizations.

Michelle Hartstrom
Columbia Financial Advisors, Inc.

Michelle Hartstrom is a financial analyst with over ten years of experience in the valuation of closely held business interests. In her analysis of client companies, she researches economic and industry information, financial market data, public company information, and merger and acquisition data. She performs financial analysis for clients for a variety of purposes including ESOP, litigation, gift and estate tax, and management planning. In addition to the financial analysis aspect of her work, verbal and written communication is an integral part of each project she performs.

Prior to joining Columbia Financial Advisors, Inc., Ms. Hartstrom worked for Willamette Management Associates in its Portland, Oregon office. She has earned accreditation as a senior appraiser in business valuation from the American Society of Appraisers and a certification in financial management from the Institute of Management Accountants. She earned a B.S. in Business Administration with high scholarship from Oregon State University. Her concentrations of study were financial management and international business, and she minored in behavioral science.

Jean M. Heilig
Jones International University

Jean M. Heilig is the director of the online library at Jones International University (JIU), the first completely online university to achieve regional accreditation. Ms. Heilig has been working full time for the university since January 2003. Prior to that, she worked part time for the university and part time for Jones e-global library (a licensed product), where she was the senior director of Research and Information. At both Jones e-global library and the JIU library she has been involved with resource development and review as well as the selection and evaluation of database vendors and content providers. She participates in client (student, faculty, and staff) outreach, support, and training and also monitors copyright issues, national and international digital library initiatives, advances in electronic publishing, and similar issues that affect the competitive environment of e-global library. Prior to joining Jones in 1999 she was the program coordinator for the Library and Information Services graduate program at the University of Denver (DU), where she managed all program logistics, budget, personnel, and student advising.

Ms. Heilig obtained her master's degree in library and information services from the University of Denver (1999), her master's degree in business administration from the University of Colorado – Denver (1992). She also holds a certificate in competitive intelligence from Drexel University (2002). In addition to her work with JIU, she is an adjunct faculty member in the Library and Information Science master's degree program at DU.

Karl Kasca
Kasca & Associates

Five years ago Karl Kasca formed his own company, Kasca & Associates, which provides top-level information research results to business and legal decision makers. His company specializes in business research and competitive intelligence, as well as market, product, and industry trends, and due diligence—information useful to businesses and attorneys in making decisions and acting on them.

Mr. Kasca was formerly with a Fortune 500 company with over sixteen years experience performing operational and financial internal audits as well as vendor and conflict-of-interest/fraud examinations in diverse business situations. As a result, he has become very experienced at finding creative approaches and solutions to problems/questions as well as performing insightful analyses of results.

Wendy S. Katz
Factscope LLC

Dr. Wendy Katz owns Factscope LLC, a research consulting firm based in Lexington, Kentucky. Dr. Katz received her B.S. in Conservation of Natural Resources, with highest honors, from the University of California at Berkeley in 1977. She has seventeen years of laboratory experience in biomedical research and has published research papers and literature reviews in *Cell* and other peer-reviewed journals. She earned her Ph.D. in Biology from the Massachusetts Institute of Technology in 1989, where her research focused on structure-function analysis of proteins. Her postdoctoral research at the California Institute of Technology used tools of molecular genetics to study how cells in a developing animal know where they are. Dr. Katz joined the Department of Biochemistry in the University of Kentucky College of Medicine in 1995 and both continued her research and taught graduate biochemistry there from 1995 to 2000. She has a long-standing interest in animal training and behavior modification and in her free time teaches dog obedience classes.

Hal P. Kirkwood, Jr.
Purdue University

Hal P. Kirkwood is currently an assistant professor of Library Science at the Management & Economics Library at Purdue University. He acts as the instruction coordinator for the Management & Economics Library, conducting workshops and class sessions on the multitude of business databases available. He has written extensively in publications such as *Online, Journal of Business & Finance Librarianship, FreePint,* and the *Bulletin* of the Business & Finance Division of Special Libraries Association. Professor Kirkwood has presented at Online World, Internet Librarian, and the Special Libraries Association's Annual Conference. His research interests are in teaching business information to M.B.A.s, Web design and usability, and concept mapping.

Jan Knight
Bancroft Information Services

Jan Knight is owner of Bancroft Information Services. As an independent research consultant, she provides a variety of business intelligence and market research services to a diverse list of companies, including publishers, corporate trainers, software companies, biotechnology firms, marketing strategists and sales consultants. Much of her work involves providing industry profiles, market studies, and competitor profile reports. Clients often commission her services when working on initial business plans, marketing strategies, or new product development.

Originally from England, Ms. Knight has a professional background in advertising, marketing, and publishing. She holds an M.A. in Information Resources & Library Science from the University of Arizona and a B.A. in Humanities/Renaissance Studies from the University of California, Berkeley. She regularly attends local business events and has spoken to various business groups on the topic of "Jump-Starting Your Own Market Research via the Internet." Her Web site provides more information on services as well as client testimonials. It can be found at: *http://www.bancroftinfo.com.*

Margery A. Mackie
Mackie Research LLC

Margery A. Mackie is an independent business researcher located in Portland, Oregon. Her firm, Mackie Research LLC, specializes in online industry research and overview writing. Other services include regional economic profile research and writing, environmental research, and specialized industry data searches. Ms. Mackie is also a contributor to "The CyberSkeptic's Guide to Internet Research," a monthly newsletter. Prior to launching her business, Margery worked in a variety of private sector, nonprofit, and government settings, always enjoying the research and reporting aspects of her work the most. She is a member of the Association of Independent Information Professionals and the National Association for the Self-Employed, and she holds an environmental planning degree from Stanford University.

Matthew J. McBride
Information Consultant

Matthew J. McBride is the president and principal information consultant of CInC, Inc. He holds an M.S. in Plant Pathology from the University of Minnesota and a B.S. in Molecular Biology from Purdue University. Matthew is currently completing his M.L.S. degree at Drexel University. He has worked as a biological research scientist for a major chemical company and as an information consultant for The Dialog Corporation. He has over seven years of experience searching commercial systems and databases for scientific, technical, and intellectual property information.

Karin Mohtadi
KZM LLC

Karin Mohtadi has participated in business valuations and business research during the last eight years. Currently she researches economic and industry information, public company information, and merger and acquisition data. As a financial analyst conducting business valuations and other analysis, she worked for clients for a variety of purposes, including buy-sell agreements, damages and lost profits analyses, economic damage analysis, enhanced earnings, employee stock ownership plans, litigation support, and gift and estate tax.

Prior to forming KZM LLC, Ms. Mohtadi worked for Veber Partners LLC, an investment bank in Portland, Oregon. Prior to that she worked for Willamette Management Associates in its Portland, Oregon, office. She holds a M.S. in Economics as well as a B.A. in both Economics and French from Portland State University.

Rita W. Moss
University of North Carolina at Chapel Hill

Rita Moss's education includes a B.A. from the University College of North Wales, Bangor, United Kingdom, with a double major in Social Theory and Institutions and History, an M.Ed. from the same institution, and an M.L.S. from the University of North Carolina at Chapel Hill received in 1988. She has worked since 1991 as a business and economics librarian at the University of North Carolina at Chapel Hill. For the past twelve years she has also conducted workshops on business information resources for

Southeastern Library Network and for North Carolina Libraries for Virtual Education, as well as giving several presentations at workshops offered by the North Carolina Library Association.

Ms. Moss recently finished revising the second edition of the *Handbook of Business Information* for Libraries Unlimited.

Robin Neidorf
Electric Muse

Robin Neidorf has provided research, writing, and consulting services through her company, Electric Muse, since 1996. She works with clients in the fields of nonprofit management, health care, business consulting, law, investment services, public policy, education, and market research to help them find and use information to communicate more effectively in print, electronic formats, and face to face. Ms. Robin holds a master's degree in nonfiction writing from the Bennington Writing Seminars and teaches research, writing, and public relations through the University of Minnesota's Compleat Scholar program. Her articles and essays have appeared regionally and nationally in such publications as *Ms.* magazine, *Minnesota Law & Politics, Corporate Report,* and *Ventures* magazine, and she is the coauthor of *e-Merchant: Retail Strategies for e-Commerce* (Addison Wesley, 2001). Ms. Robin often speaks to groups on market research, communications, public relations, life-work balance, and other topics. She is a member of the Association of Independent Information Professionals and Business/ Professional Women USA.

Judith M. Nixon
Purdue University

Judith Nixon has worked at the Purdue University Libraries since 1984, first as a consumer and family sciences librarian and since 1993 as a management and economics librarian. Prior to this she worked as a reference librarian at the University of Wisconsin, Platteville and at the Cedar Rapids Public Library.

Ms. Nixon is widely published in the field. Her works include *Industry and Company Information,* which she coauthored with Craig A. Hawbaker (Ann Arbor, MI: Pierian Press, 1991), and *Lodging and Restaurant Index,* a quarterly periodical index (West Lafayette, IN: RHIMI, Purdue University, 1985–1993), as well as numerous journal articles. Her awards include the John H. Moriarity Award for Excellence in Library Service to the Faculty and Students of Purdue University (1989) and the Gale Research Award for Excellence in Business Librarianship (1994).

Ms. Nixon has a master's degree in Library Science from the University of Iowa (1974) and a B.S. in Education from Valparaiso University (1967). She is a member of the American Library Association, the Reference and User Services Association, and the Business Reference and Services Section.

Judith Parvez
Tax Analysts

Judy is a senior information specialist at Tax Analysts. Prior to that, she was employed as a tax librarian and tax knowledge manager for several professional services firms. She is a member of the Special Libraries Association and has served as moderator of the Tax Roundtable – Legal Division.

Judy received a Bachelor of Administration/Library Science degree from the University of Wisconsin, Eau Claire.

Marcy M. Phelps
Phelps Research

Marcy Phelps is the founder and president of Phelps Research, located in Denver, Colorado. Her company offers business and market research to management, marketing, and financial services professionals. Marcy specializes in providing clients with industry profile reports and has particular expertise in online database searching. Phelps Research also offers company profiles, competitive intelligence, litigation support, regional economic overviews, comparable company research, and merger and acquisition research. Ms. Phelps has a master's degree in Library and Information Services from the University of Denver as well as a degree in Mathematics from the State University of New York at New Paltz. She currently holds memberships in the Association of Independent Information Professionals, the Business Marketing Association, and the Metro Denver Chamber of Commerce. A first-degree black belt in Taekwondo, Ms. Phelps enjoys golf and mountain biking in her spare time.

Brenda Reeb
University of Rochester

A native of rural southern Illinois, Brenda Reeb earned her B.A. in history from Loyola University of Chicago in 1987. During her senior year in college she wrote her first paper on a microcomputer, using MS-DOS and WordPerfect. She earned her M.L.S. from Simmons College in Boston in 1991. In 1993 Ms. Reeb relocated to Rochester, New York, to serve as the management librarian at the University of Rochester. With no prior business background, she was hired primarily for her computer skills. Now the director of the Management Library, she manages a staff of three, serving the William E. Simon School of Business and the economics department at the university.

After nearly a decade of business library reference work, Ms. Reeb remains fascinated by the ways students engage business sources, particularly in an online environment. She coordinates several Web interface design projects in the library and maintains a private consulting practice in user-centered design. She is a member of the American Library Association and the Association for Women in Computing.

While living in Boston, Ms. Reeb became an avid bicycle commuter, which she continues to this day, although she no longer rides in the winter.

Jan Rivers
Dorsey & Whitney LLP

Jan Rivers is reference/electronic services librarian for Dorsey & Whitney LLP. Prior to joining Dorsey, Ms. Rivers worked for Arthur Andersen LLP, where she was a manager in the Risk Management Services Group, as well as a project manager and team leader for Andersen's AskNetwork e-Products Consulting Team and a regional leader in the firm's Business Information Network. She managed projects relating to the firm's intranet and Internet sites, and she developed databases and electronic information products for groups within the firm. She also conducted in-depth research and analysis for firm personnel and leadership worldwide. Before joining Arthur Andersen, Ms. Rivers worked for the Hennepin County Public Library System. She has also presented at Intranets 2000 and at Computers in Libraries and has been published in *Searcher* and *Intranet Professional*.

Roger V. Skalbeck
George Mason University School of Law

Roger Skalbeck is the technology librarian at George Mason University School of Law. Mr. Skalbeck has worked in law libraries for almost a decade, including work in five law firms in three jurisdictions. Mr. Skalbeck has analyzed and reviewed numerous legal resources and technologies, and he frequently participates in conferences focused on law libraries and legal technology. He received his B.A. from Macalester College and his M.L.I.S. from Dominican University, and he is currently pursuing a J.D. at George Mason University School of Law.

Jen Venable
Purdue University

Jen Venable is the assistant management and economics librarian and an assistant professor at Purdue University. She holds a B.A. in News-Editorial from Oklahoma State University (1994) and an M.L.I.S. from the University of Texas at Austin (1997).

Ms. Venable has been working in libraries in the academic, public, and private sectors since the age of nineteen. She began her professional career as a reference librarian for Queens Borough Public Library (QBPL) system in New York City. After working in the branch libraries, she became a business reference librarian and later assistant manager of the business research department for QBPL. After three years in New York, she moved back to Austin as the solo librarian for Hoover's, Inc., a business information database company. Jen worked for a year in the dot-com industry; she then accepted a position at the Management and Economics Library at Purdue University, where she works today.

Patricia A. Watkins
Thunderbird School of International Management

Patricia Watkins is a business information service and resources librarian in the International Business Information Centre at Thunderbird, the American Graduate School of International Management in Glendale, Arizona. In her position she consults regularly with executives from a variety of fields worldwide to help find solutions to their business intelligence needs. Prior to her current position, she was manager of Information Resources at MORPACE International, a Michigan-based market research firm partnering with the automotive industry.

Raised in Dearborn, Michigan, Watkins now lives in Phoenix. Before relocating to Arizona in 2001, she spent a career in advertising, marketing, and market research within the automotive industry. She was founding partner and senior project director with Creative Marketing Consultants, a Southfield, Michigan-based primary market research company whose clientele included General Motors Corporation. Prior to that, she worked with the Polk Company, Campbell-Ewald Advertising, and Ward's Automotive Research. In 2000, Watkins earned a master's degree in Library and Information Science from Wayne State University in Detroit. Her undergraduate degree is in political science from the University of Michigan.

Ms. Watkins served on the board and is a past-president of Women in Communications of Detroit. She is active in several information and library organizations: the Society of Competitive Intelligence, Arizona Women in International Trade, the American Library Association, the Arizona Library Association, the Mountain Plains Library Association (MPLA), and the Special Libraries Association. She was recently chosen to attend the inaugural MPLA Leadership Institute in Abiquiu, New Mexico. She is currently involved with research on the history and economic impact of immigration between Arizona and Mexico.

Susan F. Weiler
Weiler Information Services

Susan F. Weiler is the owner of Weiler Information Services (WIS), an information brokerage business that since 1989 has provided customized business research to companies that do not have in-house libraries or information centers. Weiler Information Services provides customized business research services to a variety of organizations, including executive recruiting firms, consulting firms, financial services firms, telecommunications equipment and service firms, and manufacturers of consumer packaged goods.

Ms. Weiler holds a masters degree in Library and Information Sciences from Simmons College and has extensive experience as an information specialist and corporate reference librarian. Prior to founding WIS, she was employed by Bain & Company, an international strategic management consulting firm. Ms. Weiler is a frequent writer and speaker on topics relating to the library and information industry.

Ms. Weiler is a member of the Association of Independent Information Professionals (AIIP), New England Online Users Group, and the Special Libraries Association. She serves as a trustee of the Walpole Public Library in Walpole, Massachusetts, a member of The Dialog Corporation's Customer Advisory Board (2001–2003), and served as a director-at-large and vendor relations chairperson of the AIIP Board (1999–2002).

Samuel Werberg
FIND/SVP, Inc.

Sam Werberg joined FIND/SVP, Inc. as a research consultant in the Technology, Information and Communications Group in August 2000, after serving as an information specialist in Morocco for three years with the U.S. Peace Corps. Prior to that he worked for an information broker in Austin, Texas, where he covered the semiconductor and telecom industries.

For FIND/SVP, Mr. Werberg covers Artificial Intelligence, Consumer and Business Internet Usage Patterns, Enterprise Content Management, Information Services, Knowledge Management, Semiconductors, and Wireless Technologies and Communications. Mr. Werberg has also worked in academic libraries in Texas and New York and currently volunteers in the Queens Public Library in Astoria, New York.

Mr. Werberg received a B.S. in Sociology from Hamilton College and an M.L.I.S. from the Graduate School of Library and Information Science at the University of Texas at Austin.

Kim Whalen
Emory University

Kim Whalen is a business librarian at Emory University's Goizueta Business School. She has a B.A. in business administration with a major in marketing from Illinois Institute of Technology (1990) and an M.L.I.S. from the University of Pittsburgh's School of Information Sciences (2002).

In addition to her responsibilities within the Goizueta Business Library, Ms. Whalen is the liaison to Goizueta's Career Management Center. Through the development of Web research tools, group instructional sessions, and one-on-one consultations, she assists job-seeking students with their research of companies, industries, and geographic areas.

Prior to earning her master's degree, Ms. Whalen spent over eleven years in Chicago's nonprofit sector. Positions with the University of Chicago Graduate School of Business, Illinois Institute of Technology, Advocate Health Care Foundation, and the City of Chicago developed her nonprofit marketing, public relations, and program administration experience. She is an active member of the Special Libraries Association and the American Library Association and currently serves on the SLA Georgia Chapter Membership Committee.

INDEX

EventLine, 386
Experian, 386, 398
ExpressJet Holdings, 124

F

FAA. *See* Federal Aviation Administration
Factiva, 386, 398
  aggregator, 28, 243–246
  articles and books, 32, 33, 104
  case study research strategy, 96–98, 109, 112, 114
  compensation and benefits research, 62
  conference call transcripts, 40
  content, 262–266
  description, 260–261
  evaluation, 266–268
  investment analyst reports, 57
  pricing, 261
  research strategy, 147, 148, 164, 167, 189, 200, 205, 207
  TWST, 59
  value rating, 268
Factscope, 430
FactSet, 386, 398
  content, 340
  description, 339
  evaluation, 340–341
  pricing, 339
  value rating, 341
Fair Disclosure Express, 40–41
FARS. *See* Financial Accounting Standards Board, Financial Accounting Research System
Fastcase, 386, 399
Federal Aviation Administration (FAA), 111–112
Federal Reserve Board (FRB), 48–49, 386
  content, 342
  description, 342
  evaluation, 343
  value rating, 343
  Web site, 171–172, 173–174, 181–184, 187–188
Fennimore, Michelle, 427–428
FIN. *See* Financial Accounting Standards Board, Interpretations
financial accounting, 2
Financial Accounting Research System. *See* Financial Accounting Standards Board, Financial Accounting Research System
Financial Accounting Standards Board (FASB), 6, 77, 387, 399
  case study research, 91
  content, 287
  current text, 79–80, 281
  description, 287
  discussion memorandum, 10, 80
  Emerging Issues Task Force (EITF), 1
    abstracts, 80, 281
    authority level, 6
    proposals, 138, 139
  evaluation, 287–288
  exposure draft, 10, 80, 137
  Financial Accounting Concepts (CON), 7
  Financial Accounting Research System (FARS), 30, 386
    content, 281–282
    description, 281
    evaluation, 282
    value rating, 283
  Implementation document, 11, 281
  Interpretations (FIN), 5
  new standard, 10–11
  original pronouncements, 79, 135, 139, 141, 143, 281
  print publications, 31

resource portal, 34
staff implementation guides, 8
standards setter, 8–9
Statement of Financial Accounting Standards (SFAS), 1
  authority level, 5
  case study research, 91, 93, 99–103, 115, 116, 117, 130
  research problems, 135–136, 139–140, 142–144
Technical Bulletins (TB), 6, 11, 135–136
topical index, 281
User Advisory, 13
value rating, 288
Web site, 28, 29, 59, 137–138, 146–147
financial disclosures, 16–19, 83–84
  case study research, 103–110, 116–130
  data sources, 247
  research problems, 132, 148–160
  sources
    electronic database services, 34–41
    print publications, 41–42
Financial Executive Institute, 77
Financial Forecast Center, 53, 387
  content, 350
  description, 349
  evaluation, 351
  value rating, 351
financial hedging research, 142–147
financial market data, 20–22
  research problems, 133, 166–172
  sources, 46–47, 247–248
financial projections research, 194–196
financial research options. *See* accounting and financial research problems
financial software. *See* accounting software
Financial Times, 59, 387, 399
FindLaw, 387
FIND/SVP, Inc., 438
First Research, 387, 399
footnotes and exploitation costs research, 148–151
Forbes, 59
forecasted economic data, 52–53
foreign exchange rate research, 181–184
Fortune, 59
FRB. *See* Federal Reserve Board
FreeEDGAR, 387
Fried, Frank, Harris, Shriver & Jacobson, 425
Fujitsu Network Communications, 428
future outlook research, 196–199

G

GAAP. *See* Generally Accepted Accounting Principles
GAGAS. *See* U.S. General Accounting Office, Government Auditing Standards
GAO. *See* U.S. General Accounting Office
Gary Price's List of Lists, 62
GAS. *See* governmental accounting standards
GASB. *See* Governmental Accounting Standards Board
Generally Accepted Accounting Principles (GAAP), 2, 91
  described, 11–12
  guides, 33
  purpose, 4
  standards source, 28–29
  understanding, 5–7
  vs. England's standards, 212–214
George Mason University, 436
Gleim Accounting, 72, 88
Global Insight, 387, 399
Global Securities Information, 399